T0368372

Died Three Times Lived Once

Robert Garcia

authorHOUSE

AuthorHouse™
1663 Liberty Drive
Bloomington, IN 47403
www.authorhouse.com
Phone: 833-262-8899

Published by AuthorHouse 11/15/2024

ISBN: 979-8-8230-3789-1 (sc)
ISBN: 979-8-8230-3790-7 (hc)
ISBN: 979-8-8230-3788-4 (e)

Library of Congress Control Number: 2024924476

Print information available on the last page.

This book is printed on acid-free paper.

PART 1

Died 3 Times Lived Once

YOU KNOW THERE are things in life we can never change. There will always be negative and false issues as obstacles so we will think there is no hope to change. As many of us, with no proper guidance the road to do the right things, and to make the right choices, can be scary, to have fear of the unknown.

What I am about to show to my interested readers, as a boy, a teenager, a veteran and as a citizen, and how I lost everything, by hitting rock bottom. By almost losing complete hope, for starters, almost losing my life at seven years old. From the beginning of my life, there has always been temptatious things to do the wrong instead of the right.

Most people who would have had parents like mine, would do the right things, and make the right choices. And I did when I was a boy, and through most of my teenage years. But growing up with uneducated parents, and a alcoholic father, things were difficult, very difficult. I can't remember hardly any boyhood experiences, like most boys have. The biggest influence I had from my Dad, was taking me to work at five years old, with no choice of my own. But Dad needed my help, that's the only choice he had. You see, Dad had a trash business in the early 50s. Those were the years of the beginnings of where these conglomerate companies stand today. As you can tell as I wrote this, this experience is coming from an old man. That's right, I'm now an old man.

I'd like to think I did more right than wrong. The old saying is: "ITS A JUNGLE OUT THERE" As a boy, never knew what that meant, but boy did I find that out the hard way! Because it is a cruel world! We face corruption, liars, and cheaters, every time we put on the television, and when we look at the social media, what do we read?

Reminiscing about when I was just a small boy. Seven years of age, is my time I call a small boy. I will never forget that age for as long I live. My late uncle and my elderly father and I survived a miraculous horrific truck accident. I'm sure there are those of you that have had a family member, a child, a parent or parents that weren't as lucky as us. Because there are vehicle accidents everyday. Our accident in particular, was a Shell gas tanker and our large bob tail trash truck. The tanker collided with us, broad side. Spinning our truck, ripping our front axle from our truck, and that took us into a catastrophe, which law enforcement officers and doctors wondered how we survived. All I can remember, I'm sitting in between my uncle and Dad in our truck, my uncle driving, picking up trash from one house and to our next. There were very few people living in that part of California, which was Yorba Linda, California. With a population of about 4000. There were no stop signs nor traffic signals. My uncle pulled up to a small orange grove intersection, and as he began to pull out into the small road, my Dad yells out "LOOK OUT EDDIE" wondering why was Dad yelling so loud by my ear!! As I could barely see, what's coming down hill coming straight into us at full speed. The next thing, I awake with a neck brace, in a small Doctors clinic. With a elderly doctor. Knowing I was awaking from a coma. He informed me, "ITS A WONDER HOW ALL OF YOU SURVIVED"

It's a miracle I can remember what happened to us, on that catastrophic day. After that day, life became very different and some days very difficult for me. But I had to learn to accept it, with my young life. I think I was in the third grade, and that night mare truck accident happened when I was on a school summer vacation. Physically, I suffered a twisted neck, with some stitches on the side of my left part of my head. It's a wonder that's all that happened to me. Maybe there's more, but I can't see it. Here's a question for many that read this. How many people learn to drive, between five and seven years old? My Dad made me go to work at the age of five. No disputes, Dad told me once, "SON YOUR GOING TO LEARN TO WORK LIKE MY DAD

TAUGHT ME" Getting me out of bed, between four and five in the morning. And that went on until I was eight or nine years old. That was pretty much it for my summer vacations, from five until eight or nine years of age. So to learn to drive was no choice of mine. No, I didn't drive out among traffic. Dad would get a piece of two by four wood, push the truck clutch as he stood beside the truck cab and put the truck into compound gear, and say to me, yelling, pay attention what I'm showing you, because I don't want you to run anybody down. Scared? Oh yeah, I was very SCARED!!! You couldn't hardly see the top of my head by God!!! At times, Dad would order me to get in the back of this trash truck, my uncle would throw big barrels of trash on one side, and Dad would throw barrels of trash on the other side, and I would have to dump them, little boy me, at maybe six old. Needless to say, I learned to work hard at a very young age. There were times in those young times, when I would see boys my age, having fun with their Mom and Dad, or their brothers or sisters. Always missed that in my life. After that HORRIBLE ACCIDENT, I very much believe I became another little boy, a completely different person.

Started getting better grades, became real good in math, really getting to like school. Remembering my elementary years in school, it got easier for me. As long I would ask a teacher or two to help me with any problem I would run into. The teachers were very understanding.

If I would run into a problem, I couldn't take anything home and not understand it, because like I mentioned before, my parents were uneducated. How could they help me? Dad only went to fourth grade, and mom only went to seventh grade. Mom did pretty good for a while, but as I progressed in school, they just couldn't help me anymore.

When I wrote this, I found this very gratifying for me to advance myself to a dream, that maybe one day I would become a mechanical engineer, because that would become my major in college. I'll explain later how that never materialized. SAD, AND DISAPPOINTING. But that wasn't my time. I often think about that, especially now that I'm old. I firmly believe, there has always been a reason for everything. God's timing and reasoning. I understand that now. Maybe one day, as you read this, you'll understand God's reasoning, because I'm just starting to. Some people go through all their lives trying to do things their way, and what happens? Losing complete control of their lives, I know I did for awhile. But God has given me so many chances, which I often think, why? Why men God? I've asked. I've looked at myself, at that scary moment, we were almost killed, when I was only seven, and I changed so much for the good. And for what?

From the time we're born, for many of us, we go through life trying to do the best, and many of you brothers and sisters, never get any chances at all. I'm talking about life changing and life threatening changes, like God blessed me with. Like I say, I don't know why.

My Dad was still alive when I wrote this, and he was a World War II veteran. I've become very proud of him. But during my younger ages with Dad, he was so disconnected from me. For so many years, I've often thought, that maybe I was adopted. And I've evaluated that, that it's not true. Many people have said, we look very much alike.

I've tried to do the right thing, as a small boy, and I've heard my mother tell relatives, aunts and uncles, that I was a good boy, and they would agree with her. For so very long, that made me feel good about myself, and it inspired me to want to stay that way. On the other hand, Dad, did his thing, which was to DRINK. He was so out of touch with his son, that it has discouraged me to the point that it saddens me to think of it, even today. But what do I expect, Dad went through his own lost of love in his life. I asked him once, did my grandpa ever tell my Dad, that he loved him? I couldn't believe it, he told me, he never did.

As a boy, Dad didn't get the privilege to go to school, like he pushed so hard to make us, when I say us, my sisters and I, go to school.

As I said, Dad had me out there, working, helping him pick up trash at a young age, and we were almost killed, one early morning. Let me tell you this one, among many others. Dad comes from a very sad generation. Being born in the 1920s, 1925 to be exact. He told me so, so sad stories about his life story, as he was growing up.

I picked up this book once, called, "THE GREAT GENERATION" found it to be a very true sad generation, and wondered, why would they call it, the great generation. They went through so much suffering. That is if you're poor!!! And my ancestors come from a very poor and uneducated background. Dad, telling me, when he was able to go to school once in a while, he had to put cardboard inside his shoes, so he wouldn't have to walk on rocks. I don't know about you, but that never impress me, to think he came from a great generation.

It's no wonder my Dad wanted us to go to schooli! As I walked to school, each day as I walked, the thought of Dad having to walk with cardboard in his shoes, has always given me motivation, and it would also sadden me. And those were the days, grandpa would let him go. Because Grandpa leased a farm, and would have his sons work it, but most of the time, Dad was the one held back, and stay with his Dad, to work what had to be done, instead of going to school. My early years with Dad, were hard, and it shouldn't have been. As I wrote this, it's a chain reaction, with his Dad, and now my Dad, in my early years with Dad. Most of the time, Dad only communicated with me when he needed me on his trash route, other than that, he never wanted to talk about a son and father conversation. I remember that, it has always hurt me. Even up to this day, as I am now a old man. A life like mine has always been a tough one, because from the beginning of my life, I've never had any true support. All I knew, I had to do the best with what I had.

Little do we know, from the time our mothers conceive, and our time is coming to face this horrid world, there's no turning back. Wouldn't that be nice if we could? Like be born again. WOW!!! Later in my story, I'll explain to my readers, what it is, being born again.

As you can tell I'm the oldest and the only son of three children my parents had. And I've always had a complex, being short. I used to take it personal, but not anymore. As a boy, at five, I experienced my first fight. Tried standing to my Dad, but that didn't work out too good. God slapped down. Can't blame Dad, a boy at a small age, just doesn't get smart mouth, and say things to your Dad and think you're gonna get away with it. I'm glad he slapped me. It taught me a very important lesson. But I think Dad found out I'm not afraid of anyone. And that's me today. Like I told you, life was very hard for me growing up, with a alcoholic father, and my rebellious ways. At times coming home from school, finding Mom fainted on our living room sofa, or on her bed. That used to make me feel soo sad for my Mom.

Through my years of life, I've heard there are those few loving people like my mother, that are undeserved sufferers. And I also heard that God has a special place for loving people like my mother. I'd like to think that I will see my mother again in God's arms in heaven. Reminiscing on my Mother's love, I can remember many times, how much she prayed for all of us. Mom would make all of us go to church, every Sunday. Remembering her taking me on the first day of my school years, and how I climbed the fence, following her back home. The amazing look on her face. As she says to me, "What Are Doing Here"? "I just have to take you back to school" Never again did I leave school, until much later.

I have had a scar on my face for over sixty five years to always remind me of those little boy days of mine, in and out of school. I got this scar on my face when I was in kindergarten, chasing a girl, while running after her, our teacher sitting right at the door way, I'm running full bore when teach gets up putting the chair right in my way, and I plowed into it, tearing my left part of my face wide open. It knocked me out. The principal took me home, putting tears on my mothers face. Another mishap that happened to little oh me. By my Dad's first home, they were building another house next door. I must have been around four or five years old, I'm climbing all over the walls, like some monkey. Well little did I know, construction workers leave anything on the floor. I'm up on this wall, and decided to jump off the wall, and I landed on a twelve inch 2x4 piece of wood, with a nail sticking up out of the wood. WOW did that hurt, another incident I will never forget. Thank God, one of my uncles was there, waiting for Dad, watching me coming in hopping in our home with a piece of wood sticking out of my foot. I can only imagine what that looked like. Don't remember if anyone ever took me to the doctor, let alone to the hospital. Mom and Dad never believed in dentists, nor doctors, nor hospitals. Sad but true. That's just the way it was in those days. Things to save your life was too expensive. We didn't have it made, like America is today. Things weren't as easy as they are today. What America is today, society is spoiled. Look around you. Continuing on my early years of life, and I'm not saying I was the only abused child. There are much worse, I just know there is.

Yes I think I was abused. Never sexually, but emotionally. Dad is the one that abused me emotionally. Dad had never took me, nor my siblings to any theme parks, but he was always ready to go to a bar, or just get drunk at home.

Dad taught me how to lie. Thank God, that's all he taught me to do, bad. Taught me how to work, by taking away my childhood. Instead of being home, on the weekends playing with the neighborhood kids, I had to get up early morning to go help Dad on his trash route. Believe me, there were many times I really hated it. But there's these times in my life, that I've thanked him many times, in my old years of my life today.

I was only four when Mom and Dad brought us out from Arizona to California, I'm amazed with myself how I remember that. Could only speak Spanish. Living in a all white neighborhood was no joke. It was quite difficult for a small young boy like me, or anyone else if in my position. I can barely remember just a few times, playing marbles with a couple boys my age. Playing cowboys and Indians, running around our house. Very innocent times, and very few. Didn't know it then, but I know it today, and he knows it now as well. He had an alcoholic problem, a big problem. Because not only was it his problem, it became the family's problem as well. But the only good thing about my Dad's alcoholic problem, that he would always go to work, regardless. He never missed work. In so many ways, Dad was a very tough man, and I respect him for that today. But not then. In the long run, Dad made me tough. What I've seen him do, when I was very young and small, I've learned never to do, in my adult life.

Remembering a very violent moment I witnessed, again when I was very young. Mom had waited for him all night long, and then I heard a car pull up outside. I go running to the front door, and my uncle is right outside, looking at me, telling me, "Boy Is your Dad drunk" I stood watching from the front door, Dad having a problem getting out of the car. He couldn't even walk by himself, he needed both of his arms supported to walk up to his own front door. Had never seen him drunk, let alone completely drunk. Thought to myself, "What Ashame" His cousin and his brother trying hard to walk him to bed. He gets on top of the bed, and then he starts swinging at everything and everyone. And hits the bedroom window, breaking it, and cutting himself. Thinking to myself, "WOW Dad How Could You" Have never forgotten that. I guess as a very young boy, I sort of lost respect for my Dad. And that's sad in itself. It has taken me until now, to build respect for him after so long. Have got to say, I really felt I didn't have a Dad when I was just a boy. To me my dear readers, that was very abusive, emotionally.

After that drunken incident, I really didn't have many things to say. So I started becoming rebellious, slowly but surely. And I didn't realize it then. Looking at Dad's young life, he experienced the same life with his Dad, unfortunately. My grandpa passed on, from alcoholism.

In my younger years I slowly saw Mom go down her life of agony, like undeserved sufferers often do. Having her heart broken by her immediate family, including myself, many times, including Dad. Dad coming home too many times drunk. It got real serious. To the point, he wouldn't even come home, and when he would get home, he'd be so drunk. Mom being so worried, he would kill himself in some traffic accident. A couple of times when he did make it home, he'd get home without a wallet, and someone that found the wallet would bring it home, of course without money. I often wondered why did my Mother stay with Dad, for soo many years. She'd often told me, when I would ask her, I'll never leave your Dad, because she Loved him. Thought to myself, WOW, she's one very strong lady, to love a very weak man, behind alcoholism.

And then I have two sisters, that were always fighting, calling each other names, and that also contributed to her agony. These two sisters, were always at each other's throats. Each one of them would call me to talk about the other one. And I always told each one, "Don't call me and try to side with you against your sister. Never could stand it, because it always broke Mom's heart. I really strongly believe, we all helped put Mom in her grave. Yes, I really believe that.

Tears on Mother's face was too often, and it saddens me to admit, that I had a bad part of that, but the truth is the truth. And just knowing Dad, and these two sisters, I know they would never admit to it. But what do they say when good people crossover to another world. They're in a better place now. She's not suffering anymore. I often think Mom is sometimes around my wife and I. I'll always remember my mother's prayers. I remember Mom as a little boy as a teenager, as a young adult and now as an old man. When I was a boy, Mom would go with Dad, and help him with his trash route. Imagine your Mom helping Dad with a trash route, getting up very early to go pick up trash in a stinky truck, picking up stinky people's trash. That was my Mom, she would go all the way for Dad. This lady Mom of mine, was what ladies are supposed to do, love till death do you part. As a boy, I never saw that in my family, nor in anyone else's family. Money wasn't in Mom's heart, has always been love. Mom was always there for all of us. Yes, Dad was there for us as well, he was the one that brought home the money, but Mom was the one that would spend the money on food, clothing, pay the bills. Mama buying food for us children to support us for school. That was very important, at least that's what my Mama thought.

Remembering my young life, and noticing Mom's worries for her children and our Dad was so depressing to watch. I always wanted to go out of the house to be with friends.

Or just stay stuck in my room, either to do my homework or listen to music. Awwe music, I loved music so very much at a very young age in my life. Those were beginning times of rock and roll, when I was only nine or ten. Back then, oh man that was music, just after the jitter bug days of the forties. Mom and Dad couldn't stand the introduction of rock and roll, especially Dad, he hated with a passion. With Mom, it didn't seem to bother her. Because I would Rock and Roll in my bedroom, and did I Rock and Roll!!! I loved it. Mom was peaceful, while Dad was radical about my loud music. And Dad, of course would love his drinking, if he was home drinking, or out in some bar. Instead of trying to be with his family, or at least try to spend time with his only son, me. I always thought he would be bored being home. There were those young years of mine, trying to just talk to Dad, and he wouldn't have it. And man did that hurt me. In all in all, I became a rebel. Started to Rebel about anything he wanted me to do. Another reminisce of my youngster years. When Mom and Dad would take us visiting his cousin's or a uncle and I would get into a mischievous encounter with one of my cousins, he would literally take his belt, and whip me in front of family. And there came that time, I didn't give Dad the satisfaction, to break down and cry in front of family. I became tired of Dad trying to treat me the way his Dad treated him. My crying days were over from three or four years old. Oh yes there has always been other things in life that will hurt me more than any beating or any whipping. That's for sure my friends.

On the other hand with Mom, that was a very different story. Mom was a very respectable lady in my life. Oh she would let me know if I was being disrespectful. She taught me love, she taught me manners, she taught me respect. And people respected Mom. And Mom Loved Dad so very much. If Mom liked you, she would end up loving you. I'll always miss Mom, till I leave this side of life. Mom was the one that kept our family together, with love. My sweet Mama. It's so sad Mom started developing diabetes. She didn't deserve it, and she didn't deserve the life she got from her family, from Dad on down.

Read it somewhere in the Bible, that God has a special place for people like my Mother. I saw that these kind of selfless people are called, Undeserved sufferers. These special people do the work of God from the kindness from their hearts, not just because God is watching, but because they just want to. Remembering Mom, that was the way she was. You could see the gracious spirit in her. As I feel her around me sometimes.

I'd like to think I was an observant person, or what seems kind of weird, after that awful truck accident, my whole life changed. I was no longer the same seven year old, as I was before that accident happened. That might seem strange, but that's how I feel. From seven and onward with my young life, I've been able to remember more things than most people do. Just the flash backs I've had all my life are remarkable, from that horrific experience. Often thought, what kind of life would I have had, if I wouldn't had been traumatized, by having my neck twisted, banging my head numerous times inside a twisting truck cab.

Remember, I mentioned my Dad and my uncle. We were all very young then. But we literally died that day.

No we didn't die in the physical sense of actually dying, like most people die in most traffic accidents, as we see it or hear it happening everyday. May I ask you readers, are there any of you, that were traumatized, by an experience like mine? I'm sure there are, I'm not alone!! Those of you, will understand what I'm talking about. I will leave it at that.

Moving on with my life, after that, my life became more interesting. Some of you people, would probably ask, HOW? You have to understand, I didn't know it then. Things had to start a slow change, and become old as I am now. The following after the accident, I started my third grade class. And started an interest in the opposite sex. No don't get me wrong, wasn't having an urge to have sex. Didn't know anything about it. I'm only seven or eight, much too young and immature to know any of that stuff. But I became curious about girls. As I wrote this, asking myself, isn't being curious about girls at my age of seven or eight normal? Not knowing anything about girls. Carrying a scar on my face all my life. Being afraid of them, so I wouldn't trust them. Would later grow up over that. Remembering the third grade, had this teacher that made me think and feel that she liked me. How so you may ask. Remember I mentioned didn't get much attention at home. But with this teacher, she was very attentive to everyone in her class. It was me, started getting mixed feelings, since my Dad and sometimes Mom wouldn't give that loving attention I craved. So to me, I liked her. Oh she never knew it. And I was glad. Can you imagine. I thought I would get in trouble for liking my third grade teacher. So I never let it be known, at least to her that I liked her. I still remember her name, it will probably be hard for you to believe that, but I still remember her name after almost seventy years. Not mentioning any names, because it could and would offend of those names of those loving people in my life.

Anyway there was this one day in class with this attractive teacher, as she made her rounds to each and every student., as she always did. She stopped at my table, noticing my work, as she lingered closely. She says to me, "You're doing beautiful work, and you've come a long way,

DIED THREE TIMES LIVED ONCE ~11~

would you like to stay after school, and finish your work with me?" Can you imagine what went through my mind? Yes really!!! What could an eight year old imagine?

Couldn't understand anything what I was feeling, maybe because I've never felt that before, if you know what I mean. Of course when I arrived home, a little late for a third grader, Mom was concerned and quite worried. As she asks me. "What happened son, why are you just getting home"? That was a secret to a boy my age, what eight years old!!! So I says, "Had to stay after school to finish my work". I thought I was being honest, but was I? Not really, as I think about that infatuation, because that's what it was. After all, we all go through infatuations, don't we? I soon recovered from that hot feeling, didn't know it then, but now I know what it was. A boy's inexperienced, immature feeling for a grown woman. Can you men out there agree with me?

As I mentioned before, tried talking to Dad, about many things, but we always struck out in that department. Trying to talk to Dad, about girls, was, like trying to talk to him about Geometry, impossible!!! I've always thought, a man should sit and talk to his family. Especially when a boy wants to communicate with his Dad. Not my Dad. He always seemed too busy for me. Asking him one day. "Dad, can I talk to you about something?" He made me feel like I was interrupting him, in something he was going to do. And what that be, but just having another binge of drinking. Didn't know which one Dad was more into, being an alcoholic or being a workaholic. Dad always went to work regardless if he had a lot to drink the day before. That's just how Dad was. He was not a lazy man, by a long shot. In fact he worked two jobs, now that's tough for any man, don't care who you are. He had no education, so he sends his three children to school, with a lot of support from Mama. Oh yes, he would've never made it, without Mama. Although my Dad and I didn't have much in communication when I just a boy, I know now, his heart was in the right direction. After all, my grandpa, my Dad's Dad! In the nineteen twenties. Dad's Dad never believed in sending his children to school. School was secondary in those days. I've often wondered how my grandpa was raised. Probably much worse than how he raised his ten kids. The old saying was, in the old days, and I heard it a lot, as I grew up. The more kids a man had, the more help a man would get out of his family. Always thought as I was growing up, thinking to myself. Not letting no one know what I thought. The more kids, more of a bigger pain in the ass, and more mouths to feed. And it also becomes very expensive. In today's standards, very very expensive.

What I know about our country's history, it's been a great country. How long will our U.S. of A stay great, we don't know. All I know is, America has had its victories, sadly saying at soo many lives lost. Going to school was always interesting to me. My history teachers were very informative. Tried paying as much attention as possible. I know for Dad to go to school was impossible, as impossible as it was for my grandpa. Speaking of grandpa, can't even imagine how hard it was living in his days. Dad told me my grandpa was born between eighteen eighty and eighteen ninety. Wow!!! Like I mentioned, never had the opportunity to talk to my grandpa, my Dad's Dad. By the time I thought I would be able to communicate with my grandpa, he passed away, of alcoholism.

How sad!! Never thought I was being disrespectful, when I would refuse to go with my family to a funeral. My parents would say, okay, get dressed we're going to see your grandpa at his funeral. Many times I would refuse. Parents wouldn't have it, and wouldn't hear it. "You're going if you know what's good for you" And guess what, either I go or get whipped. Oh yes, my days of receiving whippings was pretty much a weekly thing for Dad and I.

Reason being I never wanted to go see a loved one at a funeral, I would always cry. Always wanted to remember them when they were alive, not seeing them in a casket. So what's wrong with that? My parents just didn't understand my emotions. But I didn't understand about that part of respect when I was just a boy. Understandable right? Dad would say to me, "Either you go and cry at the funeral, or you don't go, and you cry more here", "So which is it" and I would say "I'm going" Then going to the funeral was already bad enough, now I just want to sit at the pew where I was sitting, didn't want to go to the front of the church to look at whoever was in the casket. So again, Dad has to give me a warning look of terror. Then I'd get up and go to the front of the church, oh my god, here I go. I'd cry!!! Just remember a little how I would cry as a small boy. They even took pictures of me crying. Kid, get over it. It was embarrassing, my parents taking pictures of me crying, of what the heck, I was just a boy, I will have to get over it. We all should. But I'm sure there are those of you out there that never got over the cry baby personality. That's sad huh? As I mentioned about my Dad's whippings. Mmmm Mmmm!! That hurt for a long time, as a boy! There were times when I knew I was gonna get another whipping, I would run from Dad. Oh no, all that did, was make Dad more mad, from whatever I got him mad in the first place.

When it came for Mom to whip me, now that was just a spanking nothing serious. My Mom was short, like many moms were, not too much power behind her spank and were just a few times. When Mom would really get upset with me, she go after the belt, and come at me to start swinging, and I would grab her hands and hold them from trying to whip me. She'd say "Let me go" I'd say "no Mama, you're going to spank me" she'd say, I'm telling your Dad. Oh my god, thinking, here it comes again, another whipping from Dad. As I said, there were a few times I'd run from Dad when he wanted to whip me, oh but when he'd catch me, it was a double whipping, as he would say to me, "don't run from me" as he commenced to whipping little oh me. Just thinking of those young days of my life, realizing those beatings from my Dad, probably helped me for my own good. In the long run it would help protect myself, even help me to protect my life from bullies. God only knows how many times I was able to protect myself from those that underestimated me. As I mentioned I had already gotten into my first fight at five years. Started at that age to not let anyone push me around, just because of my size.

Another painful memorial painful experience I remember. Remember I mentioned about Dad having to, or maybe he liked whipping me. Started thinking after a while, he liked whipping me. Trying to weigh this all out as a boy, was absolutely impossible for me. I would have to do that later in life.

Let me continue sharing with you another unique experience of part one of my life, my first part of my life. Mentioning it before my

Dad having me work at an early age, by no choice of my own. Now, that wasn't such a bad thing. Of all the things for a man to do, was taking a boy of an age of, I'm repeating it, five, six, seven, nine, ten, and eleven. Dad had to just let me go to school when I was eight, because the experience, Dad and my uncle and I in that truck collision. Dad finally had to hire someone who could help him out. Because Dad would definitely need help. As I recall those ages, five through eleven. Dad would even take my mom to help him. Don't recall how Dad found a Korean veteran to help him on his trash business, just literally pick trash in the wee hours of every morning. Wish I could explain my relief from not having to go with Dad to pick up trash anymore. Whuuu, wheee!!! Yes it sure was. Thank God. Oh yeah, Dad was very hard to work with. So there it is, it's already hard to get up anywhere from three thirty to four thirty, to get into the grime of other people's trash. You should know at the time, there were no garbage disposals. No there wasn't any. Those were those times. So I'll put it to you this way. We would pick people's trash and garbage, throw it into our truck and take it to the dump, and Dad would of course charge a fee for each month. But like I said, that was very hard work, but when things wouldn't go as planned, Dad would get really upset, so who's the closest to take his anger out on, you got it, me. And that would hurt more. Finding out much later, that is how life is. As you can tell there's not much to my childhood, but just going to school, and Dad would take me to work. Physically learning what real work was at an early age, call it what you like, but I'll always think it's a good thing for men to be taught hard physical work as a boy.

Going with Dad, working with him on summer vacations, but as I attended school, started understanding how important school was for me, and how important school is for everyone. So, as I said, school I went, and loved it. Couldn't believe how many others didn't like it. As I would see some get bored, I would pay more attention, then it wasn't so boring. Especially mathematics and the history of our country. Some kids were so mischievous, but that will always be. Dad was I guess, a good role model, when it came to not look for fighting. On the other hand, don't let me hear you say anything bad about my family. Oh God, have never been able to control my temper on that. Speaking of temper, oh my god, this particular day, on one beautiful day. Neighborhood kids will be just that, neighborhood kids, coming out of our family home after a nice family meal. Don't remember who was the smart ass. He made a very nasty comment. Tells me. "Your Mama was sure good last night" Now Let me ask anyone out there. How would anybody react, or how are you supposed to react?

Well, I'll try my best in describing how I reacted. Turned into complete rage, and that's an understatement, I really mean it. Thought I would actually kill someone after saying something real stupid about my mother. My mother being a very respectable woman, with friends and relatives knowing the sweet lady my mom was. May God Bless my mama. When she would like you, she'd end up loving you. Well needless to say, I literally tore into these fools. Just after the comment was said, I commenced to punch, poke eyes, pull ears, pull hair, kick, kick, and kick. Just kicking four stupid kids on top on yelling and cursing them out. Yelling, "Don't you ever talk about my mother like that, do you effing hear me" One kid said, "Ok man, ok man" we were just joking "I say back, "Well I don't like jokes like that, never have and never will, and I don't talk about your mother like that, so you leave my mother alone "After that incident, they never said those things to me again. They learned to respect my world the hard way. But it didn't stop there unfortunately. On the weekends, believed that for a long time. As a boy, felt very close to Dad. But it slowly faded away, as time flew by. Sad, right? And it hurts to say it. Became a painful memory. Dad couldn't help being who he was, like we can't help being who we are. Figured it out through time, it's blood and what's in our heart. The most fun, I can remember, Mom and Dad and my siblings had together were few, but there were some. It seemed like an adventure back then. Our Mom and Dad would take us to Arizona for summer vacations from school. Big deal, right? Back then it was a very big deal and exciting, for me especially. Because it would rid the monotony. Visit our relatives. Cousins, aunts and uncles, Grandparents from both sides. As a very little boy, my best uncle, on mom's side would take me in his fancy car, would tell me how much he missed me, and buy me what I wanted.

Spoiled? You can call it what you want. Everyone called it love. Uncle was a very lovable person. He loved a lot of people, and a lot of people loved him. I must have been between eight and ten years old, when he passed on to the other side. He was about thirty six when we lost him.

But it didn't have to be difficult. And I realize now how more difficult it is for you people that might read this. Less fortunate than myself. In my situation, it has been a family's life chain reaction, but only from myself, my Dad, my Dad's Dad, and probably my Dad's Dad, and his Dad. A poor struggle from any of those generations, from the time we were born. Speaking for myself. From myself on back, we've made terrible mistakes and wrong choices, at the costs of my daughters future.

As I flashback, looking at my child self. Started off good, at least I think I did. Going to school, going to work with Dad. A kind of work that no child should go through, but what choice did Dad have. None!!! Dad, with no education, and he trying to pursue a better life for his children. How beautiful is that, and what's wrong with a man trying to do that for their future? As I said it before, alcoholism and addictions ran hand in hand, in my entire family, from cousins to cousins, uncle to uncle. Have had a few of them die from those diseases, because that's what they are. Diseases!!!

As a boy, wasn't a mouthy bad boy, as I was told. Dad had that under control. Oh yes he did. Good, right? As I grew up, I thought that was a good thing. Don't you? And when I did speak, never said anything, smart ass. Again, so I was told. And How cool is that? In grade school, have always tried asking as smart a question as I could. Of course it was hard to do that, like everything I ever tried to do right. And without strong support and proper guidance. But like I said, Dad never had that strong support and proper guidance as well. Could probably have put the blame on my Dad, and I started to. But I stopped. Why should I blame Dad, when it wasn't his fault.

Dad had always told me, we could do something so powerful together. Always with them. In a matter of a couple of hours, I would have been with them, riding in the back seat of a police car.

Naturally I told Mom what happened. She stared at me, "I don't know why, but I felt something wrong about those kids, see what happened, you would've been with them"

It broke so many hearts when my best uncle passed away. And what was the reason he passed on? Here's the sad news. Alcoholism took him away! Dyed in my grandpa's arms, in his own daddy's arms. After that happened, didn't really matter to me if we ever went to Arizona again. Mourned him, I think about two years. It's been so long ago now. Had to learn to forget and accept. Maybe accept, but I will never forget him.

So on with my life, with Mom, Dad and my sisters. Sisters!!! Not close by no means. I think I tried, maybe I didn't. They always fought with themselves. As the only son, and sisters only brother, and sisters, most of the time fighting with themselves, how could I be close to either one of my sisters. It was hard. So I became a loner, what else. Had school friends, but never brought them home. I wasn't permitted to bring anyone to the house. Just go to school and back. And I better be in my room doing homework. Good, right? Think it was good now!! But back then, bored to hell. Thank God for music. Alright, oh yes. I fell in love with a passion for music. Guess you can say, was self disciplined, with the best I could manage with my behaving myself, as Mom and Dad would like. Could have been like all others I've seen. Go with bad influences, whether meeting them at school or right in the neighborhood.

Remembering one of those bad influences, this particular one. Must have been about eleven or twelve, one of those. Dad just brought me my first ten speed bicycle. How sweet was that!! But what didn't make any sense, having a bicycle, but not allowed to go anywhere. What!!! So this kid asked me to go with him and another kid. Didn't think much of it. Just riding our bikes, to and from a shopping center. But no one knows what goes on anybody's mind, that's for sure. I tell this kid, remember I'm a kid too. I tell him, have to ask Mom. He laughs, why, you're twelve already, and you still have to ask your mom. And Mom tells me no. That absolutely aggravated me to the limit, almost beyond my limits. Mom knew it, and says to me, "You are not going with those kids, and you better not go if you know what's good for you." I was so so mad at mom. Well I didn't go, and it was a very good thing. Just standing in the front yard and I noticed a Sheriffs police car, coming down the neighborhood as I watched closely who was in the back seat of that police car. Thinking to myself, oh my god, it was those kids that wanted me to go with them to ride our bikes to and from a shopping center. They had gotten caught shoplifting, what ever it was it didn't matter, they had got caught stealing. Can you imagine, these two, ask me to go with them, really asking me to go steal just about getting into the swing of being a teenager, we just have to try drugs, I mean what the hell, what fun is it without drugs? Right? No later on I found out of course that's wrong. No, for me growing up in a dysfunctional family, alcohol and drugs was a big problem. But it hasn't become my problem at that age yet. Not as a child, and not as a teenager, thank God for me. As a teenager, I think I was thirteen, had a cousin my same age, was playing too hard in getting high. So one day I heard, he was with someone that probably didn't like him, so they overdosed him and threw him in his home driveway, dead. Always thought and never forgot about that. But remembering how wild he was, was why he was dead at thirteen. Which makes me come back to the kid that said that nasty comment about my mother. He also had the problem with drugs. Poor kid, we were all so young then. We all did drugs. Although I did too, but didn't let it consume me nor let it control my life, at least not yet. That will be in an other life.

Maybe I mentioned and maybe I haven't. Dad moved us from Arizona to start a new life in California. Was very young to remember much of anything, after all I was just four. With a two year old sibling, another one on the way. Life was hard for us to say the least. Never knew and never asked, why Mom and Dad decided to just move out to another state and not know anyone and not knowing where we're going to receive our next meal. Just the thought of it, kind of scares me, as I thought about it. But then again, Dad was a go getter. In other words, he was a hustler. But not in a bad sense of the word. But just to find a way to support his family. He was and will always be a better man than I could ever be. But my young life has only just begun, with my connection with my Dad. Didn't know it then that it would be one of my difficult journeys of my life.

Mom tells me, "See what happened" I pretty much respected Mom's intuition after that incident. Didn't ever tell momma what I should've told her all those years ago. Maybe she hears my thoughts after all these years she's been gone, too many years now. Also should've told mom at that time, "What happened mom, is you saved me from trouble, in a ride in a police car home." Oh and when Mom told Dad about what happened and what could've happened, he never let me forget it. And why would he, it was good for my own good. But things didn't stop there, I'm still on my journey, surfing my waves of life through. Don't pay attention anymore, but in those days, surf was up.

As I've said, started my life as a loner. Oh I had friends and got along real good with my peers. Just wasn't a loud mouth as I observed others to be. You know what I mean, don't you people? Oh, I could ask pretty interesting questions, and get into a great discussion, on pretty much any topic. Not as a young boy, but I started challenging life in general. After all, isn't life a challenge from the time we're born? I loved the challenge, I mean, how boring would it be, if every step of life was easy. For very intelligent people, I can imagine how boring life can be. Huh, you smarties out there? If you find this good to read. You might think, you're too smart to read this. But I'll dare you, because I think anyone can learn what anyone has to say.

Those kids that had that free ride home in a police car, well, never really connected with them very much. Maybe a hi, here and there. But nothing like best of friends, hell no, couldn't start waisting my time with that kind. Was far too young for that. But there were other kids in the same neighborhood. Good for me. There was this eight member family, that I got to know. A pretty level close knit family. All went to school, always seemed close to one another. I liked that. There was this young girl, two years younger than me. Real cute. And we liked each other, but we were too young. Ten and twelve, too young huh? We all played croquet. Loved that game, we all played and laughed and ate. They treated me like I was part of the family. That's a beautiful memory of those days with that loving family. Will never forget them.

Although I spent a lot of time with that beautiful family, my family on the other hand never spoke with them. Mom was always stuck right next door, to a nice lady and her daughters and her husband. They weren't bad people, but I was more into the bigger family, don't know why. Maybe because I liked that young girl. Mmmmm!!! And the kid that was my age, he liked football and baseball. Oh, how I still love baseball. Who doesn't, right?

Only the sad thing about growing up, loving baseball, and playing the game, never had the support of a Dad watching me play. While I noticed in all games I played, parents of the other boys, cheering us on. Would look into the stands, no body from my family around. Never. Mostly because, Dad wasn't into sports of

Oh yeah, my good young days. Many times in my life as a boy, it was fun, and exciting, weren't they people? But aren't they scary when you don't know what's gonna happen, when it comes to something, you know was wrong. But isn't that normal? As I meditate and reminisce about that time of my life, maybe it was normal and maybe it wasn't. I ask you, what is normal? Many have their own definition of normal. Like I have mine, you have yours.

Being asked the very question, "WHAT IS NORMAL?" Thinking about my feelings about a third grade teacher, which made me feel different when she would get close, was that normal, don't know, but of course I've oftenned wondered. Learned to accept that feeling as a growing up boy to a teenager and as a young man. Getting into a fight in my first year of school. Kindergarten!! Was that normal? I never thought so. My teacher then, didn't think so. First day of school, mom leaves me at school, and I climbed the fence and followed mom back home. Was that normal? No other kid did that, and never heard about anybody else doing that.

When visiting cousins and aunts and uncles, in Arizona, loveed picking on cousins that easily irritated me. By throwing my cousin's beanie to a mean dog. And laughed when I saw him crying. How cold!!! Thinking of that day, maybe I did that, just to spite Dad. Because even if I thought I was doing good, I would get spanked, excuse me, whippings more on a regular daily thing that happened to me. The way I look at it, that was discipline. I could have gotten into much more trouble than just a whipping or two. You young readers, probably wouldn't agree with me, because you'll never know what it was to live in the nineteen twenties nor the nineteen fifties. Because you kids have it made today. Kids today can put their own parents in jail, if mom or dad just threaten the kids.

Looking at my little boy days, they weren't so bad after all. And Dad has never been a bad person. He tried the best way he knew how.

How many people can say, having a Dad, as when I wrote this, he was 96 years old. Born in the 1920s, a WWII veteran. As just little boys, we don't know what is a veteran, much less knowing what a World War 2 veteran is. Until we become one.

But in my young life, I felt ignored by Dad. Feeling lonely at such a young age, is not a comfortable feeling, if anyone reading me understand what I'm talking about.

Continuing on my journey of obstacles, baring down on emotional and physical pain, that I didn't have a clue how I would ever succumb. The physical part of my young road, having my body thrown around a truck cab, not even conscious. I think after all those years, I'm finally suffering the after shock. Can that be, I was only seven, and now I'm in my seventies. Possible, right, who knows. But I can still write about it after a long time ago.

I've probably said this to you before, but I'll say it again. And I know I'm not the only one. After that deathly horrible experience at seven years old. I'm sure it's happened to some of you, right? Or maybe not. This is why, I've always thought I've always had a unique life.

Well, after that experience with life or death. That little boy, who I was before that truck accident, I changed. I really think I changed dramatically. Since it was a deathly experience, I really think I died. Not in the sense of physically dying, but I died psychologically, yes I did. Because before that happened to me, can't remember too many things. But to this day I can remember so many more things than most people. That's all I'm saying. Am I weird or what? Not so, because like I said, I'm sure it happens to some. And this happened to me.

ROBERT GARCIA

We all have our own life stories, don't we? Some worse than others. I've always thought my story was unique, until I grew up and gotten old.

Let me share with you another whipping incident of my life. Or I'll say, another whipping given to me by my dear old Dad. Another OUCH of a day.

Again at another visit of my relatives in Arizona. I mentioned, I believe I did anyway. On mom's side of the family, this one uncle who had thirteen children, there I've got your attention, right? Can't remember for the life of me, why I was whipped so terribly bad, because that really hurt. I think the real reason it hurt the most, is because, I remember Dad laughing while he was swinging the belt. Do you believe what I'm saying? You can believe it or disbelieve it, it doesn't matter, because it really happened, and it really hurt. And I'm not talking about the whipping, I'm talking about the laughing, that hurt the most. Picture the scenario. Dad yells at me, as to what I did, don't remember, he grabs me, as he's holding me in the air, like a pig, he's taking off his belt, still holding me, and started swinging the belt as hard as he could. And that's not the part that hurt, because as he was whipping, I started seeing teeth, like the devil himself, and he began to laugh. As I was crying, thought to myself, "My God he's enjoying whipping me" I have never been able to forget that. Of course I've never confronted Dad about that. Why would I do that? After all, that's how he was brought up. He didn't know any different. Thank God he never did that again, as far as I can remember. Maybe by chance mom found out about it. Don't remember, but maybe I told mom. And she complained to Dad. Of course after that, I was deathly afraid of Dad. As a thought stayed stuck, thinking, if Dad enjoys really whipping me, he might kill me, and enjoy it. Or maybe he wouldn't have meant to kill me, but some how I die by an accident.

Have heard stories, about children getting whipped, or to put it mild, spanked would be the word. Heard stories that some kids would get badly spanked, and go into a coma, and not wake up, and die.

Maybe that's why society put into law, many years later, for parents not to be hitting their kids in any shape or form.

Looking back at my young times, I'm better off being disciplined when I would get out of hand. And maybe I would. No, there's no maybe about it. I would definitely get off track. Not in a sense of hurting anyone. Never thought about hurting anyone. Well, that's questionable? Earlier I shared with you about my first fight in as early as kindergarten. As I thought, when that happened, the aftermath of that. It was always in my mind, my God, how is my life going to be. Hopefully it wouldn't continue. And it didn't happen for a while. Until!!! Just had to say, Until. Because it did happen again.

I've mentioned, that I've never liked any boy nor man hitting, hurting girls and women. And that's putting it mildly. I've always hated it. Ever since I was a little boy, always thought, any boy or man that hits and especially hurts a girl or a woman, is a friggin coward. Just because he's stronger. That's not being strong, that's being weak. And again, that's putting it mildly.

As far back as I can remember, I've never hit any female for no reason. Oh, I've had my reasons, and I have crossed that road. Didn't have a choice, when I did strike a woman. But that will come in my later life. When my life and world goes spiraling down. And tumbling down it will. So as I start my life story, my crashing down life has just begun. Try to believe me, if you will, I've never been a bad person, and my Mom and Dad, have never been bad parents. Dad always working, and not just working one job, but two!!! Mom always giving their three kids, motivation and support. She'll always be my special lady in my heart. Without our mom's love and prayers, I would have died, and I wouldn't be writing this. As I'm just writing the beginning of my life and sharing this with you. In this part, I have experienced my first death. Little would I know, I will go through two more deaths in my life. This is why, I died Three times and Lived Once.

I've had to call out these cowards, that think they're men. I almost thought my Dad would be one of them. But I never saw him put a hand on my mom, thank God for that, because I never wanted to know what I would do to Dad. What, I don't know, but I'm glad I never had to find out. I've always had a bad temper, since I was little.

ROBERT GARCIA

Continuing on my temperamental experiences. But as a boy, never tried reacting on anger, after all, I'm just a boy. Is that normal? Always thought it was.

Sharing with you, my few experiences of witnessing boys and men hitting girls and women

And I will never forget them as long as I live, because I've felt since I was a boy, women give birth. Hello, that's right!!! In case you guys that enjoy hitting and beating girls or women. And if you do, your all a bunch of cowards, a bunch of weaklings. That's what I see, in males that hurt the opposite sex.

The time when I was very young in kindergarten, can you imagine, I still remember that. But I'll never forget it, because I have a scar to prove it. There is this little girl, and as a boy, didn't understand it at the time. Out of the blue, she yells at me, "Hey", and sticks her tongue at me. And what, I go running after her, and never reach her, because this huge fat teacher, sitting at the classroom door way, gets up and pushed her chair right in my running path, I go crashing into the chair, and knocked me out. Vaguely remembering, being carried by the principal, walking to my house. Mom answering and opening the door, in complete shock, wondering what the hell happened to her little boy. My left part of my face, patched up. Mom of course crying. Her only little boy, wounded at five years old. Don't think Mom ever forgot about my scar on my face. As I said, always hated cowards, who would hit girls or women. But I've oftenned wondered, what would I had done to that girl, if I would have caught up with her. Would I have hit her? We'll never know, because I will never know. Maybe, most likely not. Who knows, maybe I would have kissed her. Would like to think so. Anyway moving on, and passing on to the following grades. And then reaching the third grade. Telling you before, I had this amazing feeling about my third grade teacher. Can't never forget her name, because I don't want to. And this feeling, started happening after my first experience with death. Nothing happened in fourth grade. But what I do remember in fourth grade. This certain teacher, my social studies teacher, telling all of us, that we could be facing a confrontation with North Vietnam, the communist part of Vietnam. At the time, which was nineteen fifty eight, I was only ten years old at the time. I'm sure I was not the only one, thinking to myself, what is this woman talking about? I wasn't even fully grown, and this teacher is throwing us into war. Thinking to myself, that's not going to happen, "I hope not" I quickly forgot about that thought, thinking, that teacher is wrong. I'll get into it later, that she was right.

Feeling good about myself, as I progressed. That same year, I became an A student in mathematics. I said, wow, all by myself. After all, couldn't get any help at home. Remember, how could anyone help me, having siblings two and four years younger than I, and having uneducated parents. How could, and who would help me. Well, I thought up a plan. Started asking teachers if I could stay after class, just to help me with a couple of practice problems, and get home and immediately do my homework.

As I started my life, as a boy, into my teenage years, into being a young man, now that I'm old. It's been an adventurous hell of a journey.

There were a few big reasons why I had to try to advance in school. I think the biggest was, just because I wanted to, and try to be something or someone.

Well, back to my outrage of cowards that enjoy beating up girls or women. I will always despise cowards that think they're men, that overpower women.

Now, at this stage of my life, I'm now eleven, in the fifth grade. And I started having a crush on a cute girl. But it was only a crush, because it never amounted to anything else. But it would've been nice if something would've come out good in that relationship, but I was too young. She was a smart girl too. And she became a queen of the high school, where I could have gone with her. But we moved out of the neighborhood. How disappointing it was for me, when I had to tell her.

We were in the same class together. She was the smartest of the girls, and the teacher made me feel I was the smartest of the boys. How cool was that? There was this time in class, the teacher had us go through a spelling bee. For some of you that don't know what a spelling bee. I'll explain it the best way I can. In this one I was in. All the girls stood with the backs against the wall on one side of the class while all the boys stood with the backs against the other part of the wall. As the teacher would pronounce a word to the first girl to spell it. If she couldn't spell it, that girl would have to sit down, and pass the word to the first boy, and if he couldn't spell it, he would have to sit down. That would go on until words are spelled correctly. It was a lot of fun, believe me, if you loved school like I did. And the girl I liked loved school as well. Check the scenario out, there were about twenty or twenty five kids in the classroom, fifteen girls and fifteen boys. Trying to out spell each other, fun if you like that kind of stuff. And we did. And imagine this, your little girlfriend and you end up the only ones standing, and now you have to try to out spell her. And guess what, I ended up the only one standing. How sweet was that for me.

I guess you know how awesome we felt that day, only if you like that kind of stuff. Both of us felt pretty good for each other.

The next thing I remember, the whole school goes outside for lunch. After that spelling bee, I felt closer to my little female friend. Always felt, I couldn't call her my girlfriend, after all we weren't dating. What at eleven years old, and in the fifth grade. A little too young, don't you think? I thought so. But it felt good to know, I liked her and she liked me. That's all that mattered to me, then.

Anyway, it seemed like the whole school was outside for lunch. Everyone looked like, we were all having fun. As I observed, everyone watching kids playing different games, laughing and girls screaming, just typical kids having fun. Everyone having a happy school day. At least I thought everyone was having a fun day, and then from the corner of my eye, I catch a glimpse of my friend with another boy. What? I'm already not liking this picture, and I still look at it. They're talking seriously, with no smiles on their faces. So now I'm staring at them, without them knowing I was looking, because there was a crowd. And all of a sudden, this coward turns fast as he swings and slaps her. Instantaneously, I mean it took me a split second to react, running towards them, can't remember if I started pushing people. Can't remember that. Pushing people out of the way didn't matter to me. I just wanted to grab this S.O.B. and beat him up. Can you see it, I felt like I was flying over people, I really felt like I was. This guy didn't see where I came from, because he didn't have time to prepare himself, when I flew into him with all fours, with eyes wide open. Both of us end up on the floor, I'm on top of this guy, as I commensed to beat him to shreds. Couldn't believe what was going through my head. And then he started crying, as I yell at him, telling him, "Don't you ever hit her again, do you understand me". He's trying to block my punches, he's trying to tell me, ok, ok man. And then we both get up, as he sizes me up. As I stared him down. Then I ask him, did you understand what I said? Him saying "Huh huh" made me think he understood. Walking away from our situation, never seen him hit my friend again. Thinking to myself, good for him. After that day, that violent confrontation gave me a whole lot of confidence in myself. Enough confidence to never let anyone underestimate me. It's been unfortunate for many whom I've encountered, which I've had to prove it to. It seems like a long time ago now, but I've continued to do that until this day. It has never been easy, believe me, growing up to a height of five eight. That's all I have. A thing my mama, always said as I was growing, dynamite comes in small packages.

You all know, life can be and can get tough and unfair. I know it's been pretty tough for me. But what the hell, learned not to be afraid of any boy or man. Or anyone that matter. So as I was growing up after my first seven years of my life, I had faced a few challenges and stand up to some idiots. And even if they are intoxicated, like my Dad at one particular day, was. So I stood up to my Dad.

Life should be a challenging experience for any man, but you get there first, starting as a boy. Those are our first steps, no matter what.

There are two sports that I've realized that I really love. Baseball and boxing.

As a boy, never thought boxing was a sport. But it is, and I've learned to enjoy it. But as a boy, always thought, how people enjoy, watching, either men or women, torchering each other. Have you people ever wonder about that? But it's an old dramatic enjoyment for people. We all love watching people spill their blood and guts out. Am I right?

You guys can believe this or not. Of course I didn't die physically but I died psychologically. Do you understand what I'm saying? For those of you that have experienced this kind of tragedy, you would understand. But it's true. It's a traumatic experience. It's like Post Traumatic Stress Disorder. Well I've had P.T.S.D since I was seven years old. And never knew it. Never even knew there was such a thing. Never would have known, that I would experience more than one P.T.S.D. experience. As I've explained, the physical part of my first deathly experience, was a twisted neck, and a couple of head cut slashes. But my mental experience would haunt me for the rest of my life. To this day, I still see that crash in my head. No, I don't let it torment me anymore, but every now and then, I think about it. But after it just happened, I would have night mares. After the spinning inside a truck, didn't know I would start having nightmares of falling and falling. It was so scary. But I had to grow up out of that, and not stay stuck on that horrific part of my life.

Episodes of life's experiences with death, can make a boy either grow up, and be a man or stay stuck as a boy. And I've seen boys my age, that never had my kind of life, had stayed just that, a boy. But they'll try being a bully with the kind of person, me!! Because since that year of my first deathly experience, I've thought it would hurt until I saw it too many times, for too many ballgames. That to me was a sense of undermining, and underestimating me, Dad's only son. But I still love my Dad. I have figured, that Dad only had what he had, which wasn't much, but the only way to love me, the only way he knew how. He was raised in hard times. How hard could it have been, during the Great Depression. And then after the Great Depression, World War 2, with Japan and Germany, if you know your history, you would know it. Dad coming out of a family of ten siblings, with an alcoholic dad, and living on a farm with lost causes. And if you studied your history, in those days, you were either rich or poor. That's just the way it was in those days. And on a farm where Dad was raised on, education was second in demand, and farm work was first. And to my grandpa, education was last in his books. He literally would not let his son, my Dad go to school My Dad would go to school like once a week, how humiliating was that for him? Naturally the teachers wouldn't pass Dad to the next grade. Well hello, if you don't go to school, you're simply not going to the next grade, it's not hard to figure that out. He told me a couple of times, that the kids around him in class, would make fun of him, because he was always bigger than everyone else.

It's no wonder, when mom and Dad moved us out from Arizona to California, which was back in 1952, which made me only four years old. And I would start school soon. And he would look into my eyes, and tell me, you're going to school no matter what. And that's what he did. Mom and Dad, sent his three children to school. Just the way Dad looked me in the eye, telling me, we were going to school no matter what. That was enough motivation to love school, and I did. Wanted to be proud of myself, wanted Mom and Dad to be proud of me. And they were very proud, for a long time. But that didn't last long. Anything good, doesn't last forever, how so many songs go, right? We were pretty much a happy family, when we were all young. There aren't too many families that are not happy when you're all young. But there are those few families, are way out, like pure evil. You people have heard about those families like I have. Like I have some family relatives, that I've heard are weird and evil, like I've seen and heard on t.v. news, or some movies. You've seen them as well. So many people have no shame, for the pain they cause to there loved ones. That's an understatement, those kind of people will never have a clue what love means.

From the times of old, kings and queens, or whatever or whoever ruled the countries of old, enjoyed gatherings of crowds of people to watch man against man, tare each other's bodies apart. It's always been a hunger of almost everyman to watch blood and guts spatter from one part of the ring to the other side of the ring. Am I right or wrong?

But as a boy, and at my age now, I've always admired the entertainment to learn from it, surely for me, I have never liked any man beat up the other man to bits. That's true. I've never challenged anyone in a fight, boy, teenager nor as a man. But I've been undermined, underestimated, and challenged, mostly because of my small size. And then that would open me up to become aggressive. Bullies have always aggravated me, and believe me, aggravation with outrage, are small words, compared to what an animal I can turn into. There have been a few of those individuals, that have told me, that I'm absolutely crazy. Crazy as I may be. Defending your own self shouldn't be crazy, it should be a must, and it shouldn't matter your size. And if it's crazy we have to turn into, so be it! And it's not crazy, I have felt outraged to defend myself against big boys, that think they can bully any small boy, like myself. Wrong!!! And I didn't always win for protecting myself. I would get my royal ass kicked at times, but I never cried. Never gave anyone the satisfaction of seeing any tears come from my eyes, no way!!!

I guess what started cooking inside my little boy mind. Is when my old Dad told me a long time ago. "Son, you're never going to be a big man, because you're going to be small like your mom", Didn't know how to react to that statement, told to me by my own Dad. But little by little, I guess it just grew on me, like a rotten apple, if you know what I mean. Always thought, who would say that to your son or anyone? My Dad, that's who. If anyone knew Dad, you'd know what I'm talking about. Very unique individual, and thank God I still had him when I wrote this. And since Dad told me that I probably never be a big guy, I had to work on my own self being. And believe me it's been hard, and I've been able to prove that there's always someone watching. For those of you that don't know who that is. It is God who is always watching, whether anyone believes that or not. It's alright if anyone doesn't believe it. The time will come, when anyone of you decides to wakeup and believe that there is a super being, and that's God. Because I had no clue for a long time. Coming to my sports part of my life, oh my God, I always loved sports, especially baseball. From the fifties to present, I've loved baseball. A long time huh?

Even in sports I was undermined, underestimated. Yeah that's right. And Dad, well, he never liked any sport, much less his only son playing in any. Never thought it would be important to a boy, to have a parent or parents come and see their son play ball of any sport, until I became that boy. Does anyone know how much it hurts a boy see his teammates's mother and father watch their son play baseball, and not have one come and see yourself play, not once. Dad never came to see his son play not one baseball game. Yeah, I never we do what we can, with what we have, and all of us should have the confidence of God's love and blessings.

And from the time I was born and until I reached the age of nineteen, never had a clue of existence of God. No connection of God at all. Thank God, Mom always prayed for those she loved, Oh my God, did she pray. Didn't know it then, but I'm God's proof of Mom's prayers. I was always amazed, and why was mom always praying and for what. See what knowledge and what faith I had with God, absolutely none. No I didn't.

Without Mom's prayers, and God's love, and blessings, I wouldn't be writing my life's story. Would have left this side of life a long time ago.

Back to my trials and tribulations of my life. Remembering another time, when people would underestimate me. My own Dad. And remember, my Dad is the first one that underestimated. Taking me to his trash route, waking me at four or five on the morning, on summer vacations. Throwing full cans of trash, expecting me to empty them. I've opened that part of my life in the beginning of my writing. Only in this time with Dad's underestimation of his son, it would be totally different.

Coming home, as usual, drunk, and Mom really upset, crying and crying, yelling at Dad. I was in my bedroom listening to what might happen. Curiosity hit me, didn't want to think, that Dad would hit my mama. Oh no, he better not. Now here I am, still very young. If I can remember, I think I was thirteen, maybe, not very sure. But young. Mama yelling at Dad, and Dad tells Mom to shut up!!! Oh my God!! Now he started walking to mama, and he's got this wild look on his face, like he's going to hit mom. And I stepped a few steps towards Dad. And I yell, "You better not hit my mama", Dad tells me with a laugh in his voice, "and what are you going to do" responding him, "whatever I have to do" A very dramatic experience for a eleven or twelve year old, and Dad, just walks away.

You better believe I was scared, and so relieved. Thinking when that happened, he could have kicked my ass. But he decided not to. What? Not even a whipping, like before?

I thought, something is completely wrong.

Let me brush up on our memory together. Don't forget my first encounter with death at seven. But I wasn't alone, when that happened. My Dad, and uncle and I, were in that bobtail truck when we crashed. And one other, the driver of the shell truck tanker. And it affected all of us.

This is why I've called this life story.

"Died Three Times Lived Once,", and at age seven I experienced my first one, At that very scary truck accident.

You know I'm going to repeat this, because it's true. There are soo many people out there, and you people know what I'm talking about. They'll tell you they love you, and then what happens, they lie and betray you. You know it, and there's not too many people that haven't experienced a broken hearted experience, am I right? You know I'm right. I've gone through it a few times. What makes any of you people any different? Betrayal is betrayal.

There should be at least two people in our lives that should never betray us. From the beginning of my life, those two people, and they're sacred in my life. My Mother and Father. Especially my mom, has and will always be the first lady that loved me, and the only one that taught me love. She was such a supportive loving mother. I will carry her love, and will always love her to my grave. And even then, in my afterlife, will love her with God.

You guys know the score. Mom and Dad will love you, we're growing up, thinking everybody loves everybody. What a joke, right?

It's not a joke. I learned how to hurt, because people that don't know how to love, have hurt me. I'm not the only one, I know that. It hurts just talking about it.

Just little boys is how we start. I mean, come on, we live through life, through trial and error, it's the facts of life, it's the birds and the bees. As the saying goes. If we don't experience trials and errors, we'll never live life to learn from our mistakes, and wrong choices. That's just the way it is.

There's an old song, and it's been around for a long time. "Love Is A Very Splendored Thing". As love was taught to me as a boy, I didn't know any other thing. Until. Yes until, I started growing up. As I/we, from the start of our lives, our bodies start growing, but many of us, the brain doesn't grow even with our bodies, unfortunate for many of us, that's true. What I'm saying, when I was taught love, then I started loving people that loved me. But on the other side of the coin, I started witnessing people in my own family, expressing love as a show. I'm sure you all know what I'm saying. People will sware to your face, that they love you no matter what. It can be unbelievable, and can hurt anyone, when one finds out otherwise. It can tear your heart to pieces, and leave a scar on your heart, like it has me. In fact, I have a few scars of a broken heart, that will I live with me until God takes me with him. I've always been a simple boy, but was hurt at a very young age. There's probably many of us out there, right? I know there are, we've witnessed them and seen broken hearted experiences. But there, I'll say it again and again. I've been broken hearted like you have too, and have learned to move on. I know as a boy have seen my mother broken hearted many times, because of Dad. But she had always been able to wipe those tears off her face, and move on, and continue loving Dad. Remembering a few times my mother had repeatedly told me. Before mom and Dad got married, his own sister told her. "Why do you want to marry my brother"? My mother's only answer was, because I love your brother. And Dad's sister says, well you can do better than that, and he's a terrible person, once you get to know him. Mom replied, well, let me get to know him. I would catch mom cry many times, too many times. Never wanted to admit to this, and I know you're out there, what I'm about to tell you. And I would get embarrassed, am I right? ?

Our moms would want to hug us, or want to kiss you in front of your friends, imagine that. Don't know about you, but that would embarrass me. And if it didn't embarrass you, then you're better than I am. But I was only a boy or a teenager, by God, what do you expect? I will always regret that, as long as I live.

Another loving thought about mom's love, when we went to church. First of all, Dad would usually be hungover or just plain tired, and he would want to fall asleep. Oh, but don't let mom catch you falling asleep in church, that's a no no. And me, well that's another story

Like I said, don't you dare let mom catch you sleeping in church. Something about mom's little hands, she had these sharp fingernails, that would catch you by surprise, and pinch the hell out of me, and she would also pinch Dad, she meant it, you don't fall asleep in church. Mom would pinch me, where it would hurt the most, it wasn't funny at all. And she would, I would want to scream or yell in church, but mom would catch me with a look of anger.

As a boy, as many other boys, I was mischievous, and yes even in church. Mostly because church for me at that time was very boring. The priest would go, on and on, what seemed to me, for hours. And then the priest would want to talk to the audience, for another hour or so. No it wasn't, but it seemed like it. So I would look for something to do, like wanting to pull one of my sisters hair, and that to me always seemed like fun, until we got home from church, and Dad would whip me again. What would I expect. We're not supposed to be disrespectful in church. And Mom and Dad took it very serious, and Dad would sometimes, unless he was one of the ones falling asleep. My sisters would love to get me in trouble, oh yeah, they loved it. It was always, awwe, I'm gonna tell Daddy, whatever little thing I would do. Started thinking after a while, I was the black sheep of the family. The oldest of three children and the only boy. Was also starting to think, that I was a disappointment to Dad. And I did for a long time. As many of you have probably heard. Things are not always as they may appear.

Coming back to being underestimated, and undermined. Must had been around fifteen or sixteen. Mom and Dad had always planned to go out on most weekends, and go singing. You all might be saying, what, singing? Aww yeah, mom would sing beautiful, with Dad being most of the time as backup. But he could sing good as well. Anyway, this one particular weekend when mom and Dad went out, was having a good time, alone with a girlfriend, yes all alone. Oh me ohh my. This is no strange thing, right? But for me, it was exciting, and was thinking about doing something, I probably would have regretted for the rest of my life. But God interfered, and I thank God for that night. So this is the scenario. Mom and Dad out for the night, all alone with a girl, that was just itching to to take me in for my life. Oh my God. All of a sudden, I get a knock at the door, and we're wondering, who in the hell could that be. Go to the door, and who's knocking, it's my next door neighbor. As I answered, I say "Hey guy, what's up" he yells at me, and says, "I want you to meet me at the corner of the street in thirty minutes, because I'm gonna kick your ass and you better be there or I'm coming for you" I ask him, "why man?" He tells me "because you and your friend tied me up to a tree and you beat me up, that's why", I tell him, you're crazy man, because I did no such thing", he says, "anyway you better be there". All I could say, "Ok" So I take this girlfriend back to her home, and just thinking about that night, this guy saved me from doing something, like I said, that I would regret for the rest of my life. It wasn't something I was proud of, because this poor kid, was always high on barbiturate pills. And I figured, he was high again. I guess what I really wanted to do, was teach him a lesson. With just one punch. And that's what happened. I go to the corner where he said he wanted to meet me. And he gets out of a car who he was with, his brother and another friend of ours. Comes running at me, and starts bouncing around like some boxer, saying to me, "Come on, come on"

I say "What is wrong with you man", he keeps bouncing around, and all I did was come up to him, and punch one good one. And he's down. He underestimated me, is what he did. So I let him have what he looked about five years older than I. At age fifteen he could buy alcohol, that's how much older he looked. And I always looked five years younger than I was. We were quite a pair, we were. Anyway, he'd been drinking, and was feeling his oats this one day. He was bedding the sister of the girl I was bedding. And he got caught up on some gossip, and he tells me, "you know dude, my Maria and your Roberta were talking that you said this and you said that." I thought to myself, dude, you don't sound very macho. He carries on, "so man, so what do you say about that" I responded, "I guess so, I don't remember" he threatened me, saying, "well if you said that, I like to take you outside and kick your ass, what do you think" I responded, "ok" he kinda laughed, and says, "ok?" That's all you got to say"? I tell him, "well you'll probably kick my ass, but I'm not running from you, if that's what your thinking" He couldn't believe what I told him. By telling me, ok, just forget about it. From then on, he seemed to always respect me. And I respected him.

I've learned, that love and respect should always prevail, don't you think? I think so. But unfortunately, there has never been much of either. Dad has always told me about respect, but some things I've seen him do, seemed contradictory. He'll say one thing and do the opposite. Shaking my head continually. I've often felt confused. So growing up, had to teach myself, about true love, and respect. Which mom was the passion teacher of both in my life. So, what do we have? As a boy, I've learned through mom, love, respect, and prayers. Naw, not right away, for sure, no one does at such a young age, no one, unless you're born miraculous, a genius and perfect. Mom has been the one in my life, starting out of my first years of life, that has been my mentor, and through God's love and blessings, is why I'm still alive after three experiences of death in front of me, that almost took me out. I'm telling you all, I've died three times, and I'm now living a life, that I don't understand why I'm living it. Which I've often thought, I didn't deserve this happy life.

Knowing the kind of life I've had, I've often wondered, why did God choose me. But then, I've also thanked my Lord many times. As the boy that I was, as I've said, my mom taught me love and respect, and to pray. And as I've also said, I believe I wouldn't be here if it wasn't for my mother's love and prayers. Knowing how the world is and how it's always been, it's hard for people to believe in God and praying. Since I was a boy, never thought I had to prove anything to anyone, but to myself, and maybe my Dad.

And what does his brother do? He comes running out of the car they were all partying in, yelling at me, "hey man, what did you do to my brother? I said, "Why don't you guys just leave me alone, and as I'm shaking my fists at him, I yell out to him, do you want one too", he says right away, oh no, no no. "I continue to tell him," you guys are all crazy, I don't do anything to you guys, so just leave me alone". A perfect example of being underestimated and undermined, is the way I've always saw it. And I'm sure underestimating and undermineding will never stop none of us, and I'm speaking for all of us that go through that.

Before I go too far down the line. After that incident with my neighbor, threatening me, to want to kick my ass. And I ended up punching him out. Well the next day, cutting mom and dad's yard, my neighbor yells out, saying, "What's up guy"? I tell him, "Screw you" And he kinda laughed, telling me, "I didn't know what I was doing" I say, "You're crazy man, you're going to kill yourself taking those barbiturate pills. And later on with my story, that's exactly what happened, found dead, overdosed with those pills and found naked in bed with another man, by his brother.

Thank God and thank Dad, for Dad teaching me not to be racist. Dad taught me at a very young age, thank you Dad. And as a boy, after that lesson giving by Dad, I felt good about it. Never spoke to and never looked down to anyone, just because they're a different color than I. And I know we've all been hit by racism, right? I know I'm right!! Because that's one of the biggest sins of our world, and as long as man lives on, it'll always be. When Dad taught me that, I looked up to Dad, because I've always seen him get along with everybody. And because of his influence, I like to think I also get along with everybody. Like I have, as you all, I've had my issues with men or women playing the race game on me. But whatcha gonna do? It's too bad, but it's the facts of life, unfortunately true.

Just going to school, I'm sure we've all been down that road. We have to prove ourselves, I know I had to. But loving school like I did, and earning good grades like I did, other races respected me for that. But they're were others, also very jealous of me. Dad sent me to school, I love school, received good grades, got respect. And receive jealous faces. Sounds like a normal life on this planet.

I have always been tested, not just because of my race, but also because of my size.

I guess I was born defensive. And also because having a Dad telling me, I'm gonna be small like my mother. Looking back, I think I built a defensive wall around me. So as a boy, any other boy looked at me funny, I'd challenge them. Weird huh? Why I'm not dead, I don't know.

Played football, baseball, basketball, tennis, against bigger guys, but I've never felt intimidated around them.

There was this other guy I grew up with, tall like most, that tried intimidating me, but it backfired on him. For a long while, he thought because he was taller than I, he could just push me around. Well like I said, it didn't work. It backfired on him, as well. He like some others, would just walk up to me, and give me a shove, like I was some punk. My reflex would be, shove him back, and almost knocking him down. And like him like so many others, geez dude, what's wrong with you?

I tell him, "you think because I'm shorter than you, you can just push me around." He responded, "ok man, ok" apparently he received my message. I'll never know to this day, why I have never looked at how much bigger, taller, nor how much stronger a man is than I. Anyone could have kicked my ass, or kill me for that matter. And kicked my ass, now that has happened, no doubt about that. Everyone has their turn, am I right?

But that has never intimidated me, by no one.

This other time, this big kid, that ended up becoming my brother in law, out weighed me, by at least a hundred pounds, oh yeah he did. He was too girlish, even though he tried being macho on me. He always in my later part of life.

Many of you know, and many of you don't know, for every step of day we take, there's no way of knowing we'll be alive the next moment, much less the next day. Tomorrow is not promised to no one.

We've all made plans, but plans can blow up right in front of your eyes.

There have been three of my upmost deathly experiences in my life, that I will never forget.

I'm trying to paint you all a picture of my first one, at age seven. And haven't been able to forget about it, mostly because, well let me ask you. Would anyone of you be able to forget it? Maybe some of you think, I can't move on. Well I have. And that's now a long time ago. I have been able to move on, thank God. I'm only writing about my life's tragedies and my times I almost got killed, that's all. Many people I've known, have advised me to write a book about my life, and that's all I'm trying to do.

But of course being very young, we're always afraid of the unknown. At least I was.

Not having any support nor ever given advice on how to do the things in a young boys world. But as I was growing, found out, fearing the unknown is a natural thing for many of us, no matter how old you are, I'm sure you can relate.

Through my life's experiences, I've been physically knocked out, oh I don't know, maybe at least four times. Maybe more times than I can remember. From being knocked out, how can anyone remember how many times. I'm sure there are quite a few people, especially men, from getting knocked out, have never been able to make it back into the normal world they were once in, unfortunately for those, it's sad. Freak accidents, strokes, heart attacks, cancer treatments, and the list goes on. For the mishaps for unfortunate people, I can only imagine, they waking up into a difficult struggling world, that for many, just give up, and pass on to the other side. And you know what side I'm talking about. To the better side of life, where there's no more pain and suffering. And as a boy and growing up until as old as I am now, I've always challenged life. Of course if you're in so much pain, and you'll be leaving the physical world, then to the other world you go, probably better for those poor souls. Maybe I speak the way I do, because I've seen death stare at me in my eyes. And believe me brothers and sisters, it's scary, for you that have been there, right? it's scary, isn't it? Here's a question for most of you. Have you ever been so scared, that you thought you would die? I know you're out there, you people that have been there. Because I've been there, more than I would like to remember. But I'll never forget it.

And for me I've had the kiss of death at age seven, for starters. Yeah, I'll write my other deathly experiences, wanted.

And as I've tried to describe, I say tried, because my life has been very difficult for me to live, only because I made it difficult, and because I've had too much drama. Like Dad, like son, you could say. But as a boy, like many boys, I looked up to my Dad. Don't we all? I'd like to think that you guys reading this, are not any different than I. Yes my life was difficult, but like Dad has told me about his, many times, don't understand how he lived, as I don't understand, how I've lived.

Since I started out on my journey, because that's how I see how my life has gone. A long journey. Where am I destined to end, God only knows. I'd like to think I will end up in God's palms of his hands. But being just a kid, what would I know what to do about trying to end up in God's palms of his hands? Entering into this corrupt world, as a kid, we all have a long way to go. I'm sure you guys can relate to that. For some of us, we'll never understand the first thing about any Godly connections. I'm not saying I understand. But through my life, I really didn't have a choice. But again, we all have choices, am I right or wrong? As I grew up, I start thinking that maybe I'm the only one making bad choices. Hey guys, do you relate with that one as well? But I had to learn, how not to keep thinking negative, or I'm gonna fall very deep and die, very young. Had to think positive at a very young age, and as if God was reading my thoughts like he does anyway. I'm heading just right there, Dead, at a very young age. Not knowing then, but I think I have something of a clue, a clue of some what. That God has always been there for me as he is there for everyone. As I think of my yesteryears, I've often thought that mom was more than just mom, she was the family's angel. That's right as I think about it now. Mom was the one that kept the family together. Of course no one knew it then, when Dad wanted to whip and beat me, who was there, that's right, mama. Even when I tried being good, my sisters would want to talk crap about me to mom, who defended me, you got it, mama. When Dad and I wanted to fight each other, when we got so upset with each other, who stopped it, mama. When my sisters wanted to fight each other, again, it was mama.

When Dad would come home very drunk, who cried, don't have to say it, yeah it was mama. My question, are all moms that way? I don't know, but my mom was the one, who kept the family together. So why wouldn't I think she was our angel. Here's another one, when some other woman wanted to take Dad away from mom, who knocked that woman to the ground, here I'll say it again, mama. When I started writing this part of my life, I couldn't believe what I was reminesing, all the times mom was the family's angel. And mom's prayers were strong, and that's an understatement of a word. I'll tell you how strong, mama only stood four foot eleven. Short huh? Now that I think about it, I very much think I got my aggression from mom, not from Dad. Coming back to mom's prayers. When mom prayed, she would cry. Wow mama, with God's love and your strength, how can I lose.

Yeah, you guys probably have already figured it out, right? Out of the three children, I was the spoiled one, only by my mother, not my Dad. That's pretty normal, a daughter or daughters get spoiled by daddy, a son gets spoiled by mama. Finding out later, that's always been pretty normal. We've all heard, oh that's daddy's little girl, which was my youngest sister, and I was mom's little boy. Aww, but those were the days of love in my family, when there was love. So my advice to all of you, take advantage of your younger years, and don't for your own sake, don't let money be thicker than blood.

I'm not saying Dad didn't love us, I'm just saying, mom's love was always so much stronger, so much more faithful to Dad. Dad has always been kinda shaky. He would tell you one thing, and do the opposite. I've always thought to myself, isn't that kinda hypocrit? Never told him, not then, that wouldn't show respect for him coming from his son. Now would it? Dad was always very strong in going to work, no matter what his condition was, half drunk or hungover.

All this time, I thought I did this all alone, about being aggressive. Not at all. Mom was the one, that showed how to be aggressive. She had never showed intimidation, I grew up, not letting no one intimidate me. Wow mama, you were the one.

Remember I told you about the youngest brother of my neighbor that came over one night threatening me, he was going to kick my ass. I'm sure you do remember. Well the other brother, which became my best friend, he once challenged me in a boxing match. Good friend, right? Yes he is.

Anyway, I'll never know why he wanted to box, maybe just something to do. Or maybe he thought he could kick my ass. For me, just one other time, I would never run from any man. Never have, never will.

So the time came along, "Hey buddy, you want to box, I only have one pair of boxing gloves, you take the left glove and I'll take the right glove." Not knowing it then, but my friend letting me use the left boxing glove, would end up being his disadvantage. As we started skipping and jumping around, like a couple of monkeys, he kept trying to hit me, with his left hook, and missing. He tried getting to close and crouching down to get me in the jaw, well got to close and within range of a swing. Now remember, he's got the right glove and I'm using the left glove. Remember that. That being said, with him having a bare left fist, and I having a bare right fist. So as he got too close, I let him have it with my bare right fist, hitting him too hard to the bridge of his nose. And that really hurt, because he practically cried. Poor buddy.

Of course we quit boxing for the day, and never boxed again.

I never let him know, that I had boxed before with a couple of cousins of mine a while before us to boxed. My poor buddy, when I punched him in the nose, he almost cried. "Oh man that hurt, you hit me hard Dude"

Like I've mentioned before, there were other mishaps, like all us guys go through, guys you know what I'm talking about, because that's all part of growing up, and there were good times of growing up and of course there were bad times. Remember those times people? We'll never forget neither. Remembering my bad and sad times. My sad times, and you know this, and that's without being said, sad times can hurt more, emotionally, than physically,

But I've described my most hurt, physically, it hurt so much, that I was completely knocked out, so I didn't feel a thing, right? My first experience of facing death. And for those of you that have been down that dangerous road. My question to you, at such a young age, how did you handle it. The little I remember of it, I didn't know what happened. It would have been a easy way to go, because I don't remember feeling anything. What I do remember, I woke up in a doctor's clinic, and the doctor noticing I was coming to, telling me, "son you, your Dad and uncle are so very lucky to be alive. You've made it through a miracle, God bless you". Now at seven, what would I know about miracles, much less the doctor telling me that we're lucky to be alive. I didn't know anything about life or death. Again I'm asking, what would anyone know about life or death at seven years old?

But as I have moved on with my life, and as you continue to read my life's experiences, you'll notice that I've lived a miraculous life, because being in that truck accident, will be only the beginning of a miracle of more to come.

But don't we all live by a miracle every day we wake up? Never knew it then until now. We all will find out, as you age, that just waking up is a miracle every morning. And don't take it for granted you're coming back home when you leave home. We've all heard it on the news, a family, a young boy, a little girl, or anyone you may hear about not making it through the day or night. Tomorrow is not to be promised to anyone. Oh we can make plans, but don't be surprised if any plans go haywire. That's part of life. But how do we know that at three, four, or seven years old as I was, of the dangerous experience I went through.

It was a beautiful day in paradise, just another beautiful summer day, on one of my school vacation days. Working with my Dad and uncle. Picking up trash in a brand new International truck, Dad bought, for his prospering business, a waste Company. It seemed like just another day to work with Dad and uncle, well it started out normal anyway. But normal wasn't even close on how us three ended up in the hospital, close to getting killed.

Never knew it then, but for those of you that believe in angels and God's miracles, that day for us, God's miracles and his angels were there for us, and that's why we weren't killed. You can believe that or not, for those of you that doubt the love of God. I didn't know anything, didn't know how to believe at seven. Would you at seven years old? Was just beginning my life, and it almost ended very abruptly. And knowing the things I know now, at seven would have never known what hit me.

Here's another dangerous experience, have you people ever go driving in the freeway, maybe at sixty five miles an hour, and blow out a front tire? Huh, have you, and how did you feel? Scary huh? It was for me. And how did you handle it? I vaguely remember, but I think I handled it very responsibility, at now sixteen. At seven many things happened and many things changed my life.

If you recall me telling you about my infatuated feeling for a third grade teacher, at eight, and then my beating up a bully after watching him hit a girl that I very much liked at ten years old. And also at ten, earning As and Bs in school, wow. Being told by another teacher, also at ten, that us guys will probably be going to Vietnam. Now I really thought that teacher was crazy, I really did. But she was right. Later on I'll share with you all, that experience as well. But right now it's too early to tell you, because I'm still only five through sixteen years old in my life.

For you older folks like me, do you all remember when Disneyland first opened up? What a beautiful place, wasn't it? The only thing is, I wasn't able to go till I was sixteen. I really felt bad when I couldn't go, from seven till sixteen years old. Because all I kept hearing was from all other kids, "Have you been to Disneyland, have you been to Disneyland, have you been to Disneyland"? That was so annoying. Guess because, when I ask mom and Dad, "Can you take us to Disneyland" the answer was always NO, NO, NO. But yet, Dad would either not be home yet, or at home drinking, or come home drunk, after a weekend binge. Didn't look too much up to Dad at the time. I had to grow up out of that, and I did. We shouldn't hold grudges against our parents, found out that's not respectable.

I had to figure it out. Dad had never been anywhere when he was young. His Dad didn't have time to take any of his kids anywhere, because Dad comes from a ten kid family. So all my grandpa knew, was work, work, work. Dad could hardly go to school, much less go to a party, a carnival any theme parks. They didn't even have them in those days.

In those days, if your poor, good luck in being a kid, poor people didn't have time, with ten kids, a man was too busy supporting his family.

Guess that's why alcoholism was very strong in those days. Most people probably used it as an escape, from reality, and wondered what kind of life will his kids have. What a life, huh. Can anyone relate, and did anyone out there reading this, have ancestors like I did? I'm sure you all know the mishaps of a struggling generation, of the early twentieth century.

From nineteen hundred through the nineteen forties, it was a mean struggle for those. You all should know your history. For those born from nineteen hundred, they didn't know it then, but world war one was just around the corner. All of you should know, any war is disastrous, I will go into much later into my life, what war I was in.

The world thought that world war one would be the end of all wars. As I went on my life, I often thought, as long as man exists, there will always be war any part of the world. Is that agreeable?

But of course when you're just a little guy, like me at the time, from five till ten, what do we know? Not much, agreeable? Right!!! And after the first world war, not long after, and twenty three years later, here comes the worst war the world has ever experienced, yes you know, World War Two. And again, what did we know, I wasn't born yet, in fact not until nineteen forty eight. I guess you can include me as one of millions of what they called us, the baby boomers. And my Dad is a world war two veteran. And again, of course what would a little boy as I was, know what a veteran was, and wouldn't know it until much later. And Dad never knew how to explain what war was, much less knowing how to explain what was a veteran.

A little about Mom and Dad, when they first met before Dad went off to war. I always thought they were a very interesting couple. Mom secretly told me how shy Dad was, but couldn't have been too shy, because once he met mom, he wanted to marry her. With all the complaints about my parents never taking us kids to this or to that. And Dad always coming home drunk, and on and on, and on and on. Our parents weren't bad people, not at all. It was their kids that were bad. If their son did that, or if one of their daughters did that or the other daughter did this, it was always something. After all the blah blah blah, I say about how Dad did this or Dad did that. He is still alive as I write this. At the end of my parents's lives, it was Dad that really got ripped off, but I never knew it when I was just a boy growing up. But all I'm telling you all, is what we all go through, don't we? It's facts of life. As I mentioned before, Dad was in the army, in world war two.

But he never once bragged about it. Another good quality about Dad. And he doesn't know it, I've grown up with that philosophy. You can be proud, but don't ever brag. Let the bragging for those that want to brag about you, but still be humble. You might want to ask those that want to brag about you, why do you want to brag about me. And just listen.

As a boy, and what I'm about to tell you all, is a very touchy subject. Molestation. Homosexuality. As you read this, it'll catch your eye, and it'll capture your thoughts. To the point, that it can piss you off. I know it has made me Gag, I wanted to go throw up, it outrage me, how a grown man can actually put in his mind and pursue it, to the point of actually committing a sexual act with a little girl or a little boy. I'm telling you, when they catch these perverts, they should hang them, but they don't. That's pure evil, and you all know that. I'll never be able to explain what goes on in a little girl or a little boy, what goes on in their minds, when something so evil is happening to them, because that's never happened to me, I can only imagine, thank God!! All you normal people should at least know, that little kids are very, very vulnerable, they don't know what the hell is going on. And the reason I'm bringing the subject up, because it's happened to my younger generation of my family.

I'll probably never mention this touchy subject again, because like I said, it's never happened to me. But it does happen, we hear it all the time. For the life of me, I've tried to remember all the times any one of my family members, if they've tried to come on to me, and I can't think of anyone. And like I've also said, thank God. But I can only feel sorry for the vulnerable children that go through that horrible tragedy, that they will have to try to figure out what happened to them, for the rest of their lives. But you gotta know, it's been going on, ever since man was created.

When I was little, I used to see things on t.v. censored. Those were the good old days.

Today nothing is censored. Television, or people in general, could care less about censorship, by today's standards. But if you think about it, it's all about money. From politics, movie stars, journalism, it's all about money, that's all they care about..

As a little boy, didn't understand then, but remembering things I've witnessed, seeing people betray their own mother and father. I'm related to one. And I still don't understand to this day.

Growing up has never been easy for a guy like me. Trying to grow up, tried having a Dad and son relationship, with a Dad that never had that as well when he was growing up. You can say, father like son. But I really don't think I'm the only one, do you guys hear me? Used to see Dad, how easy it was for him to make friends. But now I think, he was hungry for friends. Because if any of those people that he met in a bar, he called friends, where are they today? As I was growing up, as I said, from five to sixteen, I've never begged for friendship, till this day. I've seen it everyday, some people will kill for love, if you call that what they want, love.

There's a lot of confused people out there, all you people know exactly what I'm talking about, people will kill for sex and money.

During my first years of life, I can't say my first days, because no one remembers any of your first days. I can barely remember some of my first years. I'm thinking that's normal. I know it is.

One of my worst pains in my body, is my neck pain. I've never been able to rid that. People out there, being involved in a traffic accident. I mean, I'm talking about a major should have got killed accident. If you read this, you'll remember, if you're alive. Can't understand how we're alive, Dad, my uncle, and I. But I have to say, if you believe, all of us are always in God's arms. That's a strong belief, if you want to. Mother's prayers have saved my life three times. And no one has to believe that either. I've learned in my life, that all of us at one time or another, or maybe all the time, we take life for granted. I used to, as a boy, didn't we all? But as a boy, in a vague and not so sure of too many things, let alone life or death.

When I was just yeyyyyyy high, and watching how other boys and their dads got along, that would sadden me, and I would hide in some place and cry. No one ever knew that, until now that I'm opening up.

But of course I should be grateful, after all I had a Dad, not like other boys; that had lost their dads, at a very young age. So what's the difference, if you have a Dad that wouldn't talk to you, or not having a

Dad, by dying, and not being there at all. So in the long run, I should be grateful. Not understanding Dad as a boy, but now its a long time ago. But at this stage of time, I've only just begun.

Coming from a Hispanic family, or Latino family, whatever you want to call it, I felt like an immigrant, because as a boy didn't know english. But that was soon be for me a thing of the past. Mom and Dad only knew Spanish, so how are they going to speak to their kids, right?

That's right, just Spanish. So Dad tells his wife, my mama, "we better teach our son to speak English, because he'll be starting school soon". I can just barely remember that. And I vaguely remember trying to speak to a Caucasian little boy, maybe a couple of years older, with my two pistols cap guns, like I used to see on cowboys and Indians, and my cowboy hat. Amazing how I remember that, but I do. But like I said before, those were my very few days of my childhood. That also will be cut short, because Dad will start taking me with him to help him on his trash pick up business.

Think about that for a moment, trash pick up business!!! Some of you may think, how big are those businesses today? But Dad wasn't able to hang on to that business, because guess what, his own brother legally stole the business from Dad. Some of you may also think, how stupid was that. Yeah that was pretty stupid alright. But when you have a Dad like I do, you'd know he was just too nice of a guy. As I think about that time of our lives, it will always sadden me remembering how his brother connived my too nice of a guy Dad, from Dad's trash business. Can you believe that? Because I do, I witnessed it with my own eyes. Have noticed since I was a kid, how money hungry will make you do the most evilest things in the world, including stealing from your own parents. And having a brother steal your business, that Dad started. I guess I'll never be able to forget that.

I'll say it again, Dad has always lived in a world of just a handshake, and your word, and that's it. All of you know, we live in a corrupt and evil cheating world, that's the truth, especially when all those people that think of hacking, killing, manipulating, just for money.

Let me try to explain how Dad lost his waste (trash) business. Remember I told you how he started this business. Started it by himself, and then he took me with him on summer vacations when I was just a kid, at the time I was only five until I was about seven. But when I turned sixteen, something hit my heart about Dad's business, because Dad went to Arizona to ask his brother to give him a helping hand. As a result, and as a witness, for his business, that became one of two worst choices he had ever made. You'd think that would be his worst choice, huh? No not Dad, he's going to do another one, because it's my Dad that has never learned to stop being too nice to evil people. He's always been a nice guy, but people have always seen him coming, to kick him around, so sad for him.

I tried to warn him about his brother, but he wouldn't listen, after all, to him, I'm just a kid, what do I know. This was the scenario, like I said, I'm only sixteen, he's drinking his beer as usual, one weekend, and I tell him, "Dad, don't you think you should write some kind of contract, and have it notorized with a lawyer"? I told him that he sends us to school for what, to learn something right? But Dad isn't taking what his son is advising. He practically yells at me, "What are you talking about, you think my brother would take my business away from me" I told him, no not him, but maybe his wife or his kids will. And of course he's not buying that either, telling me, "You must be crazy" Can you imagine my Dad telling me I'm crazy, because I want to protect him from losing his business, I'll never forget that, he called me crazy..I'm not the one that lost a multimillion dollar business. So who's crazy? It was my Dad's loss. But in the long run, Dad and his family lost a big money making business.

But let me explain, when I was sixteen, it wasn't then when Dad lost his business. That would happen more than a decade later.

Like I've repeatedly said, my life was difficult for me, and you guys will say, no no, my life was. But we all have a story to tell, don't we? Some of us have a more dramatic story to tell, than I do.

Remembering when we first moved out from Arizona to California, I was just a little boy. And we lived in the first house, Dad first bought for about seven years. From the age of four until eleven. Had a nice time living there, but times change fast, and mom and Dad decided to move out of there. And it's a good thing we did. My peers I went to school at the time, weren't the same. Yeah times were changing for the worst, so thank God mom and Dad moved us out to another part of town. What I saw in the changing of that part of town, gangsters and with that comes drug dealings, and on and on. You guys know it, if you've been around the block like I have..

But again, when I was living there, later becoming a bad place to live. Who knows what would've happened. They called that place, the one-ways. And when you mention the one-ways, anyone knowing that city, everybody knew where you're talking about. But we all have a beginning. That first house would be my first years of a life time to describe my unique story.

No one knows from the time we start out on our journey of life, what is going to happen to us, agree? Agree!! No one knows. But if you guys are out there raising hell, and you're being bad, you should know your destiny doesn't look good. Especially if you have from the beginning, a bad example of a father, an ex-con. Wow!! I didn't have that. I'm not saying I had good guidance, but Dad was not a criminal, and that's always been a good sign for my future. And I wasn't a bad person neither.

And mom was a loving mom, like I always thought moms should be. And I've seen many mothers that couldn't come close to mom, comparing, oh yes I am. Mom was always the one that kept the family together. And when I was being bad, mom was a great pincher. Boy that would hurt. There were times, Dad would be the one to spank so hard, I felt I was getting whipped, and when Dad wasn't around, it would be mama to pinch. Dad was a good spanker and mom was a great pincher. Like I said, mom was the one that kept the family together. Once she passed, the family blew away. Later on, I'll describe how one of my siblings destroyed our family. It has outraged me, and that's putting it mildly. Anyway later on in my life, I'll tell you. There were many times when my sisters wanted to talk bad about me, but mama never wanted to hear it. She'd yell at them, "Don't talk about your brother, and he'll always be your brother, don't forget that". As far back as I can remember, my sibling sisters were forever talking about one another, or both talking to mom about me. As you can pretty well tell we weren't the closest set of siblings.

When you're so very young, what did we know about close siblings, I know I didn't. I think my younger sister and I tried, but that didn't last too long my older younger sister, well I've never wanted to talk about her, but something happened to her, and I'll never be able to explain her mental problem. And I guess I'll keep blaming her unbalanced mentality when she fell out of a car our uncle had. That will probably be her tragic life and destination. I have always felt sorry for her. No one ever investigated my two year younger sister's accident, when she fell out of the car.

It was such a horrible scene to watch. I'll probably never forget what happened on that to my two year younger sister. When I was writing this, I had a flashback on I'll always remember. Like I said, two year younger sister. She was two years younger than I, and my other sister, four years younger. Just so we get that straight.

This is what happened, how my two year younger sister fell out of the car. My uncle in the front seat driving, mom with my youngest sister in the passenger seat. Both my three year old sister and I, five years old in the back seat of the car, while my uncle driving at about forty to forty five miles per hour, on our way to pick Dad up, wherever that was, can't remember that.

It's like a bad dream to me as I flashback to that particular day. I, like many kids, loved looking out the side car windows, or like this day, I was with my knees on the back seat, looking out the back car window. Now for those of you that are not as old as I am, there were no such thing as seatbelts. So what I'm about to paint you the picture I have in my mind, as to what happened that day. And it was horrifying. It was always an amazing feeling when I as a boy, was looking out the back window, the cars around us, the desert, whatever buildings we drove by. My uncle just driving along and my mom with my youngest sister as a baby, not paying attention as to what is about to happen. I'm looking out, and I hear what sounded like a door open and close. I took a quick look and I see, what looked like a little doll flipping about the side of the road. So I took another quick look, realizing my sister is not in the back seat with me. So I yelled out, "Mama, uncle, my sister just fell out of the car. Yelling at the top of my lungs, "Stop the car" I felt helpless, not being able to do anything. My uncle slams on the brakes, and mama jumps out of the car, running towards my sister, picking her up, cradling her, with love. What I can remember, she had several scratches and bruises. If I can remember right, they only took her to a doctor's clinic. Have always thought, they should have taken her to a hospital, because she never really recovered mentally. She continued, what looked like, abnormal. But through the years, both my younger sister and I often thought, something wasn't right. As a family, my two sisters and mom and Dad, would go shopping, and this sister, would get off the car and start walking wherever she was going. Dad would yell at me, ordering me to go get her. And I finding out, she often sleep walk. Say some peculiar things, and do some not so normal things as well. As I remines on that terrible incident when my sister fell out of the car, I often felt sorry for her.

Everyone is different. Some of us are very unique, and some people are very strange. I often thought I was strange, but I don't think so anymore. Because I've heard some very strange stories, what people have done to their own family. I mean down right evil.

As I was growing up, heard stories about a boy killing his own sister, or more evil, a grown man molesting his kids. Evil and too weird for me. And who likes talking about those things, no I know I don't. But it happens right? It's all part of of things that really happen, good or bad.

Overall I can say our family stayed together because of mom, Dad always worked, his three kids went to school. But no one ever talked about the strange things that happen to our family, hardly anyone does. Dad had a cousin that was very flirtatious, and she was very disrespectful. She would hug and squeeze to the point, I started wondering. Is this woman going to let me go or what? You would think that would be it. Not our family, I'm just beginning to open up my family's corrupt relations. And do I have some story to tell you, if you want to know. That's what makes the world go around, am I correct? Some stories take the cake. You all have heard the worst stories, in many families, and many results of the evilness that have landed the criminals in prison.

You know it, I know it. It's no secret. But I think, and it's only because I think so. Nobody has to agree with me. But I think I've seen and witnessed betrayal, that it would make most people gag. Maybe that's why I've grown old, a loner. I mean, what the hell. You know. You all know it. Because that's no secret either. And maybe I have never met the right people. Honest and good loyal, down to earth individuals. Those of you that have been with me, the wrong road, going the wrong direction, you know what I'm talking about. Another reason I've come up with, being a loner, is when you become close to someone, a sincere friend, and then he or she betrays you or they end up dead, maybe you understand and maybe you don't.

So you may ask, so who do you talk to, and have a good time with? Oh I've survived, and I have all I need. God. But as a boy, you're pretty well lost. Growing up in different neighborhoods, gave me the opportunity to make good and bad choices, haven't we all? Some of us as little boys, that's all we've done, was make wrong choices. If anyone of you ever read this, and you're in prison, then you know it. They call those institutions, D.O.C. Department Of Corrections

I feel sorry for you all, because we all have or have not a roll model to look up to. Well there again, I didn't have much of a roll model either. But I grew up with a praying mother, and maybe many of you didn't. That's the biggest reason I feel sorry for you. Mom made sure we all went to church. Not just go to church, she made us pay attention. But then again, as a boy, I've seen guys, no matter how well parents raise their children, they still end up losers, and in prison. For the life of me, we don't know anything about jail or prison, parole, probation. That's why my mom and Dad were so strict with us.. it's either mind or get whipped. Very simple.

And boy oh boy, things have changed drastically since I was a boy. And all for the worst. You old guys know it. For you younger generation, if you've threatened your parents, that you will call the police, because they want to raise you properly. I'm telling you all, something is not right. Now, I've also heard people beat their kids for practically no reason. And some kids getting so beat up, they end up dying. Well Dad never beat me up, he'd whip me pretty bad, although there came a time when I threatened him. You people might say, say what. I started getting aggressive towards my own Dad, ain't that something. Never thought that would happen. And neither did he. I think it surprised the both of us. Remember I told you, my Dad had a drinking problem. That's right, he did. And at the time when I wrote this, he didn't drink anymore. That's right, he quit drinking. He had to, or it would kill him, like it killed his Dad, my grandpa.

??? know, my turn would come in facing war.

As I've gotten to know Dad, as we've gotten old together, we relate and come pretty close in our boyhood experiences, as he's told me how it's been a miracle, in the things he's seen and the things his Dad had him do. I always thought we were different, in so many ways, yes, and in so many other ways, no. I'm just an advanced replica of him. For so many of us that's true, but there are so many of you, that can't even come close to your Dad, and of course that could be good or bad. It depends upon so many factors.

As for Dad and I, I've never wanted to do the things I've seen him do. Like come home so, so drunk, but I did that too. But I've never been so drunk, I couldn't drive nor couldn't walk. He would be so drunk, he would get pulled over, and get thrown in jail. He felt so embarrassed about that, and he never drank again after that embarrassment. And I've never been so drunk, I couldn't get home, like he couldn't, and he wasn't able to get home for a weekend.

At the first house Dad purchased in California, I never forgot when Dad got home with his brother and his cousin. As a little boy, hadn't seen Dad be so drunk, he couldn't get out of the car, they brought him in. Being just a little squirt, my uncle walked up to the door knocks on the door as I opened it, he looked down to me, and says, "Hello Mijo, boy your Dad is so drunk he can't get out of the car" and uncle laughing about it. Then as they helped Dad walk into his house and try to get him into bed, because it was about five or six in the morning. They carefully put him into bed, as though he was a little boy. I just wanted to cry. And you think that would be it. No not Dad, all of a sudden, he starts swinging with both arms, and hits the bedroom window, and breaks it into pieces, cutting his hand. It was quite a sight for a boy my age.

Have you guys ever see your Dad so drunk, at an age like I, age four, five, or six. Horrible isn't it? I know it was for me. After witnessing Dad drinking and drinking, and wondering that he'll probably follow grandpa to his grave. I really thought so. Because he really had a serious problem. Just like his Dad did, that took grandpa down under.

Those of you that remember, I telling you, when I wrote this, Dad was still alive.. that's right, he had reached his nineties. You're reading it right, he had reached to ninety six. I'll tell ya, to see Dad go through what he went through, life time miracles, it has been amazing.

Facing death together, facing our utmost differences and arguments. I often wondered if we would ever talk as a father and son should. I had been thriving for Dad and I, to come on peaceful terms, and I never thought it would happen. But it did, and that's a miracle in it's own.

As I mentioned to you, Dad and I facing death together. Yes we did, along with my uncle. As I mentioned before. Died Three Times Lived Once. It was a very unlucky day for all of us, especially uncle. Just ten years before that horrific disaster, my uncle faced death in world war two, stepping on a mind in France. When being young as I was, my uncle tried to describe what it was like, when he stepped on a bomb. Just a little boy when he was telling me about it. What would a boy know at my age of, again very young. But little did I because maybe because he wouldn't want to talk to me or what, till this day, I don't know. As he has always told me about grandpa, his Dad, that he taught him how to work. Other than that, he doesn't say a whole lot of anything else, about his Dad. And I only saw, that grandpa was too busy with nine sons, and one daughter. The old customs of back in the day, was, the more kids a family had, the more help you'd get out in the farm. There was no such thing as going to school. There were no laws back then, for a parent by law had to send his child to school. And so my grandpa did just that, didn't make any of ten children go to school. Especially if a family comes from poverty, and could barely feed his family.

I would often wonder, was everyone like that, in those old days? By not sending their children to school. Well if that was true, where would America be?

Have to admit, things were very tough to live and try to raise and support a large family, during the nineteen twenties. It's no wonder Mom and Dad only had three of us. Hell of a lot cheaper to raise, three compared to ten. Mom came from ten brothers and sisters, Dad came from ten brothers and sisters. Maybe that's why, I find it hard to understand, why Dad couldn't give support and be more attentive to just one son, when I just a little boy.

My description of a war in the one I was in, will come later in my life.

We've all been exposed to the dark at one time or another. Wasn't it scary? That doesn't scare me anymore. It fact, there's not much that scares me anymore. That's of course, right? Once I got old!!! And again, that has been a long time ago. But let us flash back together, when I was only five.

In my first house, Dad bought in California. It was this weekend, which I will never forget as many nightmares and memories have passed me by, so quickly in my life. What's been the old saying. Time flys when you're having fun. Everyone knows, there's two meanings to that statement. True, time flys, and it's false, you don't always have fun. In a perfect world, that whole statement would be true.

There was this one weekend, Dad and I were spending together, in fact, my whole family were spending a weekend together. There were few, but this one in particular. Television was showing previews of a scary movie, called "The Werewolf of London" It was a very old movie, but it was scary looking. Well, during the day, they were previewing this movie, which will show that night. I didn't know if I really wanted to see that monstrous hairy animal. Long nails, long jagged teeth. A man looking wolf. Wow!!! Night time creeps up on us. And I've fallen asleep. It was about nine or ten in the evening. What does Dad do? He wakes me up, saying, "Son, you want to see that wolf movie?" Thought to myself, do I? Again I'm only five, remember? As soon as that creepy hairy wolf man movie came on, I started sweating. At five, have never seen a monster movie. Through out that movie, I had no control, whether to tell Dad, if I wanted to see that movie or not wanting to see it. Had no control, believe me. I was too young to say yes or no. After the movie, I would try to forget that horrible looking wolf man. That face, hair all over his body, his long ugly claws, his long sharp teeth. I'm telling you, it's scared the hell out of me.

Let me tell you how I tried to sleep that night. Needless to say, I didn't. Let me ask, wouldn't you go through the same? Yes I think you would. Don't kid me, you know you would. And I know it too. We all know it. Another question that comes to me every now and then. Do any fearful events ever come and haunt you? It did come and haunt me for a while. But when mom would take us all to church, that ugly movie, like it would run from my mind. To me it looked like the devil running from God. Isn't that the way it's supposed to be. Through my years, I found out the hard way, that God has had control of all my life, since I was born.

Coming back to that horrible sleepless night. Like I said, when Dad and I watched that "The Werewolf of London" Dad, Mom, and my siblings all went to bed. Let me describe that one bedroom little house. Not much to describe. A living room, a kitchen, one bathroom, and one bedroom, and that's it. That's all there was with Dad's first house. And where did everyone sleep? Everyone else slept in the only bedroom we had. And where did I sleep? Take a guess, there's only one place I could sleep, you got it, the living room. Dad completely forgot about that movie we just watched. Well I couldn't, all I saw was that hairy ugly, jagged toothed, long clawed werewolf in my mind. Don't forget, I'm only five. I think after that, nothing will ever scare me again. And nothing ever did. Because as time went on, my sisters would rely on me for protection, when mom and Dad weren't around. That started giving me self confidence, and positivity, and security on how I would live my life.

Speaking of self security, and confidence, and I can't forget aggressiveness. That's right I became aggressive. I had to, I've never been a big person. Watching those old movies, gave me just that. Aggressiveness. Oh, it didn't always work, but I never ran from anyone either. Sorry to say, Dad was my first experiment. Started challenging Dad, by being aggressive. Yes, I know you guys, that was very disrespectful. And I never should have done that to Dad. Don't know if you can say, I was starting to build resentments, Let me ask you people, has your mom or dad ever ask you to drink with him or her? I must had been eleven or twelve, when out of blue, Dad asked, "You want to drink a beer with me"? Well of course I didn't know how to react. If your Dad ever asked you that how did you react and how did you respond. My first thought was, what the hell, he must be drunk, or maybe he misses a drinking buddy. Just standing and looking at him, and I told him no. He responds by telling me, "Why not, one day you'll probably drink out there with your friends". And guess what, he was right. Very obvious right? Bad influences are always in our lives. And it will always depend on how we respond to them, and influences good or bad will one day decide our fate. And just after Dad asked me about having a beer with him, naturally I had to remind him, "Dad I'm only twelve" It didn't seem to bother him, he says "well ok, I just thought."

As I moved on from being a boy. I had to learn to over come my first deathly experience. Or I'll be in paranoia through my whole life, and it wasn't easy getting over my life or death catastrophe.

As I look back then, as I couldn't understand Dad, when I was a little one. His Dad didn't give much attention to any of his siblings, and grandpa couldn't give much attention to just one. Dad wouldn't know the difference, when he was a little boy, so Dad tried giving more to us, more than his Dad could give to them. Makes sense to me. So I say like this, it was much tougher to live during my Dad's time, than it was for me when I was small.

Am I right, you guys reading this. We have become spoiled rotten. But if you read this, and you're either in jail or in prison, you're probably going to blame your Dad anyway. You cowards.

If you were born during my time, then your probably a baby boomer. Maybe you guys always knew what that was, but I didn't. We don't know things automatically, but I started understanding what a baby boomer was. And I finally figured, hey I'm one of those boomers. In my yesteryears, after world war two, America was having a population explotion. Guys from the war, during Dad's days of coming home, couldn't wait to come home to their girlfriends or fiancee, or wives and kids, for those that had families to come home to. So the results were, having kids like me, during the forties. I'm only too glad to come from a smaller family, than the size of families Mom and Dad came from. There aren't many people that have more than five kids today. Financially speaking, can't blame anyone, not having more than five. Unless you're one of those elite ones in society, the upper class.

When Dad used to take us visiting his cousins, or his uncles, kids everywhere. Seeing kids coming from everywhere, all over the floor, coming out of different rooms, out of closets. And these were my cousins. My generation, my mom didn't have no more than three of us. The way we've grown apart, my siblings and I, feel so blessed, there weren't anymore of us. Later in my life, I'll describe to you, how bad, and why my siblings and I grew apart.

I think everybody, when you first start growing up with your family, it has some kind of connection, at least I always thought so. There are those few that stay close through out their lives, my hats are off to you, may God bless you. Because that's a blessing.

It's sad to say, but I've grown to speak my mind. Being in a family of three, and I being the oldest and the only boy. And I'm probably speaking for so many of us.

When we're all tiny tots. With us, growing up and my parents appointing me as my sisters guardian. I say sisters, because I had two. Both of them, one being two years younger, and my other sister, being four years younger. And being appointed as a my sisters's guardian, believe me, that was tough. Being blamed by my sisters for things I didn't do, and get punished for it. Didn't happen all the time, but the times when they would get me in trouble, by lying to mom and Dad, it was uncalled for. I would get punished in different ways. Either ordered to my room, spanked, and sometimes whipped. Oh, the good ole days. For you guys that can recall, and relate, remember those days? They were fun, weren't they? I'll never forget those days of my life. I'm an old man now, and remember them very well.

But for all the bad memories, there are good ones as well. And the old saying goes, there's a reason for everything. Of course as a boy, we wouldn't understand that. Unless you're a genius, then it's physically impossible for a boy or girl to understand anything and everything about the reasoning behind all things that's in store for each and everyone of us. Sometimes when it's too late.

Let me bring you back to the day we almost died, when I was only seven. After all, that's what this is all about. Died Three Times Lived Once. So it's very obvious, this has to be my first experience of death looking at me, face to face. Scary? Very much so. But it only scared me after the fact. How could anyone be scared if you don't know what happened in the first place?

It was just another beautiful day in another day of my school vacation. As I am where I am with my age today, have learned the hard way not to take life for granted, because reality will sneak up on us and terrorize us for the rest of our lives. It has to me, but only when I think about it. It happens when you least expect it. There's catastrophes, that can destroy our future and lives. But if you want to believe there's no hope, then for you that believe that, then there is no hope for you. Then that could be your own catastrophe. God can help you, if you reach out to him.

And on that particular day of our near death of a gas tanker coming straight at us, slamming our brand new, nineteen fifty seven international truck. With a forty foot long staked bed, hitting us broad side. There was no slowing down from that huge tanker. Our truck approaching an orange grove intersection, with no signal light or no stop sign. Still remember Dad yelling at my uncle, since he was the one driving, yelling close to my ears. It freaked me out. Believe me, it really put the fear of death, that day, which I'll never forget, as long as I live. And I'm now an old man. And still remember like it happened a few years ago. I'm sure there are you that will read my life story, that either happened to you, or know someone close that experienced the same deathly day, of your life.

Anyway Dad yells "Look out brother" like I said, very load by my ear. The next thing I know, is nothing, because I was knocked out cold, not knowing what happened. Temporary in a coma, is where I ended. Waking up in a doctor's clinic. Wearing a neck brace. Pretty much in la la land. Confused as hell. My whole body sore.

What the doctor tells me next, is not what a seven year old would want to hear. "Son, it's a miracle you all lived through that ugly accident" What I'm told later, right after the accident, Dad stepped out off our now twisted truck, people coming out of their orange grove homes, Dad looking at all these people, asking them, what happened?

See if I can describe this disaster correctly.

When that gas tanker barreled into our International truck, they said, we went twisting in a circle, immediately ripping our front axle off the truck. My uncle being thrown out of the driver's seat, his pant leg catching on the driver's door handle, saving him from flying into God's nature of orange grove trees, and maybe he would have gotten killed, with hardly any chance to live. Dying immediately from the impact hitting any tree.

Now people, in those days there weren't any seatbelts to be worn. No padded dashboards, no green and red lights to stop at, not even a stop sign. So with no seatbelts, I was sitting in the middle of our truck cab, while our truck was in a twisting motion and at seven years old, yelling for "daddy daddy daddy" Maybe the truck twister, is why my neck is now in so much pain as I deteriote with age.

Now on the other hand, my uncle had already suffered a near deathly war incident. He was in combat in world war two. Just ten years before this truck accident happened, he had stepped on a field mind, tearing him up, and nearly died. And almost lost both eyes. Coming home with just one eye, for visibility. In other words, half blind. And then this horrific disaster nearly killing him. But this time, by the impact of our twisting truck, and my uncle being thrown out of the driver's window, and by God's loving protection, his pant leg caught the driver's door handle. And about half of his left ear was torn off. You see, while the truck was twisting in a circle, uncle being thrown, his left part of his head started dragging on the ground, as the truck came to a stop, because that's how they found him. When I heard the whole scenario, as I stood listening, I froze in amazement, astonished as to what happened to us, and could have happened. Wouldn't have ever wrote this story, and I've only just begun, because there's more to my life's deathly experiences, than what I've opened up to you so far.

We don't all believe in miracles, I know I didn't use to, but I do now. No one has to believe what I write. But whether you believe it or not, everyday we wake up it's a miracle, we've been a miracle from the time we're born. Like I said, being very young, didn't know what a miracle was, much less if there was a real God. But life's ups and downs, and wrong and right choices, we go through trials and tribulations. And we should all learn from our mistakes. But here I go again, mentioning my mama, because my mama, at my younger years, she was the one that kept the family together, my sisters, Dad and I. Mom taught me how to pray, made the family go to church.

Mom was very strong in keeping promises to God, and made sure her family did as well. Making me, very early in my life, to go to catechism, every Saturday morning. To teach me how to receive my first holy communion. You guys think that was easy? No it was not, because I didn't want to go. Arguing with mom, because why did I have to catechism, when I went to school all week. Her answer was, because she wants me to go. Simple as that. It's either, and it was easier to do what mom wants me to do, or get spanked by Dad

Thinking about back then, about my younger self, life was easier, as I think about it. All because of Mom and Dad. I'm sure, with you people reading this, you'll agree. But as I remember those younger years, I noticed others my age not have it as well as I did. Did I feel blessed? Not really, because I didn't know what blessed was. Probably feeling too sorry for myself, how Dad wouldn't connect with me as a father and son I always thought should be. As I reminese, I didn't have it so bad. Actually I was very much spoiled by mama. Didn't know it then. But with my mama spoiling me, came discipline, with Dad. Thinking at the time, I thought it was abuse with Dad, thinking like it was all the time, receiving a spanking, feeling like I was whipped. Now that I'm an old man, very glad he did that.

I have a question for all of you, and I'm sure there are plenty of you. Do you have a friend, that have stayed connected for over sixty years? Is that unbelievable? For me it is. Never thought I wanted any friends, after seeing and witnessing betrayals within our own family, over money. I have to say, I have one friend outside our bloodline. Have to say, he's been like a brother, or a cousin, he's been closer than my own sisters and cousins.

Does anyone have a friend like that? Because this best friend of mine, has always been there for me, through thick and thin. There are very few people like that, and maybe anyone reading this, may have or not have a great friend like that.

That's right, I'm now in my seventies, and my friend and I have spoken since we were in our early teens, and he lives in another state. He still lives in California while my wife and I live in Nevada.

He has seen our family rise and fall, especially myself. But he has never left me out to dry. But I also saw him and his family, including his wives, rise and fall.

We've all been there. Haven't we? Or maybe not everyone has ever had a special friend like this spiritual friend of mine. Awe, of course we didn't start as friends, we just went to the same school. And we didn't start as spiritual friends either. And we never had anything bad to say to each other, now as I wrote this, I found that amazing. To not have anything bad to say to each other, never speaking behind each other's backs. Although my friend, since through the years didn't know we would become old and stay as friends after all these years. I believe all or most of us from times of our young lives meet up with good people that show consideration for others, from parents that raised them. And this friend of mine and I come from the same kind of roots. Not saying we're from the same family, I'm saying we were both raised the same. His parents became friends with mine.

But that's not where we first met. Everyone have their childhood friends, as I thought I would. But this particular guy, has continuously portrayed a much better example of a better man than I..

But I've never told him, I'd be letting myself down.

And never wanted to see a man's head swell, in thinking he's better than me, when I've thought he was.

At my age at that time, not realizing how good I had it. Guess for the most part, most of us do have it pretty good. Let's think about what I just said, having it pretty good at that time. We've all taken our lives for granted, haven't we? I know I used to. Not anymore.

Thanking God after all those years, for someone like this friend of mine, sticking beside me. Nah, I'm not saying we know everything about each other. I'm just saying we've always been there for each other, whenever we've called one another, is all.

As I've mentioned, we were in our early teens, playing in a complete different neighborhood. When I said early teens, I only being, if I can remember about thirteen, my friend, I think fourteen or fifteen. Man, that's a long time ago. A lifetime ago. Hello, over sixty years. Wow.

Just like any or most neighborhood kids. If you like playing games like baseball, basketball, or football, right? And that's what we enjoyed playing. We dared ourselves to play football in the streets. That was rough, but we played it anyway. Buddy and I, with others, in the neighborhood, to come up with at least six or seven kids to play either baseball or football. Just thinking about it, when I first wrote this makes me go back to those times. Oh, my buddy and I still talk about those days, not all the time, but every now and then it's brought up. Those days came and went, like whoooo, zip Gone. Where'd they go?

And I know, every generation feels the same thing. We're born, little kids, teenagers, young adults, and we're off to old age. How many of us like the facts of life. No one, that's for sure. For some like myself, it went by soo fast, it's been too quick to enjoy. Through the years as a boy and up, I've noticed, I'm almost repeating what Dad has been through. But my generation has been more luxurious. I didn't go through a depression, although I went to a war, it wasn't a world war, thank God. Things were just harder for Dad's generation. My grandpa was harder than Dad was on me.

Since grandpa had ten kids, he wasn't too keen into sending any of them to school. When Dad was one hundred percent into sending his three kids to school. That made a lot of difference with where I am today. Where as, poor Dad was only able to go to fourth grade. Sad huh? Yes sad but true.

When I was five, I didn't have it anywhere near like my Dad, when he was five. When Dad was five, not everybody had a car. Now when I was five, mom, Dad, and the kids could hardly wait till they learned how to drive.

At five, I really didn't have anything to say, whether I wanted to drive or not. I had no choice in the matter. Always thinking, if I didn't do what Dad wanting me to do, I would definitely get punished. Scared of Dad? I guess I was, didn't recognize fear at such a young age. It's an impulse, I was a little boy, Dads are grown men, we're intimidated being little as I was.

When we're all little isn't it natural to have fear? But as a little older than a toddler, how do you feel scared? Didn't know how, did you? Believing not knowing the answer to that, I became to believe, that I either cried or got mad. You with me, guys? Because I became rebellious, later on in my teens. Becoming outrageous with bullies, or just bigger guys than me. After at about eleven years of age, became aggressive towards people thinking their better, because they're bigger. But I wasn't aggressive towards everyone, I considered myself a respectable boy, or I would have heard about it from Dad.

And doing something wrong, and Dad hearing about it. He would have heard about it loud and clear, believe me there would be heavy consequences, and I would receive bodily injury. At least that's what I used to think. Again we're just little kids.

Don't know who was more scared of their Dad, my Dad of his or I, with mine. As I concentrate on that, I think Dad was more fearful of his Dad. Because Dad's Dad used mostly his fist to get a message across any of his sons, and my Dad would use his belt, to relay a message to me.

Becoming resentful, and rebellious against Dad, didn't help us for any close son and Dad relationship, believe me. It didn't work for a hell of a long time. Anger never helped us neither. They all went against us, resentments, rebellious attitudes, and anger.

I'm sure you all have heard, "God works in Mysterious Ways" and the day came when God proved that mystery to us. Even if it has to put our lives on the line. Saw death right there, right in front of me and just about took out all three of us. Dad, uncle and I. As I meditate on that for a little while, realizing now that I'm old, that wouldn't be a bad way to die. It is what it is, the bare facts. Either it's our time to go or it's not. You've all heard that too. If I have, so have you. Many cliches have been overly abused.

So much for cliches. The point I'm trying to make about bad and sad father and son relationships, is that makes your lives rather sour, and miserable, and many of us take it everywhere we go.

As a boy, I took it to my first day of school. Getting into my first fist fight. How old was I, five. Did I start out rebellious? I don't know, and probably never will. But what's another old saying, "the survival of the fittest" yes at ages, from the time I was born until sixteen, I've survived my life's ordeals, but little would I know, I've only just begun. And I don't believe many others would have. But people like Dad, uncle and I are very unique people, but not because it's my story, just because I feel it is unique. We all have survival stories, and this one is mine.

Although we survived that catastrophe of that disastrous day of my life at seven, I'll probably take that day and my injuries to my grave. Because as an old man now, I'm starting to feel the aches and pains within. Back in the fifties, you all know, technology wasn't no where near, where it is today. In other words, my Dad, uncle and I have been alive all these years, and I wonder all the time, and always ask, how? Because after that happened, I wasn't the same. And you say. Of course we change, and I didn't know what hit us, and how I've changed. And as I've thought about it. It happened for so many good reasons.

I guess that's why my best friend and only friend I've only had, have never changed to one another. And that's why, at my age, and married to my wonderful wife, they've become friends. It's a beautiful relationship, that as a boy,. I thought would never have happened.

We've all heard of this statement, I'd rather have one good friend, than a bunch of liars and theives, and call you friend. You've got that right.

Noticing things when I was growing up.

Bad things. Within my own family, especially in my family. Why do you think I've only had one friend. Because most people are not trustworthy.

As I keep bringing you back to my seven years of age nearly getting killed experience. I became very fearful of trusting anyone. Can anyone blame me. Not really, right?

Not that anyone betrayed me in particular, but watching and witnessing my parents get lied and betrayed, right in front of their own eyes, and mom and Dad never having a clue. So sad. Looking back at that time of my life. Mom and Dad were so innocent to fall into bad relatives traps of lies, for their financial gain has always made me feel resentful towards those people.

There's only been my best of friends, my only friend. For over sixty years. Through my life, my friend has never lied to me, has never told stories about me.

This will seem rather strange, I've had many arguments with Dad, but never with my friend. Isn't it normal, we live with our Dads, not our friends. But even friends will argue with you, but not this guy. If he a disagreement with me, he wouldn't say much, he'd would want to talk about it. But that's still unique, don't you think? Here's another incident. After we moved next door to my buddy's house, we were playing football in the streets, pretty much in front of our homes. We had this arrogant family. There's always somebody right? Here we all are playing in the streets, my friend, his brother, a guy around the corner, three from within the neighborhood, and that's it. Our football being thrown around, like the game of football is played. And this arrogant inhabitant had done this before. What did he do? As we throw the ball, sometimes it would land in his yard. And everytime it would land in his yard, he would keep the ball. Piss us off? You better believe it, because it happened too many times, this idiot kept our ball just too many times. We kept having to buy football after football after football, too many times. After the last keeping of our football, and having to stop our fun, this got out of hand for a couple of us.

Buddy's brother, came knocking on our door, wanting to talk about a plan. Thinking, now what kind of plan. He asked me, if my Dad had any kind of paint in the garage. Telling him, I wasn't sure, but we'll look. Just had to ask, what's on your mind Bud? He says, "I can't stand this guy, every time we play ball, and it lands in his yard, he keeps our ball. And we're going to do something about it, do you want to?" I nod, with a glad to hear of his plan. Dad never heard us in the garage, picking any bucket of paint we could find, and go sneaking over to this angry idiot, and without waisting any time, we poured about four buckets of paint all over his car, and all over one side of their house. Bad as it sounds now, at the time, we felt great about it. And get this, within three months, that family moved out of the neighborhood. All us kids, thought, good riddance. And then another interesting family moves in. During which time, always thought, from one extreme to another. Now this family moves in, and a couple of kids were pot heads, and it was so sad, a young teenage girl, died from drugs. Won't forget that like so many things in my life.

But I recall, that family was too loose. Just the mother herself portrayed herself too whory, if you know what I mean. And I know you do. She was about ten to fifteen years older than I. But showed very little respect.

In the long run, our whole family felt sorry for them. My friend and his family were super. I'm not talking about them. I'm talking about the other side of our house.

Felt real sorry for the father of the family. He hardly said much. Always kept to himself.

But all those days of my life had very little bearing on the life I almost lost, again at age seven. Through my years, seven has been my favorite number. In case any of you don't know, it's also God's number. And seven has been a significant part of my life, and I'll be writing to let you know how the number seven had saved my life more than once. Twice to be exact. For now I'll keep describing my first deathly experience. Because remember, That's what I've been trying to share with you all. And because, "I've Died Three Times And Lived Once."

Through my first years of life, never knew it would come to this. And as my years have slowly creaped up on me, I've had many people advise me to write a book of my life and my deathly experiences. Because you have an experience you should share. But I'm not alone, cause I know there's far more worse life and death experiences than mine.

But this one is mine.

As I've tried to explain to my past psychiatrists. My truck accident experience, it was like it never happened. But it did. Never felt anything different, right after that. But I'm starting to feel it now. Remember, that was my first death I experienced. What I'm trying to explain, and it's always been hard to. It was a nightmare.

Dad, my uncle and I, walked away, on that day, when I was seven, back in nineteen fifty five, from our dead bodies, in a sense. And I must say, in a sense, because I'm still alive. No, I'm saying, I wasn't the same after that day. Impossible, many of you might say. I say, you're wrong. Because as others have been through as I did, or others have experienced much worse. Understandable. And what happened to you, that experienced much worse? Strange right? Exactly understood. Psychologically, of course not physically. This is not a horror story, it's a scary experience of my life. I'm trying to portray, is all.

Don't know, and probably never know, about you others that have experienced what I went through, or for you all that have experienced much worse. What I'm saying, after that scary day of my life after seven, I changed. You ask, in what way? Miracles just started happening to me. But I also had nightmares. Was, like it seemed, I was constantly dreaming I was falling and falling, with no end. And I would wake up all sweaty. Frightened as to what I might see happen the next day. So as I said, we have to move on, or we'll build a very bad sense of insecurity. Did I? Yeah, for a while.

Mom and Dad never thought about going to a doctor, much less to a psychiatrist. That's just the way they were, what could I say. Nothing. Little would I know, at such a young age, I had become my own psychotherapist. Do you believe that? Probably not, and that's ok. Because later as a teenager, I had my friend's brother tell me, I should have been a psychiatrist.

Don't get me wrong, and only if you believe in them. We're all living miracles. I know, there are a lot of you out there, that don't believe in what I'm saying, much less believe in miracles or believing in God.

Can't say I knew how to believe in anything at all. But we had christian catholic parents, what they said, we had to abide by what they would tell us to do, or we would get punished. But we didn't have to get punished, because we went along pretty much what mom and Dad wanted.

Believing very much, what could have happened on that horrible day of nearly getting killed

And how I've tried to survive that horrible day of my life. Even the doctor couldn't understand how we lived through it.

As I've said in my first part of my writing, non of us, meaning, uncle, Dad and I were never sent to be diagnosed under psychiatric therapy. And why, I'll never know. Because, and not just because it was us in particular, and just because, it was a very dramatic dangerous experience for anybody.

After that happened to us, I don't believe I was ever the same. Didn't cry anymore, wasn't afraid of anyone. I think we all lost a little bit of ourselves that tragic day. Even mom. I can only imagine how she felt when she first heard what had happened to us.

Now think about that, you're all out there, think about what I just said. Everyone is at first, in shock when you first hear of any of our loved ones have been in a tragic accident. Well, this one was a truck accident. Since we were in that truck, truly believe, that was much worse. But like I've also stated, when that exact second on impact, we didn't feel a thing. I know I didn't. Not mentally anyway. Of course I felt it physically, because I heard later, that I was screaming for my Dad. And I woke up in a doctor's clinic with a neck brace, and I received numerous stitches on my left side of my head, just to the side of my forehead. Do I suffer from them today? Not my head stitches, but from my neck. I'm in constant pain, now as an old man.

Noticed how I'm selfish, I think we all get selfish when we or a loved one gets into an accident of any kind, don't we? And how do the families of the victims of the ones that get hurt, or even get killed react? I can't even imagine how I would handle that. But my mother went through many dramatic experiences, more than she should have.

Yes I really believe that, just because I have never been a mother. At that time, I was just a boy. How did I know how or what my mother went through. Because I realize now, that's how.

Noticing at such a young age, when I was, my mother, didn't know it then, but I know it now, mama was such a special lady. And how I used to see other boys mistreat their parents, especially their mothers. Boy, that used to piss me off. It would piss me off so much, I would pick on them about it. No way I would talk that way to mama. As a teenager, visiting a school mate, just around the corner from our house, and I hear him shout something to his mother, and then yell at her to shut up. And that outraged me. And I say, "Hey dude, what is wrong with you man, talking to your mom that way", his own Dad, motions me, "Good for you young man". Naturally, my school mate didn't like what I had to say in his house. Can't blame him I guess, after all it's his mom and his home. That's just the way he lived, and respect for my parents was the way we lived.

Being a Catholic and having love and respect were the ways of our household were in those young days of mine. Or else.

And looking back at those days, I have no regrets. Because I've looked at it this way, for those days of learning how to love God, having love from mother and father, and respect, is what makes me the man I am today. But it was never easy, right guys?

On my continuous survival after that day of almost getting killed, that's right, when I was seven years old, my first encounter with death. Went on with improvement in my life. Of course I didn't know it then. But on my daily routine, it wasn't an everyday routine at all, it was an improvement. As if I was older than I actually was. Becoming more advanced than my classmates. Can you believe that? Because for me, it's hard to believe, and I'm the one writing this. Going through my maturing of life, like I could see things will happen, before they would happen. Doesn't that sound weird to anyone out there? I'm sure it does. Because it's always been weird and strange to me.

But it was to my advantage, to improve my life, and for my future. And another thing, maybe one day I'll look my age, because I've never looked it, even now I don't.

After seven years old, I also improved with wisdom. Started receiving As and Bs. What? I know I couldn't believe it.

I truly believe I've lived a miraculous life.

Moving on through my years after seven, were amazing. Let me repeat that, my younger life years have been amazing. But very hard on me, for the most part.

But isn't life hard on all of us? Especially if you don't get any support from anyone that says they love you.

Since the time of my younger years, I have always tried to understand how people really see what love really means to them. My mom taught me, the true meaning of love. I mean it with true sincerity, because mama was a very sincere lady, which I will forever cherish in my heart.

Since I was a boy, started noticing people, even within my own relatives, what false representations they showed what love meant to them. With those people, money, sex, drugs or alcohol, was what love they had for anyone. Found out no one will ever be able to buy love. We've seen it a million times haven't we? And maybe you're one of those kind. Well, ask yourselves, are you? It has always made me sick and sad, to see that happen. To see a relative do something so evil and conniving.

As I've said, many things changed, after my first head on with death. Thinking it would go away and that would be the end of it. Well it continued on. Writing this story of mine, I have always wondered how I've lived to end up, much closer to God. Always tried to make my mom and Dad proud of me. And what's wrong with that? If you're reading, you guys that understand what I'm saying, didn't it hurt? When your Dad wouldn't give the time of day. I remember it used to hurt me very much.

Some questions to all of you, do you believe in God? Do you believe in miracles? And do you believe in angels? Just think about that before you answer. But if you look at it from my point of view, you might understand what I'm trying to tell you. No, I didn't even know there was God, much less knowing about miracles or angels. You've had to have lived the life I have lived for you to understand or to have a clue. Many of you won't believe me, much less understand me.

Like I said, didn't know there was a God, much less knowing about miracles and angels. And I also said, that I've had a mother, that taught me well. Yes my Dad did too, but worked two jobs, so it was very hard for him. And I understand that now. Too blind and too naive, when we're too young. Ain't that right?

Going through the waves of time, whether the time waves you in the wrong direction, or time waves you to the right direction. Now what do I mean by that? What it means to me, either you make right choices and right decisions, you will prosper tremendously. But I don't think there are that many people that are perfect, and maybe there are. And I don't mean that in a perfect sense. Because there is no one in this world, that's perfect. And being a boy, is just a start of time, making mistakes and making the wrong choices. But I'd like to believe that I didn't make many wrong choices, and go the wrong way. Because that's why I had my mother and father, they were always there to correct me. To discipline me, to punish me, if I deserved it.

Aww, but once we start our teenage years, I started thinking I'm smarter than my parents. Oh, how wrong we can be when we think like that. Right guys? I've heard it before, and we still hear those people. Every generation have their smart asses that think they're so smart. And maybe they are, in a evil way. And I'd like congratulate those that have never abused your parents, my hats are off to you. Because I believe there are very good people out there.

From my young life, from my first encounter with death, and slowly getting closer to my second encounter with death. Don't know if I should say I wasn't scared, because that would be lying, and we would know, I'd be lying to myself. Remember, Died Three Times, Lived Once. As I've gotten old, I know there are programs like, anger management, and pain management. And as I started my teenage, never heard of any program of fear management. I'm asking, is there any program like that? Soon enough I'll be opening up my own fear management, to control fear for my own self. It's either that or stay paranoid all my life. And I've seen that type, and I know, so have you. Always freaked out, cry at every little thing. That's not me, and it has never been me. Thinking that Dad probably tried to keep me, as maybe his Dad had him. What I mean is, Dad told me some stories about his Dad, how mean and arrogant, and very violent. As well as all his uncles were. Oh, I was a shy little kid from the get go. But learned quickly not to be afraid of anyone. Shy all the way up to my first year of high school. After ninth grade, I was done with shyness. But don't we all start off kind of timid, and shy? Remember no real moral support, from especially Dad. Mom tried, but I always thought moms can only do what they can for a son. Right? Mama was a strong spiritual parent, and Dad was a strong working parent. But Dad couldn't help being who he was, because of his Dad. Sad but true.

I mentioned my first year of high school. And remember I constantly talk about my first deathly experience. Because I will never forget it, and for you that have come close to the kiss of death, you just don't forget it, that's a natural thing. But the sad things that happen, there are those that don't make it. There are those that are killed instantly, and there are those that end up disabled. I think I would rather die instantly than suffer, in a pain, or worse yet, end up in a wheelchair. What do you think? Maybe I feel this way, because I faced death at such a young age and by God's blessings, nothing major happened to me physically. And I'll say it again. Something psychologically happened to me, and I'll never be able to explain it perfectly. All I knew at seven years old. After that truck accident, I wasn't the same person, from eight years old, until I went on experiencing my second death. And I'm reaching that part of my life slowly but surely. Maybe there are you out there, that think I'm psychotic, and maybe I am. Never really cared about what people thought, especially what people thought about me. Am I wrong in thinking that way? I've learned through my mom and Dad, as a boy, respect. I had to learn, from the time I was a little boy, it's either I show respect, or get spanked by, yea you know it, by Dad, who else.

Of course who's going to like getting spanked, or worse yet, whipped, would be the proper word for me, because it happened more than a few times. Quite a few times.

Well there you have it, from my boyhood days and starting to reach my adolescence. We all should know, it has and and probably will always be hard being a teenager, unless you're born with a silver spoon. Being born rich, in other words. For me personally, and for my family relatives, as far as I know, there has never been any silver spoons. I come from a very hard working ancestry. We either work very hard, or I wouldn't get too far in life. But that goes with all of us, that's just how life is, no buts, ifs, or ands about it. And thank God, Dad taught me how to work, and work very hard, is how he taught me, at an age of only five years old. Didn't know it then, but found out, that was very lucky for me, because it turned out to be, my best feature as a man, which it would become to my advantage, as to how companies would see me as a hiring person. Because the time did come for me to go out into the workforce, as a teenager. I've heard many people say they had to work themselves through college. Well, I had to work myself through high school and a little junior college, until the war of Vietnam stopped me

ROBERT GARCIA

into advancing any career I had in mind. So again, thank you Dad. Because of my working hard, made me hirable.

So, starting at my big age of thirteen, I started cleaning a parking lot, and can you believe it, I was cleaning a parking lot of a hamburger stand, and got paid five dollars a week. After graduating from junior high school, which was very close to us at the time, but would soon be walking close to a mile to high school. And I got tired of mom buying me used clothes from a goodwill store.

I always thought back then, if Dad wouldn't had drank so much, he could have given mom a little bit more money to clothe us better. I say us, remember I had two sisters, and mom would buy them used clothes, also at a goodwill store. Never knew if they liked that, but I didn't. Like I said, got tired of mom's taste for me, of the kind of clothes she wanted me to wear.

So one day after on my home from school, stopped by this fairly new hamburger stand, with a name, John's hamburgers, asked the owner. Remember I'm only thirteen. Walking up to his ordering window. He says to me. "My I help you"? And I asked him. "Sir can you hire me"? He wondered about that. "How old are you boy?" I tell him "Thirteen" He asks me, "Now what could you do for me? I'm looking at his parking lot, and I tell him, "I could clean your parking lot every day I walk from school". He was amazed, I think because I had accepted five dollars a week!!! To me that was a lot of money, after all I wasn't receiving anything to buy nothing. And I felt so proud of myself. Well I guess so. It would become my plan to buy my own clothes. And start wearing new clothes, and new shoes. To dress better for high school, and of course for the girls. After all I'm gonna start high school.

Being thirteen years old, felt pretty good about myself. Walking into mom and dads house, and giving the big surprise. I got me a job. You should have saw the looks on their faces. They looked at each other, and imagined, they probably thinking, who would hire a thirteen year old, that looks like ten? "Who hired you?" I say "Johns Hamburgers" "and what are you going to do there"? "I'm going to clean the parking lot every day walking home from school for five dollars a week". To you all of you that are interested enough in reading this. The day of my first job, being only thirteen, it was the first part of the sixties.

Feeling privileged to going to school, compared to the times of my Dad, which he only went up to fourth grade. It was so very hard in those days. I can't even imagine.

While Dad wasn't able to attend school, Dad made it perfectly clear, his three kids were going to school, and that was a must. He wouldn't hear of it, that any of his kids didn't want to go to school. And the greatest thing for Dad and I, that I started loving school. Especially mathematics, and the history of our country part of school. And I don't remember many classmates liking or even coming close in loving any part of school.

So when I started high school, I started my first job. I felt like I was on cloud nine. Building more confidence within my spirit, what little I knew about spirit within. I knew zilch. None.

I only know now, as an old man.

Continuing with my life as a high school boy. I had so much fun, I'll never forget it. Why would I forget something Dad, wanted so much for his kids. Working two jobs, most of the time. I never disappointed him, during my high school days. He showed a lot of pride in me. Walking everyday from school. Like I said, walking home from school, was near a mile, and then clean a hamburger stand's parking lot. That part of my life, was no fun at all. But we can't have everything. Being able to learn, was the fun part, but cleaning a parking lot, was just something I had to do, to be able to purchase my own clothes and shoes, and have some spending money.

ROBERT GARCIA

Oh, and on the weekends, with the little money I would save up, I was finally able to go to a party or some place special.

Only being fourteen, wasn't driving yet, but I'm getting there. So I had to continue cleaning a parking lot. But when I turned sixteen, oh wow. Not only did I get my drivers license, Dad bought me my first car. But I finally stopped cleaning that parking lot. And now what would I do for money? Couldn't remember for the life of me, when I was writing this. Had to had made some kind of money, after all now I'm driving a car. Money for gas, money for food, and yes, now I need money for girls. That's just the way it is for a teenage boy. And finally having money, to take myself to Disneyland and Knots berry farm. Those were the greatest theme parks in my day. And very popular they were. Where I couldn't go as a boy, was able to take myself. Go to, and take anyone I wanted to, and who wanted to go with me. In my high school days, there would always be a girl that wanted to go out with me. Mom and Dad were always warning me, to watch out for those fast girls. There'll always be around. Fast girls that wanted to be taken out with boys with cars. I don't think that's anything new, in any generation. Mom was constantly monitoring me about girls coming home with me. Mom didn't like it. She would scold me like I was a little boy. Mama was always right, and I thought I knew it all. Finding out much later, I was so wrong.

Having my first car was very exciting for me, wasn't it people? You remember!! And of course, by having a car, comes responsibilities. Car maintenance, checking the oil, making sure your tires have enough air. Being ready if you're involved in an accident.

Coming back about being ready if you're involved in an accident. Well there was this one day of my life. Wasn't in any accident, but I was driving in the fast lane, going at sixty five or seventy miles per hour. For any of you that know Los Angeles, California, there has always been, what they call the grid lock, in other words, bumper to bumper. If you can visualize going at a fast speed, and then one of your front tires blow out. Now I've always heard, if you have a front tire blowout, you may flip your car, or worse yet, create a car pile up. Killing your self, and possibly killing many others. Well that almost happened to me. With a chevy corvair. If you know what a corvair looks like, it had the back engine, which makes it harder to control, when a crash happens.

Like I said, I didn't panic, and as scared as I was, was still able to control my little corvair. But as miracles have happened to me, as surprises happen to all of us.

Can't remember who was with me, but I suppose he or she freaked out as well, and wondered what the hell happened. Because when my front tire blew out, I almost lost control of the steering wheel, but I was able to grip it hard with both hands, looking around me very quickly, was able to get my car from the fast lane and swerve clear across to the slow lane on the interstate five freeway. If anyone can visualize where that freeway is in California, then you'll understand the situation I went through.

Coming to a screeching halt on the freeway shoulder, as I took deep breaths, as I wondered how in the hell did I pull that off. It was a close call, for a lot of people.

As I've lived my life, and seen many crashes, often flashed back with that incident, front tire blow out, and thought, what a miracle that day was for me. And how disastrous crashes, which I've seen so many times, and I'm sure you all have too.

Here's another flash back for me and for you. Just another day with Dad, after a few years after our dangerous deathly truck crash. Dad had another truck, picking up trash from commercial accounts, driving down the road, and Dad all of a sudden, starting pumping the brake foot pedal, and yells out to me, son we don't have any brakes.

I really believe Dad didn't stop that truck, God did. For you that don't believe in God, are probably thinking and saying, why would I mention God. The biggest reason being, because there is a God, and I wouldn't be talking about this close call, if I would've died, the day we were broad sided in fifty five by a gas tanker, when I was seven. Now there I was at ten, almost crashing again. Scared? You better believe it, and so was Dad. My eyes almost fell out of my head, when Dad yelled out, "son I can't stop the truck, we have no brakes." Was starting to think, I'm gonna go through life, paranoid, insecured, nervous as hell. But I didn't. I'll mention it again, I'm alive, because of God. No, I didn't know it then, of course not. But at ten, started thinking, and paying attention to mom's prayers. Mom's faith, and prayers, is why I'm here, writing this today. And being seven and ten years of age, is now long gone. From those days, never paid any mind to write anything about my life, because I've never thought anyone would read this, and I still don't. Only time will tell, and only God knows.

Going on with my life, as if nothing was wrong, and that's how I went on. As I've said, was great in school, especially in mathematics. At ten, was receiving As and Bs. Continued on with great grades through middle school, up until the eighth grade.

Never wanted to feel too confident. Always heard if you're too confident, you can fall, and fall hard. So I tried watching that, as I noticed others fall and fail, especially in education. Smart? No I never thought so, but friends did tell me I was. So I let my friends tell me that. And of course it felt good to be told you're smart. But that was just the beginning of my life, as we all start. You know it.

Man oh man, it sure felt great to start high school, into my freshman year, didn't it feel good, you people reading this? Remember I mentioned confidence? Yes I had and still do have my self confidence. Guess because I faced death at such a young age. At my young self, had confidence and will power. As my years continued on, during my middle school years, and going into my high school years, mom and Dad were so proud of me. Don't believe I was the only one with parents being proud of one self. But those are stories left for you all to tell, and this one is mine.

By having self confidence, was able to defend myself from others. Finding out from then, we all need that self defense, if not, we'll be pushed, shoved, and stepped on from bullies. And I've always had issues with bullies. In fact I couldn't and still can't stand those maniacs. I have other choice words, but why stoop low to their level. Have, and still see, and probably always witness bullying, from those low life, thinking because they're big, feeling that power trip over smaller guys. Maybe it's a complex I've had all my life, and maybe I can't help carrying around. Believe by having that complex, it's helped me survive with aggression. That's been my advice to guys, in the same boat as I. Sorry to sound offensive, but I've had my share of attacks from people, because I'm short, they can just push around, well coming from me, they're wrong. And some have found out the hard way. You can believe it or not. But it's been me that would pick on bigger than me. Funny huh? Its been a surprise for many bullies. Surprise, and attack.

Guess from the time Dad told me, that I would probably be small like my mom. What man, having a son, tells his son that? And maybe that was a positive thing for me. Because I have been able to defend myself, since I was a boy.

Little did Dad and I know, from the day he told me about my shortyness, I would use that aggression against him. Because he was taller than me. Not by much, but he felt like he was much taller. But for me, it's never been about how big or how tall the bully has been, it's always been about how well I can counterattack the bully. And that's helped me up until now.

Coming from the time I was in the fifth grade, having an infatuation for a girl, and watching another kid hit her, outraged me, to the point of aggression, and aggressive I became, by running at him, jumping him, and beating him till he cried. I couldn't help myself.

It's funny, after that incident, during my later years in school, didn't have any violence, or I didn't have to use aggression against anyone. Thank God for that. But I did have a couple of violent problems with a couple of neighborhood kids, my neighbor next door, and a kid around the corner from our house. And later having a problem with one of my sisters boyfriend. And also later, a big kid wanting to throw me over a second story balcony. Oh, by the way, also later on, an older brother of my first wife. But that I'll explain later on in my life. But in school, no trouble at all. Whew, thank God.

Have you ever heard, that it's hard being a teenager? Well I wasn't any different, but I not only had it hard as a teenager, but as a younger boy as well. In fact didn't much have a boyhood. During the days as a boy, and wanting to play with my neighborhood kids my age, it was off to work at four or five in the morning. To help Dad pick up trash, in Yorba Linda, California. Anybody ever hear about that city? If you know about it, then you also know, that it's a very rich place to live.

I know there are many of you, that have had many friends, and I probably could have had many friends as well, but I didn't want that. Especially in my life time, witnessing comrades die in a war we were in.

Don't really know why I've never had close friends during my teenage years. Oh I've had a fraction of my time as a teenager, with some acquaintances. And maybe it's because of trust you have to give, for me to call you my friend. Don't really know why, I'm just guessing. And I've became to accept the life I've had for many years.

During the fraction of my teenage years, for a while, with a few neighborhood teenagers, we played baseball, basketball, football, even pool. Can't say I didn't have any fun, because I did. But my biggest attention I focused on, was my education. That was my biggest concern, that I had to do, for my life. And I'll tell you later, how that all fell apart. I felt that was my own empire I was trying to build. It's just like, it doesn't matter how big your house is, it's still a man's castle. Remembering my young life, from the time I was four years old. Being born in Glendale, Arizona. And I can't for the life of me, remember anything before four years old. Can any of you remember anything from the time you were born until you were four? I think not. Dad moved us out to Norwalk, California, into mom and Dad's first purchased home. Even though it was a one bedroom little house, it was still Dad's home and castle.

Don't know about anyone else in my family, Dad, Mom, and my two sisters, but from the time I was only four, only knew the language of Spanish, until I reached thirteen, I had become fluent with the English language. Doing great in school.

Also at the age of thirteen, Dad had purchased his third home. Dad never knew this, but I was very proud of him. He probably thought I never understood him, that he constantly repeated, only went to fourth grade. How could I forget. He always reminded us. As I've grown old, I became more proud of him. When I wrote this, he was still kicking at ninety six years old.

From the time I was very young, I've always respected my parents. Because Dad wouldn't have it any other way. And he would let us know if he didn't like it. Personally, when I wouldn't show respect to his eyes, he would pull me off to the side, and he would let me know, and I would have to agree with him or else. And I think you all know what I mean by, or else, without going into the formalities.

And that was pretty much the way things were up to, as I started approaching my teenage life. And now that I write about it, I appreciate God's love, and mom and Dads ways on how they raised and supported the three of us.

Although I have always loved my parents, my coming teenage years will prove, that I would become rebellious and manipulative. As I've said throughout, Dad wanted his family to show respect, and I had no problem with that. But when Dad starts showing his other side of himself, I started a rebellious life. And a rebel I would become, especially against Dad. As it was, we weren't close as I always thought a father and son should be, as a little boy. A rebellious young teenager I would become. In other words, his policy was, you do what I say, not what I do. Like I said, as a little boy, I had no problem accepting to learn respect, but as I approach the teen ages, and Dad continued to try to teach me respect, but he would show his other side of himself. Which to me, was wrong. Am I right guys? How would you feel?

Don't know, and probably will never know, why my mom told me things, what Dad would do behind our back. Because if Dad did betrayal things behind Mom, I think those were betrayal things behind his family as well, don't you think?

Try and visualize this scenario. Dad always swore he loved mama. And Mom and the family would believe him, and why would we not believe him? Right? He always seemed sincere. Would put a good show. But Mom would catch Dad in betrayal actions around the neighborhood. In my Dad's second purchased home, in that neighborhood, there was this floozy, loose with herself. I would notice her talking to different men, most days, either coming home from school or from somewhere. She was always talking to some guy in the neighborhood. And Dad was one of them. But he preached respect to me. Huh? Hear me guys? Does anyone understand what I I'm saying. What would you do? To this day in my life, will never know why Mom told me those things about Dad, and I will never bring that up to Dad. It just wouldn't be fair to the both of us, we're old now, he's in his nineties and I'm in my seventies. We both have had many tests in our lives. Not knowing as a boy and as a teenager, what Dad actually went through when he was a boy and a teenager. I know now not then, I'm no better than Dad. And I've never thought I was better than anyone. Because no one is. Dad has pretty much lived his life, and I'm still trying to live mine.

Like I've said, started having issues, and resentments towards my dear old Dad. Looking back at it, that sounds sad to say, much less to write about it.

It hurt when I wrote this. But I'm being honest with myself and to my life's experiences. And most of all to anyone that will pick up my book and read it, and pay attention.

Moving on with my teenage life, it was fun for the most part. And my life as a high schooler, was beautiful and exciting. I think I had more sense then than I do now. I'll tell you later why. Because we all experience our ups and downs, don't we? I know we all do. In a perfect world, our life would be, and Tom Hanks once said. Tom said, life is a bowl of cherries. What a joke.

So what I couldn't do as a young boy, I tried to catch up as a teenager. And of course that proved to be impossible. Thought by having a car, I thought I had freedom. Becoming a teenager, there's responsibilities, like following traffic laws. Here comes my first speeding ticket. Yep, I got my first speeding ticket at sixteen. Driving sixty five miles per hour at a twenty five mile zone.

And I almost got a ticket making an illegal exit from my high school parking lot. When I say, almost, that's what it was, almost. As I was exiting, didn't notice a police car parked, just waiting for anyone, especially a high school kid, like me to drive out illegally. And the illegal exit I did, and here comes that police car. He pulls me over, and as he started pulling out his ticket book, he gets an emergency call on his radio, ordering him to go to wherever he was needed as an emergency. As he informs me, it's your lucky day son. And drove off. I sat in my car, thinking, whew, oh my God. Thank You. But I don't think that was as lucky as the time I told you about my front tire freeway blow out. And luck had nothing to do with my most scariest, and my most dangerous deathly experience in my life, and here I go again. The deathly truck accident.

You people probably think I'm too repetitious, going on and on, about the truck accident that almost killed me. Well how would you process it? Would you have forgotten it? I don't think so, and if you would have, then I don't think you take your life very seriously. I personally to this day thank God for that miracle. And little would I know, my life would be overwhelmed with miracles. But aren't we all living a miracle from the day we're born? Well just ask yourselves, aren't we living miracles from the day we're born?

As I continue writing to you about my life, and it's hard to put it all in writing about a lifetime, to put it into words. Living a life, and putting it into words, are two different things, don't you think? Dad of course had a very different and difficult life as a boy and as a teenager. But I still can't remember a lot about what he told me, but he had it very hard, like most of the people did in that day in time. I truly believe that Dad and I are very unique people. When I wrote this book, to say I still had my Dad, at my age, and him being ninety six years old. Wow!!! And me in my seventies. How many of you can say that? There are very few, I know. In my last neighborhood, where I grew up, and left the house, my first time. All those kids I grew up with, have long time lost their moms and dads. And I still have Dad to this day. And I wrote this book in two thousand twenty two. Life moves on, and time doesn't wait for no one. And no one is promised tomorrow. There's a song I truly admire, it describes love and life beautifully "Life can be short or long, and love can be right or wrong" Do any of you remember that song? Because I'll never forget it.

Not really knowing the meaning of life as I started my young life, often wondered, what's our purpose? Writing this when Dad was alive at ninety six, he often wondered what was his purpose. Probably many of you out there, maybe thinking the same thing. Well guys, what's your purpose, because many of you didn't know it when you were young, and probably still don't get it. And where do many of us end up, I think either dead or in prison, or probably in a nut house. That is if you never find out what's your purpose is.

Dad has been reading the Bible, everyday for the past ten years, just after Mom past. He finally came to a conclusion, that he's supposed to inform others about God, everyday until he passes. When he told me that, he sounded so happy. I didn't know what to tell him, so I've left it at that. If that's what he thinks, believing he's a messaging child of God, so be it. And maybe he is. And maybe we all should be messengers of God. I've also thought that maybe Dad thinks he a messenger of God because he's very old.

In my younger years I've often noticed things about real old people. To be wanting to be better than they've ever been to be forgiven by God.

As I said before, Dad and I are unique. He'll try teaching you something, and he'll go doing the complete opposite. And outright tell me, don't do what I do, do what I say. Don't you think I found that quite odd. Of course I did. And who wouldn't? From five on up until my teenage, I've wondered, what's wrong with Dad? Nothing was wrong with Dad, I just didn't understand him is all. Understanding Dad was not the easiest thing for me to do, after all I'm still trying to figure out where am I going with my life. And trying to understand Dad, and keep my grades up was hard. And I think you'd agree with me. So I did the smart thing, focus on my education, and quit trying to figure out other people's problems, even if he is my Dad or my Mom.

So it's off to school I continue going, because as you all know, or should know, without an education, life will be a complete disaster. But as I wrote that, my best friend and only friend I've ever had, also a very unique individual. Quit school at seventeen years old.

When I first heard about that, thought to myself, oh my God, what is he doing, why would he quit school? And I asked that exact question. "Hey buddy, why did you quit school?" "You're only seventeen man" And what was his answer? A responsible one, and as long as we've known each other, a responsible person he's always been. What did he say. "I'm going to support my girl friend, she's pregnant", I tell him "but you don't have to marry her, he says, "oh yes I do" That's just the way he was, loyal to his responsibilities. I thought he was better than most guys. He never thought so, but his neighborhood buddies thought he was a very good person. And I still do. Knowing him for over sixty years now and still going when I wrote this. He's been as I've said, a unique man, and a very good supportive friend that I've had the pleasure of knowing. It's too bad the relationship with that girl friend, he impregnated wasn't as loyal as he was. Because she was a very flirtatious girl, remembering the kind of girl she was. She flirted with me by God. Cheap. That's what she was. And he didn't deserve her. Look what he did for her, he quits school, got a job as fast as he could. Worked his butt off for that cheap woman, and for his child. Even his mother and father and his brother thought so. And even to this very day, wondered if that child that girl was carrying when she was pregnant, if that was his child. Never found out any different. Since I strongly believed that education was first, before anything else, it's was so hard to not do that sex thing with any girl. Came so close. I mean, I actually put it in, but I pulled it out just in time, just before I ejaculated into the girl I was with. Will never forget that. Had a girlfriend once, that wanted my baby, during the time the military draft was out, when the Vietnam war broke out. That girl was so hard trying to cling to me, no matter what it took.

But I stuck to my guns, and kept my whistle buckled up, by not falling for any girl, so I would not end up paying with my life, supporting any loose chick. And you guys know damn well what I mean, what I mean, by sticking to my guns. Had to keep standing tall, with education, on top of everything else. And that included women, spreading their legs to trap me. Because that's just the way life is. And all of you know that, or should. Hell, after seeing my friend get suckered into a relationship that didn't mean anything to her. He's still suffering as to how he is putting up with those children he had from that loose woman. And get this, after my friend married that flirtatious woman, he wasn't married to her too long, because next I find out, he's divorcing her. Was I surprised, not one bit. Never really knew why, maybe he found out the baby wasn't his.

And maybe it was. It didn't really matter to me, after all, that wasn't any of my business, and he'll be the one that will be suffering. Right! That's right. But one day after all of that bologna, since it was his younger brother that was always upset about brother marrying that woman, and divorcing her, he's standing in front of his yard, tapping his foot like he was tap dancing, and smoking like a train. Came up to him, asking him, what's wrong dude? He responds "Do you know what my brother is going to do? He's going to marry that bitch again", he sure pisses me off. Did some name calling to his brother. And it didn't take long, before I knew it, my buddy married that loose woman again. Thinking to myself, poor guy, he didn't learn from the first time. And got suckered in again, and married that woman again.

Life is the way it is, and will continue being the way it is. And I started figuring things out for myself, or at least I thought I was, in what I wanted to do with my life. Was just another guy thinking I had the world by it's tail. What a joke that turned out to be.

Well, day by day, continued going to school, and it wasn't just school for me, as if I could see a big reward at the end of the tunnel. Oh I had my good times with friends in high school, parties and all. Girls here and girls there. It was fun, but I was careful. I was never missing school. No, not me. Went to class, school, and my junior college everyday. That was me.

Thinking to myself back then, if I start missing a class here, and missing a day of school there, then I'm going to start falling down. And in my mind, with God's permission, that wasn't going to happen to me. Working myself through high school and junior college, was very hard for me, as I would expect to be hard on anyone else, am I right, guys? Flash back, remembering my algebra class, the first year of high school.

My teacher was a good and strict algebra teacher. From the beginning I was receiving As and Bs, in algebra, but too many parties will make anybody fall if you're not careful. Because parties and education don't mix well. It's either one or the other, not one with the other, or they can do without each other. But he let me have it straight. My algebra teacher tells me, "What happened?" I look at him, with eyes wide. I say, "What?" He tells me, "you're falling", "but if you want, you can make it up by going to summer school" and I did. And picked my grade up to an A minus. Very proud of myself? Of course I was. And who wouldn't be? You would be, and should be. Because we only have limited chances at life. We all have to try and take advantage of the time we have on earth. What am I trying to say? I didn't know it when I was so young. And I don't even know if I know it now. I just think I do.

But my buddy's brother, his younger brother didn't believe in school. He was completely opposite than I was. He thought I was a book worm, because I was always carrying school books. He also called me a nerd. He seemed bothered that I loved school. When he hated school. I felt sorry for that kid.

Get a load of this next incident I'm about tell you. This kid hated school so bad, he comes knocking on my door, and says, "Hey man you want to go with us?" I say, "go where?" I asked. The next thing he tells me, amazed me, as to how hateful he had for school. He says, "we're gonna go and vandalize that school" "so do you want to go with us"? I was bewildered, when he told me what they were going to do. When I say they, because it was going to be him, his brother, and another dummy from across the street. I felt so bothered, because here I was with a girl in my parents house, while they were out on a night out to sing at some place they usually went to have a good time. I was very comfortable, when I got this sudden knock at the door. So when I told him, I didn't want to go. I say "Now why would I want to go do something stupid like that"

Thinking to myself, my buddy already impregnated a girl, he thinks he has to marry, quits school, gets a cheap job, and now he chooses to go vandalize a school, thought to myself, boy, how stupid can people get. I'm sure glad I was never involved in that ridiculous stupid idea

ROBERT GARCIA

of vandalizing a school. Well anyway I'm minding my own business, having a sexual encounter with a girl I thought would one day marry. Whew, that was a close call, because I'm sure glad I didn't marry that. But that's another story I'll open on later down the road of my life. But just because I didn't marry that girl, I ended up marrying the same kind, cheap.

Let me continue with my life with the boys of our dead end neighborhood, because that's where we lived, three houses from the dead end. And there's that middle school, that went from sixth to eighth grade. And living right next door to kids that vandalized that school. Well this story continues, because after they destroyed that nice school, and while they were swinging off ceiling lamps, and marking on the walls, and breaking windows, the boy, that I call my best friend, now an old man like I am, while he was swinging off one of the lamps, his drivers license fell out of his pocket and onto the classroom floor. Can you imagine? But that's karma for you, what goes around comes around. Repeating to you, I'm so damn glad I didn't go with those idiots. One of those idiots is no longer an idiot, he's well, and has been fighting prostate cancer, and so far he's ok. The other idiots are dead, one died a drug addict, the other a alcoholic, nice huh? No not nice, but very sad. In the mean time, I continued for my future, going to school. And remember this is years after the deathly experience of that truck accident, that people say we should have died. And here I am, focusing on my education, instead of following these knuckleheads. And I've already told you about the younger brother of my buddy when some other night, when he came knocking on my door before. Only to want, like he put it, wanting to kick my ass. And it was just another night of pills, which sadly to say, he was addicted to. Boy did he love taking those high pills. He just could not stay away from them. And that's what took his life. Poor kid. The real sad part is, I had always thought he liked girls, but his brother told me when he arrived at his house, something was very strange. Music was on full blast. No one in the living room. He goes into one of the bedrooms and catches this other guy in the bedroom with his kid brother, with their clothes off. And his brother laying still under the blankets. He was always talking about girls, and how pretty this one was and how pretty that one was. That shocked me, and I really think that shocked my buddy as well all to hell. Well I don't have to tell you the rest of the part he wanting to kick my ass. Well that never happened, because he was too weak from the drugs to fight anyone. And I was never proud when I punched him in the face. But it was just once, maybe once too many. Because like I said, wasn't proud about that.

Back to the time when we were all young.

Another dramatic incident we got ourselves in, and letting this kid control us to vandalism, and yes, burglarize, Burglarize? What the hell. When I thought I was smart, well I wasn't. I thought I was. We let the devil into our lives at such a young age. Yes we let my friend's young brother talk us into breaking and entering into a record store. It was like, we got sucked into some bad influence, and very evil. No, my buddy and I weren't the ones that actually broke in, but we were the look outs, it's the same thing. The way I look at it. When his brother and the kid from right across the street from us, broke into a record store, my friend and I were the look outs. Boy were we scared. He was so scared, he was shaking and crying. Telling him, calm down buddy. We'll be ok. And by pure luck and the love of God, we got through that night. That was so close. Oh dear lord. If anybody knew. My friend and I telling each other, what the hell were we doing there.

Never again did I or we, and I'm talking about my buddy and I never again did we ever do anything stupid like that again. Always wondered what possessed us to follow and let his young brother to talk us into doing something, like burglary. Burglary? Never in my life, but remember we're only teenagers. Fourteen, sixteen and seventeen year olds. Stupid right? Always thought that was one of my most stupidest thing I had ever done. I mean, aren't we supposed to get smarter as we advance in years? In a perfect world, yes, but in a real world, people are just weird. Our wrong choices and our wrong decisions will take us straight to hell. If we don't look at ourselves as to what are we doing to our spirits, because didn't know it back then, but through my bad choices in my life, just had to change, or I probably be dead by now. But in this time in my writing of my young life, I've only just begun.

Alright, back to my school days of my life, and how I look at it now, that will be one of my best times of my life, but not thee best, and I'll get to that part as I write this down.

Awe, my school days of my life, those were the days, long gone but not forgotten. My buddy, to this day reminds me, of how smart I was, I never thought so, but he reminds of that. And I thank him about that.

Remember writing to you about my algebra class in my freshman year in high school, and went on to trigonometry in my sophomore year in high school. So proud of myself, and so were my mom and Dad. Dad telling me, I'm very proud of you son. And mom, you all know how moms are, sentimental and emotional. And get this, I felt it was another promotion, yea, going into my junior year in high school, started calculus. Wow we. Can you believe it? Because I had a problem in believing that could happen to me. We all plan for our future, by taking our prerequisites. So I was planning on entering junior college, and having my major being mechanical drawing, and to continue on to a university, and becoming a mechanical engineer, to work for a major construction company. Yea right, but unfortunately you will see by writing this out, that I would get no where close to ever becoming that dream I had, that I thought I would one day become.

Was attending my classes on a everyday basis, even with some classes, on Saturdays. But that's how many of us start out, you out there reading this, does this remind you of yourself? I'm sure it does, I'm not alone, you know who you are. Well with me, this is how it was for me. And now that I'm old, it kind of makes me feel bad and sad. But back to high school.

Remembering I had joined a car club, after being a member of this particular club, sometimes I thought, that wasn't a good thing. There was too much violence, too much partying, oh yeah too much of the wrong things for me to handle. Uncontrollable. Would go to some of those parties, and all I saw was sex, and drugs in all these house parties. Filth. No don't get me wrong, I liked it, because I was just a kid, and like many of us, we seem to like filth when first introduced to it. At this part of my life, I was introduced to pot, (marijuana), at sixteen years old. And I thought everyone smoked pot, didn't we, or should I ask, didn't you?

Smoking pot made me feel smarter than most, didn't it make you feel that way to you? At sixteen, started drinking, and smoking pot, and of course continued going to school. But I never became an alcoholic and I never became a drug addict, during those early teenage years of my life. But the way I look at it now, that's still was not a good way to start my life. Was nibbling on pot, and hardy drinking alcohol. It wasn't bad yet.

And hadn't got caught by mom and Dad, nor the law, thank God for me. Didn't want to spoil my good education reputation, but I was starting to live on the edge of destroying anything good for me. Because all that had to happen, is slip a little to the left and I'll fall into the hands of the law, and I probably flunk out of my classes. Wow, what a disappointment that would've been for my parents, especially for me. After all I'm only just sixteen and seventeen years of age. Too too young to destroy something I was just starting. Really? Thank God nothing got out of hand, then. Yes I say then, but it would be decades later before anything drastic would happen to me. But I leave that part of my life to show you how twisted my mind got out of control.

Back to how I first said it before, concentrate on priorities. Now ask yourselves or better yet, let me explain what priorities meant to me, and what it means to me today. And I started to get unorganized with my life, by opening the door to evil and bad influences. Don't know about you, it's easy to let your guard down if you let evil and bad influences control your life, at such a vulnerable time of your life. I'm asking, isn't it? And I know, we've all faced that at one time or another.

Didn't know it then in my young life, and I've only just realized it lately with my current life, that there's a reason for everything.

Priorities was never on my agenda for a long time, and I know now there are those of you, that live a much better organized life than I have ever lived, and know their priorities, and live a very organized and happy life than I had. And that's why this is my story, even though I'm exposing my stupid choices and decisions. But I had to learn it the hard way, like probably many of us, but not all of us. That's just life, the way it is.

And I told you, didn't have a very guided life at the beginning, this is why I say, I had to teach myself about life the hard way. And very hard it was. And remember all this happened to me after my most tragic accident at seven. Facing my life's first death. Remember, Died Three Times Lived Once.

Will never blame anything on my parents, because they had it harder than I did. Mom and Dad were born from the greatest generation in America's history. The generations after them have had it much better, basing on America's way of living. And I know, from the history I was taught in school, other parts of the world, are third world countries, with bombarded territories everywhere. Sad but true. So I believe I've had an amazing life, from my childhood and into my story approaching my teenage years. Even though I say I had it hard, I still consider myself blessed, compared to other parts of the world.

Everyone has a story to tell, don't you?

While I started my teenage years, like everyone has or at least had the opportunity to live life. So many others aren't as lucky as we are. Agree? Agreed. And then there's others that have a rich life. That's left to the politicians, from the president on down, or like I've seen other countries have dictators, or kings and queens. Then there are those that start an average life or born poor, and become a celebrity, that's an opportunity in some few countries. But especially in America. With that said, you may know and maybe you haven't figured it out yet, but my generation comes, being born in the late forties, and actually started living life during the fifties.

Coming from transistor radios.

For old guys like myself, and maybe some younger people out there, remember the transistor radios? When I wasn't at school or wasn't doing homework, had a transistor wrapped around my head. I loved them, listening to my music, oh man, those were the days, weren't they guys?

By that time, we were living at Dad's second house in California. What a marvelous time of my life, to be able to listen to music, and sports. Oh yes I was a fanatic, especially when it came to sports and music, huh, what did I say? Oh well, loved both, and crazy about both. What can I say. It kept me at peace, when I hardly received any attention from Dad, especially from Dad. So by having my leisurely time either one or both to pass the time, and enjoy myself by myself. People say, I had a very shallow life, maybe to them, but looking at it from back then, glad I was bored and having a shallow life, because I could've gotten in trouble for being bored.

Mama was my savior, and was the one that raised me, because Dad didn't have the time, how could he, he was always working, or out drinking, and at times come home drunk. So what time did he have, none. And he couldn't help it, he was constantly pressured. So mom had me shut down from going anywhere in the streets. Didn't like it then, because I was too young to understand what she was trying to protect me from influential people that would get me into trouble for sure. Felt sorry for mama, she had a heavy and responsible burden on her shoulders, that I didn't have no clue. She knew there was evil close by our neighborhoods, and she was just trying to protect me from that. Now that I'm old, thank you mama.

Going back to my school days, and my music and my sports days, and mama raising me, was how I stayed out of trouble when I was much younger.

And to this day, I'm still crazy about baseball as I was then. And Dad wouldn't have anything to do with music or sports. Well that didn't help me for support, when I wanted to play baseball. How could Dad help it, his Dad wasn't supportive either, and how could my grandpa safely support ten kids, during the early part of the twentieth century? The time when all my uncles and only one aunt, the only sister of my Dad.

Life is a struggle isn't it? Finding out much much later in life, life is a struggle from the time our mother conceives, and on to our day of birth. And then it doesn't get better, it becomes more of a struggle from the day we're born. And then if we don't take advantage of the little time we have on this side of life, there's not too many chances left if we don't realize what is it we're doing wrong. So, from just being the only son, with my two sisters, and my parents, don't know how you guys think, but life was pretty lonely for me. But was able to grow up out of that, and I did, or who knows where I would have ended up being so young.

Looking at other families, my Dad having brothers, my Mom having brothers and sisters, and many of my classmates having brothers and sisters. I felt I was the only boy and the only son in a family in the whole world. Childish right? Looking at it now, that was childish.

So on with my life I had to go. Or bore my self to death.

Like I said earlier, at Dad's second house in California, there were bad and good influences. There was this one kid, had a Dad that was a little league baseball umpire, and that impressed me, and motivated me to join the little league team. And join I did just that. So with school and now baseball, I was very busy, I'll say. And Dad didn't like it. And at the time, Mom and Dad didn't even like my style of music, What? I say what?

As baseball being my favorite sport, and music being my most spiritual fantasy, I enjoyed my life by myself, but I have never felt like I was alone.

Oh, I had my opportunity to become a professional baseball player, but I didn't take it, and my wife as I wrote this tells me I could have been a professional singer. I said what?

I say, I don't think so. But what I thought and how and what could've happened, are two different things completely.

So, as the world turns, as to how that movie series went. My world turned as how God would have it. Or should I say, as to how I thought I would go, with or without God. What a bad scenario and a sad destination that would've turned out if I didn't listen to my spirit. But that would come later on in my life's writing. So we'll see, as Dad always said. Boy that would bother me every time he said that. We'll see!!!

As I said, As The World Turns. And everyone in that time era were either doing something for themselves or doing something against themselves. But, that's been true for thousands of years, and this story is about me, and the people around me.

Coming back to man's latest invention when I was eight and ten years old, the transistor radio. The fifties, the nineteen fifties that is. I was so hooked with that little radio I carried around, when I wasn't in school or doing my homework. That wouldn't of mixed too well. That would have been a big distraction for me. So I had to have self discipline. I was good at that. Having self discipline. Able to control my choices and decisions, was for me one of my great traits. For a while, good doesn't last too long, unfortunately. Mentioning God again in this part of my life, because when you lose that connection with God, you're bound to fall, no doubt about it. For you guys that don't believe, what I'm talking about, don't believe it, and see what happens. Because I speak from experience.

Paying attention to my education, like I said was very important to me, and that only lasted up until my junior college days.

Since I'm now up in age, I can't remember all my days, much less all my days in school.

But I do remember my first day in school when I was just a little boy, up until my last day in J.C. In between those years, no way I can remember all of that.

Just trying to paint you my disastrous day of my life, on my first face of death, that's all. This is why I'm writing this, and calling it, Died Three Times Lived Once. Because I really believe we change, after facing death, and I faced it three times. And became a different person each time. The person I was each time I faced death, I became a different person after words. Believe it or not. That's me, that's all.

As we all go through our struggles with life in time, as I did with mine, there had been times I just wanted to stop, just quit, and give up. You know what I'm saying? But I didn't just yet. Not yet I say. I was too young to stop, quit or give up. Wasn't even twenty one, why would I want to do that. But you know as well I do, there are those that do lose themselves, so sad.

As a teenager I would hear or would read it on the news, someone commit suicide. And would think, they are cowards, until later in my life, I became one. To think along the border line anyway. By what I mean, when I say borderline. Because I did contemplate suicide. Thank God, he had always been there for me, to pull me out with my feet dangling part into hell.

Here's a question for all of you, have you ever experienced De'Ja Vu? I mention this, because I've experienced Deja'Vu. I'll leave that for now, and you hold that thought.

Now let me fantasize my music with you all. As I've said my time started in the late forties. And my life of course started in the fifties.

ROBERT GARCIA

The good old rock and roll years. That was such a beautiful time of our lives, wasn't it? I'm sure it was for so many lives, no matter what color you were. And the king of Rock and Roll was debuted. Elvis Presley. Wow!! For those of you that were or still are Rock and Rollers, it was awesome and so spiritual. I say spiritual, because it was, and because, he was one of a kind. Dying at such a young age, forty two. He was provocative, a sexual image for the women, and he brought people of all colors together. Agreed, agreed. I still have all of his records. My friend I grew up with, at one time had a picture of Elvis painted on his living room wall. Picture hell, he painted pictures of Elvis all over the his house. My buddy was a Elvis Presley fanatic, and that's putting it mildly. Had an old fashion jukebox in his living room, full of Elvis's records.

Elvis came out with his first hit record, "That's All Right" in nineteen fifty four. That only made me only six years old. I don't know how many of you started listening to music at six years old, but that was me.

And I continued on with the love for music into my teenage years. My teenage years began in nineteen sixty one, I turned thirteen years old. Wow!!! As I graduated out of eight grade, to go on into my freshman year of of high school. At fourteen, as Elvis is coming on strong. If you older guys like myself remember, and if you loved music with a passion like I did, then you would know, as Elvis continued rock and roll, in the early sixties, it was just before the English invasion of pop music. And I loved that time as well, with the Beatles, The Rolling Stones, and the list goes on. At this time in my life, couldn't continue playing baseball. Feeling better just to concentrate on my grades, go to concerts. Music would have to be my secondary interest. Because, it became impossible to play ball, keep up with my grades, and work my way through school. Not coming from a well off family, I just had to work, no choice in the matter. It is what it is. Not how we would like it. Right?

The years of my high school years were becoming intense.

By no fault but my own. And why, because teens will be teens. I just had to join a car club. No I didn't, but I did. Guess I wanted attention, like so many people do at that age. Want to see and be with girls. Girls girls girls. But as I remember those days, our car club had politics, and organization. I was appointed as treasurer, what, that's right. We all had dues to pay every week. We threw dances. An L.A. deputy sheriff would come to our weekly meetings. It was very impressive, as I think of the time. And the Sheriffs department was impressed as well. Would advise us to donate to charities, and we would. The dances we would have at a ballroom, we would have the battle of the bands. Such a beautiful memory of those days of mine, when I wrote this. All car members, and our dates, would dance the stroll, if anyone of you know and remember the stroll. It was so much fun. And of course, with dancing, there's romance, and now we're in the middle of what we should do or not do, when you have a hot girl with you, right? How many of us get stuck, and I almost got screwed, oh my god. Almost.

All of these things are happening to me, as I'm approaching my last two years of high school. Had a girlfriend mom didn't approve of, when that girl wanted me to impregnate, close, but I didn't go that way, kept my pants on, zippered closed. Came close though. But not close enough.

Being in a car club, some members would have parties. Parties, more like a bunch of teenagers, having a free for all. And girls, awe, all the cheap ones we could screw, in the back seat of any car. Looking back at those days of partying, as a teenager, and now as an old man, the good girls wouldn't go to parties. They were much smarter, and much prettier. Because they were clean girls.

And so those were my car club days. Those days were part of my life, I can't deny that, because it was a very impressive part of my life, and I had a lot of fun. Since I was good with numbers, the car club president appointed me treasurer. So why wouldn't I feel good about myself. As a teenager, I felt that was a huge responsibility.

And I will remind you again, all of this happened about ten years after the day I should have died. That has always amazed me.

And to also remind you, my head was badly hit, had stitches and my neck very badly twisted, to the point, it gives me extreme pain today. But that has been my life, and I've had no choice but to accept it the way it is, instead of wanting my way.

As I look at life today, and think about how I used to look at life, they are two completely different people. Because I have changed after each time I looked at death straight into it's face. And believe me, each experience had given me a more open mind. If you understand what I mean. My first deathly experience gave me the openness to succeed in school and into a life I thought I would never survive, because of my head injuries. But it has been a complete reversal on how most people would have recovered. After each deathly experience, I had to recover, that is if I lived. You should know, it's not a quick process, it took some time for me, like it would anyone else. In this first part of my first part of writing, I've tried to describe how I've survived but I did more than that, I succeeded, where as I should have died like most would have. Blessed, yes I am. And if anyone has been through and what I've experienced, or more, you are blessed as well.

Going through the first part of the sixties, there was so much racism, oh there still is, but in the fifties and sixties, oh my god, it was so evil. But don't get me wrong, there will always be racism and evil, but it seems that much of it has subsided. After too much blood shed, only after too many people died. And I'm sure there will be many more people that will die, before the world ends. Oh yes I truly believe God will end the world. But in this part of my life in my writing, I didn't know it then.

Going back into what I was talking about the fifties and sixties, when the golden years of Elvis Presley began. It wasn't just because I liked his music. He had a huge spiritual reason for being who he became. An icon. He was a race gatherer, because of his music, he united all of those that loved life and music, spiritual music. Elvis started out as a gospel singer, for those of you that didn't know. And died because he loved people and music lovers.

As ten years go by, in the year of nineteen sixty four, and after Elvis's stardom in nineteen fifty four and while I'm now in my sophomore year of high school, the British Invasion of pop music invades America. And what an invasion it was. Was it a competition for Elvis, no it was not.

Two different types of music entirely. There was the King of Rock and Roll, Elvis Presley, and then there was the British Invasion, pop music. And I loved them both, as millions did too. I really believe Elvis

Presley was all by himself, being the king of rock and roll, no one could compete against him, no one could come close. That was a fact.

So we're talking pop music, with the Beatles, The Rolling Stones, Donovan, The Dave Clark Five, and on and on. And they were a smash.

And where was I in all of this? Enjoying every bit of it. But most of all, attending to my grades in high school. That was my priority, to do well in school, to go forward into Junior College. Awe yes, and I did well, because I was able to accomplish that. My high school graduation was magnificent. Felt like I was on cloud nine.

So it was school, music, and going to baseball games, in that order. School was top priority. I'm sure you book worms as I was called, would agree, that school should have been top priority. I was able to attend concerts, like the Supremes, the four tops, the Jefferson Airplane, if any of you remember, or even ever heard of them. But those were my days my friends. And able to go watch a baseball game once in a while. The Los Angeles Dodgers, which I've been watching since nineteen fifty nine, that's a long time ago.

As I'm writing this about my life, like people have always said, time flew by so damn fast. It's funny though, and you all might agree, but maybe not all. When I was just a little kid, time seem to drag. Then there's a song by The Rolling Stones called, "What A Drag It Is Getting Old" maybe some of you remember and maybe some of you won't. The point I'm trying to make, it hasn't been a drag for me. Because as I am old as I wrote this, I've enjoyed every part of my time. As an old man that is. But to get to this current life of mine, which has been a dream, I had to go through three life times. Because I Died Three Times Lived Once.

Don't know how many times you guys graduated, because I've had more than my share of graduations. Yes, good and bad graduations. You may ask, good and bad graduations? Will you believe this? I went through four graduations. Wow, what a journey it's been. Of course before any graduations would happen, I would have to bang my head severely, with stitches on my side of my head, and with a twist of my neck, to where I suffer with a lot of pain today as an old man. But I don't let it get me down, because I'm enjoying life so very much, to let

ROBERT GARCIA

any pain bother me. There's one graduation I would have loved so much, and that one would have been, graduating from an university into the major of becoming a mechanic engineer. A dream right? Well I can't live too many dreams

Anyway after my high school graduation, with great grades to enroll into junior college. Supporting myself working part time at a machine shop, which I had started while in high school. Had to do something to support college. Dad couldn't help me, but I had no problem with that. That's life with me at the time. Just move on with myself. Taking prerequisites, for whatever I needed to move forward. Taking mechanical drawing classes, in a two year J.C. And was going the right way, with a lot of momentum. Will never forget it.

But as luck will have it, because we can't have it all. Some people like I did, thought I could have it all.

Working my way through school, from the time I graduated from eighth grade, and through about a year and a half in J. C. And here comes my interruption, Uncle Sam. I received a military drafting notice, thought to myself when I received that. S.O.B. It nearly tore me apart. Oh man, how can they do that? It's simple, that's the government for you. Sometimes things happen when you least expect them, isn't that right? That's just part of life. Didn't know it back then, we have to learn to take the good with the bad, and teach ourselves to accept which ever order, but accept the law how it is written. None of us will never like it, I know I don't. Who does? We have to go with the flow, or we're going to run into walls, and have a very bumpy road in life. And guess what happens if we didn't take that drafting notice seriously, some ended up in jail. Disobeying a drafting notice, was like going awol, or committing treason.

With my notice, the draft had given me a hundred and twenty days, four months, to report to boot camp training. Thinking it gave me time enough to join the Air Force. What a joke that turned out to be. Yeah because now I wasn't paying attention to my J. C. education. I was paying more attention of how to dodge the Army. To this day, will never understand, why I didn't want the Army. Guess it just sounded too common. If you ask every veteran, nine times out of ten, they'll tell you they were in the Army. Remember I'm only nineteen, for me, receiving the draft notice, it kind of put me in shock. Don't know, just didn't want the Army. And I wanted the Air Force so very bad. And I didn't get the chance. Was so disappointed. Yes I sure was.

Had to get over it, or it would swallow me and chew me up and spit me out. That's just the way life is, or you'll die disappointed. But at nineteen my disappointments have only just begun. Can you guys imagine how a guy feels, here I am planning a super future, and as I thought I was the only one being drafted. Selfish, oh yeah, maybe because my heart was so much into who I wanted to be. Is something wrong with that? Don't think I was the only one feeling that way, when this war broke out.

Flashback!! It seemed like only a few years ago when I was nine or ten, sitting in a fourth grade class, our teacher telling us guys, don't be surprised if we end up in Vietnam. Now at nineteen, thinking about what she said. I thought she was ridiculousness, with another thought, she's crazy, that's a long time from now. But time just swooped up on us.

Had received my Army draft notice, I'm seriously studying in my Junior College, for a super future. And also received in the mail from the Marines, two year enlistments Don't know why, I decided to keep that two year enlistment in my back pocket. And I'll tell you later why I'm glad I did that.

Now at this time, thinking about enlisting in the Air Force, telling you already how that fell through. Still attending J.C classes. So I go to the Armed Forces recruit office. Go into the Air Force recruit office. The gentleman explained to me what kind of exam I'd be taking. And I passed it with flying colors. I felt great, but to no avail. Because it didn't matter if I passed that entrance exam or not, because I wouldn't be getting sworn in until three hundred others were sworn in before me. And God would only know how long that would take.

Have you guys ever feel like your world is falling down on you, because that's what was happening to me. What a mess I was in. Can't continue my education, couldn't enlist into the Air Force, I didn't want the Army.

So what's next and what's left. Not much.

What could I do, absolutely nothing. I have a girlfriend wanting to get pregnant. Being a member of a car club. Mom, Dad and the family, we all had to go to a funeral all of a sudden. Returned home after a few days, but just after we arrive home, there's this sly boyfriend of one of my sisters, that came rushing to our house, yelling for me. "Hey, hey bud, we've got a big problem with our car club." You have to take down your car club plaque off your car." Naturally I asked him why, and he says "One of our car members shot a guy from another car club". Thinking to myself, what the hell for. Next he tells me "We were all cruising the boulevard like we have always done, and out of nowhere this guy throws a beer bottle at our guy hitting him in the face." "And of course that pissed him off, and goes home to go get his Dad's shotgun, goes back to the boulevard to look for the guy that threw the bottle, finds him, and shoots him "Without hearing another word, I go out running to my car and take off my car club plaque, without wanting to hear anymore. Have never known if the guy that got shot ever died. Really didn't want to know either way.

As I said, my world was crumbling all around me. At nineteen years of age. Something had to give. But isn't that the way it goes with many of us? Life has always been tough for many. And so it was tough for me, and this all happened during the sixties. Oh yeah the good old sixties.

But as I look back at our time during the sixties, as I moaned and groaned, and cried, cried, cried. Thinking we had it bad during that time. For us people in our generation, our generation before us had it much worse. As I wrote this, still having my Dad so far, at ninety six years old. He survived the Great Depression. We didn't have so bad. Compared to that generation. During Dad's time, when he was very young, there were no jobs. Not everyone could afford a car. No television, not everyone had a radio, and to have a telephone, not everyone had one. So for you that read this, America was a very sad and hard place to live, during the early part of the twentieth century. But the whole world was suffering economically. And every world leader was confused as to how to solve the worlds problems. And if you know your history, Nazi dictator, Adolf Hitler, took advantage of the worlds confused problems. And that was times of my Dad.

Continuing on with my story, thinking I had it bad. Well I did have it bad, like everyone does when we're just starting out with life. So didn't you have problems fighting for your future? Of course we did. That's just nature, the facts of life. Unless you're born with a silver spoon, you're going to have to do what the government wants you to do. While those that are born with gold and silver, they don't have to worry. I always had a problem digesting that policy, and I still do. What makes the rich any different when it comes to following the rule of law? But that's not for me to figure that out, because I wasn't born rich. But I'm pretty satisfied how I've come out, not rich, but not poor.

On the day I tried to enlist into the Air Force, I repeat, I was so disappointed, when I couldn't get sworn in after passing the entrance exam. And I thought it would have been a whiz. I get into the Air Force, no Army, no combating the enemy in Vietnam. How sweet that would have been. But I wasn't living in reality. Reality should have been in my head, that during the Vietnam era, I enlist in the Air Force right after high school, not go to junior college for a year and a half and then try to evade the Army, that was a wrong move I did and it almost cost me my life. And I'll tell you later why it almost cost me my life.

So as my life continues, when I walked out of the Air Force recruiting office, and in my mind, I'm now going to become a Marine, at least at the time I thought I was. Could see my whole life disappear right in front of me. My little boy days. My self confidence, my determination of becoming an engineer. My rock and roll days of Elvis Presley. Pop music and the Beatles with all others that I'll probably never see again. Felt so negative about myself.

I'll try to explain as how I felt, by feeling negative with myself. And this is all after feeling positive with my schooling after high school. Because I was disappointed. Wanted life how I wanted it. Isn't that the way we want it? I'm sure I'm not alone here. We all want it our way. We're selfish by nature. We have no clue in what is in store for us. Finding it the hard way, God will always know what's in store for us, from the day we're born.

And into the Marine Corp recruit office I go. Remember I told you, I had received in the mail a two year recruit enlistment letter.

And I walk into the recruit office, there was this big Marine gunnery sergeant in his nice blue uniform, with a shit eating grin on his face. What's the first thing out of the sergeant's mouth. "Well hello son, have a seat, right now we have four and six year enlistments, which do you want"? And for the life of me, couldn't remember when I put that two year enlistment letter in my pocket. But I pulled it out to show this sergeant, and I tell him "and you also have two years, which I can enlist." Right? He developed this funny looking face, which made me laugh on the inside, but I didn't show it. He says, "oh yes we do." I tell him, but you weren't going to tell me were you? He says, oh yes I was. I just starred at him. Signed all what I needed to sign, and sign my life away I did. After that, I thought to myself, my new life has just begun, and also my new deathly experience might end my new life. But again didn't have a clue. Getting home and telling my parents, that I just joined the Marines, wasn't the happiest thing they ever heard in their lives, and I didn't feel good telling them either, because I'm their only son, that they could lose in a war we didn't belong in. But like they say, it is what it is. And this is how my life was, and not how I wanted it. And finding things out how life really is, can be very amazing. And can be gratifying if we accept the things we can't change, and knowing the things we can, and being able to know the difference. It's too bad that it takes a man like me, many years to learn the facts of life. But also what do they say, "Better Late Than Never" Even that took me forever to understand what that meant. Well it did take me awhile, but I think I've taught myself a whole new way of living in my last sixteen years of my life than all my years before. Does that sound strange, maybe, but I wrote this, this is the story of my life. And all others that have wrote before me, have written their life stories. And you have an opportunity to write about your life.

Many of you know, and then maybe many of you don't know. But God and life is very mysterious. No one knows from the time we're born, what our life is all about, what's our purpose, and where we're going with our lives. Any of you that know where you're going, then you're better than I am. And God Bless You, because you're going to need all the blessings God can give. And I didn't wake up suddenly knowing everything about where I'm going in life. Being born, going through my little boy days, going through my teenage years, and up till now, I still don't know where I'm going in my life. And don't think anyone knows either. Thinking that when people start thinking they know it all, they begin to run into walls, and the road of life starts to become bumpy I speak for experience.

Back to my neighborhood teenage friends. Out of five of my friends, I was the only one that enlisted into the Marines, and only one of my neighborhood friends, just around the corner, went into the Army. He got drafted.

And when I got home, after signing up with the Marines, first informing mom and dad, and because I couldn't take mom's tears, I just had to get out of the house, and go tell my Army neighborhood friend.

Walking up to his door, my friends mom greeted me, was always nice to me, tells me her son is in the garage with other friends, as many times before, playing pool, table tennis, or throwing darts. Or we could just sit and watch a small T.V., that they also had in their garage. As I flash back to those days of my life, with friends and neighbors I grew up with. Will always miss those days. And as I sat not saying absolutely nothing for a while, my buddy, tells me, "hey dude you're sitting there and being too quiet, what's wrong with you man" And quietly I say, "I joined the Marines today" In my thoughts, couldn't believe what I was saying. I actually enlisted into the Marines, and not knowing at the time, will probably be deployed to the front lines in combat in Vietnam. But in this part of my book, I haven't been to boot camp yet. And started to get paranoid, and mentally started to freak out. All of you guys got to understand, for those of you that are tall, us short guys have to psych ourselves out to accept the idea that we can do the same things you taller guys can. My friend going into the Army, was over six feet, and I was only five feet eight inches. Because after I signed up into the Marine Corp, was starting to feel butterflies.

Back in my friend's garage, when I told him I had joined the Corp, he says to me, "Oh my God man, are you crazy, the Marines are the first ones in the front lines in combat. Oh God we'll probably never see each other. I responded by saying, "probably so, but I've already signed my life away" Because, if anyone that doesn't know, once you sign up into the military, you either report for duty, or face treason, or awol. Don't know which is worse. And I didn't want to find out. And so I had to start psyching myself out. And psych myself I did. It goes without saying, it wasn't easy. I personally never had any problems I couldn't handle. When things got physical, and about to get violent, I would go head on with any man, and didn't care how big he was. And believe me there were times, I thought I might hurt someone. From the time I was a kid, I never cared how tall or how big any man was. To me size didn't matter. What did matter, is how a man could handle himself.

Things got more sad when I had to withdraw from my junior college classes. That was so sad, when I had to tell each of my teachers. Telling me they hated to see me go, but they understood why. During the Vietnam era, and during the draft, I believe it left a lot of J. C.s and universities practically empty. Unless you're rich, or the only sole surviving son, then you probably didn't have to go to Vietnam. Consider yourself bought and paid for.

As a boy and into my teenage years, have always tried to give it my all and my best, no matter what I did. In school, during work, and when I played ball games. Tried playing as hard as I could. Now, just about to report for duty. Into the United States Marine Corp. should I feel proud. Don't know how to feel yet, because I hadn't reported yet, at this part of my life. Remember I'm still nineteen years old, at this part of my writing. Haven't started training. I guess it's the man in me separating the boy in me. Will I become a man once I'm in the Marines, or will I be kicked out. Because I've heard that happens. At that part of all males's lives, we will or have gone through the part of maturity, but some don't ever get there, that's unfortunately sad but true. I started seeing that as I was growing up, from my boyhood to my teenage life.

Life is hard for so many people. Isn't it? I know it was hard for me. Heard of many committing suicide. When I heard about that, it's sounded so disappointing and it was demoralizing, if you let it get to you. Going through my young life, even hearing about people not knowing if they wanted to stay a man or a woman. Weird, and I also thought that was evil. And maybe I'm wrong to think that way. Because

I have a couple of those confused relatives. Never understood why they acted funny. But growing up and seeing that, it wasn't funny at all. It was shameful for the family, and humiliating for themselves.

So now I only have about a month and a half of freedom. That's right just about to lose my freedom. Accepting the responsibility that I have to report to the Marine Corp recruiting depot at Camp Pendleton for duty was a big challenge for me, don't know about you guys, when you had to report. What did you guys do, how did you handle it?

Now I sit and wait for my day to come to report for duty? Of course I'm not just going to sit around and wait, and do nothing. That's never been me. I'm a hyperactive person, have always been. Awaiting for my recruiting date, I continued working for a machine shop. A shop I had worked at from the time I started junior college for my own expenses. Mom and Dad didn't have to pay for anything I wanted. Including beer, no I couldn't buy beer on my own, I was still only nineteen, we had guys that were twenty one to buy beer for us. Partied a little bit. But most of all, did a lot of running. And doing push-ups, sit-ups. Was just trying to get myself physically ready for boot camp. And most of all get myself mentally ready as well.

It was kind of funny how time changes things with a man's relationship with his only son. Yes I'm talking about my Dad and I. Had already wrote earlier in my life, that Dad and I weren't close as I would have liked. And I also wrote, how can I blame Dad, because he didn't have a close relationship with HIS Dad my grandpa.

It amazed me, when I finally talked Dad into filing a VA claim, because he didn't want to. For us Veterans that went through a psych questionnaire, and you know it. A hundred question form we all had to fill out. There's a certain question. "Do you remember when your dad said he loved you" simple right? Not for Dad, he had a hard time trying to respond. I had to repeat the question, as I put my hand on his shoulder. And as I repeated it, I say to Dad, "Dad don't you remember when my grandpa told you he loved you" What did he say "No" with his hand partially covering his face, like he wanted to cry. My emotions wanted to scream. I had to ask him again, "Dad you can't remember when your Dad said he loved you" he says it again, "No I can't" at that very moment, I thought, now I understand you my dear old Dad. Inside my heart I cried for him. Without saying anymore. That was a big psychological obstacle both Dad and I had climbed over.

And as I await my recruitment date to arrive, Dad finally tells me, son I love you, and I'm very proud of you. That wasn't like him, he couldn't remember his Dad telling him he loved him, but I remember my Dad telling me he loved me. Yeah Dad and I had come a long way, from disconnected love to love connection. But as you will know later, I destroy that, with bad influences. Evil was getting between Dad and I, and our love for one another. And again, I know I'm not alone, you know who you are. It's happened to you as well. Evil has always been good to separate loved ones. But no matter what, my mom had never disconnect her love from me. She would always be there for all of us. And of course for Dad. Dad had been first for mom, and then children. Point being she had never betray one for the other. She loved all of us equally.

That's how I am today. Loving all my daughters equally the same. Later on I'll open up about Dad actually admitted how he loved one of his children more than his other two. And also admitted that he was confused and that he didn't know what he was doing. You see how evil betrays. If you let it in.

I'm just about to report to, hurry up and wait. Because that's what the military is mostly about. No they never actually say that. But that's how it works. Hurry up and wait. But the waiting has come to a halt. The day has arrived.

Flash back!! A memory of mine. There has been a few of my peers tell me I was aggressive, and some have said, I was crazy. Believed the aggressive part, not the crazy part. Yes I do believe there are crazy people out there, but for me that some people have said I'm crazy, not so. The fact being that my life has been crazy, I believe that.

So it must had been about a year before going into the Marines, working at my machine shop job, three of us guys went to a huge carnival. That carnival was called the pike in Long Beach California. When I was a kid its was a fun place to go. There were rides, games, girls, and prizes to win. And there was this tattoo shop. We just happened to take a stroll into this shop, looking at different types of tattoos, and one caught my eye. It read, "MI VIDA LOCA" as I started to walk away from the wall of tattoos as I stared at that one, "MI VIDA LOCA" one of the guys that came together with us, tells me, "Hey dude you ought to buy that one and put on your arm" I tell him, "No way" thinking of my Dad, oh my God no way. This co-worker rides and continues to nag me. Telling me, "come on man, it'll look good on you, I'll even pay for it" I respond "no man I said no" and he continued on, "What is it dude, are you chicken" and I say, "no I'm not" he says, "yes you are" "chicken, chicken, chicken" and I gave in, alright alright. Ok, I'll put it on. Thinking, why this asshole just talked me into something I didn't want to do. Put a tattoo on my right arm. And put a tattoo on my arm I did. And "MI VIDA LOCA" on my arm has been on my arm since I was nineteen years old, and I'm now in my seventies. When I first put this "MI VIDA LOCA" tattoo on my arm, one day at my mom and Dad house, doing my face in front of the mirror, trying to see if I could grow hair on my face, Dad walking by the bathroom, and catches a patch on my arm. Asks me, what is that? As he yanked off the patch, he yells out, what is wrong with you. And then he yells towards mom, "you know what, our son has a tattoo" didn't ever forget about that, Dad was so scandalous. That tattoo has pretty well branded me, describing my life as being true. Because my life has and was very crazy. My life has mellowed out since then, thank God for his miracles. I have experienced God's presence, and many of his miracles. And this is why I'm writing this, to open up to you all, how I've died three times and now living a life I would have never dreamed of.

Well, time flies by as it does with all of us. Mom and Dad forgave me about the tattoo on my arm. I guess so, I'm about to get bused out to Camp Pendleton, to start my bootcamp. In case any of you read this, and don't know what boot camp is. First of all, everyone wears boots, and it's the beginning of a brand new world. And a brand new world it becomes. Because, whether you were drafted or if you enlisted, the bottom line where you signed your name, you have become the property of the military government. All personnel that becomes inducted into the military, you answer to either your drill instructing sergeant or your platoon sergeant, and to no one else.

No, I didn't know anything about this boot camp training. I'm just writing to you about my life, as to where I've been, and I'm about to describe my life's mishaps and my three deaths I experienced is all. And only because I was encouraged and motivated, by many, including my psychiatrist. I'm also going to try to best describe to you all my God's miracles, on how he saved my life by reaching out for me, like he probably has to many of you.

Well get ready get set, let's go. My time has arrived. What I'm about to write it will have a profound insight on who I became after my military service. And how I faced death numerous times. But I'm not there yet.

On the day before I was to report for duty, I think mom cried forever, and kept Dad in an emotional state as well. Really felt so sorry for them. I think mom cried all the way to the bus depot to Los Angeles. Poor mama. Oh don't get me wrong, I cried too, but I think I cried more for my parents than I did for myself. I'm thinking they're feeling very sad, because they are going to lose a son, in a war I'll be facing.

Don't have any idea how many of you, if you even read this, know about the Vietnam war. Because if you don't know a whole lot about it, then no matter how much I explain it to you, you still probably won't understand it. I tried to understand it, but all I think I know is, it was a political upset with China, Russia, North Vietnam, and the United States. And over fifty thousand american troops were killed. When I say troops, I mean we were all just kids. It was a sad, bad experience. Like I said I was only nineteen years old. But I can still remember it, like it just happened last year. My mind may not be as fresh as it was when I was about to report for duty at nineteen years old. But I can tell you that I can remember what happened to me during my Vietnam tour. That word "TOUR" has always gave me a chuckling amazing thought about it. As if going to fight a war in Vietnam was a tour. What a joke. I've always thought to go on a tour, was a pleasure exciting trip to go on. This war that many of us had to go to, was no pleasure, I'll be one of many to tell anyone, it was a disaster for those that experienced deathly incidents as I did.

Seems like I got off track, sorry about that. It's just when I start with my flash backs, I get into a trans of when I was there.

Back to when I was about to get bused out to my Marine Corp, Camp Pendleton, to start my boot camp training. Was in complete awe, I'm telling ya.

Well Dad drove my mom and I to downtown Los Angeles so I could catch the bus. Will never forget the looks on my dear mom and Dad's faces as I got on the bus. It was so sad. As I got on the bus I ran back to the back of the bus to look at my dear mom and Dad's sad faces. You could see mom's tears as I cried for them both. Dad tried not to show any tears, but he couldn't help it. How can anyone help it, when your only son will be deployed to a war. Much later, I found out, we should have never been involved in that Vietnam war. Before I was deployed, had always thought we shouldn't be fighting in Vietnam. But I'm only one person, and I've been ordered to go, whether I wanted to go or not. I've always looked at it this way. All countries have always gotten into wars, because of politics, why would Vietnam be any different.

From the beginning of this war, In the mid to late nineteen fifties, it was just another political dispute, like all other wars. As I mentioned the nineteen fifties, I only being nine or ten. And never believing I would be in Vietnam to fight for my country, but most of all, fighting for my life, and for the man next to me.

As we were traveling on bus to our Camp Pendleton, for our first day of training, to be received by the sergeants for our duration of our training. It would become at the time, it would start as my worst nightmare of my life. I really thought so. But I would find out after three decades, I would become to realize that enlisting into the Marines, would become my most and best decision of my life.

Seems like you could drop a pin on the bus floor, and everyone would hear, because that's how quiet it was while we were on our destiny to Camp Pendleton, California

As I sat on that long bus ride, as we all did, in suspense, I kept thinking about my fourth grade teacher. Thinking intensely, remembering the look on her face, how sure she was, that we would go to war. I'll never forget that. She spoke to us how the French Army tried to help out south Vietnam, by helping them fight the north Vietnamese Army. But was unsuccessful, and the French were being overran. So America started sending journalists to Vietnam, and American military trainers, but that wasn't going anywhere as well. Couldn't understand why the French couldn't handle the small country of north Vietnam, which was a very small country. Being young and naive, of course I wouldn't understand. And would never understand, until I would end up in country. And it's too bad I was watching on the T.V. the French were being overran, and American journalists were getting killed as well.

I know I'm not alone, when I think, there has always been evil in the world, and will probably always be evil in the world. But then, there has always been God. And he is much more powerful. Amen to the truth. I mention evil, because war is and will always be evil. Instead of a peaceful world, that we should live in, evil people around the world continues to take lives.

As our bus journey arrives at our destination, the Marine Corp recruit depot, Camp Pendleton California, you could hear, oh no, oh no, we're here. It seemed to me, in my inner self, something within me was already changing, already starting to accept. It became a very good thing for me. Because on that bus there weren't many of us that felt the same.

Here's a funny. As our bus entered Marine Corp property in Camp Pendleton. Almost everyone were behaving themselves, like I said almost everyone. There's always one, right? There's employees of all sorts, female employees included. Maintenance people, men and women. No surprise. But there was this female shaking something out some window, and this guy in our bus pokes his head out the bus window and yells, "Hey baby lets fuck" His words must had echoed all over the base. Because that's all everyone could hear. Thought to myself, Wow. Also thinking, this kid, better stand the fuck by. Because when the bus came to a halt, there was a drill sergeant waiting for the bus, with his new recruits inside with a look on his face that could kill. And kill is what this drill sergeant almost did with this idiot, yelling out obscenities. When the bus came to a complete stop, the sergeant rushed the bus doors. Gets in the bus, and with a look of hate and murder on his face. As he is in, yells with a voice that could shatter the bus windows, and at the top of his lungs yells out, "Who in the hell yelled out, hey baby let's fuck, and you all better point him out, because if you don't, you're all going to get your asses kicked" And point him out we did. Well I didn't have to, with all others pointing at him. He was tried and convicted. Really felt sorry for that kid, because he just made a spectacle of himself. The second this kid was pointed out, the sergeant grabbed him, and literally dragged him through the bus floor and threw him out, like he was some dead animal. We all didn't have to laugh, because it wasn't funny. Thought to myself, what a way to start your first day of boot camp.

So on my way on my first day of Marine Corp boot camp. And already witnessing a dummy do something so dumb.

As I said before, my inner self prepared my mind for the upcoming psychotherapy, physical Marine Corp boot camp training. And there's probably been many as well. I'd be silly to think that I would be the only one. That would be bragging, and I've never believed in bragging. Yes you can be proud, but don't brag.

But that's just my opinion. Because I've seen, as you probably have as well, many self flattering, selfish, self centered people out there. And they can be so self humiliating, and the whole thing is, they can't see it. The evil spirits within those kind of people, will twist their minds, making people believe their ok with what they do. Whether they're wrong or evil. Like this kid, on our way to military training, arriving at a Marine Corp base, yelling at the top of his lungs, at some female marine corps employee, some obscene gesture. Humiliating himself, and again, he probably didn't think he was doing anything bad. But I'm sure the sergeant that threw him out of bus let him know he was wrong. And I never laughed at him. Because it wasn't funny. Can only imagine how many people humiliate and make a spectacle out of themselves. It's unfortunate I'm related to some of those type of people.

After the evening of arriving at Camp Pendleton, California, it was our first introduction of rules from our platoon sergeant, that I have

ROBERT GARCIA

stored in my memory, for over five decades. Wow!! It's amazing to me, on how I can remember practically every day of my time in the Marine Corp. It's an experience of a big part of my life that I will cherish for the rest of my life. Later on I'll write to you and tell you how by enlisting in the Marines would become the biggest and the best decision I had made for my entire life. At only nineteen years old.

But that will come later in my writing of my life, and another part of. DIED THREE TIMES LIVED ONCE. Right now I've only just begun Marine Corp boot camp. And wondered at nineteen, what the hell did I sign at the recruit office.

Well so much for spilled milk, as the old saying goes. Had to stand there and listen to this platoon commanding sergeant on our first day of boot camp training. And little did I know, it would become my first day of having the Marine Corp brain wash me. Because by listening to my platoon commanding sergeant, my life would depend on it. And listen to this Marine Corp platoon sergeant I did, because my life would depend on how good I listened.

Remembering the first day, as our platoon sergeant spoke to us on top of a platform, informing us, that he will become our mother and our father, and that we would listen to him or else. This sergeant wasn't a big man, but he was stocky built, and well proportioned, with muscles where there supposed to be. And he wasn't afraid to tell you, if anyone of us thought he could kick his ass, to come on and let's see if he could. And all fifty of us didn't move. Told us he had been to Vietnam three times, and wounded four different times and showed us the wounds at all four different spots on his body. And showed us and told us that he had a black belt in martial arts. Noticing as discreetly as I could, every man's look on his face. No one flinched a muscle, or blink an eye. This sergeant was very serious and very interesting. Like he said, he would become our everything, in training us, for our lives. And training us for our lives, he did, and did very well. I remember these words, that still echo in my memory part of my mind. "You all look like a bunch of girls. And by the time I'm done with you in thirty days, you will be a Marine, or you will no longer be here" "you either become a Marine or you will be kicked out, discharged out" And he carried on, if I can remember, until almost midnight, and what does he say about that time. "Now you will all be dismissed and get in different lines, get haircuts, shower down, will be issued training uniforms" "and revile will sound off at o'four thirty. The next thing, "platoon dismissed" couldn't believe it, it was almost midnight, and we'll be woken up by four thirty A.M. We all were probably thinking, man, this Marine Corp is crazy.

But as I laid on my first night on my rack, in a quonset hut, because that's the way the barracks were in those days. Don't know how they are now. But in those days, like I said, over five decades ago, those huts would get really hot. But what could anyone say or do about it, not a damn thing. At least that's the way I felt. If anyone would make a spectacle out of themselves, by giving attention to themselves by bitching, and moaning, boy oh boy, man oh man, you're in for a rough road, and a rough ride. You would be picked on. You would be volunteered on purpose. They will and would make an example out of you. Thank God I went through a smooth training experience, with the Marine Corp. I shall and will hold the Corps dearly in my heart and soul. Boot camp training, and advance training was the most important part of my life, at Camp Pendleton, California. God and The Marine Corp, is why I'm alive today, that gave me the opportunity, to share with all of you, that for those of you that might have gone through the same thing, or worse. You know who you are.

The first night of silence on top of my bed rack, oh my God. Being away from mom and dad for the first time, was kind of strange. Being nineteen, not ever being away. Wasn't that scary for many of you? It was for me, I'm not gonna lye. If your scared your scared. Didn't ever pretend to be someone else. Haven't you seen, or maybe you were one of those kind. And you know what I'm talking about.

Flash back, I'm going back to my freshman year in high school. Remembering when I took a speech arts class. Was so shy. I was scared then. But that became a far cry of differences. Wouldn't you think? It's one thing to be in a class, being taught how to speak in public., and being taught how to kill in the Marines, is completely different. During my fourteen years, in my speech class, and not knowing that in five years, I would be Vietnam, it's a big difference.

ROBERT GARCIA

On my first night introduction, it seemed like that platoon sergeant would never let us go to bed. But he did let us go to bed. Bed my ass. That wasn't bed. It was borrowed time, in pause, pending if I pass the Marine Corp boot camp training or not. That's all that was.

My adrenaline hitting me in all the parts of my mind, that's for sure. No bout adout it, is how they used to put it.

After a few hours, the platoon sergeant wasn't kidding, revile blew the horn, loud and clear. And three drill sergeants and a platoon sergeant waiting to see if any late comers would stay in their bed rack or stay sleeping. Of course there would be stayed sleepers, after all it's only the first twenty four hours. No, it's only been a few hours, but at that point it felt like eternity. Was it really that bad? It felt that way at nineteen years of age. Between a man and a boy. You know how it was. If you were in the military. And if you've never been, common sense should click in. As I mentioned, the Marines took the boy out, to turn me into the man I am today.

But my life would take numerous twisted turns, feeling like the trials and tribulations, we all go through. Is that how it went you guys? Maybe some yes and maybe some no. Maybe some about the same, and maybe some much worse. That's for sure, we don't all go down the same road. It's so unfortunate, many of us choose the wrong side of the fork of the road. But that's always been about how life is. Many of life's happenings are not how we want them. That's just been how life has been since man was created. I'm sure we've all heard someone say, "God Only Knows" Think I've heard that all of my life, by mostly my mama. And it's true. And if you don't think it's true, and if you don't believe in God. Then you may wonder, and it may explain our wrong turns in life, and taking the wrong side of fork of the road.

And taking the wrong side of the road, I have. I'm not gonna lie to you. My whole life I've written so far is nothing but the truth, so help me God. Another old saying. "Honesty is the best policy" ninety five percent of the time, that's true, but there's that five percent you might want to stretch it. If you know what I mean.

So the beginning of my boot camp has only just begun, with the first day starting with only four hours sleep, but I don't think I got but only two. Maybe that explains my insomnia I have today. So be it. That was the life I chose. No body's fault but mine, if you call it a fault. Because as I said, looking back at my life today, joining the Marines, during the Vietnam era, has been my most important intelligent decision of my life. Not saying I never worked, I've worked my butt off, but only God and myself know that to being true. So no one can vouch for me, and that's okay. Because I don't have to prove anything to anyone. God has seen my actions, and God has been there for me, every step and day of my life. I just didn't know it. There are so many things we think we know, but actually we practically know nothing, we just think we do.

Continuing on my first part of my Marine training days, which I had no clue about what was going to happen to me. When revile sounded off, oh my god, I thought the world exploded, when the Quonset hut door busted open by a drill instructor sergeant's boot. As he yelled his obscenities, to get the hell up and out of that hut, and in formation in two minutes or you'll wish you were never born. With the look on his face, we didn't dare to test him. No way, anyone would dare him. When he said in formation, half of us wondered, what the hell is formation? We all rushed out of the hut, and standing like a bunch of lost souls, or maybe like a mob. No one told us what to get in formation was. So how were we to know. But by finding out the hard way. It was hard for the first days of a Marine Corp boot camp. Oh man, should have saw the look on the platoon sergeant, he looked like a pissed off Rambo. Didn't even know what or who was Rambo was then. He rammed his strong bully body through the four squads of about fifty young guys. He pushed and shoved like we were a bunch of light weights. Compared to him, we were. And we haven't even started the day yet. It was only four thirty in the morning, of our first day, of boot camp training.

For the majority of the time time, I really felt I had made a big mistake. But in my mind, I was going through with this, no matter what. But I also thought, I'm too young to quit now. What would I say to my family, If I had quit all those years ago. It would have never been a good ending story, that's for sure. And I probably wouldn't have written this, if I would have humiliated myself, by quitting the Marine

ROBERT GARCIA

Corp. As it is, there will be things I will write, that really put shame to my family and myself especially my three daughters. But I will reveal that part of my life in due time, towards my part of my, Died Three Times Lived Once.

Don't know about the other armed forces but the Marine Corp taught me determination and self discipline, with a lot of motivation. Which I didn't know I had it in me. Couldn't concentrate on anyone else, but myself. Had to listen and pay attention, or else.

As our Marine training continued, you'd think it would get tougher, and it did for many of us. And remember I'm not a big guy, and have never pretended to be. It had begun a brand new world for many of us. But not for all of us. Physical training was every morning, every day, and every night. Beginning at four thirty in the morning and it would end about seven in the evening. And we would be exhausted by each and every day.

And just piss off any one of the drill sergeants or worse yet, piss off the platoon sergeant, and we would be in a world of shit. Oh yes we would.

What I soon learned, to be exhausted in the first few days of training, especially, Marine Corp boot camp training was normal.

Remembering the platoon sergeant, what he said to all of us.

"From the start of Marine Corp training, on your very first day, I am going to tare down each and every one of your bodies, and rebuild it back up. This is how the Marines have done for hundreds of years. And continue to do that today."

In order to tare down our out of shape bodies, two drill sergeants, and the platoon staff sergeant. When the platoon sergeant said he would break down our bodies, that is exactly what he was going to do. And they did, and I passed it. What, little old me. But before that would happen, we would have to endure extreme training and pain. Don't have to tell you, that not everyone passed this Marine Corp training in my time. Some of us were too fat, and some of us were too skinny. But all of us were out of shape.

Just the first day, came to a complete shock for many of us. As revile sounded off, and a drill sergeant slams the door wide open, with a tremendous kick of his boot. That in it self, put us all in shock. Awaking from a deep sleep, after going to bed after midnight, and being awoken by a slam of a door. And that was just for starters. It would become more intense as days went on.

Not one drill sergeant nor the platoon sergeant gave in, they weren't supposed to. That's what they were trained for. And they were pretty damn good at what they did. And to this day as I think and remember those days, I am very grateful for what they did. It probably saved my life. Let me say it this way, no probably about it, their training did save my life? And what happened after the slam of the door, you're wondering, as all fifty four of us stood in a disorderly stance? We were ridiculed, called turds, girls, fagots, and about anything that would make us feel like shit. The platoon sergeant started demonstrating by example, different types of Physical training.

And I'm not gonna describe to you everyday of my Marine boot camp, because that would be monotonous. Will do my best to describe just the hi lights of my military training in the Marine Corp, is all. After all that wouldn't be the point of my life's experiences, or should I say, deathly experiences.

The Corp has been, as what I have studied about it, that it's the most extreme military force in America. Now I don't know that for a fact, but I have been told by many, they've been the first in battle in the history of our country. Meaning that when all out war is on going in any part of the world, the Marines would be the first in line to face a battle. And it's written in our history books of America. Am I proud, maybe I should be, but I won't brag.

As day one began, observing our platoon sergeant commander, on how every physical exercise would begin and completed. He would order us, that it be done properly, or keep doing it until completed properly. Or be punished for it. We'd be punished for not being able to complete any certain exercise, by doing them properly. It seemed fair to me. After all it's a military academy. The list of physical exercises upon a daily routine, were extremely physically exhausting, for the first week to two.

Thank God, I used to do a lot of running in high school. Running had become to my advantage, in not just the Marine academy, but in another academy I'll write later in my life, that I'll later reveal.

There's been a few people I've met through my life, good or bad, that have told me I have or have had a unique life. I've never thought so.

As I said, thank God for my motivation to athletically run. Because running was a must for my Marine Corp boot camp. Self disciplined myself to be able to run longer and faster than most men. That seemed to amaze me growing up, because of my size. There I go again, with my complex. Couldn't help it back then, it doesn't bother me anymore. It is what it is.

While going through my boot camp training, found out who I was and what I could and couldn't do. But doesn't that happen to everyone else? Very true, but as I've said it before, I don't know about anyone else, and at that time, I had a struggle finding out who I was, and wondering where am I going to end up. Dead or alive. And we all end up that way anyway. Dead.

Looking back at my life going through my military boot camp training, believing I was spiritually motivated through my mama's prayers. And I know many of you won't believe that. And that's okay, you can believe what you want. Remember I'm writing this. This is my life, and my life's experiences, with death, as I faced it three times. Died Three Times Lived Once.

Each morning at my Marine Corp boot camp training, there was always something the drill sergeants would think of to motivate us through endurance and motivation, and with that, adrenaline. Awaken at four thirty AM, and do our fifty pushups and fifty sit-ups, and fifty squad thrusts. And then double time to the mess hall, is how they called the cafeteria.

Mama's prayers have always been there for me, way before the military.

But mama's prayers being there for me in the military, I think literally and physically saved my life from harm's way. You see, my mother's prayers were of course to God to send one of his angels to shield me from anything happening to her son. But I'll never be able to understand that. Because it was a miracle, and I've never understood miracles. And If you understand miracles, then good for you. All I know, God Loves us and I love God. I've learned never to question God's will. Because I believe when we start questioning God's will, we start tripping and falling and running into the walls of life.

The first day of boot camp training awakening to hell, and the drill sergeants drilling us into a hole I thought would never be able to crawl out of. Didn't know it then, it would become my life saving training as I reminisce on those days of mine. Double timing to the mess hall, and then double time it back again to the barracks. Fun huh, we all thought it was complete hell. But we were very young then, what did we know what was that all about. All I knew, I signed a dotted line with the Marines, and God only knew what was in store for all of us.

And remembering the sergeants only giving us ten minutes to shit shower and shave. Wow!! But that's just the way it was. To prepare us for a tour, a tour my ass, a war going on in Vietnam. If anyone of you reading this, have been in the military, whatever armed force, and went to Vietnam, and were in the front lines, then you know. No need to describe and explain to you how it was. And you might've seen much worse than I did. And God Bless You if you even lost a close friend or maybe you lost a limb. God forbid. God Bless You again.

Here's another hi light of another torturous hell day in the Marine boot camp. Can't forget too much about it. After all I was always sore as hell.

But we were all physically sore, I'm not being selfish, just stating a fact is all. Some of us were more sore than others, because our bodies had never did one push up nor even ran in their entire teenage years, so it's only normal to feel bodily sore. Our bodies screamed of pain. And the younger guys, seventeen or even eighteen, some of them cried. They were so sad to look at, because it was so demoralizing. Don't want to sound like I didn't want to cry, because I think my crying days were over when Dad used to spank and sometimes whip me as I was growing up. And I just knew from how much I heard how tough the Marine Corp was, I was going to have to not cry no matter what. And I didn't. It was weird. Because all of my crying days were over when I was seven.

In fact my crying days were over after that terrible truck accident, Dad and uncle and I experienced, when it nearly killed us. Guess all my fears anyone could humanly feel, just disappeared. Well almost all. But going through a boot camp training in the Marine Corp, just couldn't phase me. And I think any of you won't believe that, and that's okay too. I felt pain as well as the next guy. But to cry while in boot training, it never happened. Never gave any man the satisfaction, when anyone tried to intimidate me. And still to my old days today, no man has intimidated me. This I swear.

Any sergeant, lieutenant, or captain, never faced anyone higher rank than that, couldn't give me any fear. Especially when they would yell right in front of our faces, at an inch away. And believe me, the drill sergeants and my platoon sergeant tried to give us the element of fear so very hard. And it did scare the hell of some of us. But it just couldn't scare me. And I'm not bragging about it, just stating a fact as to who I was, in particular compared to my comrades. Like I said, the younger ones did cry.

I'm not saying that the training wasn't challenging, of course it was. Especially hard for guys my size. Remember I said I'm only five foot eight, and small in stature. But again, that didn't matter to me. And I'm not saying, I've never been beat up, yes I had my time of getting my ass kicked. And vise a versa.

And to eat at the mess hall, literally changed my eating habits. How could I help it. I mean it wasn't like eating mom's good cooking. Maybe that's why they called it a mess hall, because it looked like a mess. Especially when new Marine Corp enlistees would eat at.

Found out in just a few days, from the time I enlisted in the Corp, I had enlisted into a whole new world, and it would take a whole lot of changes to get used to. And we won't like it. Oh well!!! That's life. That's why the Marine Corp was also the crotch, and we all should know how that stinks, shouldn't we.

Another hi light of our training, but I can only describe it to you from my perspective, from no one else's. Can't assume what others went through, because then I would be wrong. Because then it would make an ass out of you and me. Huh?

From my stand point, I completely underestimated myself, from the time I signed that important piece of paper, called the Marine Corp contract.

Anyway back to my list of hi lights of boot camp. Didn't know it at the time, mostly because I' was young and naive, like everyone is at as a teenager. We're awaken up at four thirty am, like it was from the beginning. Done all of our exercises. Doubled time to breakfast, and doubled to the bathroom. Then, the sergeants get another sadistic idea. They order us for each one of us pick up a white five gallon pail, and fill it up with water. And we're all to have two pails.

Can you guys picture that? I've had that picture in my memory for over five decades now. So on we go. Each of us, had to fill up two five gallon pails of water. To this day, have never known how much five gallons of water weigh. Maybe you guys know. But we had two five gallon pails, filled with water, and then run about fifty yards and back. Now can you imagine? Because like so many memories of that time, have never forgotten about that one. It was painful. Can't remember being sore, because I was too numb. Sleep, can't remember ever sleeping while in boot camp. Guess I did. Would've had to, or I probably would've died.

This all goes without saying, but I've written about it anyway. The drill sergeants and platoon sergeant were right. From the beginning they were going to break us down and rebuild us better than we have ever been. And that's exactly what they were doing. If some would make it or not, that's just the way it would happen. Some pass a Marine Corp boot camp training, or doesn't pass. Fortunately for each one of us, we all passed. Platoon sergeant, was so proud of us.

Moving on with my beautiful memories while I was in the crotch, the stinking term of being in the Marine Corp.

All along this training, we did a lot of marching. Oh my God, if we weren't doing a whole lot of PT, we'd march and march. And we would get it right, if our lives depended on it. That was the platoon sergeant's specialty. We better get perfect or we don't pass boot camp.

One of many number ones these sergeants love doing, was run, run, and run. And run up and down the dirt hills of Camp Pendleton we did.

Check out this one recruit. As I said, the sergeants would run us up and down the hills of Camp Pendleton. Well one of many hot days, running down this one hill, and this guy running down in front of me, was attempting to trip the guy in front of him. Thinking to myself, what an asshole. So I yelled at him as we're running down this pot holed hill, like we've done other days. Yelling at him, "Hey what are you trying to do?" He yells back, "F**k you, it's none of your business." Yelling back at him, "You better not do that" again he says "F**k you" so as he continued trying to trip the poor guy in front of him. Now let me again try to describe to you, the kind of terrain the Marine Corp would take the new recruits running in. Desert hills, pot holes everywhere and anywhere. Could be rattlesnakes. We're all dressed in combat boots, green gym shorts, white t-shirts, with the Marine Corp logo on the front. We're all sweaty. Aggravated. And this asshole wanted to put more misery to the guy running in front of him. Thought to myself, if this idiot succeeds in tripping the innocent guy, he could get seriously hurt. Could break a leg, an arm. He could be in a world of hurting pain. And I also thought, I'm going to stop this from happening. No way I'm going to watch this happen. So about his third attempt, he missed tripping the guy in front of him, and on my first attempt, I got him good, going straight down, and he almost hit his face on a rock. And I'm glad he didn't get hurt seriously. As he went down, I yelled out, "how does it feel f**khead" He in turn, yells out, "you motherF**k*r, and my way I went. As I kept up my running with the rest of the unit, I heard a drill sergeant yell at the out of ranks private, which was the one I tripped. Unbelievable, the asshole and I never had a confrontation. Good for the both of us. On our way we all went on. After that long ten mile run, it would be an understatement to say, we were tired. I wasn't tired, I was exhausted, bushed. Whatever other words there are to describe, I'm super beat to hell.

During our boot training, I heard through the grapevine, that the drill sergeants always pick on one enlistee, to make him an example.

Never wanted to believe that. Thought to myself, no sergeant would make anyone an example. But they did. There was this one guy, just another private like me. They not only made him as an example, they humiliated him, and put him to shame. Poor guy. Another thing I never forgotten. Thank God they didn't pick on any of us short guys. Because I probably would have made a big scandal, and probably end up in court. As it was, there was this one drill sergeant that didn't seem to like any of us. In fact he was sadistic, and hateful. He seemed like he loved to give pain to take out his anger out on. And he did it with pleasure. We'd all talk about him in our barracks. Saying things like, "What is wrong with this guy, he's a maniac" We all thought, maybe Vietnam made him crazy.

Probably and very importantly, to become a Marine, the biggest part of our boot camp training, was qualifying on the rifle range. That was and has always been thee most biggest thing to become a Marine. I mean come on, that's been history of the Marines. And to qualify with the m-14 rifle was a must. And if we didn't we won't pass Marine Corp training, and you get dishonorable discharged disqualified, and kicked out, and put shame to yourself. On the first day of trying to qualify with the m-14, I failed. Oh my God, now what is

Coming back to the sergeants example. Like I said, we really felt sorry for this guy. They would call him, "private joe, front and center" and he would come to front and center.

They would order him, "private Joe, you're gonna be our private of example. Through your endurance of your boot camp training, what do you say" he'd respond, "Yes sir" and they would yell, "can't hear you private Joe" and he would yell back, "yes sir" If you can see what I'm trying to describe to you reading this. This poor guy is standing in front of approximately fifty Marine boot enlistees. And he didn't have a clue as to what was happening to him. A lot of us thought, something gotta be wrong with this guy, and the sergeants were probably wondering, when will he wake up to reality. As this guy was letting himself be treated as some object, I think we all saw him as a big dummy.

I'm sure many of you know, that boot camps in all armed forces are at least thirty days. It doesn't seem very long, right? Wrong. Unless you've gone to the military, then you would know, that thirty days of being beat down, and building back up, can be a painful experience. And sometimes feel like you're going through hell. Because I felt that way. Wondered what the hell did I do to deserve this.

So for some boot camp enlistee, let anyone abuse him and let humiliate him and let shame be put to himself. The next thing this poor fool goes through, is one of the sergeants orders private Joe that today he's going to be a duck. The sergeant tells him, "so when I call you, you're to come to my office as a duck. Understood" he responds, "yes sir" "and if we're all in formation, Your to quack like a duck as well, understood" he says "yes sir" And then it happened, he's called, what does he do, he started quacking like a duck. "Quack quack quack quack." All of us just stood looking at this guy, we couldn't believe what we were watching. Was this real. At one point, I thought, am I in the Marine Corp, or at some circus show. That's how unreal it seemed to me. So for one whole day, this fool was a duck. But the show is not over yet. Because it's only just begun. Now that I remember, he was a duck for at least four days. After that, they would make it look like they would leave him alone. But only come back at him again, to change him to another kind of animal. How cruel. And how weak that fellow recruit boot was. Couldn't and wouldn't stand up for himself.

And like I said, this poor weak individual, kept being picked on. A long time after I was back from Vietnam, I've thought about that guy. And how did the Marine Corp let a guy like him enlist. Wasn't there any amount of entrance exam, for common sense? And why would I focus on that poor guy? Right? Maybe I'm being too dramatic, and maybe I'm not. Because after boot camp training, and sent on our after boot camp leave, we're supposed to return back to advance training. Well as we all returned, and a sergeant reads off names off his roster, he came up to this one name, as strange as the look on his face was on that day. He just stared for a minute. And he says. Maybe many of you knew private Joe, well he won't be coming back, because apparently he shot himself. And like you could hear a pin drop amongst us. I immediately thought he couldn't take it, he blanked out.

Because he followed what he was told to do, like they wanted him to act like a duck, one week, and then about a week later, they wanted him to act like a pig, and then they tell him to act like a dog. But we all thought, it was his fault by letting himself to be abused. Because it didn't happen to anyone else. I guess he felt ridiculed. And I really think that made us more psychologically stronger. I don't know about the rest of the guys, but that gave me more confidence. To not let anyone push me around. And that's worked for me all my life, after that incident.

Continuing on our basic training. I've mentioned in my writing, that there were a couple of youngsters, within our platoon. What I mean by that, a seventeen year old and a eighteen year old. They hadn't finish crying, before they enlisted in the military, especially the Marine Corp. Thinking to myself when we saw these kids cry, man oh man, what a place to cry out like a baby. Because the sergeants had a ball with these kids. I call them kids, because that's how they acted, and the sergeants were trying to build each one of us from the boys we first landed on Marine Corp property into fighting men, and to be ready to be deployed for war. From my point of view, and probably how the sergeants were looking at the recruits there wasn't one really individual to call a real Marine.

About to get real serious, when they took us out to the rifle range, because we will qualify today. Because if any one of us did not qualify, the sergeants would be all over us, and we only have three try's to qualify. God forbid if that happens to any one. We'd become history. Our name would be on some wall, explaining what a coward this guy was, that couldn't pass a Marine Corp boot camp training. Sad and ridiculed.

As I said, we only had three try's to qualify at the rifle range, and on the third time if we didn't qualify firing a M-14 rifle, anyone would be dishonorably discharged. Well on the first day out on the range, I with four others didn't qualify. All five of us were really scared, better believe I was scared. I won't lie. Might be sitting here proud writing this now, but back then, I was scared shitless. Oh yes we were. Because with by not qualifying, we're on our way to severe punishment. What?? Oh yes, the sergeants didn't let us off the hook so easy, because they hated any of their recruits not being able to qualify firing a rifle. That was against their rules and regulations. That was a No, No. And what was our punishment you might wonder. Get a load of this. We were super motivated. Because when each recruit is called out by name, because we didn't qualify, we're into a world of hurt.

I always thought, growing up, Dad was the only one that could put me in a world of hurt. But so much for the days of my childhood. Now I'm in the Marines, and I have to try to step out of the world of the boy I was, and learn to cross over to the man, the Marines to change me into. Thought to myself, I could've learn to be a man out in the streets, like most men.

Yeah, but I just failed to tell you something you probably already know, or maybe you don't. The military creates something much more than a regular young man doesn't find in the streets. Self discipline, and courage, and the best of all, self satisfaction. That's what I found out for myself anyway. But, the Marines are not for everyone, you either want to be a Marine or you don't. The drill sergeants and the platoon sergeant will find out where your mind is on the first day. You can't fool them.

Like I said, get a load of this. For me, and the other four that didn't qualify on our first day, learning how to fire a M-14 rifle. Well, let me put it this way. Anybody can pull the trigger on any weapon, right? Being out on the rifle range wasn't about pulling a trigger on the M-14, it was all about how well anyone can hit a target. Anyone can pull a trigger on any weapon. It's as easy as ending up in prison. We hear it all the time. Any law enforcement agent, from a police officer on up, by accident shoots an innocent person, a man, a woman, or a child. Will be investigated, and could be found guilty, and convicted, and put in prison. Same goes with qualifying on the Marine Corp rifle range. Back to our punishment, when we didn't qualify, shooting the target accurately. This one drill sergeant loved to prove a point. So he called us out by name, we all lined up in front of him. Yells out, you will qualify with the M14 by tomorrow. Next he's yelling out, all of you maggots get on your knees, and put your arms stretched out in front of you. Next he's dropping two pencils in front of each one of us. He says, you will see pencils in front of each one of you. Put one pencil under each one of your knees. Didn't know what the others were thinking, but I thought, this guy has to be the most meanest sadistic individual I have ever heard of. Can anyone imagine how painful pencils feel, standing on top of them under each knee? You probably think I'm exaggerating. You can think what ever you want to think. Because I remember the pain. Who knows, maybe that's why I have bad knees now.

But through my life, I've always tried looking at things, on the positive side, why people do things what they do.

I mean after all, we were being trained for war. Vietnam. And we were all going. No doubt about that. So when drill sergeants are trying their best to train future Marines to the best of their ability, just in case anyone of us were to get captured, becoming a prisoner of war. The drill sergeants tried training us to endure pain. Once deployed, I understood the sergeants philosophy. Although being scared when we were punished for not qualifying out on the rifle range on the first day, I had to psych myself to try my damn best.

The next day, was just another great day in trying to qualify to shoot a M-14 accurately. And I did it. Mentally it was a great accomplishment for me personally. I'm sure it was the same affect to my fellow comrades.

So going on to our next phase of basic training. But one thing that I noticed, whether it's the beginning of training, or advanced training, something never changed. We were always running. The sergeants called it, double time this or double time that.

The memory of my experiences in the Marine Corp boot camp, left the biggest impression in my heart and soul. I will never forget them. Mostly because I never want to. Even if I'm suffering the pains the Corp gave me. The pains remind me where I've been, with pride. I'm proud, but I never brag. I've always thought, leave the bragging to the ones that are stuck on themselves. Dad has told me, time and time again, "Son you should be proud" I've always responded, "Maybe I should be, but the real heroes never came home Dad. They're the ones that gave their lives for their country. May God Bless them all, that have lost their lives in all wars of America.

On our boot camp graduation, that was so awesome. Should have seen the looks on all of our faces. Marine Corp boot camp training, was so rough, and tough, and we all graduated. Even the cry babies graduated. We were all United States Marines. We were real men now, so our platoon sergeant told us after graduating. Telling us how proud he was. Also telling us, "I don't have to tell you, that you're all going to Vietnam, and all of you should know, that not all of you are coming back. All of us graduates, looked at each one of us.

After graduation, we're given a two week leave, and to return to our next phase of training, which was called, advance training.

Advanced training became more technical, what I mean is, more in detail. With advanced training, we were taught, close hand to hand combat. Had to learn how to operate many more weapons. We were taught how to throw hand grenades. It was either you learn or blow someone up. It didn't take no Einstein to figure that out. We either take military training seriously or get someone killed, including yourself. Went through some dangerous shit. Because there's always some dummy, that just couldn't grasp it, when given a weapon in their hands. It was scary, let me tell ya. Anyone being in the military, in combat training would know or should know, when having to pull a pin of a hand grenade, you only have three to five seconds. That was scary, and I took it serious, to learn about that weapon. We were taught how to use mortars. Another one to take serious. In fact, all weapons training was a serious matter, and I took it very seriously.

And so for me to take weapons training seriously, it became pretty basic. Because after all, it's either you learn or you don't. It wasn't hard to figure that out for me.

As I mentioned, hand to hand combat. I can only imagine how we looked, fighting one another, with make believe rifles and bayonets, us with helmets on. The instructor partnering us up, and trying to choke out our partners out. First I would get behind my partner and pretend on choking him, and then his turn. But my partner almost choked me out for good.

And running, no it wasn't just running anymore, it was now running and jumping over or crawling over walls. And six to eight foot walls we were ordered to climb over and keep running as fast you could. I had a lot of fun. Huh, yeah right. But I knew it would soon be over, and go face reality, real war, real live enemy. Targets that shoot back, and fight back.

By the way, I really believe the Marine Corp is and has always been the toughest armed force in America. And not because I was a Marine, but because it's written in America's history. You don't have to believe me, just read it's history, like I have. Like I've said, I may be proud, but I don't brag, and never have, like I've seen and heard others. My opinion on people that are too proud, let their pride tangle up themselves from reality. And that's too bad, because people look at you as a selfish, self centered person. Oh I can be an arrogant asshole, but I've had to be, to prove a positive point.

On through my life, I've heard guys claim they went to Vietnam, and on, on. But when you ask them about a certain territory of Vietnam, they have no clue. And for those of us that have actually been there, we don't like talking about it. That should be just natural, when you've seen your own comrades get killed. That should be natural, right? I've always thought so. But I've noticed those that have never been in Vietnam, talk, and talk, and talk. Because they've never been there. Well I knew a guy like that, and he was so humiliating. To stand in front of you, and lie. And then here's the thing, I trusted him in the beginning. And believed his story. Thinking about that later on, boy he was such a manipulator. And a big liar.

Then I heard about those same kind of people tell very similar stories. You know the stories. Trying to get all the glory about a war they were never in.

As my military training was coming to a slow halt.

But first let me describe two flashbacks I just heard in my head. Told you about the cry babies, that the drill sergeants had a wonderful time with. Even threatened them, that if they wouldn't stop crying. Calling them every name in the book. You name it, that's what they were called. Starting on our climax of our training, advance training that was. And I've also said, what ever training it was, the drill sergeant still double time, and double time it was. And how about getting vaccinated, walking through a hallway, and we would get vaccinated by two doctors, one on each side of our bodies. On the arms, legs, thighs, everywhere, and right after our vaccinations, the sergeants would have us run, and run hard.

Before I forget to mention about the time we were all supposed to report to our advanced training after we graduated from boot camp training. As I just said, we were all supposed to report. Well unfortunately there's always at least one, right? Maybe in a perfect world, everyone would. And if we didn't report on the day we were supposed to report on that very day, well may God be with you, because you're going to need God's blessings, for so many different ways Of course my only real concern who reported to my advanced training, was myself. Don't have to be very smart to figure that out.

Like I said, on the day we were supposed to report on our first day, it took this one fool, and through the years I've forgotten his name, but that's not important anymore. The important thing was, for all of us to pay attention what we were all going to see, to this poor fool. Because that's what he was, a fool. For me, on the day I signed my name on that Marine Corp contract. That started my honest obligation, with a commitment of following orders. And if anyone of us had a problem fulfilling that contract, be prepared. Because the Marine Corp sergeants and even the Marine Corp officers, from their end of fulfilling the contract, would have to go hunt down whoever's AWOL. Absent With Out Leave (AWOL) Here's where it gets touchy and unfortunately very violent for the poor fool. When they caught up on with this poor guy, it looked like the sergeants were soo happy that they caught this lost fish. The leading sergeant, yells out, "Company Attenthuh" and by the looks of things, the AWOL fool, he'd been on the run, his clothes all moist, him, looked like he'd been running for a couple of weeks.

Sergeant yells at us, "we finally caught up with this son of a bitch" "and he's not going anywhere but to the brig." Have always heard that to be in the brig is much tougher than a regular jail. Especially a Marine brig. They have no mercy, and probably never will.

Next thing we saw what happened to this poor fool, he gets the wholly shit kicked out of him. The sergeant in charge, smashed him in the jaw, he goes down, then the sergeant kicks him. But that's the Corp for you. No one defies the Corp. The Marine Corp that is.

Remembering much of my boot camp training, I only had a couple of issues with the platoon sergeant and a drill sergeant.

The first one, we were out on the marching parade ground, as many days that we would march. Perfection was a must with the platoon sergeant or we would hear about it at the end of the day. And on one particular day, he thought I screwed up his march. When it was someone else's fault. Will never forget that day. He grabbed me, and was about to kick the hell out of me, and was stopped by a drill sergeant, informing him I was not the one. In my head, thanking God. And the platoon sergeant actually apologized, as I was.

The next thing that happens, I received a letter from the girlfriend supposedly going to marry, thank God that never happened. Which was the girl I first mentioned that wanted to have my baby, wow that was close. Anyway, received a letter from her, and was told to double time to fetch my letter. Well on my way running to fetch my letter, this one drill sergeant catches up with me, and what does he do, he started yelling at me, telling me I'm not to receive any mail. And commenced to try to poke my eyes out. And I'm dodging his poking. And he finally lets me go. Another part of my boot camp training I've never forgotten. Always thought that was kinda weird. But I got over it. Had to, because I'll inform you later in my life how I became very proud being a Marine. As I got older I noticed other comrades, former combat Marines, were as proud. Our training kept on, up and down the hills, running through obstacle courses.

On another particular day, our platoon was on a run, and running through obstacles, and there was this one obstacle, that we had to grab ourselves with our hands as we hand climbed over muddy waters and some of us would slip and fall into the mud. And this one seventeen year old is humiliated by our platoon sergeant, and what does this kid do, he started crying. He should have never done that, because he was humiliated even more.

The Sargent grabbed ahold of him, and yells out to everybody, oh we have a pussy in our platoon. As I've said, thank goodness my crying days were over, since I was a boy. My crying days with Dad spanking me, paid off when I enlisted into the Marines. Mom would tell me, when I was little, son you're such a cry baby. And those days were long gone, since my first experience with death at seven, as I've constantly have repeated. I guess there were just too many times, Dad made me cry, and one time, I saw him laugh, as he dangling me while he was basically whipping my ass. Now I'll never know for a fact, if he was laughing, because he was spanking me or whatever he was laughing about. just don't know, that's a long time ago. And glad they were over for my military service. Because finding out later as I turned nineteen, that wouldn't have been good for me to cry during my Marine basic training. For you that might read my life's story for what ever reason it might be well worth it to many of you, to learn how to grow up. Oh, no one is going to try to stop you from crying, but yourself.

I'm not saying, crying is bad, I'm just saying, it depends what you're crying about. As all of us boys, should grow up into manhood, some boys never grow up, psychology speaking that is. Have noticed many of us boys, just our physical body grows, but the mind lags behind. You've seen them, I've seen them, we've all seen them. They'll blame all their wrong doing to everyone else, but themselves. Like I said, the day we're born, and I speak for myself, we start growing, and the days go by, as the years fly by we all should be progressing, as our bodies expand.

As the days have gone by, as the years have flown by for me personally, it has been a journey, and that's an understatement, as I write my struggling life's experiencing's journey.

For men and for many of us, we'll always find crying is not such a bad thing. But if you're like me, after a while, physical pain will eventually go away a little, and you've probably experienced emotional pain. When I say emotional pain. Like seeing your mama pass away, someone in your relation pass on. Now that really hurts.

One more upset while in Marine Corp training. We were just about finished with most of our training. And remembering this one exercise. They called it reconnaissance. That was very important that we knew how to recon in combat training. Well on this particular day, our company of Marines, before we trained for the recon training, we were to stack our M-14s like a pyramid, which was so cool. It looked like a standing tree of rifles.

This was a big reason why I appreciated, that my crying days were over. Take a load of this one. So we did our reconnaissance, we had stacked our rifles, then after hours like an actual experience out in the bush as we combat veterans called it. We got into formation, and then ordered to retrieve our weapons, and marched back to our barracks. We were all dismissed, and we all went to our assigned bunks. But dummy me just had to notice that I didn't have my assigned M14, because we had to be responsible for the M14, by a serial number, we had in our possession. And so I go to our company commander, which was a captain. And knocked on his door, and he of course, yells out, "What the f**k do you want get in here" Continues to yell, "well private what the hell do you want" and stupid me responded, "sir the private would like to inform the captain that I don't have the weapon which was assigned to me." He yells back, "what the hell did you just say to me" then he says, "follow me" "stand beside me" then this is where it gets real bloody for me. I stand at attention, as he yells out to a company of Marines. In case you don't know, that's two hundred and fifty men. Men my ass, we were all a bunch of kids. The commanding officer, the captain in charge, commenced to yell out, "what this private has just informed me that he lost his weapon" Thinking to myself, I didn't say that, what an asshole, he's trying to get me in trouble. Reminiscing when I wrote this, will always wonder why did he do that. So I prepared myself psychologically, because I think my spirit knew what was about to happen.

And the captain continues to inform our Bravo company. "And since this private has lost his weapon, there will not be any weekend liberty for no one in this Bravo company, is that understood"? "Yes Sir" And through most of the night, until about midnight, the four right guides of the company. Let me remind you all, I'm only five foot eight. And each right guide is at least five foot ten or taller, weighing around two hundred pounds or more.

After the captain informs Bravo company that no one is going anywhere for liberty that weekend, you should have seen the looks on every man's face. If looks could have killed me that night, I would've been dead since then. But here I am today alive and in pain. In pain

ROBERT GARCIA

for so many reasons, and not just from what I'm about to tell you what happens next.

What happens next, I could say at that time, it would be my worst nightmare, but through my life, that couldn't compare to what happens, continuing on with my life as I write on. Remember, DIED THREE TIMES LIVED ONCE

I'm not gonna lie, of course I was scared, as to what was going to happen to me. And it happened. The four right guides came looking for me, asking everyone, where is the son of a bitch? The upper man, from his bunk, points me out, watching his finger pointing at me. All four guides grab me, and push and shove me into the large shower stall. Pin me up against the shower wall, one man on each one of my arms, which the other two, took turns, punching me, and then they switched and continued to beat me to a bloody pulp. And what did I do, you might I ask. Well I didn't cry if that's what you all think.

As three of the right guides took turns beating me up. Hitting me in the face, nose, cheeks, my chest area. I stood looking at them, tasting my own blood. My own platoon guide didn't want nothing to do with it. How would I know that? Well as the other three commenced to beating me. As they slowly stopped, I started laughing at them. I mean really laughing out loud at them. As I wiped my blood off my face, I tell, "hahahahaha, you're all a bunch of cowards. Each one of you is bigger than me, and it would only take just one of you to kick my ass, but you're beating me up, you're all a bunch of cowards.", my guide tells me, "hey bud I wanted nothing to do with this." I responded, "Oh f**k you too", we all head back to our bunks, I'm was a bloody mess, tasting my blood running down my face. After all these years, have always wondered, why the captain never heard us with my loud voice calling these guys cowards. Guess he thought he was teaching me a lesson. But it was all well and good. He did teach me a lesson. How to manage fear. Maybe he didn't know that at the time, but I took it as a positive lesson to absorb. I didn't know it at the time, but that would become one of my tools for defense, where we would all be going. And all you old guys should know by now, because many of us went to Vietnam.

Well that's all I can remember how my training came and gone. The Marine Corp turned me from the the boy, when I enlisted, and the training and the war we experienced, came back a man I am today. But that was a long time ago. From the time going to war, returning, and all the time from then until now, has made me the man I am today. But it's been very easily said than done, because I will have to experience two more deaths before I would arrive to my current stage of life. Remembering my deathly truck accident, that I psychologically died, that literally changed my life, becoming a different young boy after seven years old. Now at nineteen am about to face my second death. War.

As I've said before, everyone has a story to tell and have all the right to write about your life, but this one is mine. And I can only explain to you all, where, what and when it happened. That's perfectly normal, right?

I'm not saying that I'm the only one that bad and sad things happen. There are far more mysterious and more dangerous things that happen to others. But for many of us, and maybe all of us we've put ourselves in the place in where we're in right now. Am I right or wrong? I think I'm right about myself. I've put my own self in the life I live now. And that's because of God's love, blessings, and his miracles. And I know there are so many of you, that don't believe in God, blessings, much less believe in miracles. But that's you. I wasn't a very strong believer myself, but I'm a stronger believer than I used to be. Because God had been knocking on my door for a long time, before I finally opened it. And I'm not pretending that I'm better than anyone else, because I'm not. I'm just saying that I'm a better person than I used to be is all. God has taught me things that will be hard for me to put into words, but I'll try.

We live a miracle in everything we do, and with who we do them with.

Many people live in the dark, and I would like to believe that many people live in the light. Under God's light. I know he's my sunshine. Because I've died three times and lived once. Hell, the life I lived before I opened God's door, I had only flown in a airline when they flew me to Vietnam. And later on I'll write you about the places I've been to since Vietnam.

Don't want to bore you non believers out there. But I've had an amazing life, and with that lives' catastrophes, like anyone else. I'm about to write and describe to you all, with the best of my ability, how I barely escaped my second experience of death.

Here I go. Still remember my mom and dad when they cried, when they saw me get in the bus. Destination, Marine Corp boot camp training, Camp Pendleton. But that was all behind me. And you should have seen the look on both of their faces, when they saw me get on the airline, destination, Vietnam. Wow, a sad thought. I thought Mom was gonna die right then and there. Here's where my mind blanks out. I remember getting on board the C-130 airplane to be transported to Vietnam, but from where did we fly from, can't remember for the life of me. But remember landing in Quang Tri, Vietnam by a six by, which was a troop carrying truck. Like a cattle truck, but this was a open bed, with about ten Marines being delivered to various short manned units. And short manned they were. If you as readers, try to imagine, if you've never been to Vietnam. At the time, bombarded ruins, bomb craters practically everywhere. I'll try to describe it the best way I can. Picture yourself a nineteen year old kid, it was spooky for me. Eyes wide shut, is what I wanted to do, because my inner self didn't want to look at to what my eyes first saw. First Quang Tri's dirt was a red clay, which made me feel the dirt was Red, because of the blood shed. Gory, and frightening to start my first day in country of Vietnam. Not only feeling paranoid, this kid comes running up to me, but he wasn't a kid. He was a Marine, no helmet, with a 45 pistol in his hand. His face was full of crusted dirt, his clothes torn and filthy. What would anyone expect, after being in the bush for over thirty days, so of course he stunk, like anyone else would. This guy looked to be at least thirty five or forty, but he was only eighteen years old. I was immediately in shock, can you picture that? When he ran up to me, could have sworn, he had been crying all night long. He yells out at me, as I jumped off the six by truck, he yells out, "is this all of you oh my god" I say "I guess so" he replied, "we were overran last night dude and all through the night we were attacked, it was aTet Offensive", attacked by waves of men, women and children with everything they had, and we weren't receiving any support of any kind in time" So this is why, the way I look at it that the military draft was in full force at the time. And guys like me were enthusiastic to enlist into the military.

I will never be able to imagine, what it would be to get overran. And for many of you that don't know what being overran is. I'll try to describe it. Say you're within two hundred men as a fighting force. You're all camped out in a big perimeter. One big circle, dug in trenches. And you all start receiving gun fire, and you return fire, and goes that way for a matter of hours. Then you start receiving more intense firing, and mortars and grenades. And men start to die more than you thought, so you try to retreat, but to no avail. They keep attacking you, and now you have to run for your life, watching your comrades die. A very ugly and a very sad sight to witness. And this was what that Marine was trying to describe to me what happened. And what a devastating nightmare that was to him. Poor guy.

Remembering what that fellow Marine told me how old he was, thinking he had to have been only seventeen when he enlisted into the Marines. But he looked far more in years than what he was. All along with thoughts to myself, man, I can only imagine what's in store for me within the next thirteen months. At the time it seemed like eternity. Didn't know it then, being a rifleman in Vietnam, would be my most ultimate experience of my life. Because everyday in combat in Vietnam would keep me on my toes, and not for my life, but for my comrade's life. Because that's how the Marine Corp trained me. To save the man next to me.

The Marine that greeted me on my first day on my arrival in Quang Tri, has always been in my memory all my life, since my first day in country.

A flash back which I've had since my boot camp graduation, reminiscing what our platoon sergeant told all of us, after graduating, that it's been the history of the Marine Corp, in war situations, we look out for our fellow comrade to come home alive. I didn't think much about it then, but I think a lot about it now.

ROBERT GARCIA

Reminding you all, I'm alive today, writing to whoever wants to read this and pay attention to it, it's all been an amazing life, because of God's love, his blessings and miracles, or I wouldn't be here, and sanely living a life, I wouldn't have imagined. That's God's truth, in words I have been doing my best to tell you all, but I don't believe it's easy for anyone to put a life story into simple wording. Maybe it is for professional writers, and that I am not. And won't pretend to be. You all can see, I'm not even close. But I'll try to paint a story to what happened to me, and I'll try not to be too dramatic. Just truefull.

On my first day in country, to do my utmost and to the best of my ability, to save my comrade next to me so he can return home to his loving family had become my focus.

Assigned to Bravo company along with the Marine, that had faced an overwhelming situation. He had faced an overrun situation. Attacked by an enemy that out numbered his Marine unit. That was behind him now. He had to move on with a new unit that gave him support to at least save his life. After a while he was able to handle that pretty good. Because he became my fire team leader. As he became a short timer. A short timer is a ground pounder, in the Marines, a short timer was a foot troop, that went on patrols, day or night. And well involved in long and far operations, that most of the time it would take anywhere from thirty to forty days. And right at this very moment, of my arrival, short timer was a far cry from thirteen months. Finding out later, after the Vietnam era, all others that went to any other U.S. conflicts, troops were deployed for six months, without saying that's far short than thirteen months.

Remembering my first night out on a patrol as a fire team size, is only four troops, and as a new boot, first twenty four hours in country, I needed to be trained. And my overwhelmed comrade Marine had become my team leader. A year younger but well informed, I trusted him. Did I have a choice, no.

But my question to all. Everyday we wake up, if we do wake up the following morning. Some people don't wake up. And when we are awake, we have to trust someone. That doesn't mean you trust everyone. And a man like many, I had to trust my comrades, especially in a war environment. I understand, not everyone goes to war. But I respect everyone, and anyone. But to trust everyone and anyone, that's a no, no. Do I live insecure, maybe, but maybe I'm alive today because of my own insecurities. There are people that live with positive insecurities and there are people that live with negative insecurities. I've seen both kind throughout my life, and I know you have to. With us veterans, I can probably speak for many of us, but not for all of us. Because we've all been in different experiences in war.

I'm not going to try to bore you readers on my everyday in country stay in Vietnam. I'll just write you the hi lights of my nearly death days.

Started out on our daily, nightly patrols, rain or shine. And anyone knowing about tropical weather, would know about monsoons. Because in Vietnam, when it rained it poured. Oh my God, did it rain.

My first part of my life, with my deathly experience as a kid at seven, thinking I died then, but I woke up, and I've taken you up to now, where many as myself that had to go by law to the war of Vietnam. And the thousands that protested that war and also the thousands that ran off to other countries so they wouldn't get drafted, called, dodging the draft. But if you would've gotten caught at that time, and many did. And by getting arrested or trying to run from America, you would be charged for treason. Wow, would I want that on my head, being charged for treason, and what kind of time would I be facing in prison. So what did I do, I enlisted.

Proud, yes I am, like many should be. But I'll stick to my guns, anyone can be proud, but try to not make yourself look like a fool, by bragging. To me whenever I saw or heard someone bragging, many people would just turn around and walk away. People that brag about anything entirely about themselves are self centered, and selfish. Thanking God everyday, and giving him gratitude, that he gave the heart I feel I've always had. At least I think I've always had. I say this, because I've been told at least a couple of times, that I have a strong spirit. Do I feel that within myself, no I don't. And never have. But I truly believe in the afterlife. Maybe that's why others have said I have a strong and good spirit.

ROBERT GARCIA

A lot of things have happened to me in my life for me not to believe in the afterlife. Many of course don't and probably never believe anymore than the life we live physically. People will always and have never believed in anything but themselves. That's been always unfortunate for greedy people. Because our time is only a very small fraction of God's time. And we're all God's little children, no matter how old we are. We don't live long in this life. And I've waisted a lot of time, trying to get it right. Haven't we guys and gals? I mean look how fast time flies in our lives. We're born, then in just forty years, people start to feel old. It's a shame, how we waist time. But how is anyone to know when we're too young. Time will never be on our side. As Mick Jagger, sang, "Time Is On My Side". But that was just his song, probably about a romantic relationship with some girl.

Read this story once, about a troop in world war 2, being in a deathly situation, as many of us experienced. But as I continued reading this one, it was almost exactly the same. People say, how so. Because this guy thought he was with a fellow soldier beside him. And his name was Mike. Well if you know a little about the Bible, there's an angel by the name of st Michael the archangel. So this guy continued on his patrol, thinking he's with his buddy Mike. The next thing that happens falls nothing short from being a miracle. All hell breaks out, ground mines, soldiers getting killed. And bombs exploding, heavy gun fire everywhere. As the end of that hot battle came to an end. The troop gets back to his unit, and starts looking for his buddy Mike, and asking about him. His unit informs him, that there is no one by that name. Well in Vietnam that happened to me, and I also knew a Marine named Mike, and he was beside me, only he got shot and bullets flying so close by my head, and my ears began ringing. And they still ring today.

Although I wasn't far from my Marine unit, the scenario was basically the same. See if you can see the difference. From the day I had arrived in country Vietnam, you could hear gunfire, naval cannons going off, hand grenades exploding near by. At that very moment remembering, as I had a flash back, of my fourth grade teacher, telling us we would be going to war, thinking to myself, sitting in class on that very moment, she's got to be wrong. Being only ten years old, and now being in Vietnam, am now nineteen. Wow, I thought, I've arrived to reality to my worst nightmare, and many nightmares to come. For you as for all of us, reality can be frightening, and I'm not going to pretend I wasn't scared when I was. But as our fore fathers have done in previous wars, we have to, as I had to manage fear.

Because if we can't handle fear, fear itself will kill us. I know it, as well as the next man that went to war. Being I was trained a Marine, that was my utmost, and my most proudest defense, which pulled me through my time in Vietnam.

Had heard so many and too many horror stories, about getting yourself or your comrade either hurt or killed. From the time I left the states to my Vietnam arrival, was told, don't expect much sleep, because you better be alert or your dead. From all the stories I heard, they weren't far from the truth. And that's probably why I have insomnia today. No doubt about it. Because I didn't get much sleep at all.

And by the way, what about propaganda, oh my God. Don't know, and it doesn't matter anymore, who was creating stories about U.S. troops killing babies while we went on our patrols. When I heard that, thinking, how can they lie like that? Because that's what that was, pure lies. Also heard, that some troops were raping Vietnamese women. Now of course there was prostitution, that's always been in all wars. But rape, I've never witnessed that.

Returning back to my experience with st. Michael the Archangel, as the one I read about the troop in world war 2.

I had been going on on our patrols, being trained, and trained well, but in war, trained well or not, if there's a bullet with your name on it, it's gonna get ya no matter how well you're trained. Well, on this one night as many others I will be facing, my comrade Mike was beside me, on a reactionary force. I had only been deployed going on two weeks. It was one of our squads out on a night patrol. The rest of our company spread out, guarding a bridge that had been used for the NVA, north Vietnamese army, for in and out of south Vietnam. I had been invited to our machine gun tower, to smoke. Guess what that was, that so many troops smoked. I'll give you three guesses and the first two won't count. Pot. Marijuana. There are so many names for that drug. Although they've legalized it in a lot of the states, I don't think they should have. And on this night, we're smoking pot, passing joints around the gun tower, when all of a sudden we heard pop pop pop, explosions of different kinds everywhere. Fright hit us all. Especially myself just being deployed two weeks before. We climbed down that tower so quick, running back to my squad, while my squad leader ordered me with the others to get all our gear together, and prepare to help save lives. Guns firing, bombs exploding, it looked like fourth July celebration. But there was nothing to celebrate about, we had to get out there where we were needed. And we were needed badly. We ran out to save lives as fast as possible, and we were running like a herd of bulls. But no one knew what was about to happen. Lives were going to be lost.

The sergeant in charge ordered us up to a bush line, to commence firing into the bushes, and firing we did. A lot of crackle pop, boom boom boom. And right in front of us came back right back at us, crackle pop, boom boom boom. That was such a surprise that hit us hard. I thought I died that night. But I really believe that part of me did die. Throwing myself back and into a bunch of dried branches that tangled my left arm with my weapon and couldn't untangle myself to shoot back. Finding out later, our radio man was shot in the head killed instantly. He was focusing to use the radio, instead of hitting the ground like many of us did.

That night was a catastrophe for all of us, when I say for all of us. But the Vietnamese had lost more men. That night personally for me, would end up haunting me for the rest of my life. Although it's been over fifty three years ago, it still feels like it happened last year.

Like I was trying to describe it to you readers, I had gotten tangled up in dried branches, trying to twist myself out of that mess to shoot back. But as I was twisting and turning, bullets were flying by my head, by my body, bullets flying from one side and to the other side. I honestly thought I died. It was a night battle, so it was very hard to see. So Marines were shooting night illumination from mortars, and I could see rounds flying by me. I'll never forget that night. It has left a frightening scar in my heart. After that night I wasn't the same, none of us were never the same. Today they call it P.T.S.D. I didn't know what they called it back then, all I knew was, a good part of me died that night, and little did I know, my war days had only just begun.

Oh, and my buddy Mike, I never saw him again. I thought I heard him suffer pain, like he had gotten shot, that night we were taking fire. thinking all these years, he had taken the bullet I was supposed to get. And after reading about that world war 2 story about being with st. Michael the archangel, I believe I experienced his presence as well. But not just that night as I move on with my deathly experiences. And let me say this. That night all of us taking fire of bullets, as like I said, trying to untangle myself, God was holding me down. Another miracle about God protecting me that same night, as bullets were flying everywhere from one side of me to the other, physically I would be dead, but my spirit tells me God held his hand from me being shot.

What I'm about to tell you all, many of you won't believe it, but that's okay, to myself I believe it very strongly. Like I've said before, this is my life, and I'm writing this about my life. And maybe it can relate to many people and maybe not. Because different things happen to all of us.

Having Dad still alive when I wrote this, he's told me time and time again, that Mom prayed for me everyday I was gone to Vietnam. Well, as time has flown by, that night in particular all of us getting shot at, I could feel mama's prayers. How about that for spirituality, believe or not, it doesn't matter, God saved my life and many others.

Here's another one for you. Another believe it or not. Feel strongly blessed by God's love and blessings, that he strongly protects those who try to save lives, we're not just out there to take lives, we're saving lives, and that's what the Marines are all about.

After that night of battle, like I said, it changed all of us. Remember, we were soldiers, and young men, at eighteen to twenty five years old. Our lives had been changed until we leave this physical world. Unfortunately for the enemy, they took more losses. And I was given the order, since I was one of the new boots having only two weeks in country, of collecting the dead. Say what? Yeah, I with others were assigned to collect the dead bodies, by dragging them to where all other dead bodies were. Thought to myself, what an assignment. I Well never forget dragging this one, a dead young Vietnamese soldier, with his eyes wide open staring up in the sky, with a perfect hole, like the size of a silver dollar, through his forehead to the back of his head. Wow, what a frightening look. I just had to stop dragging, and look at this dead guy, and the look on his face. There were probably about forty dead bodies in all, including three of ours.

Another old saying. War is hell. Know it was for me for us, during our time fighting the communist Vietnam, 68, 69. Over fifty eight thousand troops perished during our involvement in Vietnam, sad but true. And those like myself lost our sanity, and then there are those that lost limbs. Men losing their lives, limbs and/or your sanity. War is hell. All I wanted, was to get home and try to live a normal life. A normal life? What's normal? Did we have a chance? No World War Two veterans, nor Vietnam veterans had what new veterans have today, to transition from the military to civilian life. Some military personnel don't leave that life, because I think they like it. I think it can be a very beautiful career. But I wouldn't have lasted, because they would have sent me back to war, Vietnam, and get killed. There were those few comrades I met in some of our notorious battles, claimed I would immediately get promoted to sergeant if I would re-enlist, because of my performances they witnessed of my capabilities. My response to their claims, no extra stripe is gonna get me killed. It wouldn't be worth it, a little more money and another stripe for my life. Some had no choice nor a chance. There were those few Marines I met that had enlisted for four and six years, always wondered and thought to myself, wow, that's crazy, and suicidal. War is hell. Remember, DIED THREE TIMES LIVED ONCE.

Long before I was deployed to Nam, I had already experienced my first death, and lost what sanity I had then, at seven, remember? Now here I am, slowly experimenting my second death, and losing my sanity at nineteen.

Remembering, just before we were shipped out on a transport airplane, we were in a room of about a hundred of us, with a gunnery sergeant asking us one big question. "Does anyone think they shouldn't have to go to Vietnam?" I was starting to feel some butterflies in my stomach, so I raised my hand. I raised my hand and the gunny asked me "Oh yeah what makes you think you shouldn't go?" I responded, "I'm my mom and Dad's only son, he asked, "is your dad still alive"? I say "yes he's a World War Two veteran" the gunny disappointing me, "well you're still going" Some guys beside me, had some giggles, you thought you weren't going, but it didn't work. I asked them "You find that funny"? They didn't laugh anymore. Because it wasn't funny, someone like me already had P.T.S.D., and I didn't know it at the time.

So now I'm off to see the wizard, and check on my sanity, in my Vietnam experiences, if indeed I came home with sanity, or come home at all, other than in a body bag. Thinking negative? Who wouldn't, for a guy like me.

After just a couple of weeks in country, and after my first facing death in the face, I started to become snobbish. Arrogant. And started getting smart ass with even my lieutenants, and that was not cool at all. I had been very lucky, and lucky I was, because of the things I had said to my superiors. By all means, I could have been court martialed. I even threatened to hit one of them. Thank God I did not. Cussed out one of them, only because he cussed me first, because I was attending to my squad that were almost having heat strokes. Another lieutenant, will never mention names, so I won't mention his, actually got us lost, because I discovered he couldn't read the map he had in his hand at the time. Can anybody imagine, why would they put someone in charge that couldn't read a map. You probably won't believe me, but I had to make a decision to save our platoon's lives.

And a big decision to save my platoon's lives I did, with my lord given me a will and a way. I felt sorry for this guy, our lieutenant, that I had to put him in a vulnerable position, which I didn't mean to do. When we put trust into our leaders, we, I, put our lives in their hands, assuming they're doing the right thing.

With this particular lieutenant, our platoon commander, after confronting him about, accusing him not able to read a map. He pretty well admitted it. His body language told us that, what I accused him of was true. Because when I came at him aggressively, he was turning the map in his hand, like he wasn't understanding it, and I became very suspicious with him. So I say, "Jesus lieutenant do you know how to read that map"? He wouldn't respond. So I grabbed the map out of his hand, "give me the f**k**g map", "Oh my God," pointing at two different spots on the map, "Oh my God we're supposed to be here, instead we're way over here, lost". Looking at my other comrades, keeping the map with me, "you can stay with him, but I'm going back to our main unit", the rest of the platoon followed me, with the lieutenant lagging behind. Nothing was ever said from anyone. I kept my mouth shut and so did everyone else. The lieutenant when I confronted him, he didn't know what to do or say, so he liens back against a big rock boulder and slidden down to the ground, and sighed, "Oh my God" after that incident, thinking that if he was to charge me with insubordination, what could I do. But the thought in my mind, was much stronger, to save my comrades from harms way. And our return back to our main unit, realizing our company of Marines were taking fire. Wow, in my mind, having a horror thought, if the NVA, would have known our little platoon of Marines were lost, and had gotten detached from our main unit, they would have massacred, and slaughtered us into pieces. What a horrible thought, and it kind of demoralized me. Never understood myself why I became aggressive with that lieutenant. Guess I was just doing my job. Save lives.

Never saw or heard of that poor lieutenant again. Always thought that maybe someone reported him, or maybe he reported himself. That would've been the wisest thing for him to do. Instead of getting humiliated right out of the Marines. Thinking at the time, don't the military teach wanna be officers how to read a map? That would, and should be a big factor to saving lives and being an officer, no matter what branch of the military you're in.

Writing my life story, and describing my three near death experiences have never been an exciting thing to put into words. So it's tough for me, but I'm trying. One of my best features in my character, and my image, is having self confidence, my second one would be, self discipline. Or vise-a-versa.

Being in Nam for thirteen months, seemed like eternity. Everyday seemed like a month, every month seemed like a year.

And I had an issue with platoon commanders, because they would only be in country for only six months. Couldn't understand that being fair. All three lieutenants that took command while I was there, I never gotten very well with. I had two lieutenants in charge while I was point man for eight months. To you readers, you might ask. What is a point man? Let me show you how terrible that was being the first man to get killed. Isn't the greatest ambition to want to do that. Well I did it. To be able to write this and tell you what men like myself went through, and makes me feel like going through it again, I had flash backs writing this. So some times I had to lean back and take a break. I'm back. Had to write this. And I had to keep on poking at it, no matter what. Remember: DIED THREE TIMES LIVED ONCE

In this writing of my three facing deaths during my life, it seemed many more times I could've have gotten killed. But these were my intense times and moments of my life, as a kid, in Vietnam as a young man, and my last one, with a very negative motivation in committing suicide, as a much older man. I'll try to describe my highs and my lows of my life. Like we all have. And my writing could describe parts of your life, I don't know, maybe, and maybe not. Experienced some crazy times, that I often wondered why I'm still alive.

Any of you guys that have experienced combat in any war, in your lifetime will definitely understand what I'm saying. But I can only describe my experience. We all face different types of battles and we all have different reactions, and we all have different types of scars. Either physically or psychologically. And I'm describing mine. But there's one that stays the same, is love for fellow comrade and love for country.

And we're going to meet some of the strangest people, even if they are our comrades. Am I right about that? Because I know I think I met some guys, that I thought, what are they doing in the military? Well, when I wrote this, the Marines will enlist practically anyone.

As I said, I was ordered to be point man for eight months of my time in Vietnam, and only because I made a small target. Sergeants and lieutenants told me not to worry about being the main target if attacked by the enemy. Thought to myself, yeah right!! Try convincing someone

ROBERT GARCIA

else. But what was I to do. Disobey orders, that wasn't happening with me.

I was put into very difficult situations, that sometimes I wondered what would have happened if I would have been court martialed. What a catastrophe that would've been for the future I'm experiencing and living now. Because I had been very arrogant to two of my lieutenants, and came very very close in getting court martialed with one of them.

This one of my times I cussed out this one lieutenant, didn't feel too good about it after I had yelled at him, and cussed him. We're on an operation, company strength, hottest as hell. A hundred and fifteen to hundred and twenty degrees, and ninety to a hundred percent humidity. I would call that hot, would you? Of course. We walked, it seemed like ten to twelve miles in such heat. My God. I've recently researched, and asked which is the worst, humid weather or dry weather? Received an answer, dry weather is the better of the two bad conditions. All of us were extremely dehydrated, and water wasn't all we needed. We needed rest. I was our platoon's first squad leader, and was monitoring my men very close, and a couple of them were getting over heated, to the point of passing out. And I was trying not to let that happen. Thinking at the time, this lieutenant would have that into consideration. So my radio man informs me, he thinks he's going to pass out, and he's completely out of water, so I slow my squad down to give him and another one of my men some of my water. And what's wrong with that, right? Well apparently that was completely wrong with this lieutenant, so he takes advantage of his commanding position and yells at me, "hey you get your f**k**g squad up there", which blew me away, I couldn't believe what I was hearing, so I respond, "what did you say" in return he says it again, "I said to get your f**k**g squad up there", and the next thing what comes out of my mouth and I couldn't believe it either, "f**k you, and he tells me, "what did you just say" so now it's on, I repeat it, "I said f**k you" and I thought something seriously was going to happen to me. Because he yells back, "you and I are going to talk about this, when we get to our destination, I say, "yes sir" I thought, oh my god, what did I just say. What's a man to do in that situation? Leave your men to pass out from heat stroke, or obey this lieutenant? So I thought I was doing the right thing, trying to not have any of my men have heat strokes.

Yes I was doing the right thing, by helping my men to prevent them from getting heat strokes. But I was not doing the right thing by yelling and cussing the lieutenant out. I was completely out of line. Because he would have had all the right to court martial me. So now I'm either pissed off or very worried. Always thought, since boot camp, we're supposed to help our fellow comrade to save their lives. But now I'm about to find out what's really in store for me and my future. Worried, yes of course I was worried, and pissed at myself because I let my temper control my emotions. Men in my squad of course were concerned, and I appreciated that, what is this lieutenant going to do after my anger flared up. There again my mama's prayers were at work again, even in this extreme situation. My life's future in all of my experiences in the Marine Corp, were all in the hands of this platoon commander. At the snap of his decision would all be over. Wow, imagine that. But my mom's prayers were answered by God's will. Unbelievable? Yes I couldn't believe it. We all get to our destination according to our lieutenant. Hours of hiking, and humping up and down sand dunes, in and out of elephant grass. Elephant grass? Giant leaves of grass, over eight feet tall, and about three to four inches wide with razor sharp edges. Cut you up in an instant. And don't let it get infected, you're just getting into more danger. Infection and decease. Took on sniper firing from different locations, from the enemy, it wasn't easy, and it's never easy in a combat situation.

Having very close encounters with death has always been difficult to accept, but what are we to do, can't run from it, we have to face it head on, kill or be killed. That's just the way the Marine Corp trained me. And the Corp has been in existence for over two hundred and fort years. And I never thought I would be very proud to be part of that history. But I am very proud. So why shouldn't I be, didn't know it back then, somebody was looking at me, as to what was I was doing. And awarded for my service.

So after we took on sniper fire, and trying to get to our destination, as quickly as possible, getting dug in, forming a perimeter. And after all of that, and as exhausted as we all were, not wanting to, but I had to face my predicament, to see what was the lieutenant going to tell me, and what his decision to do with me. Nervous? You damn straight I was. But I had to face him anyway. Just a man facing another man. Difference being, at war, one man is a platoon commander and the other man is just a corporal. As I approach the commander, as he was just dug in. "lieutenant, did you have something to say to me?" So surprised, and so happy what he says next, "No, get the f**k out of here" Could care less when he cussed me again, because this time I kept my mouth shut, and this time I was a wise smart ass, to not put my foot in my mouth. Because if not, my mouth would and could get me in serious trouble. And trouble I didn't need at this point of the war game. Because that's what all wars have been, old men's war games. At the expense of young men's lives. Am I right or wrong?

No one will ever know how relieved I was, when the lieutenant dismissed me. Getting back to my squad, one of my squad members, informs me, "hey corporal, the lieutenant likes you, the way you confronted him and stood up for your men."

It continues to amaze me, when I think of those times in Vietnam, and I know we all have our own stories to tell. But for now this one's mine.

Being so lucky and blessed while being in the Marines, with my platoon commanders. My first encounter with my first lieutenant not knowing how to read a map, which was so scary. Nothing ever happened with that one.

Then I reminisced about another encounter, my second platoon commander. We didn't seem to hit it off as well. He didn't seem to understand why I wouldn't salute him, right in front of God's creation, where the enemy could see and know who's a commanding officer. Couldn't believe it, he asked me, "corporal, why don't you ever want to salute me"? I responded with confusion. "What, can't believe you're asking me to point you out in front of the enemy that could be watching us this very moment. You should have seen the dumb stupid look on his face. He says "Oh my God" and then turned around and walked away. With no response, guess he knew I was right. Like I said, he and

I locked horns with disagreements out in the field, or like we all called it, out in the bush.

With disagreements with commanders, I had disagreements with squad members as well. Don't we? Here I'm just a squad leader, but I can't imagine how hard it is to command a company, a battalion, a regiment, or a division of Marines. Na, I was ok just being a squad leader, that was enough for me. It can even make you crazy.

Going back to my first fire fight, when I was just two weeks in country. Didn't mention this one important of that night being shot at, and almost getting killed. I was stuck in dried branches, all tangled. When I was finally able to get myself up, completely in chaos, kept feeling rounds flying around me. Although when I wrote this, didn't seem to self realize, that during that night battle, in nineteen sixty eight I was literally walking on the edge of life and death. Bombs exploding everywhere, we could hear mortars being fired, and the continued rounds flying everywhere. But the look on my squad leader's face, while shooting the enemy I have never forgotten that look for over fifty four years. No I will not forget that look on his face. It didn't look human. Since this was my first real fire fight, having that scenario in my mind, thinking about it as I wrote this, what was I to expect when we were involved in making decisions to protect your fellow comrades, and that he did very bravely. Little did I know, I would become like him, gung-ho. Who-raw. Semper Fi, Always Faithful.

Moving on with my love for God, my comrades and country, exactly in that order.

I believe it was a blessing to be a Marine, because it's not all about being a soldier, it's about loving to help anyone that needs help. I've pretty much been that way all my life.

And thanks to God and thanks for my Dad for being a good roll model in showing me how to respect people no matter what race they are. But we will always run into others that give a hoot about anyone other than themselves. They're simply born that way, they can't help it. Just like evil can't help being bad. Don't take my word for it, but I've had people tell me, that I'm a good person. Found out that to be true, because after seventy some years, I've been happily married to a better person than me. And that's what makes us one, a molded loving couple.

During the Vietnam era, the draft had come back again after World War Two. And I'll never understand that choice of enlisting into the Marine Corp. It completely threw me off my rocker after I realized what I signed, back at the recruiting office. There are many guys that think, still today, that we were all drafted, I've had to correct a few of them.

As I was saying, we have to put up with all sorts, even at war. Trusting everyone and anyone with our lives. From the president on down. Well while I was in Vietnam, in all the operations I was in, we're ordered to perform or else get charged with disobedience, insubordination, and even treason. Wow. And thank God I obeyed every order. But like I mentioned earlier, I had disagreements with all three of my lieutenants while over in Nam. It was quite difficult to obey a commander when he's just arrived, and I've been there more than three months. Then one of them wanted me to salute him, in the middle of a site, where the North Vietnamese Army would know he's an officer. What a joke. Often wondered, what kind of training do Marines go through, to become an officer? Because the way I see it, with how these three lieutenants were, I could've become a lieutenant.

In an other incident with this lieutenant that didn't know that he would be putting himself to be recognized as an officer, had been calling me for a while on the radio. We were guarding a bridge for several days, and he wanted me to let him know if everything was okay. And I was ignoring him, which could've gotten me into a lot of trouble, and it almost did. And during our time there guarding this bridge, we had some encounters of the enemy. Took on some sniper fire here and there. So I finally respond to the lieutenant, and what does he say, "Get your ass over here" What he didn't know, that we were all smoking pot. So now I have to get my ass, across the bridge and to his headquarters on the double. I knock on the door, the sergeant opens the door, and the lieutenant grabs me, and throws me up against the wall, thinking to myself, wow what is this asshole doing. I had immediate reaction, I shrugged my helmet off my head, and about to slam the lieutenant, he immediately says, "What are you gonna do" I say "I'm gonna hit you, to defend myself from you." "You just threw me against the wall, what do expect me to do" He tells me, "get your ass out of my hut" I say, "with pleasure"

The platoon sergeant couldn't believe it looking so surprised, as I walked out. There we go again, underestimation. I had many experiences of bullies and bigger guys than myself, underestimating guys like me. And have always surprised them, with aggression. I'm not saying that all big guys are bullies, but I think most of them are. And that's too bad for them, because why can't we all get along. That's impossible, men will always be who they want to be, evil. There again, I'm not saying everyone is a bad evil person. Thought many times about that confrontation with the lieutenant, but he learned to respect me, like I had respected him.

With the same lieutenant that I had a confrontation with, we were on an operation and gotten into some shit, against the enemy, just another day at war.

Again he wanted my presence asap after having a severe battle with the N.V.A. Didn't have a clue what he wanted to see me about. But in turned out peaceful, thank God. So I'm at his presence, at attention. He tells me, he's really honored to have me as his first squad leader, and wanted to know how I felt about that. "Corporal, I'm real honored to have you as my first squad leader, how do you feel about that"? I surprised him, "I don't like it" He was amazed, with a response, "You don't like it, why the hell not" My response "But I don't have a choice, I wouldn't want a fresh boot coming from the states ordering me how to fight a war when I've been here six months, he might get me killed" he says "Dismissed corporal" guess he got the message. Have never liked the idea that new replacements, or new officers coming fresh from the states, but that's how war has always been. Guess it just made sense to the lieutenant, and couldn't deny what I said to him.

That lieutenant might had been about three or four years older than me, but when fighting a war, age has never made any difference, it's about common sense, if you don't have common sense, you can get soldiers killed.

But If you really think about three quarter of the things we do in life, it's all about common sense, because if we don't have some, we're pretty well doomed, on this side of life.

Don't know if you've noticed, but If you have, I'm a real strong believer of the afterlife. As I've said before, you don't have to believe what you read and what I write. And I wasn't much of a believer before, but I'm old now. And this again has never and never will make any difference how old we are. But the sooner we read God's message, the sooner we'll see clarity of this short life and the life after, for eternity. And believe me, at nineteen or twenty, I was already ready, or should I say, ready or not to go into God's arms, as I am now. At least I think I'm ready. There again I'm showing doubt. We have to be ready for God's coming.

Guess I've been ready since I was seven years old, of course I wasn't ready at seven, and at this war at nineteen where our government sent us to, wasn't ready either And I was ready, when I enlisted. Just didn't know about either facing death, at seven, nor at nineteen, twenty nor twenty one. I spent two birthdays in Nam. Just thought I'd mention that. Because it's true, but since every Marine that went to Nam, it was a thirteen month stretch at war. Wow, another forget me not. Didn't have the opportunity to celebrate my twenty first birthday back home. But I made it home alive when I was twenty one, so that's fair, right?

Another forget me not, whenever a chaplain had the chance he would announce that there would be mass at the risk of getting shot in Nam. And I would be one of the few that would show up. And I felt good about it. Maybe I felt good about going to mass even if it was outside, because I felt like my soul was clean. But I also felt my mama's prayers within my soul, and spirit. Spiritually speaking, God has been with me all my life. Just like he has with others.

For all the veterans, because it's not just about the Marines, when it comes for God, your fellow comrade and country. We all should be thankful for the country we live in. And that my brothers and sisters, is why I enlisted into the Marines, back then at the Vietnam era, to save my comrades. As I've mentioned we all had our problems not only with our commanding officers, but our fellow squad members, but I only had one. One of my squad member accused me of being racist. What? What? Couldn't believe it, because I had the happiest squad in the platoon, can't imagine even saying that, happiest squad!! And many others wanted to be in my squad. And was proud to be their squad leader. But this guy thought I was racist against him. Couldn't understand him by a long shot. And he was scandalous about it, because he kept repeating it, to the point, I had to tell him to shut up. And I kept telling him to shut up, until I couldn't take anymore, so I charged him and hit him square in the mouth. But that didn't stop him, it only made him mad. And in the nick of time, came another squad member of mine, asking me if I needed any help, I say, go ahead, and he charges the guy that accused me of being racist. And my side guy took care of that mess. And even came back to this guy asking him, do you still think I'm racist? He was just one of those guys that shouldn't have been in the military. But who am I to say, who is supposed to be in the military or not. No one, that's who.

And he became my weakest link in our squad, which was first squad of our platoon, of Bravo company. But that's how the Marine Corp has always been, you're only as strong as your weakest link. And I was okay with that. The thing that bothered me was when he accused me of being racist, because that was simply not true, and I'm still not racist today. I thank Dad for my philosophy of racism. God created us all equal, from the beginning. Unfortunately there is still racism today in the world. And probably will always be. Don't know about you guys, but since I was very young, when I would see a few guys talking and laughing, and noticed close to see, a white man, a black man, a hispanic man, and a asian man having a good time and enjoying each other's company. That would amaze me, thinking what a beautiful view when people of all colors can be happy together. I've only seen that maybe three times, in my over seventy of my age of my life. Sad isn't it? Because we live in a corrupt and difficult world, because man makes it difficult. With this guy in my squad, that was different, and not because he was black, but because he was different in the way he thought. He stood out compared to his squad comrades, because there were other black members in our squad. And we all got along, but he wouldn't accept that. He would point me out, saying I was treating him different compared to the others.

Never knew if he continued with his attitude, probably so, because the other members were not accepting him. One day another member of our squad came up to me, after a long hump of walking, we all would take advantage of any bomb crater that had any water and wash ourselves the best we could. Well he didn't want to wash himself, and if we didn't wash ours, we would stink very badly, and would disrespect your fellow comrade. So this other comrade comes up to me, "Hey corporal can you order this guy to wash himself, because he stinks too bad. I responded "well how many of you guys are there, to him" he says "well there's ten of us" I say "well wash him up, take some soup and a brush, and some water, and have a good time washing him up" and they did wash him up. Boy was he more pissed off at me. The old saying went, it's better to be pissed off than to be pissed on. We hardly ever spoke. Well he was making things harder for himself, because instead of going with the flow, he was going against the wind.

As time goes by in the middle of time at war, things became worse, by no means did it get better. Especially for my own self, started to feel burned out. From not eating properly, not getting enough sleep. But still I had to perform no matter what. A few times more than a few, we had been put on alert, and by orders by the top, by no means no one was to sleep for thirty six hours. In case some of you don't know, that's a day and a half. I'm now suffering the side effects of putting all of us at one hundred percent alert by ordering us not to sleep for thirty six hours. Even though none of us liked the idea of not getting any sleep. Appreciated that order, because that's a big factor why I came home alive. Among many other reasons why I didn't come home in a body bag. Not letting us sleep was one of many other reasons why I came alive. And one hundred percent of being on high alert paid off, because we were attacked, and of course there were casualties, that's always unfortunate, in all wars.

Any one of you have all the right to brag and be proud, if all of you veterans did a honorable service to our God, fellow comrade and country. And you know, or you should know, FREEDOM IS NOT

FREE. And freedom has never been, it never has been, and it never will be free. Evil will always want to attack America, because we live in one nation under God.

As long as the world is and has been, and as long as man exists, Jealousy, Racism, Greed, will always want to attack the free part of the world. Maybe that's why I see messages that are out there, that the world will come to an end sooner than we think. But there's a lot of disbelievers, that will not agree with me. And that's okay as well.

Mentioning before, about that lieutenant that wanted me to salute him in the middle of no where, and possibly where the enemy would see him as an officer. Well in this other incident, our company had been in a battle, and of course there were casualties on both sides, but the enemy suffered the most. And after that catastrophe, the lieutenant noticed that american grenades that had detonated by his bunker. Boy was he furious and scared. And furious and scared he should've been. And who did he ask, what was the meaning of that, yours truly. When he wanted to know, why detonated grenades were targeted by his bunker. I had to tell him. "Sir, don't you get it, your unit doesn't like you, and they want to kill you" But I'm not mixed up in that". You should have seen the look on his face, he looked like a little boy, scared to death. He asks me, "but why do they want to kill me"? "You're too arrogant, and you're too into showing your authority" "We know you're a lieutenant and we know your our leader, but you should lead as a team member, or things happen, that's unfortunate "Can you imagine how that would've looked to the higher ups, an officer being found dead, killed by his own men, and not by the enemy. Going home in a body bag, and your family finding out how he was killed.

Needless to say, he changed his attitude or he would have be found dead. All that attitude he had before, had changed, thank God for him.

Even before I was deployed to Vietnam, I had read about men turning on their own leaders, all through history, mutiny being a very bad thing to happen within your own unit, and was so glad that didn't happen in our unit.

I was very glad that this platoon commander had changed his way of leading his platoon. We ended up becoming close comrades.

We didn't like each other, nor didn't dislike each other, just became close comrades. We were in more firefights as our time continued as a fighting unit, and as a fighting team. And from that time of my life at war and to my current life I live now, have never applied for a position to be liked, just respected. And to do the job I was hired to do.

Continuing on our war effort being a squad team leader, as how I liked to be referred to. There was this one battle we were in, and was so glad I wasn't point man at that time or I probably would've gotten killed. Because the point man got killed. We were only company strong, meaning we only had about two hundred men. Well we were on a mission on a very hot day in Nam, and we were on the very border of Vietnam and Laos. That was a very close call for our unit. Being about a hundred and fifteen degrees hot, we stopped along the ridge for a quick snack break, when our point man walked maybe ten feet away from his unit, when suddenly an enemy soldier appears out of nowhere. When they both realized who they each were, the reflexes kicked in, pulling out their weapons and shooting at each other, killing one another in an instant. I'm suddenly crawling with a claymore mine and setting it up as quickly as I could, and blowing it up, and we gave them a run for their lives as how we wanted. Because finding out later that the NVA were battalion strong, which meant we were outnumbered four to one. But they didn't know that, because of our fire power, we had them on the run. Thank God for another miracle.

Comparing Dad's World War Two experiences and my Vietnam experiences, it's been quite an ordeal how I finally realized, as father and son we came back home alive, from two different wars of course. Twenty five years apart from each other. Dad being in Okinawa by the end of World War Two, in nineteen forty five, and if he would have arrived like he said in nineteen forty three, he might not have survived the war. and I arriving in Okinawa by nineteen sixty nine after serving in Vietnam for thirteen months, and almost getting court martialed.

As old men as we both were when I wrote this. Him being ninety six, I being seventy four, never thought we were similar, but we are, whether I wanted that way or not. It's always been how God wants things on his will, not ours. God's will, to us can be catastrophic, and it can also be miraculous, but God has always been miraculous.

Not too long before I decided to write this life story of mine, Dad informed me that he felt lucky he didn't go to war sooner than he did, as I he told me, when WW 2 was going strong. Because the fact that he couldn't speak English, what slowed his process of going to Okinawa. The very fact that he couldn't speak English, and the Army having to send him to a English class, and was sent later to Okinawa when World War Two was just about declared over. Is why he came home alive. With me, I was closer to getting killed, by a day, during the Tet Offensive in Vietnam, but the Tet Offensive kept right on with continuous aggression, even after I arrived. And being point almost by the beginning of my arrival, because of my stature in size. Had to accept that, it was an order I had to obey. But there again it was God's miracles I survived. Because, and I'll repeat, I walked point for eight months. If you think that's not very long being the first man to get shot in case of an attack, for you youngsters, hope you never are put in that predicament.

Here's another scary incident I went through, and for the life of me, will never know how my comrades were able to pull me up and out of this muddy cliff I had slid down I'd say at least five hundred feet down, and slipping and sliding I went. It was no joke, but my whole time in Vietnam, had never been a joke, day or night. But that's war right? Just have to take life or death situations seriously is all, and I think I did, after all, received an award for how a Lieutenant General described my actions in different battles, to try saving lives. But had always thought any other soldier would have done the same thing. Because that's how all of us are trained to do. Save our comrades lives not our own.

Anyway on the night I slid down about five hundred feet or more, I wasn't counting, down to, I thought to my immediate death. Another day of my life or death, walking point, but all I did was take a forward step. And monsoon rain was very heavy, could barely see. Company strong, am ordered to pull out, forward go private, and that very first step caught me by a big surprise. So I go sliding down, down, down, through muddy vines just barely missing getting hit by many rocks, oh lord, I was petrified. Just another day thought I was gonna die. For all of you combat veterans, do you remember those days of close to death? Because for me I've never forgotten those close days facing death right in the face.

Like I said it was very muddy, feel like I was sliding down in shit, literally cried and screamed, because I was going straight to hell, to my death. Or even if I would have survived, how in the hell is anyone going to get me out of this hole. Thinking by trying to pull me out, someone else can fall and end up with me. Wouldn't that have been fun. And another thought, what if we would have gotten into a serious fire fight with an on coming enemy. I would have been left and forgotten. Wasn't that a nice thought. Nothing nice about it. I think I've had that nightmare of my life all of my life. And that's probably just another reason why I have insomnia.

Literally this was an act of God right beside me all the way down this hell hole.

A part of me died in that hole I slid into, that night in sixty eight in Nam. That scared the shit out of me. After that and through my life and up until now, nothing has ever scared me like that again. Thinking I'll be long forgotten about. Then it seemed like an angel over me, could barely hear some soldier's voice. Probably yelling from the top of his lungs. "Private, are you okay?" Responding I say, "Someone get me out of this hell hole, help me". And I really thought they would try to make it look like they tried their best and then just report it, as just a private missing in action. I really thought that. I really did. But I was wrong, boy oh boy, I thanked God I was wrong. "Private we're going to connect all of our rifle belts together and pull you out, okay" quickly responding, "okay" thinking, I couldn't believe what I was hearing, that they're going to try to get me out of that hole cliff, a part of the ground that just disappeared from beneath me.

That sliding hell, and getting pulled out by my fellow Marines, I wasn't the same, for the rest of my stay in Vietnam. Could you blame me. I was asked after getting pulled up, "are you okay Private, do you still want to go out on patrol, because you don't have to." I tell him "no no, I'll still go, nothing can scare me now, no man can scare me now" my comrades laughed about that, but I wasn't laughing, because I didn't think it was funny.

But in war, anything else can and will scare the hell out of you or should I say me. Like watching a comrade get shot and die right before your eyes. Now that's scary. Don't you guys think? I mean we're supposed to save lives, not see them die. That demoralizes you, and that's the whole enemy's plan. Demoralization is a weapon we can't shoot at, because it's within our own spirit, and that scares us the most.

As I've remanence waking up my flash backs through my life, I've oftentimes thought to not talk about these war incident experiences just to anyone. And I've oftentimes also look at that time of war in my life, that I make myself blank out. Does that sound weird? Probably so, and then when I start writing it down like I did when I wrote this, I start remembering many things that happened to me. And they're not good happy memories.

But we all have many sad and bad memories, if you've been in war.

So how do we handle this life of transitioning from military combat to civilian life? Today for the young veterans the VA has a transitioning program to help you manage from the military and back to civilian life, because it's not an easy change. Maybe that's a good program for them, I wish them a lot of luck. But in our time, coming from Vietnam all psycho, there was no such thing as transitioning. Not for us, and not for WW2 and before that. This is an improvement for the veterans, about time, right? Better late than never, is what I say.

The government draft us, including during WW2, for Vietnam, send us to a war, that according to many, we weren't supposed to be in. I just thought I'd enlist anyway. Didn't think much about it at the time, but looking at my life, how it's been kind of upsetting, by no fault but my own. But the best part of my life was enlisting into the Marines. Because I wouldn't be where I'm at today. Thank God, and thank the VA, for approving me, from my disabilities.

As I continue my life's writings. Have to be grateful to God and grateful for my wife as well because I wouldn't be where I am today, without neither one of them.

After that scary night of falling into that hole, or maybe it was a cliff, I became more aggressive with less fear. If I'm going to die, I'm going to die.

I became more of a God fearing man than ever before. And God was with me everyday and every step of the way, in Vietnam. Little would I know, and learn to realize and maybe because I'm now an old man, God has been with me all of my life.

Continuing on my duties as a Marine. Didn't know it over fifty years ago, that while I served my deployment, I would become less focused on my life and become more focused on saving my comrades lives. And that's exactly what I did. Didn't really think I would return home alive anyway. I really thought I wouldn't come home alive.

Unfortunately not every Marine or any soldier for that matter focus on saving any life but their own, and sometimes not even their own. And there were those that didn't take war seriously. One evening as I was ordered as I was appointed as a fire team leader to take myself and three others, on a reconnaissance location. Before we headed out to our destination, I was warned about one Marine, and to be very cautious about him. In other words, do not trust him. Rumor was, this man, I'm not gonna call him a Marine, because Marines are not to do what he was doing. He was labeled a sleeper. Rumor was, this guy would fall asleep when he's supposed to be awake as a guard on watch for any enemy movement, including to be aware of maybe attack us. And you veterans should know, to be labeled a sleeper is not a good label, and a terrible reputation. Well I planted that information deep within my head, because that kind of information, we should take very seriously. And I did. And we're on our way on our journey and to our destination on our reconnaissance patrol. And didn't dare forget what I was warned about this guy. We finally arrived about two clicks from our main unit, and we were getting settled and to be done very quietly, and quietly we had to be, or our whole purpose would be compromised, and could get us killed. Especially if one is supposed to be awake and alert, while his comrades are relaxed and asleep. So when it was this sleeper's turn to be on guard. I got along side of him and whispered close to him, "hey dude, I've heard you like to fall asleep on watch", "please I'm warning you, don't fall asleep on us tonight" and how did he react, he threw a hand gesture at me, like he was saying, f**k you. And how did I react, "oh yeah" Then I point at my boot and I say to him, "You see this size eight boot, if you fall asleep tonight I'm planting this boot into your face". Needless to say he didn't think I would kick his face when he did fall asleep. And I didn't get any sleep that night as usual. Because I kept my eye on him to see if he would actually fall asleep. And I catch him nodding out, bobbing his head around, as he's about to fall asleep. I sneak up on him, and I cock my leg keeping my eyes on him, and I kick him as hard as I could. His body goes down and back up again. He kind of looked funny, but I didn't laugh. It wasn't a laughing matter by no means. My point I was trying to make to him, was not to kick him, but to stay awake and not to get us all killed. After that incident on having to kick this poor fool. That he thought I just wanted to kick him. So he try's to scowl me and try's to cuss me and threaten me that he's going to kick my ass. I scowled him instead, "shut up you, I just saved your life, you could be dead, we all could be dead, you have anything to say, save it to when we get back to our unit. He quieted down, for all of our sakes. So we make it back, and I approached this fool, "you have anything to say to me", he responds, "No I don't", I say "didn't think so"

Researched many times in my life, and even before I was deployed, and I still do a lot of research to this day. But while I was over there in Vietnam, commanders were constantly telling us all, and always reminding us, to stay awake while we're out there, because Charlie was on the look out twenty four seven to watch us make mistakes.

"Stay awake people, or Charlie is gonna kill ya, by slashing your throuts when you fall asleep on your watch. Please stay awake" Well that stayed echoing in my head, because I didn't want to die that way.

From that night that I had to do something wasn't proud of, by kicking that guy. That taught me a lesson, to not trust just anyone.

First having to trust a lieutenant that didn't know how to read a map, which left an imprint in my frightening moments in Nam, then this guy that falls asleep on watch. Felt like death was following me everywhere I went. While in Nam, had the flash back of that truck crash in nineteen fifty five, that still haunted me while in Nam. Don't think much about it anymore. Too old to worry about those things. Physical death is gonna catch me any day anyway. That's the death I'm not afraid of anymore, its the second death I'm deathly afraid of. We're all physically doomed. It's not if we die, it's when. Guess I've been ready for God's judgement since I was a boy. Ain't that something. Didn't know it then. But since then, I've evaluated my life, and I've been in so many scary moments,n that I've finally let go of fear of leaving this physical world. God will judge me accordingly. That's why I'm a God fearing man today. for just a few years now. I finally woke up. And I finally answered God's knocking. I firmly believe I'm alive today because of God. If I go deeper, we're all alive because of God. Just trying to describe to all about myself in particular. Facing death as a boy until my present life. Remember DIED THREE TIMES LIVED ONCE. I say three times, and I know we all face death more than three times in our lives. I'm trying very hard to show you the scenario of the three times I died psychologically, because each time death nearly touched me, or to put it in another way, each time death nearly took me. The time as a boy in that accident, and during my thirteen month deployment in Vietnam, and in my return from my serving my country, having a great reputation as a civilian. Then something fell out of my life.

God. Became completely disconnected from God. God didn't ever close the door, I closed the door on God.

I'll continue on my life's writing, and try not to bore my readers. And maybe I'll still bore some of you. That is if anyone dares to read this.

The term, TRUST, and someone you might call, FRIEND, is a very sacred thing in my heart and soul. On the other hand, Dad trusted anyone and called anyone friend. Guess you can say, Dad was a great teacher for me, to not do anything he did. It seemed like every time he trusted someone, he'd get betrayed. And I heard about this one time, my mother told me, he called someone friend, that wanted to take him outside and shoot my Dad. Wow, so you see what I mean? Within our own relations, Dad was betrayed, manipulated and lied to. When I wasn't a loving son, I would manipulate and lie to my Dad. The day I wrote this, it makes me emotional, because I really feel sorry him, my own Dad.

Continuing on my deployment in Vietnam. And as death got closer, but as I said, wasn't afraid of death anymore. What's the old saying about fear? Especially being in a war situation, the enemy is not going to kill you, but fear will. My philosophy was and still is, fear management. Everyone has fear at one time or another, but it's how we manage fear. That could and will decide our fate. And if it's our time it's our time, no way of getting around it. You can agree or disagree but that's the way I've lived practically all my life, my philosophy of living or dying.

Here's another life saving incident, it wasn't from someone saving my life, but I made a choice to save a wounded comrade. To this day can't come up with a reason why I decided to save this Marine's life, while we were all held down by a sniper. Can't find the reason, but motivation took over my decision, when no one else wanted to.

Now I know you can picture me, a five foot eight inches tall shorty, weighing approximately a hundred and forty pounds, and this Marine I'm about to go get out of the sniper's range of fire, and I know none of you won't believe me, well then don't believe it. But it happened. This guy stood six foot two inches, weighing about a hundred and eighty five pounds. And when I wrote this, reading it to myself, it's unbelievable to me as well. Others called me crazy, but I didn't care. That was not on my mind. Saving lives was our training, and saving my friend was on my mind. Anyway, there were a couple of snipers, maybe some mortars being launched at us, and this poor guy was laid out wounded. I couldn't bare the thought he laying down with pain, and we're just on the side lines watching him die. I just couldn't stand it. We were even ordered not to go any further. I thought, what, what was that I heard? Out of no where I make the decision, and take off running towards our comrade, even he thought, "What are you doing, I out weigh you, and I'm much taller than you." I say, "shut up hold my neck, as I used the military hold. No I didn't and couldn't pick him up, of course not. But I did the best I could, and I dragged him from harms way. And saved his life. Am I bragging, yes I am, because to save lives is a big reason to brag about. No matter who you are.

ROBERT GARCIA

As I mentioned about how we all let fear control us, until I came to face fear and death right to his face. Was it easy, no it wasn't. It took practice after seeing some of your own comrades die. When I returned home from my deployment from Vietnam, there was no transitioning. Didn't even know what the word meant.

After saving my comrade's life, received a tongue lashing from my captain, couldn't blame him, no higher ups want to see more lives lost..

But you think I stopped there. Took my training very seriously. To save lives, and that's what I'm going to do. Didn't know when would I save more lives, but I knew we were going out again on more operations, because I still had more time to do in Vietnam. And I also thought, maybe I'll die before my tour would expire. That was a nice thought. But as we all should know, especially if you're close to my age, if our time is up, it's up. In other words, if it's our time to check out, then it's time to meet our maker. You can be stillborn, or live to over a hundred years old, and between those years pass and leave this world. But age has nothing to do with how we live or die. What I'm saying, to have death brush by you so closely, like it did me, it's had a tremendous affect on my life, and how I behave today. Because I faced life and death experiences that I literally thought I died, and the third and last time I should have died, God gave me another life and will never understand why. Oh I have my own idea and belief why God has given me numerous chances but that's my belief. And you people won't believe it, at least I think some of you won't.

At this part of my life I'm still not finished with my obligation of my life as a soldier in Vietnam. Had been promoted twice and getting shorter, shorter in time in that is, not my physical height. Funny funny. During my promotions, Private First Class, to corporal, which by then, I'm now a nco, (Non-Commition-Officer), and a few times temporary sergeant.

As I've mentioned earlier, as long as man exists, there will always be Jealousy, Greed, and Violence. Well, during my promotions, there were a few comrades that hated when I would receive a promotion. Jealous, damn right they were. But those are who they are, they can't help it. Just like those that are evil, they can't help it they're evil, it's in their spirit, because I believe they're possessed. Sad thing for them, right? They're all over the world, and I have a few in my family.

And you probably do too.

My thirteen months of my obligation to my country, as a Vietnam Marine, will stay in my heart and soul as a right to serve honorably for the rest of my life, even if many say it was a war we've shouldn't have been in. Well, that could be a matter of opinion if you look at it from all angles. That's like saying we shouldn't have been in any war. Doesn't anyone remember WW2. According to the president at that time, when Prime Minister Churchill, and Communist president Stalin were practically begging the United States to help Europe, fight against Hitler. But our president said that we didn't belong in that war. But of course the Vietnam war was completely different than WW2. But it was still a war of blood shed because I was there and saw blood spilled. And over fifty eight thousand soldiers lost their lives. So as far as I'm concerned, we don't belong in any war, if people are going to die. But that would be impossible, by saying that we wouldn't be in any war, that would be like living in heaven, in a perfect world. And we're not even close to that in this physical life we live in.

If we lived in a perfect world, we wouldn't need God. Well you and I know that we're far from living in a perfect world. And since we live in a corrupt society, God gives us an option to choose where we want to be for eternity. I choose to be with God, my lord and savior for eternity. Don't know about you guys. If you believe it or not, the lord is coming to judge the living and the dead. Mentioned earlier we had our differences, my officers and my squad members and I.

During another battle with the enemy, we were being heavily attacked from all sides, but somehow we were able to get a regiment of the NVA have them on the run. Unbelievable. We were chasing and shooting a regiment of North Vietnamese Army. With our air support and naval cannon gun trouble." And I'm glad I didn't shoot, because like my comrade told me, I could have gotten into a lot of trouble. Shooting an unarmed NVA soldier. So we just stood around this hand coming out of the ground. It must had been around nine or ten pm, when this was happening. Being patient was my problem.

Because I didn't know what to expect. We waited and we waited. We witnessed the first NVA come out, a very skinny man, no weapon, no ammo, no food, and no water. And a regiment of NVA came out of the ground all suffering from thirst and hunger, and no ammunition for the weapons we found in the tunnels. We were watching a catastrophe, and a defeated communist army. Who knows how long they had been down hidden from civilization. The look on all of their faces told a sad story, on each one their experience of this Vietnam war.

Life wasn't important living in Vietnam during war time, survival was. But it didn't matter whether you lived there or were deployed there. Life was indispensable back then in that country, Vietnam. From what I've read in today's living standards, it's much easier to live there today. But I'd never live there. It's in my blood as a Vietnam veteran, too many Americans lost their lives over there. And I would never live in a country where I saw my comrades die. That's called respect, is how I see it.

Have any of you Vietnam veterans ever see a bunch of orphans starving? It would almost make me cry. Vietnamese children running behind us, while we were driving a small flat bed truck, taking a bunch of food us Marines were throwing away, and these children were running right behind us. It was a sad sight to watch. And I was one that saw those poor children starving. There Since the Great Depression in our country, we've pretty well have had it made. People starve out here, because they want to, but they don't have to. We've all seen young and old alike stand in many corners in this country of ours asking for money. And if any of those homeless people in our country stand at the right corner, they can probably make a good living. Only in America.

But don't get caught inside of a bunker for even a hand grenade to explode, it'll kill you, from the concussion. Concussion is so powerful. Had seen what happened to a soldier when a bomb of some sort exploded while he was he was inside a bunker. Blood coming out of his ears, his eyes, his nose, and the shrapnel made him look like hamburger meat. And even if he would survive, psychologically he would be torn.

For you Vietnam veterans, combat veterans that is, remember the Viet cong, and their booby traps? Very barbaric and very inhumane, oh did I mention evil, yes very evil. Made out of bamboo spikes, either they would have these traps being held by a thin rope and when a soldier would be patrolling along he would trip off another thin string, and here comes the spiked, either a huge ball or a tree, coming at terrific speed. And leave any man with huge holes in your body. Another horrible sight to see.

Personally the enemy really pissed me off. We were dug in, in a perimeter, one big circle, the best we could. Different parts of our unit going on patrol, on reconnaissance, to see where could Charlie be. But we had a big spooky surprise, right in the middle of our perimeter, and underneath our company of Marines, there were tunnels. Wow, what a flash back I had when I wrote this part of my deployment. Well, in the middle, a hand started coming out of ground. Say what. Yes I'm telling ya. A hand out of no where creeping up through the ground. Scared the shit out of us all. What did I do next? I got my m-16 into a firing position ready to cut down whoever was coming out of ground. Well, I'm glad I didn't, as I hear a yell, "Corporal don't shoot, you can get into a lot of food. I would rather die than to see any child of mine in that predicament. I wouldn't be able to bare it. Later on of my life, fortunately by the blessing of God, I'm blessed with children. But that will be later in my life's writings, and how I'm not fatherly connected with one of them anymore. Sad.

As a soldier in Nam, we would face the enemy, diseases, or for some, they would commit suicide. Remember this one Marine getting bit by a mosquito on one of his feet and never keeping the mosquito bite clean, and so it got infected. The next thing in just a few days, his foot was swelling so big, that he could hardly walk on it. The doctor told him he had gotten elephantiasis. I remember getting dysentery, man oh man. And how did I get dysentery? It wasn't very hard to catch any disease in Nam during the war. I've had diarrhea, but getting dysentery, felt I was going to die a painful death. Stomach ache, nausea. Everything I tried to eat, I would shit it out. Got so very weak. Felt like I wanted to die.

War can be a very lonely place to be, where life is not important, feeling homesick. Life was very cheap. We were all just a number, where we could be replaced. And some that lose their lives are replaced. All the time at war. Ever since man has been created, it's no big secret.

Here's another remanence of my life in Nam.

We were given C rations to consume as our dietary nutrients to satisfy our hunger everyday. But it just barely satisfied our hunger. When they only gave us one little box of C rations. We were always hungry, at least I was.

One day, and remembering those little orphans running behind us to get the food we were throwing away. So I decided to go food hunting from a bomb crater, where we used to throw away food no body wanted. Using a ammo bag and picking up canned goods. Then this fellow comrade, finds me along with others, and asks me, "hey bud what are you doing" I respond, "picking up food that everyone threw away" he says, "whatever dude" So I went about my business picking up as much food as I could. And having heating tabs to cook food during the day only, not at night. For obvious reasons.

In America anyone can migrate from any country of the world, can go to school, and if you have money coming from another country, you can start your own business and become a millionaire. Only in America. The land of the free and the land of opportunity.

We've all heard, FREEDOM IS NOT FREE, not at the cost of military lives, in all the wars America has been in. Thanks to the heroes that gave their lives for America's freedom, that's why us veterans say FREEDOM IS NOT FREE. America's freedom has never been free and it will never be. America learned the hard way, just when Japan invaded Pearl Harbor on December 7th 1941. Even though I wasn't in that war, I still know our country's history. It was a corrupt attack by Imperialism government. And it's too bad the whole country of Japan suffered, because not everyone wanted catastrophe, and that's exactly what happened.

Some countries call America the police of the world, and Japan's behavior is what caused America to behave that way.

As I mentioned witnessing Vietnam orphans, running behind us as we trucked hundreds of canned foods, on our way to throw them in, a bomb crater, we called a dump. The orphans we saw, were from three years old to about ten years old. And they were starving, and they didn't know where their parents were, presumably dead. I had one little girl come up to me, begging me for some food, it broke my heart. I gave her what I could give her, which wasn't much. And thinking to myself, even though I didn't have any children yet, how would I react if I had a child begging for fire, we had them on the run. But I had a flaw within my squad, of course. The lieutenant let me know about it. As we were on pursuit and attacking, the lieutenant came along side of me, and advised me, "you have a man missing, and you have to go look for him, it's your responsibility to find him." I already knew who my flaw was within my squad. The one that accused me of being racist, the one I punched, the one that wouldn't shut up. As I ran back to look for this idiot, and risking my life in doing so, and maybe get killed. It was overwhelming for me, thinking I probably won't find him, and if I do, he'll probably be dead, if I don't killed before I find him. Luckily for the both of us, I found him. He totally pissed me off, by finding him hiding in a deep hole, shaking like a little boy, being a tall bully of a man, that he portrayed himself. And when finding him shaking inside this hole, I yelled at him, "get your ass out of there before I shoot you myself and no one will ever find you" Fortunately for me he crawled out of that hole, because I wasn't really going to shoot him.

And fortunately for our platoon, that man was transferred, to where, will never have a clue, and didn't care. That was a God send, for a man that I thought should have never been in the military. Those kind could get men killed, including himself. I guess the lieutenant realized that and requested that man to get out.

Question to all of you veterans. How's your hearing? Because mine is all shot to hell. Wonder why. It's very obvious, in all fire fights and close bombardments well make you eventually deaf. Very hard of hearing. I experienced guys shooting their m-16s very close to my ears, and one guy was shooting so close to my head, and wasn't watching where he was aiming at. For a while our platoon rode along with a tank platoon, and the tank canons were, it seemed like one hundred times more louder than small arms, of course they are, they're canons.

Took the canned food to my bunker and as I cooked my food, the delicious smell coming out of my bunker, drew attention to my comrades. And I hear one say, "hey dude what's that I smell" I say, "the food you guys threw away." Felt sorry for them, come on in have some of your food. And they said, "oh my god this is delicious", I respond, "when it's cooked"

And that's the way we survived in Nam. At least that's how I survived.

As I was describing to you all, the booby traps, Communist Vietnamese, which we called Viet Cong, would set up barbaric dangerous traps to kill any American soldier. And unfortunately it did kill anyone walking along a jungle trail. And that's what happened to a good Marine. I say a good Marine, because he was loved by so many of us. He had a great sense of humor. Would listen to anyone that had a story to tell, and cry with you if the story was emotional. He was just one of those type of guys you could trust, and we all loved as a brother. So nice of a guy.

Almost from the beginning of my deployment in Vietnam, I had been appointed to walk point man. And for eight months I walked point, and fortunately for me nothing ever happened, close but nothing serious, nor no bodily injuries. When we were attacked by a regiment of NVA, we were attacked within the main part of our unit. Like I said I came close

As I had said, walked point for eight months, which would be an understatement to mention, it kept me on my toes, because I'd try to walk a point so quiet so we weren't heard. And many times it was literally impossible. But I was never shot, shot at. But not shot. And every time we would get into a confrontation, rounds and shrapnel fragments were on the fly, flying ever which way, and hair line close. I could feel all rounds and bomb fragments fly by my head and body. Scared shitless. Who wouldn't be.

And this poor guy, a lovable person, and a booby trap had his name on it.

Will never expose anyone's name in my life's writings, so I've left this Marine's name out of my writings on purpose.

Didn't think much about it, our comrade, our buddy, our friend, taking out a fire team to a certain location as all patrols do, to recon for information of the enemy. Well all's well love and war. Right? We've all heard that before. And nothing has never come out of it. Because of war. "All's well love and war" When I first heard that bullshit, it discussed me, because we all should know, there's nothing loving in war. So this poor guy takes his patrol, as he commenced as point man, his first and only time he's ever been point man it didn't take but maybe ten minutes, and we all hear a loud boom, can't describe it with enough words, but it was so loud. That it froze us all. Because we all knew what happened. Poor guy never had a chance. The most important thing about this good Marine, he had been bragging about going to Hawaii to be in his sister's wedding, he was so happy and proud, and anxious to go see his sister. So when we heard that loud bomb explosion, we all froze looking at one another, with disbelief. What a terrible thing to happen to a guy that didn't deserve that.

Immediately when we heard the bomb, many of us volunteered to see what happened to our buddy. When we pretty well knew what killed him. He's walking along a booby trapped trail, and he was the very first soldier to trip the bomb, point man, and it blew up in his face, ripping his head off and he was taken away in a body bag. We all were either pissed at every Vietnamese, or like myself, crying for this poor guy. Thought to myself, what a sad disaster. We could only imagine what his sister's face looked like when they gave her the sad, bad news.

I have carried that sad sad, and one of many of more bad experiences that happened to me and to others, for over fifty four years. Can you relate guys? I'm sure you can.

As sad things happen, so do scary ones within our own unit. Although my combat experience in Vietnam, thank God I only decided to do it once. And I didn't enlist for more than two years like some guys did. Because during the Vietnam era, if you were drafted or enlisted like I did, and if you enlisted for more than one tour, you're bound to go see Charlie, or the NVA, again. Although war won't take you down physically, it's bound to take you down psychologically. I've been psychotic before I went to Vietnam, if you remember my truck crash I told you about. And now here I am in Nam, facing the communist, the NVA. And facing the enemy I did, like so many others did.

ROBERT GARCIA

Hopefully those of you that read about my life, won't miss the meaning of my whole message, because it's not just about me, and my life, It's about all of us that have gone through difficulties throughout our lives, like I have. Believe that others have gone through much worse experiences than I have, that are either dead, in jail, or in an asylum. And if you're not in a asylum, then you have a tight noodle, if you know what I'm talking about. You know it. I know it. We all should know it. If we're not born with just a little bit of common sense, then we won't get far in life. We can go to college, a university, or a trade school, and graduate for the career you want, but if you don't have just a little bit of common sense, you won't be any good to anyone, including for yourself. Sad but true. Because it happened to me. I'm living proof. And was still alive when I wrote this, in my seventies. Why I've never wrote this before this, don't know why. Guess it's been eating me inside to write it. My own Dad told me, "Son, you ought to write a book, you've been through a lot more than I have", and never paid attention to that. I've had a couple of psychiatrists advise me to write this, and didn't pay attention. A little slow, yes I am. Guess that's why I'm where I'm at today. Alive and happier than I've ever been.

Meeting other Marines while in Nam, some smart and some very dumb. Again it's all about common sense. No matter how smart you are.

Met this one that thought he would try all the armed services, and by the time he became a Marine, he was twenty eight years old, the oldest in our unit. Thought to myself at the time, what is wrong with this guy? And he would have a picture of his wife and brag how beautiful she was, and on and on he went. No I wasn't jealous, I thought he was stupid, thinking what the hell is he doing in all the armed services if she's so beautiful. Never told him anything that would make him feel bad, didn't think that would be right. But one day I finally had to tell him, "you know you show everybody your wife's picture and brag how pretty she is and I've wondered why are you in the military, when you should be home with your wife" He didn't know what to say. But I think he thought about it. Time goes by, and then he requested a short leave to go see his wife. "Corporal you think I can go see my wife just to see how she's doing" I respond, "I think I can arrange that" And he's gone for a while, and comes back divorced. I just had to ask him, "So how was your trip" He wasn't too happy telling me, "Well I'm now divorced, because I didn't write to her to tell her I was coming out to see her, I surprised her as she surprised me catching her in bed with another guy" But it's happened many many times. We used to make fun, telling guys that had girlfriends or wives, "Bet Jody is bed with your girl" Boy some guys would get so pissed off.

This guy that came back divorced after discovering his wife in bed with another man, looked disgusted, heart broken and pissed at what he found. And who wouldn't be. Don't know what I was feeling when this poor guy was showing me his pretty wife's picture. Right away felt she was betraying her husband, and using him for support. That's common, right? People get betrayed everyday, all the time. But this guy's wife used him for a fool, and had probably talked him into trying all branches of services. Well he sure did, as what he told me, the navy, the army, the Air Force, and now when I met him, in Vietnam, now a Marine. It's too bad I had to punch him one other day. Because he didn't take war, and my warning to him, seriously.

Had many thoughts about this guy, in how he thought life was. Especially in a war situation, which what I saw, sucked.

This guy sure gave me a bad day, and maybe gave many of us a bad day. I say that because I found out he wasn't taking war security for the safety of fellow Marines serious. Seriousness and safety should always be the first priority in all war situations. That's how our squad had become. But this guy had a problem with that.

Let me try to describe how this guy had the problem of taking the Vietnam war serious, which by being in our squad, me and other members of our squad had an issue with that.

As most American wars have been in history, we send units from fire teams, which go out as a four man team, squads go out on patrol as a twelve or fifteen man team. All go out on a patrol, reconnaissance, which was with us at the time, in Vietnam search and destroy.

On this day as I was assigned as squad leader, and to take first squad out on patrol, we're all just doing what we were ordered to do, at least that's we all thought. No not this silly guy.

At this time being in the Corp, I thought every graduated Marine, actually thought they were true Marines. What a joke. Because it wasn't so. I mean, I know no ones perfect, but come on. At least be a better man than you were, before you enlisted in the Marine Corp.

Found out too many times, my expectations have always been too high. What I mean is, I'll expect something from someone I may love very much, and get completely disappointed. That shouldn't be anything new. But it has always knocked me off my rocker. And let's get one thing straight, when I say love anyone, I mean just that, loving brotherly. Loving for brother and country, trying to save a fellow comrade, is all I'm saying. And that's how the Marine Corp trained me. And it has always disappointed me how others don't stand up to SEMPER FI. (Always Faithful)

With all of that being said.

This disappointing of a guy, that was now in my squad, kind of surprised me. As I was saying, we're out on a patrol, and I'm walking behind my point man, with my radio man behind me, trying to be as quiet as possible.

Patrolling as quietly as we could possibly be, but that was very far from this guy's mind.

As we were patrolling by a village, I could hear him from up front of the squad, rattling on like he was walking down his neighborhood, with not a care in the world. Can anyone realize how pissed I became? I give the order to halt. I run back to this idiot to warn him to keep his f**king mouth shut. "hey dude, I can hear you way from the front of the column, quit talking, and don't make me come back and tell you again" "shut the f**k up" And do you think for one moment he listened and payed any attention? Hell no. Because as we continued on our patrol, this asshole started continuing talking his ass off again. Now this made me go nuts with rage. I practically ran back to this imbecile, now I'm gonna kick his ass. And I attack him, "didn't you hear what I told you, I've already warned you" I tore into him, I punched him so hard, I almost knocked him out. And I've never been proud of that. And I never heard a squeak from him again. In fact, since I had more time in Nam than him, I went home, and never knew what ever happened to him. But all I can do is imagine what might've happened to him, and who else's life he could've been responsible for. That's always been a scary thought.

Had felt sorry for that poor fool, but we're all suckers when it comes to relationships, right? I was engaged to get married to a every man's girl. What!! Yes, and I had already been warned about her, but I still didn't listened. Yeah, back in my teenage years, I had been dating this one girl, and it was just another girl my mom didn't like. Mom didn't much like any girl I brought home to introduce to. She would call them all whores. Yeah, I never showed mom how it bothered me when she'd say that. But later I found out that she wasn't far from the truth.

As I kept dating the girl I was planning on marrying, and then I got deployed to Vietnam, received a couple of letters from one of my sisters, letting me know that this fiancé of mine was cheating on me. Didn't know why I was surprised, after all other guys warned me against her. And I didn't want to accept the truth.

And so what's the difference, I had another girl on my mind, so I was cheating too. Had really wanting to marry a girl I had met in Arizona, and I had been writing to her. So what was I engaged to someone else? But unfortunately one day I received a deer John letter from her, saying she didn't have any plans on marrying me. And tells me not to write to her again. Heart broken, I guess you can say that, but not serious. My whole focus had to be, and it was, on where I was between all of these letters, war. Had heard some bad sad things about some guys receiving deer John letters from either their wives or their fiancé or even from their girlfriend, that didn't want to marry them or not wanting to continue with the relationship. And some guys could not accept rejection, and go off into the deep end, and commit suicide. Or be too much in deep thought about the sad broken hearted letter they just received, and wouldn't be paying any attention to the war they're in and get shot or blown away. Sad but true. Just in case, you don't know what a deer John letter is. Well there's a lot of Johns, Joes, and Jerry's, right? So they created the letter as a deer John letter to a soldier while he's at war. And it's never been the right time to receive a deer John letter. Because some guys would end up dead.

ROBERT GARCIA

Relationships!!! Many of them bad, and very bad. But you and I know there are those few that are good. Some people don't know what they have until they're gone.

Remembering this one Marine, he had been in Nam, months before I arrived. His girlfriend had written him to inform him that she was expecting a baby. Oh man, did he get excited about that, he sure did.

He was not only excited, he became desperate so desperate, that he wanted to rush home to be with his girlfriend, to support her being by her side, to watch his baby being born. But I couldn't believe what he wanted to do, to get home. Then I heard this scuttlebut, about him wanting so bad to be with his girlfriend, that he was even wanting to jump off the machine gun tower. Thought to myself, wow, this guy is crazy, naw he's not gonna do that. Yeah right, the hell he's not. Well days go by, and maybe a week went by, and then I hear a medevac chopper arriving to our location to medevac this desperate young man to go see his girlfriend deliver their baby. And how did he do that? Well he pursued what he said he was gonna do. From what I was told, he took a flying jump off the machine gun tower like he said he was going to. Breaking his leg when he suddenly hit the ground. And sent home. Have never forgotten about that, that how some people can get so desperate to get what they want. And never seen him again. Just so you all know, this machine gun tower was over fifty feet tall.

And then my thoughts went back to the guy that went home to go see his wife, that had tried all branches of the military, including the Marine Corp. Showing her beautiful picture to everybody, and bragging how pretty she was. And I agreed with him, that she was pretty. But I also told him, that if she's so pretty, what was he doing going into the Army, Air Force, the Navy, if in fact she's pretty. Guess something clicked inside this poor fool. Requesting to go home and surprise his wife, and what happened, he's the one that was surprised. Oops, I can only imagine how he felt when he got home to try to surprise his wife, only to catch her in bed with another man. Wow. And this other guy jumping off a fifty foot tower to go home to be with his girlfriend have their baby. And what about me, when a sergeant offered me a second R&R to go to Hawaii, to catch a flight to Los Angeles, to go see my parents, only to see this girl I had planned to marry, but I decided to cancel the wedding off. And by coincidence see her at my parents house about to drive off, pissed at me, because I canceled the wedding, cussing each other out. Good riddance. Go to hell. Later on in my life's writings, I'll have to reveal that I still fell into the entrapment of whores, no matter how I tried not to be mixed up in with them. All along my own sister being a whore. And getting home safely from Nam, and my sister introducing me to another whore. What a world I was trapped in.

Let's go back to love and war, and war is hell.

Yes let's go back to where I had experienced my second death. Remember, DIED THREE TIMES LIVED ONCE

That was the biggest reason why I didn't want to get married, when I was about to get deployed to Nam. Being away for a while, and maybe get killed, or wounded, or worse yet, come home without arms or without legs. What a psycho and scary thought, if that would've happened. How would any woman want with a limbless man? Much worse if I would've had a child. What a disaster that would've been.

As I said back to where I left off. I'm still in Vietnam, in my present part of my life's writings. You do remember what I thought about trust and devotion? Especially putting trust within your own unit of comrades. Trusting another comrade with your own life, can be a life or death situation. And believe me I had to punch out a couple of Marines to knock common sense into them to make them realize how serious it was at war.

First I'll start with a guy that shot at me, for no reason at all. Didn't know the man, didn't know why he did that. But I had to show him I was just a little crazier than he was. And it worked. At that time I had been assigned first squad leader, and maybe that's what it was, maybe jealousy, I'll never really know. Just the thought of that memory when I wrote this, gives me a dreary feeling. Because what if he would have shot and killed me. The shot fired came real close. But I couldn't let him feel that he won and had control of my fear. So I shot back at him, which freaked him out. At first he thought he was crazy to pull a freaked out idea of shooting at a fellow comrade. Thought about it after the incident, what a fu**k head. He thought he was funny. Here's how it went down.

We were both squad leaders. I think what bothered him, that I was first squad leader and he was fourth squad leader, when I had arrived for my first and only time in Nam, and this was his second time in Nam. We had both taken our squads out on patrol, he taken his squad and I taken mine. We had all arrived simultaneously, our squad and then his squad. I was starting to settle down and prepare for some rest, when all of a sudden, I hear this guy yells out, "Hey dude" as he started laughing, and points his M-16 and fires off a shot by my foot. My immediate reaction and reflex was to shoot back at him. Right after he shot by my foot, I quickly raised my M-16 firing back at him, only much closer by his foot. If only I would've had a camera to take the look on this asshole's face. Because he looked frightened to hell. He says, "Hey asshole that came too close" thinking, he had the f**king nerve, so I yelled back, "yeah the next one will be your head, you're playing games, and I'm not playing" All he did was walk away, and I thought, wow it worked, my immediate reaction by acting more crazier than him. As time in my life had continued on after my Nam time, acting crazier than most assholes, gave me control for bullies to leave me alone. Oh it has not always worked, there were times I had my ass kicked, like anybody else.

It was sure weird about that guy shooting at me, thinking, aren't we supposed to be shooting at the enemy and not at our own men. Like I've repeated, there's probably been many guys that shouldn't have been in war. But that's never been for me to decide. When there's crazy individuals in war with men that are normal, it can get anyone killed. And I'm sure it's happened many times. But war can also make normal men go crazy after a while. Am I right you guys, you combat war veterans? I'm sure there are guys coming home like I did, all f**ked up. With PTSD., on top of being sprayed with agent orange, but no one paid any attention about it. And I believe that no one could help it.

But we ourselves as U.S. soldiers, had to rely on the training we were given. And its perfectly understood, not everyone will pass the strict training. Thank God I graduated from the Marine Corp Academy Boot Camp in Camp Pendleton.

Graduating from high school is one thing and graduating from the Marine Corp boot camp, is completely another thing.

Coming back to my extreme experiences in Vietnam, and not my everyday thing, because that would be very boring. Sometimes boredom would set in among us guys like anyone. Especially in very vulnerable situations, during our guard watch. When it was anyone's time to stand watch, there was never a good reaction. But when shit would hit the fan, then the fight is on. Start shooting or you're gonna get shot and killed.

So taking war as serious as I took it, is what I did, and I thought everyone else should do the same. Not really, there has been idiots sent to a war situation, since man's first war. I think so anyway. As I had said, unfortunately I had to punch a few guys, to try and knock some sense into these imbeciles, if it worked, I've often wondered if it did. Just knowing those characters, I doubt if it did.

I only had one Marine try to punch me, while in Vietnam and it was one of my lieutenants. As I've said it earlier in my writings. But as I described that one that shot at me, you probably think, isn't that bad enough. Yeah that's real bad. That's worse. I'm just saying, for anyone that tried to physically punch me. No. And I've never been proud of punching anyone. Because after each incident, I felt like shit. But I've never applied for any position to be liked or disliked. Whether it be just a job, or this Marine Corp. I've admired people for their accomplishments, whether in war time or in a work environment. But I've never had any ambition to start a liking for anyone during my working days of my life. Much less during my war time in Nam. Ain't I right guys? And of course I understand that everyone is different.

Extreme experiences. Well oh wow. Yeah. Like I've said, still to this day, have never been proud of punching any fellow Marine. But I think my justification on punching anyone of them, I think I had just cause.

I'd never mention it in public, or brag or broadcast it, about my assaults against any Marine. This is why I'm writing about it.

Now, I've written what happened to me in my advanced training, when I went to our captain, to inform him, that I no longer had my assigned M-14. And he turned me in, by announcing what I had done, in front of two hundred and fifty Marines. Telling them, that there wasn't going to be any weekend leave for anyone. It was like the captain was siccing me to the wolves. So I'm not going to continue to elaborate on this. And to make a long story short, four right guides literally kicked the holy shit out of me, to a bloody pulp. Because I was a bloody mess. And at the time, didn't give them the satisfaction by they expecting me to break down in tears. Instead I laughed at them. Believe that or not. Because that's what happened to me. So I was already ready, when I was deployed to Nam. Physically punching ready. When we were airline transported to Nam, looking out the airline port windows, thinking to myself, I wasn't going to take any bullshit from anyone. And that's the way it went down. Through my thirteen months in Vietnam.

The sleepy head incident, when this other Marine had a dangerous reputation of falling asleep on watch. And that wasn't going to fly too high with me. Falling asleep on watch has never saved lives. Especially when we're all given a warning about not to fall asleep on watch by our commanders. The Viet Cong, North Vietnamese sympathizers, and all other enemies would sneak up on watch sleepers and catch all Marines asleep and slash their throats. That's always given me horror scary feelings. And I obviously didn't want anyone of us falling asleep and get me killed, by having my throat slashed. A so frightening way to die in a foreign country. Vietnam. Even when it wasn't my time to stand watch, I still couldn't sleep. I was paranoid. So when this guy had been transferred to our unit, I know I had to tell him something. Even if he didn't like it. To me, it wasn't important if he liked it or not. Warnings from commanders should have always been taken seriously. And when I warned this guy about what we had heard about his sleepy head dangerous reputation, all he did was shrug it off, like it was nothing. Telling him, that don't let me catch you sleeping, because I'm gonna plant my size eight boot into your mug. He got real pissed at me. I told him, you're lucky I kicked you, and not the enemy slashing your throat asshole. You want to talk about this behind the lines, and see what the captain says about it.

That thought about that fool, I have never felt bad about it. After all I very possibly had saved all of our lives, including his. Even though I kicked him very hard. He surly didn't want our commanders knowing he had fallen asleep again. Maybe because of those kind of carelessness type of soldiers, I have insomnia today.

Fire fights after fire fights, because we're on a roll. We received a change of orders. Our unit was being transferred from a land unit to a floating unit. And it pretty well disappointed almost all of us, that didn't want a change of orders. But who are we to say shit. Right? Orders are orders. Or pay the consequences. Maybe that was good for me in the long run. Who knows how long I would've been point man. I had already done eight months. And because I made a small target. Being a short guy. So off to a helicopter aircraft carrier destroyer we go. Whether we liked going afloat or not, following orders was a must. And dealing with it was a big part of being a Marine. Following orders was the life I lived back then.

We were all choppered to our destination, the helicopter aircraft carrier. And no I don't remember the name of that ship. Maybe I just didn't want to remember that. I don't know.

There were over five hundred men on that ship. Half Marines and I guess the other half was Navy men. That's never been important to me. The most important thing was what battles we had to fight. And who would live and who would die. The importance of saving lives was the upmost important to me, and I think that should've been on everybody's else's mind as well. Don't you think guys, comrades? But unfortunately that's hardly the way it goes.

War is and has always been hell and evil. I can't look at it any other way. Killing or being killed is a fate that only the results of war will determine. It's been that way since man's first bloody war. Which has been going on for thousands of years. You know it, and I know it. Everybody should know it. When I was in war, the things I saw really saddened me when innocent women and children die. They use a painted word, when innocent people get killed, they call it, COLLATERAL DAMAGE. Evil is just plain evil, I don't care how you want to paint it. Another one we all see, at least I saw it, little starving

ROBERT GARCIA

orphans. There were many times, I'd go hide somewhere and just cry. And I did. I don't care who you are, and I don't care how bad you think you are, if you would've seen what I saw, you couldn't have helped it, but I bet you would have cried too.

This is why it's so important that every body, and in every generation in America takes freedom very serious. And don't assume freedom, defend it. I'm only one voice. And there are many voices out there that are screaming for freedom, and don't do anything about it. Especially the younger generation, that mom and dad have always given them what they want.

When we were transitioned from fighting a war on land, and to fighting a war from a ship. Everyone hated it, as far as Marines were concerned. How could you blame us, hardly had any room to breathe. Everyone was in everybody's way.

Can still remember when our commander announced that we were being transferred to a afloat unit. Thinking at the time, what the hell, why?

Our company of Marines would become an afloat reactionary unit. Which meant, we would be the Marine unit to back up any Marine unit that would get hit by Vietnamese Communist Army.

Which most of the time would be complete chaos. And chaos could not be helped, because that's always been in all wars. If you don't believe me, read the history. And again it's not about chaos, it has always been about the lives that are lost. That's the sad truth.

But isn't that how evil works? Of course it is. The prince of darkness has always loved the killing of innocent people. And Jesus, our lord and savior will intervene, on his second coming. Look what happened to the innocent Jews, during the holocaust. Look what happened to Africans or anyone that had black skin, or for that matter, I'm brown skinned, how others have treated us. Racism has always been around, and it's not going anywhere, no time soon until Jesus returns. And that my friends I believe one hundred percent.

As I said about chaos, it's an instrument that the enemy has always used. And they still use it. And always will.

When I wrote this, I started gathering my marbles together, the few I still had, and was able to reminisce and do a lot of flashbacks, as to what happened to me through out my entire life. And it wasn't easy, I tried.

As I recall the five months we were afloat. Afloat, is what they called it, sitting off shore from the main land of Vietnam, just floating, and waiting to be dispatched. In other words, waiting for a loud huge speakers to announce, and to report to our living quarters, and that we have only ten minutes to be choppered out to our brother company of Marines for back up. They're in distress, and they need our help right now.

As I also recalled, I was on a few reactionary missions. And it was so scary and frightening, which I've never forgotten. Where do you think I practically lost all my hearing. I've had hard of hearing since Nam, but I think I lost most of it, when I was afloat, during my last part of my deployment. For about a week, our company went on patrols with a tank company. Now that was dangerous, interesting, and loud. Imagine sitting on an armored tank, and they're blowing off their cannons. Do you guys know how loud an armored tank sounds like, when they blow off their cannons? I felt secured riding with these guys.

The first part of my hearing loss, when we were in a fire fight, trying to shoot our way out. And this Marine was maybe a few inches away from my head, rattling off his M16, inches away from my head and ears, with his eyes closed. And crying. I just had to yell at him, to tell him to watch where in the hell he was shooting at. I must had woke him up from his paranoia, and the nightmare he was maybe experiencing at the time of this catastrophe we were going through. Often thought, what if I wouldn't had yelled at him, could he had shot and killed me by accident. Who knows. Just another day in paradise. What a living hell, we all went through, right guys? Remembering a certain Fourth of July, and how we celebrated it. Throwing grenades off a cliff, close by off shore. We not only did we have to watch out for the enemy, but we had to watch out for our own comrades, that could shoot you by a catastrophic accident. Many times thought, what a way to go home, and your family finding out how you died. The families would receive terrible news.

Here's another one for all of you. There were always some ex-cons, even those coming out of the brig, a Marine prison.

This guy had been released from the brig, on a day after many lost their lives. And this one Marine comes up to me, asking me what would I want him to do. Out of the blue, and I had never seen this guy. I tell him, pick up a working detail, and gather up the dead, and bury them. And he tells me, that he had already done that. I just stared at him, and asked him how did you do that. I was amazed, and it just flipped me out, asking him, how did you do that. He had his bayonet in his hand, and informed me, that he cut up all the bodies he could gather and he buried them in one small hole. Wow, I made sure I was not close to that guy And every morning after meeting him, I looked for his face. And I never seen him again.

War can make people nuts, to an extreme. Didn't know who was more dangerous to be around, either the guy that took a shot at me, or meeting up with this guy out of prison, that decided upon himself to cut up dead bodies and bury them in one hole. He must had already been dead and had crawled out of hell.

All people come from all walks of life. We all should know that. But some people can be very peculiar and very evil. Very mentally unbalanced. Screws loose. And I'll remind you, I don't pretend to be better than anyone, just better than I used to be. And maybe some guys went to the Vietnam war when they were stable but, somewhere along their time on duty, something happened to their mind.

Oh, I'm not saying nothing happened to me, that would be lying to you. Because I came back unsecure. I tried being low key, keeping to myself. Spoke only when spoken to. Never tried being a smart ass. Tried showing respect to everyone. But I had a gun with me, after Vietnam. And that wasn't good. Didn't trust anyone. And today can't say I trust too many people. And that lasted from the time I was twenty one until I was almost thirty. And that's a long time, to never getting caught with a gun. Never shot anyone, although I wanted to. But thanks again to God.

All wars are, how can I describe them, very political, violent, and disastrous. All wars are so inhumane. They've always been and always will be. Where there were once a beautiful part of the world, wars have destroyed that. And when I was in Nam, I witnessed too much bloodshed and bombardment for me, in my life time. And I pray I never see that again. God only knows.

Before I met that ex-con, and how did I know he was an ex-con, because I asked him, why didn't I ever see him before. And the magic answer, he had been in the brig, for man slaughtered. He called it self defense. Didn't know if I should believe him. Later found out he belonged to another marine unit.

When I was nineteen through twenty one, and during my war duties in the Nam, I was an obedient soldier, or I wouldn't be writing this life story. And needless to say, we shouldn't go to war, with the idea and expecting we're going to receive praises, awards, and medals, because I sure in the hell didn't. And doing what I did was not for receiving any war medals. Us Marines are all trained to save lives, meaning we should always look out for our fellow comrade next to us. And here's how a Marine Officer witnessed me do what I did. When I didn't know. This was the only AWARD I have ever received in my life.

THE SECRETARY OF THE NAVY TAKES PLEASURE IN PRESENTING THE NAVY ACHIEVEMENT MEDAL TO:

CORPORAL JOE M MARINE

UNITED STATES MARINE CORPS

For outstanding achievement in the superior performance of his duties in the field of leadership achievement as set forth in the following:

CITATION:

"While serving initially as a Fire Team Leader and subsequently as a Squad Leader with Company B, First Battalion, Twenty-Six Marines, Ninth Marine Amphibious Brigade in connection with combat operations against the enemy in the Republic of Vietnam from 19 July 1968 to 13 May 1969, Corporal Marine performed his duties in an exemplary manner. Participating in five major combat operations, including Operations Mameluke Thrust, Houston IV, and Houston V, he repeatedly distinguished himself by his courage and composure under fire. Exhibiting exceptional professional ability, he skillfully supervised the tactical deployment of his men during engagements with the enemy and contributed significantly to the accomplishment of his unit's mission. Constantly concerned for the combat readiness of his unit, he tirelessly trained his men and molded them into an effective fighting force. Corporal Marine 'leadership, professional competence and steadfast devotion to duty reflect great credit upon himself, the Marine Corps and the Naval Service."

The Combat Distinguishing Device is authorized.

FOR THE SECRETARY OF THE NAVY

J.J. DOE jr.
LIEUTENANT GENERAL, U.S MARINE CORPS
COMMANDING GENERAL, FLEET MARINE FORCE, PACIFIC

PART 2

Died Three Times Lived Once

RECALLING AND REMEMBERING every day and night, of my duties in the Nam. Memories of those days and nights gave me nightmares. And couldn't get rid of them. Thinking all along it was just me. In those days, as I've said there were no such thing as transitioning from military combat life to a normal civilian life. And don't know if it would have helped. I'd like to think it would. Compared with the kind of life I came home to, transitioning into a civilian life, from the VA, could've probably helped. But I'll never know, because I never went through a transitioning program. Transitioning program? As if I would've went to one. I don't think so.

Just the helicopters alone. Coming home and realizing, law enforcement now uses choppers for patrolling the skies. The first time I heard one, I ducked, wow, just gone a little over a year and choppers are flying around civilians, around our city limits. Amazing and interesting.

Coming back to my nightmares. I've been having nightmares, since after that tragic truck crash, since a doctor wondered how we lived through mangled twisted steel. Fortunately for me, I was able to move on, because if I wouldn't have been able to move on, I probably would have lost myself, through mental problems. And some kids, that I've seen through my life, depression have taken them down. Because they couldn't cope. I'm understanding why many of us couldn't cope, now that so many years have gone by. Life will always be hard for anyone and everyone, if anyone wants a peaceful and financial career, you have to fight for it. And life has become very competitive, as to what I see today.

But anyone that's been in my position, during war situations, knows or should know, we certainly try to save lives, for no damn medal, my

God. Wasn't looking around, as to who was looking so they would give me some kind of praise, awarding me a medal. God has always known me and my heart. I'm the one at nineteen, that did something, God noticed. I didn't know what I was doing. God instructed me to save my comrades, even if I had to eat the bullet. And eating bullets, came mighty close in eating many of them. Meaning, I came so close in getting killed. I just have to get over it.

What about when I became a short timer. What does that mean, right? When one is getting closer to his time, after he's seen enough war. For us Marines, during Vietnam, it was thirteen months. All grunts, 0311, riflemen, all of those Marines, are infantry, are ground troops. And once we all graduate the Marine Corp boot camp, you've made it. But only to go to war, if in case there is a war. And after we do our war time, and rather we want to go home or not, we're going home. And who wouldn't want to go home, you'd be surprised.

I was squad leader up until I was choppered out, but before that happened, I lost a good Marine, by the enemy with a ricochet. That was just another sad day for me, when I went home. Marines were getting prepared for a day patrol, and they emphasized that I was not to go on no more patrols. And I didn't go out on this one, and what happened. We all heard rounds flying. I didn't care, I ran out by habit, as I was being yelled at. Only to inform me, my youngest Marine in my squad, had gotten hit by a ricochet. What made it so sad, we were just talking him and I about our future when we got back home. Eighteen years old. And he was dead. So depressing.

When I was evaluating what I was writing, and trying to be as honest as I could, first to myself, and then to my readers. You all ought to know what kind of family I came from.

As you know, I only had two sisters, no brothers. Could I had developed some kind of complex. Maybe, but I'll never know the truth behind that life with only having sisters. Mom and Dad had sisters and brothers, and I repeat, I never had any brothers. Looking at it from a different perspective, and maybe we become dysfunctional and not know it. Well I didn't know the dysfunction, and naturally speaking, when I was so young.

ROBERT GARCIA

I'm trying not to be so scattered, by writing what happened to me in Vietnam, and then I jump back, as I flash back to another time. I know that can be confusing. But if you knew anything about the kind of life I've lived, you might know something, or someone that's lived as I have. I've known worse. My wife and I met this other Vietnam veteran, boy did we feel sorry for him. And he didn't know why he was telling us his story. He had heavy P.T.S.D. Horrible nightmares. Apparently he had been involved in hand to hand combat with some enemy soldiers, and he killed them, but of course he was almost get killed. But badly wounded. So his story went on, and telling us, that when he was honorably discharged, that the nightmares continued through many years. And then this one time, while he was at some public place, years after he leaving the military, all of a sudden, in a vision, broad daylight, some woman approached him, and he grabbed her by the throat and almost killed her. And someone called the police and they took him away to jail. And they kept him there, awaiting trial. And a judge threw a conviction of attempted murder, and sentenced him for ten years. In the middle of the story, he started crying. As he was telling his story, we could see his frowning face, as he was reliving what he almost did, to kill someone, thinking it was the enemy. And he tells me, I didn't know who this person was, all I saw in my mind, it was the enemy, so I was defending myself. He also told us, in my mind, I saw it was another enemy soldier trying to kill me. As he repeatedly says to us, and I don't know why I'm telling you all of this. That's always been something in me, that I have no explanation for. Why some people I've briefly known, and tell me their whole life story, why, I'll never know. Because it's happened a few times, which I can't explain why they have. Thought, maybe because I'll listen and try giving them advice. Don't really know. But people have put their trust in me enough to open up with their issues, about someone or something they're having problems with.

Eventually as time went on, we see this poor guy again, and he must have had a smile from ear to ear, to tell us really good news. He had already told us that he was released from prison and the attempted murder charge was dropped, and the V.A. Had approved him one hundred percent compensation. That guy looked like he was flying on cloud nine. His face looked so bright with happiness.

You civilians in the norm, does anyone know or can anyone realize what it's like to be a combat veteran with so many traumatic experiences from any war, and then get charged for murder. Thank God for me, when I had recently been discharged, and coming home from Vietnam, I had to carry a gun. And almost shot someone a few times, so I definitely understood this poor guy. Telling my wife, in my current life, can you imagine if I would've shot someone, during my whole life, anytime in between, and from the time I was discharged from the military and now. I wouldn't be telling this story, I'd be telling it, behind bars. Prison bars.

There's never been any excuse for murder. But only people like myself, when you're in the military, and you're at war, in a war zone. And then it's not murder, it's war.

I really believe that almost all combat veterans mentally snap, after being in a war zone, I know it's happened to me, and then we bring it home with us. And put danger to ourselves and to others. Because I know there are probably many combat veterans in prison than there should be. And that my readers is a fact. Do your own research and you'll find it. It's also sad for a mentally sick veteran and for the victims involved.

When the time came for me to be choppered out of war, and to prepare myself to be discharged. Was so excited, after a hell of a year, thirteen months of a year. That's the time in country, Marines had to do. Have never known how long the Army soldiers had to do in Vietnam. Maybe because it didn't matter to me, if you had to be in war, one day or one year, it's all bad. And all too long to maybe kill someone or maybe get killed. It's all bad.

And what about the veterans that come home depressed? Oh they're a danger to themselves.

Unfortunately I used to feel that way, until I got some help. But also it's unfortunate that not all veterans seek help. Then they lose themselves by committing suicide. So sad but true. They become a statistic. Because depression can really take you down, way down. After

I finally found out who I really am, I've oftentimes thought, who in hell was I.

This is why I feel, DIED THREE TIMES LIVED ONCE. As I was writing this life story of mine, my whole life came back to me, from the time I was a boy to present. And it's been quite a journey. As I'm sure your story have similarities to mine, and maybe not even close, and maybe much worse. Everyone has a story to tell or to write about. And for now this one's mine.

Just before they were going to chopper me wherever, at the time, I didn't know. They made a big announcement, telling us, that for anyone that had six months or less going back to the States, would be automatically be discharged. Can you guys come close into imagining how I felt. No you can't, because you're not me

And so I got choppered out of war and to a place to prepare me to discharge me. That was another experience, because get a whole of this one.

They flew me to Okinawa, and I again almost received a court martial. Have never received a court martial, but came close, while in Vietnam, and then this time in Okinawa. And the captain at the time, had ordered all of us to shower, and have chow. And after chow we would all be permitted to have a day leave. Noticed I said, Day Leave!! No No, not me, I thought I deserved a day and night leave, and that would soon become a problem for me, and almost a big problem. So we're off on our day leave, and I guess I was just acting like a dog, too long in pound, the dog pound that is. Because I took a day and night leave. I'm only twenty one. Spending two birthdays while in Vietnam, and releasing this dog loose, would be detrimental for me. And men will be men, and we're all turned loose from a corral, and go looking for women. So what's new, right? Well little oh me, didn't just find one woman, I ended up getting drunk and high with, if I can remember, I think their were four women. Crazy, maybe. But after being in a war, how are men like myself supposed to be like? I've always thought it was normal. But here comes the horror part of my reality. Because after spending a day and night of perverted sin, like a man hungry for sex. I wake up the following morning, and amazed I still had my money.

Really. Putting my clothes on, picking up myself out of a fantasy. I started wondering, oh my God, what's gonna happen to me. On my way back to the barracks, arriving there, and knocking on the captains door. He yelled out, get your ass in here. And sit your ass down. And continued yelling at me, telling me, I'm going to receive a court martial. I'm sitting all stunned and in a stupor. And he asked me, do you understand me Corporal?

I had to respond, letting him know, I didn't understand. He looked bewildered, asking, why I didn't. I go off by saying, "Captain I don't understand why I would receive a court martial, when I just did thirteen months of war, and now I may receive a court martial for being gone for one night. He looked all stunned, and yells at me again, "get your ass out of here you smart ass" I didn't waist any time getting just what the captain ordered me to do, and get my ass out of there as soon as possible, before he might change his mind. Oh my God, did I feel so lucky that day, you better believe it.

Unfortunately for all of us, luck is not around as much as we would want. Ain't that an understatement. And this would be a whole new world, as all of us veterans, at this Vietnam era would soon find out. Because depression would soon set in our civilian life, that veterans like myself would be too shameful to even to admit, because this next part of my life, would turn out disastrous to many as I will soon reveal to you all, that read this. I know it's happened to many of us. Always thought I was alone, and that I was the only one that bad things happen to. Boy I was wrong. But I was just too young to realize reality of life. Like we all, or most of us go through. Transitioning would be a new word for me, because I sure in the hell didn't know what it was, nor did I know what it meant, and no one else during my time knew what it was either. And maybe some of you guys did.

Did anyone of you Vietnam veterans have a hearing loss after arriving home? Because I did, and didn't know what it was. And since arriving home, couldn't figure it out why I couldn't hear, and kept having ringing in my ears. Maybe you guys knew what it was, but I didn't. I was so dumbfounded. Had stomach ulcers, with vomiting. I was only twenty one. And wondered why was I feeling so bad at such a

ROBERT GARCIA

young age. Had no clue. But before my Vietnam duty I had been told that I was smart. What now, after war, now I'm dumb and stupid? And that's how I felt, when there were times people would laugh at me. And after Vietnam, unfortunately I became arrogant, and that wasn't a good thing. Who likes an arrogant asshole? I know I don't. And I didn't then, and now here I am, I've become one.

Looking back at how it was back then, when I arrived home from war, thought I would be very happy, but I was wrong. Had tried to forget things that happened in war, but it was hard to. It was hard to just forget about my comrades that lost their lives for our country, we call U.S.A. Because freedom has never been free, and it never will be, without lives being lost. Freedom and liberty will always be tough for America to survive. And God will forever be there for our country, because as you should all know, this is a one nation under God. Home of the brave.

Don't get me wrong, I looked happy to be home, but I've pretty much been one of those kind of guys that looked happy and always laughed on the outside and did my crying on the inside. Remembering what I wrote earlier, when one of my sisters wanted to introduce a beautiful girl when I arrived from Nam. At the time it sounded so good and exciting. And little would I know, it would be my beginning of my fall and disaster of my life. You know who you are guys. I'm sure some of you, have been down that road as well I have been. And what did you do about it, because I didn't know what to do. I felt stupid, because I was very much in love with this girl. So that's how easy it was for her to do whatever she wanted to behind my back. Has that happened to you?

When you think you're in love, with your partner, your girlfriend, or your wife they can abuse you, and use you up. And that's exactly what happened to me, and I couldn't help it.

So my sister threw a welcome home party for me, and so I invited a few of my comrades to the party. Natural thing to do right? I thought it was. And I have to admit, I couldn't wait to meet this girl. That my sister had described to me, that she was a very attractive girl.

Thinking all along this was normal. Being in war, and not seeing an American girl in over a year. Not knowing that my body wanting a woman's body close to me, and just going with that feeling alone, would throw me into a loop of a lifetime. We all go through that, don't we? Thinking about that guy that requested a leave from Nam, to see his wife, and what happened, she surprised the hell out of him. He catching her in bed with another man in bed. And it happened to me, although I never actually caught her, but I didn't want to accept that she was always cheating on me. An old song, what a woman can do to your soul. All along thinking I had married the woman of my dreams. What actually happened was, I ended up marrying a fantasy, by thinking with the wrong head of my body. In other words, I wasn't thinking with my brain.

Back to the home coming party my sister threw for me, which was a warm home coming party. At the time I thought that my sister was a very loving sibling. Later on through my life's writings, I'll paint you a ugly picture, what kind of a woman my sister really is.

Anyway, my comrades and I arrive at the party, with this sister of mine, having open doors and open arms greeting us very warmly. Remember not everything appears as what we see upon the surface. Underneath the surface is pure evil. Later on I'll also paint you this sister of mine had been a curse from the time she was born. You all may think I have hatred for this sibling, and maybe I do, for what she did to her Dad. Because she didn't do anything to me.

So we arrived at the party, as we all waited for this so called pretty girl, to arrive. Being as young and naive as I was at the time. Oh by the way, did I mention, me being stupid. Oh yes I was. Very. I knock myself by calling myself stupid because I was, and maybe I still am. But I'd like to think, maybe I'm not as stupid as I used to be.

We're all at the party, waiting patiently, while we all had a few beers. Sister and I exchanged a few words and some laughs. Typically like most parties go. But with this one, maybe a little dramatic, with the wait for this girl, that would become my first wife, and be my worst nightmare of my life. So the night slowly drifting away, and maybe an hour and a half goes by, when all of sudden there's a knock at the door, and you could've heard a pin drop, how quickly people shut their mouths, and starred with awe. Sister opens the door, and in comes this girl, dressed

ROBERT GARCIA

up, long black hair, ruby red lips, with high heels, and wearing a pair of short bright pink hot pants. As I think that's how they used to call them. And men will be men. By this time my comrades and I are half drunk, as this girl walked in, our mouths dropped open, as if we've never seen a girl in our lives. As I reminisce as I wrote this. This girl was dressed like a whore and I was terribly blinded by the light. And what did I expect, as I look back at my life, this sister was just as much a whore as that girl was, that would become my wife. Wow what a fool I was. Because I actually fell in Love with that girl. I went through a disaster and no one will ever know what kind of life I had with that, I called wife. But in the long run, and in my life's mistakes, I wasn't any better. And I'll show you later how I continued to fall deep into a world of hell, that I thought I would never recover. But we can all recover, if we seek help.

Don't know if any of you have ever lived in the kind of world I lived in. But I literally lived in a world of whoredom, since I was a younger teenager, about fifteen or so. When I started High school, my life was peaceful until I started really looking closer and closer at women. That's normal and nothing's wrong, right? Well the way I see it now, there's nothing normal if we put sex in front of education. Well, try talking to most kids about what should be first, sex or education. They'll just listen, but not pay any attention to you or anyone. Hey that sounds like me when I was a kid. It's happened to many of us, so what else is new. It's same old story, generation after generation.

What's the old saying? When it comes to women, you can't live with them and you can't live without them.

The wife I'm married to now at my old age, have to admit, she's got to be my best wife out of three marriages. They've always said, the third time is a charm. Neither one of us is perfect, by no means. We can have our ups and downs like everyone else does.

When I was lost and locked in a world of sin, and as I wrote this, started thinking about how I would like to be with another woman. But that's my evil side that speaks within me and then I start feeling bad about how I think.

The world I was locked in, it consisted of women, alcohol, and drugs, and guns. What a dangerous chain connection to evilness, don't you agree? Never been the kind to have much money. Coming from uneducated parents, that's just the way it was with us. But that's no excuse for why I didn't continue my education when I arrived from Nam. Don't know about any of you guys that were in combat, if you faced battle like I did. Something mentally happened to me. I just didn't come home normal. Normal to me, was finding a woman, find a job and have a family. But when I found my first wife, there was nothing normal about my life. She fooled me.

As I've mentioned in my earlier part of my life, I was once a very good kid. And being almost killed in a tragic truck crash at seven years old, which turned me around to become someone different. And then get deployed to Vietnam to have death stare at my face again for the second time. And then become another person differently again. Well what did I expect, when I was lost in a world of sin. And I'm still kind of lost, but just a little better than I was before.

I mentioned before I was deployed to Nam, I was engaged to a girl, when I was warned that she had been with other guys, but didn't want to accept nor listen to that. Was just being a fool. Asked myself, what kind of fool was I? But we're all fools, aren't we? Reminds me of a old song, "Fools Rush In" But as long as man exists, we'll always be fools. That's just a fact of life. All of you know that's true. That goes for everyone. We hear it all the time.

Rich or poor, fools will always rush into the game of love. Unfortunately I never thought it was a game. Thought, love should be a serious relationship between a man and a woman. That's my old fashion self. And I was taken advantaged of. Oh poor me. But I would pick myself up and start over.

As I said, was a fool, engaged to a all man's woman, and didn't want to accept the truth, because I liked her too much. Now that's a real fool. Just didn't want to believe anyone about this whore, because that's what she was. Looking back at my life.

This is a fair question, as I think it is. I don't think everyone is, what I'm about to ask. Why is it we have to get old to know what we learn in life. That's what happened to me. I didn't start out slow, but I became slower than most, after war. People said I was smarter than most, before I was deployed to Nam. And when it came to women, I was very dumb and stupid. I'll admit it, can't hide it, too old to lie.

We all should know, beauty is only skin deep. And so we're off and going out, after meeting this girl of beauty, when I thought she was normal. Time will tell. And I was determined to keep this girl and marry her. What a stupid fool. And I'm sure there were guys behind my back, and probably even some girls that would giggle and laugh about me. Can't blame them. Most people, when you see something comical, they laugh. That's about one of the only things I have never done, is laugh at people. I've laughed with others, but I've never laughed at anyone, just to make fun of someone.

There are those few men and women, that meet up, and get married within six months or less, and a lot of those poor fools don't make it. With my first wife and I, we actually dated for five years. Unbelievable. You'd think it would strengthen our relationship. But it didn't. And it took me five years to find out, and I never found out until after our divorce. Five years of dating and ten years of marriage. Divorce?? No not yet, I'll come up to that when the time comes. But that would've been the normal thing to do, right after you find out who you're married to. No not me, I just wanted to keep f**king. Thinking all along, she loved how I f**ked her. It actually took me ten years to find out, she was an unfit mother and an alcoholic. What a waste, and what a shame. For who, for her or for me? A waste of time for me, and shameful thing for her. And who suffers between all of this. The kids, that's who. Poor kids, we had two daughters. It's happened many times with others. But while it's happening to me, I'm not thinking what's happening to others. Because my kids and I are the ones that suffered within this relationship. And what am I to expect, when all I'm focusing on, is sex and not love. Because both this girl and I loved sex, and never once fell in love. What? That's right. Thinking all along this woman wouldn't cheat on me. Yeah right. Another foolish thought. She came out of ten kids in her family. Nine siblings. And didn't know it then, they would all perish from drugs and alcohol. That family would be the first family,

I thought would be the most corrupt and dysfunctional. Later in my life, my family would prove me wrong, with what I thought back then. But when I first met my first wife's mother and father, and her brothers and sisters. Getting to know them closer by the day, I would find out what a disaster that family was. It's no wonder this girl was already f**ked up when I met her. I was just too focused on sex, and stuck on stupid. I should have stayed focused on my education, when I returned home from Vietnam. That's what I should've done, that would have made more sense, and my life probably would've been much simpler, and much smarter. That's too long ago now. Just forget it about now dude.

There was this certain motel that had gotten used to seeing us two, every weekend. Would sign and pay for a room as a married couple. We started f**king at that motel almost right after we were introduced. And who introduced us. My whore sister, that's who. And again I didn't know it back then.

Can anyone ever be able to explain what's the meaning of normal? Somewhere through my over forty years of life, got into a world of shit, and have never been able get out of this whirlwind world of hell I've been in. Until, and I repeat it, until I answered God's knocking within the door of my heart. And then everything seemed to change. Weird huh?

But that wouldn't happen to me until my acceptance of God, my lord and savior. And I'd be suffering until that happens. Oh, we all suffer until we go into the other world. And I suffer much today, from all the falls and bangs I went through. But what I'm saying, I go through my painful world with better peace of mind. Believe me it does wonders, how I can manage pain. You guys, you ought to try it, it's called, pain management. But I've learned that physical pain doesn't hurt nearly as bad as heart break pain. Am I right? But we should learn to get out of that hurtful world or it'll destroy you. And learn to move on.

So this first wife of mine and I are in and out of this motel constantly, and consistently, for the love of sex. We were both sex maniacs. Oh yes we were.

After that coming home party my sister through for me, and I started dating that first wife of mine, my uncle had invited me to apply for a job where he worked. He was a foreman of a steel tank fabrication welding company. Which was hard work, but uncle knew I was a hard worker, or he wouldn't have encouraged me to apply. He also knew, I arrived from Nam, and of course he knew I was in the Marines. We were really close, that uncle of mine, which was Dad's youngest brother. Dad had probably told him that I wasn't afraid of hard work.

Remembering my uncle and my aunt, his wife, had previously had taken me just nine years prior to Fresno California to pick grapes. I'll never forget that. And I'm sure my uncle noticed how hard I worked., at only twelve years old. So now here I am at present time, now twenty one years old. I'm sure that's why he invited me to apply at this company he had worked for, at the time, maybe nine years. Uncle tells me, all you have to do, is apply, and you'll be hired. So I tried it on for a while, and it fit me real good. It was money in my pocket. Money to go out with. And if men want to take out women out on a date, we all need money, so we need to have a job of some kind. Even though, looking at my life back then, it was a waste of time, and money. Just wasted my life away with the wrong women. I should feel so lucky this first wife, didn't think of killing me while I slept.

Meeting up with this woman, the mother of my two daughters, had turned out to be a catastrophe. She was only eighteen years old and I was twenty one, when we met. A meeting, for my own good, should have never happened. I can only imagine how many of you have wasted your time with wrong people and bad influences. I'll admit I have. But when we're young, and while we grow without guidance, only God knows where we're going to end up. But God knows where we're all going to end up. Because he's God. You can believe that or not. During this life's journey, I've become to believe everything God has done for me. Because of the life I live, never thought I'd enjoy where I'm at today. Oh being who I am, I still need a lot of improvement, by all means. I'm just saying, I'm better who I was before.

Looking back at that life I lived. But that wasn't living, I was just barely existing. Working, going out with that woman. That wasn't living. I lived a very shallow life. If you called it life at all. I had my plans with her, but she had no plans. Her plan was just to get laid. And what can I say, I loved every minute of it. That's how it is when we're young. Ain't it? There came a time in that relationship, when she would disappear, and no one in her family knew where she was. As I looked at it later, it was bullshit, someone in her family knew where she was. They just didn't want me to know what she was doing behind my back. And it would happen more than it should have. Like a half of dozen times. I was completely wrong by staying with that girl. And then marrying her. I was blind by being sexually involved with her. How perverted, because that's what it was, perverted on my part.

I thought through time our relationship would improve. What's the saying, people think, like I did, that we can fix people. There's no such thing, of being able to fix people. And I, like many do, found out the hard way. Isn't that right guys, we enslave ourselves by being stuck with a girl, by pure sex. And those kind of relationships never go anywhere, but straight to hell. What kind of relationships go right, when we don't have God in our lives? I never read the bible, much less go to church.

And everyday during the week I'd go to work. Get off work, and take a break, because it was hard work. Shower down, and once in awhile go see my buddy that went to Vietnam, when he was in the Army. Then I would prepare a date with that girl, for the weekend. Go to her house, and no one would seem to know where she was half the time. Have always wondered about that. Why wouldn't anyone in this girl's family know where she was?

Oh have I mentioned alcohol and marijuana, of course we would smoke pot and drink beer. So why would I expect a serious relationship with this girl, when we used drugs and alcohol every time we got a chance. Seriously I was stupid.

Most guys that go out with any girl, that do drugs and alcohol, don't ever go out with them, much less plan on marrying them. No not me, I was just plain dumb. And she took me for a ride. A ride to hell and disaster.

We put our ownselves in every situation we get into. No one told me to go out with that whore. I wanted to go out with her. Even mom told me, stop going out with that puta. Would I listen to mom, hell no. The more mom told me not to be with that girl, the more I wanted to be with her. Crazy huh? Yeah crazy and I suffered for it, and later on, our two daughters suffered as well. I think they suffered the most. I dated a girl that was just a whore, can't put it any simpler than that. You would think I would not marry that woman, but I did.

So that was my life. Worked hard as hell, go out and f**k hard as hell. I was literally a crazy kid, and on my way to doomsville. Yeah literally living a life of hell. A fresh honorably discharged Marine Vietnam veteran, and a crazier than hell citizen. Citizen? I was a complete crazy jerk is what I was. There were times Dad would think I was a little off my rocker. And he wasn't shy to let me know how crazy I'd become since I arrived from war. Looking back at that time of my life, Dad wasn't completely wrong. Thought about it, and it seems like I had been in the pan, and jumped into the fire, to make things worse for my life. And that's how it was for me.

So far disconnected from God. God had always been there for me. It was me, that didn't want to acknowledge him. But he's been there, all the time, and he'll be there for everyone.

I dated that loose woman for five f**king years. What a waste of time. Don't you think?

During all of this dumb founded life of mine. You'd think I would have enough with whores.

I was working at my job, where my uncle had had me hired to get myself into the working world, which was my first employment after my Vietnam war service. Worked with a few older men and there was this one other young guy. Working for peanuts. He gets my attention and invites me to a crystal party. What a crystal party!! That sounds weird right? Well this poor guy tells me he's going to be the only guy there and tells me I could join him with some beer, and that there's going to be some women there. And that caught my attention. You can come on over if you want.

It's obvious what my response was. Of course I'll come to your crystal party. Expressionless I tell this guy, ok I'll try to make it over. In my mind, I'll be coming running. Joke right? Now like I said, I'm dating the first wife of mine. But half the time I can't find her and no one in her family never seem to know where she was. What's a man to do?

Well it's a Saturday night and I arrive to the party, crystal party that is. And like this guy said, women would be at the party. Thinking all along, of course women are going to be at the party. I thought only women went to crystal parties. That's what I've always heard anyway. Now here I am, invited by this guy, which his wife was the one throwing the party. And this guy was going be the only man there. Change of plans, I guess I'll join him. Ha hah hah. The man offers me a beer, and we started shooting the breeze. About life in general. After a while I noticed a girl looking from afar from another room at me. It was like going out fishing. Boy meets girl. Girl likes boy. And we shot that breeze pretty good, her and I. We started and ended our meeting very sweet. And never thought I'd see her again. Boy will size up girl, and girl will size up boy. And this boy doesn't realize yet, but he's about to get caught up in another spider web, by a black widow. Another whore. Well I'm not married yet, and I'm not even engaged. So I'm still a free man. Don't know about that. Looking back at it, since I'm now a old man. I wasn't free. I was locked up and enslaved by sex, under the control of whores. It was so easy for practically any woman to control me when it came to sex. Am I hitting it right guys? Because I don't think I'm alone on this subject. I've seen it all the time, and you've seen it all the time as well. Would meet up with any girl anywhere. I would start a conversation, the next thing I'm inviting her out for a meal. Just so I could get her to bed. Trying my best to be sweet so she won't turn me down. Does it sound familiar? We've all been there. But you'd be surprised, there are those few men that have never been with a woman. You've seen them. And I've seen them.

Well God created man and woman, and God created man to be with a woman. But society of today is so corrupt. And only in America can a man change himself to be a woman, or if a woman wants to change herself to be a man. As I just said, this can only be done in America, because if you're a homosexual or a lesbian in some other parts of the world, they'll kill ya. They won't put up with it. Coming back to what I said about God creating men to be with women. And there's been times in my life, that I have followed the Bible. Who me? That's right, I wasn't always bad all the time. I have a few good toes on me. In

ROBERT GARCIA

other words I have a few good bones on me, and some goodness in my heart. After all, should show some gratitude towards God.

But looking at myself as to who I was before, with the things I did with women, I know God has never approved that. For any man to be a whoremonger, or any woman to be a whore. That's completely against God. Any of you guys that has read the Bible, any woman goes to bed with a man, that's it, you're supposed to be together till death do they part. That's not even close with today's standards.

And this girl that I met at that crystal party, as I said, thinking I would never see her again. Like I said, I wasn't married yet. And all of a sudden, one morning, and living with my future brother in law and sister, I get a call. Unbelievable, it was that girl I met at the crystal party. We both talk for a while, asking me how I was, and so forth. Just some small talk. Then she says, "Why don't you bring some clothes and come over here and spend some time with me" Whore will be a whore. But what makes me any better. I agreed, so there I go running over to her house. To me at that time twenty five years of age, to go be with a girl at only eighteen years of age was impressive. She wants me to go over to her house to f**k her. And I did. It was like I disappeared from earth. Once I went over to that girl, no one knew where I lost myself. And my family were worried. Of course they'd be worried. Family is supposed to love family.

This girl that I had met at that party, well she wasn't any better than all the women I've been with. What did I expect, if all we want is sex, that's all we're gonna get. It shouldn't be of any surprise. What's Love Got To Do With It. Does that sound familiar?

And when I wasn't going out with those two women. Where would I go to? Topless bars, that's where.

Remembering my good friend, when I first arrived from Nam. Have never been to any bars, because before I was deployed to Nam I wasn't twenty one yet. Makes sense. So when I arrived from war, he asked, "Hey buddy, want to go out for a beer" I respond, of course, why not "after all this is a friend of mine, who I grew up with. But I never expected a topless bar. Since I had never been in one. And all I saw was naked women walking around the bar. Thinking to myself, wow unbelievable. My buddy asks me, "Well bud what do you think"? "I thought I would surprise you" and he did.

Little would I know, my buddy taking me to a topless bar, would add to more pervertedness on my part. It wasn't his fault, it was my fault. I could have stayed out of those places, but at the time, I didn't want to.

So in between dating my future first wife and this other girl, I was going out to nude bars or topless bars. What a life, and what a joke. Wasting my life away.

You can get killed in those places. And I came close in getting shot.

Looking back to my life then. I could have done something much better. How about you guys, how was your life, when you came out of the military.

DIED THREE TIMES LIVED ONCE

Living the life I live now, with my current wife I will never regret. Why did it come so late? That's not for me to ask. How do they say that? Better late than never. I sincerely believe, God saved my life, numerous times, not just three times, like my title of my life's writings suggest.

Maybe war brought a lot of corruption into my life, after my time in the Marines. I'll never know, and probably never figure it out.

From the time as a boy, in the truck crash, that they say we should've gotten killed. Was my first death. And then facing my second death, in the face of the enemy in Vietnam. In the coming up with what I'm about to get into my third death. Will take a while, because I temporarily straightened out. I wanted to live a normal life, and of course it wasn't easy. Nothing has never been easy, when I tried to be good.

Found out much later in my life, nothing will ever be easy, if we want things our way. That's just the way life is. You can believe it or not. And if you don't accept God's will, you're gonna have problems all the time, because I'm telling you that's just the way my life was. Until I accepted God's will, as you can see, my life was miserable.

Continuing on with my misery, because misery has always loved company. So they say, right? But when I was young and naive as hell, life was miserable for me. And I know there are some of you out there, that have had a much more miserable life than I have. You're either dead or in prison for life. And I could have been there too. But we're all young and naive when we start out on our journey, aren't we?

Just like as I continue on this journey. Eyes wide shut, is how I lived.

Because I continued dating these two. And I was juggling as to which one I wanted to stay with. Can you believe that? Juggling between two whores, or to be more civilized.

Juggling between two women. Ok, that sounds better. And that's how my life went for five f**king years.

What I should've been doing was continue my education where I left off before I went to that war in Vietnam. That's what I should've done. And for the life of me, I'll never know why I didn't. I've come up with a few Vietnam veterans, and they seem to have the same answers. By not knowing why they didn't continue down the right road, instead of the wrong one.

Later on I'll let you know, how I could have been either a drug addict or an alcoholic. You might or might not believe what happened to me after I walked the straight road for a long time. And then I fell, and fell deep I did.

Dating two women or more, and going to nude bars. Was my life style. My life was in the gutter. I've sometimes thought that maybe I would've been better off if I would've stayed in the Marine Corps. But I'd be dead for sure, because they would have sent me back to Vietnam, for sure. Five years of disastrous experiences with this woman, the mother of my first two daughters. Poor daughters of mine, they're the ones that suffered the most. But that's always been the case. Dysfunctional stupid people having kids. And the chain goes on.

In my family's ancestry, I can't go any further back than my grandpa, my Dad's Dad, who was born in El Paso, Texas, with Dad's mom He was a very hard worker, and had ten children and was also an alcoholic, and died an alcoholic. My mom's side, her mom and Dad came from somewhere in Mexico. And I never found out from what part of Mexico. All of them, sorry but they were all uneducated. What can I say, but tell you the truth. And then comes along my Dad and Mom, also uneducated. Intelligence wasn't too popular in my family. Maybe before my grandparents, but I didn't see much of any smarts, when I came into this world. And all during my life. Oh, there's a cousin, that was a doctor. But never seen him again after we all grew up. That's another thing about my family and relatives from both sides of my parents. After we all grew up, never heard from them. But that even goes with my own siblings. And when you find out what kind of siblings I've had, you wouldn't want to stay connected with them either. They have always been good at blaming everyone else. I even feel shameful to call them my sisters. And as I get deeper into my life's writings, then you'll know why. Remember my youngest sister was the one that introduced me to my first wife. Just a whore introducing me to a another whore. Wouldn't have never spoken like this, but I've said, this is my life story. And I have nothing to hide. I'm old now. I've recovered. Now all I have is some time to wait for Jesus to come. Because there's no doubt, he's coming back.

Moving on with my infidelity, from bed to bed, from one woman to woman That was my life, and I enjoyed it, what can I say. Young and naive, and immature. And I didn't know who to blame. I've tried to blame it on the military. But would that be right? Don't know. Won't ever know if the military would have helped me, if they would have had a transitioning program, like they do today. Maybe, it might have. It could have motivated me to continue my education, from where I left off, to go back to junior college for what I wanted to do. Which was to be a Mechanical Engineer. It's a dream I passed up, a long time ago.

So I went on and on and on. It's seems like I was on a merry go round. Going round and round, looking for another woman opportunity. And this was before I got married. The girl that my sister introduced me to, this other girl I met at a party. Once in a while go out with a woman from that topless bar. And the list goes on. Perverted. And I wondered why my life turned out the way it did. Well f**k dude, what the hell did you expect. And I thought every woman was a whore. Only when I would look for them, and then how easy are they to get what you want.

I was literally living a disastrous tragedy. But By no fault but my own. Friends of mine were pretty much the same, but not quite as bad as mine. The best friend of mine married a whore twice and divorced her twice. My other friend that went to the Army married a whore as well. He felt because he impregnated he had to marry her. Now that girl would not leave this poor buddy of mine alone. She was always around him, day and night. I knew something was going to happen. Babies are born all the time.

I had been so wrong, thinking that every woman was a whore. Of course I was wrong. That's disrespectful to think that way. Because not every woman is a whore. There are those women that are ladies. But what I have always thought, if I looked for a lady to date, it would take too long to get her to bed. Crazy right? But that's how I thought.

So in between these two particular women, I was actually testing each one, to see which one I would I stay with and wind up marrying. Looking back at that, I think about it now, what a hell of a choice. Which one would I marry, which one of the two evils. I mean I was back and forth. A couple of days with one, and later on, a couple of days with the other. If I wasn't a whore monger, don't know what you would call it. Thinking now, maybe that's not what I called it. They weren't whores, and I wasn't a whore monger. That's funny, because now I think, that was an up side down world I was living in.

I actually moved to Burbank, California so I could be closer to the one I met at that crystal party. Can you believe that? And I got hired at a tile store in Burbank. Which was another experience completely. And this girl started f**king around behind me. She thought I wouldn't catch her. What a bitch. Wondering to myself when I wrote this, who was more itchy, these women or myself. I think now, we all were. We all wanted to get f**ked. Living in my f**ked up world. And nothing is going to change unless I want to change myself.

So now the girl I met at the party, and I have decided to move in together. Wow. Into an apartment. As time went on, I decided to become a truck driver, because I wanted Dad to buy me a truck, and he did. And this girl and I were doing real good, up to a certain point. But up until my current marriage, I never had a true relationship with any of my former marriages. How can anyone have a true relationship, when we don't have a Godly connection. And I didn't find this out, many years later.

After being together, that woman and I for an ex amount of time. I thought I tried to be devoted and loyal, but there was too much drama, and drama has always pushed me away. Her mom and dad liked me, but out of all the women I've ever known, their parents would end up liking me, and wanting for me to marry their daughter. But I've always felt they didn't really know their daughter, but me. Her father and her and I once went to Las Vegas for a couple of days, as she thought by getting me drunk, she might get me to marry her. She even asked me, "while we're here in Vegas, wouldn't you like to get married to me" I couldn't believe it, she and maybe her Dad were trying to get me married to his daughter. My response immediately, no, no, no. I'm not ready for marriage. She looked very disappointed. From then on she started changing. I'll admit, I only liked her temporarily, but not to marry. She had already had a baby daughter from some other guy, at only eighteen years old. The more I got to know her, the more I thought to not stay with her too much longer. But before that was to happen, something drastic was coming my way. And if I would've pursued what was coming at me, I would've went to prison for sure.

As I said, this woman I was living with, before I got married to that other loose woman, with who I later had two daughters with. She always had sneaking suspicions about I having another girl on the side. And of course she was right.

I guess the real reason I moved in with this woman, was to find out who she really was. Fair reason right? Well, like I said she had a baby from a former boyfriend. And that would soon become almost fatal for her ex and I. Because her ex and her ex's mother didn't like the fact that I was being called daddy by the baby. And I think they didn't like me because I was brown skinned. Not white like they were. Big reason to not like me, I guess, because I've never been racist. But they're not like me. People that are racist, have and always had a big problem in believing that we're equal in the eyes of God. Because most of all there are those that don't believe in God. They want you to think that there is no such thing as God. And you and I know that has been going on for a hell of a long time. Since the creation of man.

ROBERT GARCIA

Equality has always been my focus and my philosophy of life. Not that I'll try to convince anyone to believe what I believe. If I'm asked, I'll state my views, but that's all I'll say.

And while living with this girl, woman, of whatever you want to call her. It doesn't matter anymore. She made a comment about God that eventually turned me against her.

With my dangerous experiences with death, with a truck crash, that nearly took my life at seven years old, and then I nearly got killed several times in Nam, for me to be with a woman that didn't believe in God, would be worthless to carry on a relationship, of a negative sense.

So one day, out of the blue, this guy, the father of this woman's baby daughter, comes barreling through our front door, points at me, and tells me he wants to talk to me. With evilness in his eyes. Pure hatred. There was something his mother had told him about me. Can't remember what that was anymore. Which doesn't matter anymore, because I'm alive to write this down. So I go outside with this big asshole, and big he was. I'd say he stood at about six foot seven inches. while I stood five foot eight inches. Is that big enough for you, it was for me. But I have never ran from any man, and I didn't run from this guy. Now picture this. We're both standing on the second story balcony, and he commenced to grab me by the shirt and picking me up, and making the movement like he's going to throw me over the rail. As he picked me up, we're both starring at each other. I looked straight into his eyes without a flinch and said to him, "if and when you throw me over board make sure I'm dead, because if I'm not I'll be looking for you." And that definitely worked out for the both of us, because he gently put me down, and walked away. I was in shock. While I hear a voice, "hey man shh shh, come over here" there was a next door neighbor, as he says to me, "you know I saw what just happened, and what you told him, but if he were to throw you over, you might not die, but you could end up paralyzed and end up in a wheelchair." And then he shows me a gun. "Here take this, you're gonna need it, and if you use it don't give it back to me, because it's not registered, just throw it away" And as I thought to what he said to me, it made perfect sense. How I could wind up paralyzed and in a wheelchair. Wow, that sounded more scary than dying. So I took the gun. And waited, and sure enough he came back like a fool that could get himself killed, and I'd wind up in prison for the rest of my life. Can you imagine that? Because I've thanked God a thousand times since then. And the reason he gave me why he came back was to apologize to me. Thought to myself, that's bullshit, he came back to kick my ass or might want to come back and finish what he started earlier. As he came closer, he says "hey dude I want to apologize to you" as I respond, "don't get any closer" he asked me, "what" as I stood sideways looking at him and repeated "I said don't get any closer" and now I was the one with evilness in my eyes. Feeling too confident, and the decision in my head, that I'm gonna shoot this guy, and I might end up killing him. Oh my God, what a desperate thought. But he decided to walk away. That scenario has played in my mind for decades. Something must had clicked in that young man's head, because It saved both of our lives. He might've gotten killed and I would've gone to prison. Little would I realize that won't be the last time I pull out a gun on anyone. That was the first time. Didn't know it then, what I know now. What I've experienced through my life will forever play over and over again and again till my dying day. Only when I remanence those days. And wonder where I am today.

Only because of our loving and forgiving God, is the reason I'm where I am today.

Oh I believe there are us and maybe a few others that believe God will return. Oh he definitely will be a big surprise for millions of people. It's funny, those millions that will be surprised, are the ones that don't believe in God, and his return.

When that young guy walked away from a desperate situation, and could've gotten him killed, the woman I had been living with, asks me, "What was that you were holding in your pants? I couldn't answer her, but I just starred at her. Her mouth fell open and her eyes were in shock, as she said "oh my god, was that a gun" I responded, "What did you expect, look at him and look at me"

But she doesn't stop there, because we continued staying together, why, I don't know. But when we're young, people stay together, when there's no spiritual connection with God. Am I right? So when young people stay together, it's only because of sex. It's got to be, what else is there? And when that runs out, you're both finished. That's when age creeps up on you. But when we're put in a situation like I've been, having to pull out a gun on someone, that can be devastating. Guessing because I was in the military, was the reason I liked having guns around, and that to be dangerous for myself and for others.

I loved what I accomplished in the Marines. Satisfaction. Just to know in my heart, I served my country honorably. But there's good and bad side affects after the military. I'm sure you're out there, as you read my life's writings.

Back to where I was with this woman, and preparing to leave her. And the coincidence that was so strange, my co-worker was about to get shut down as well, by his girlfriend. His girlfriend found out he was f**king some other woman, God only knows how she found out. Women will be women. So when we were at work, these two bitches are planning an ambush. We both worked together, running a retail store in Burbank. We closed the store and head out home, and when I get home, opening my front door, I noticed my big television console is gone from the front of the living room. This woman I'm living with, looking at me, as if she wanted to laugh, and I turned red hot, pissed at this woman. Asking her, "where's my f**king television" she laughs and says "it's for me to know and for you to find out" Well, she thought she was so smart. But I knew where her mom lived, and so I go over there, as her mom greeted me to lead me where my television was. In the garage it was. Thinking, her mother was a nice person, but this bitch was bad. Her own mother tells me, I don't know what's wrong with my daughter, she should treat you better. I thanked her and went on my way. Meanwhile my co-worker calls me, "hey buddy how's everything with you, told him things weren't too good, but that the good thing was I was able to recover my console television, and that this woman still didn't know I found my t.v. at her mothers house. With my buddy, he wasn't as lucky as I was. He tells me, to come on over and I'll show you what happened to my stuff. I arrive at his door, the door is open, and this guy is sitting in the middle of the living room, with a bottle of ten high in his hand. A very powerful drink, in case some of you guys don't

DIED THREE TIMES LIVED ONCE

know. His face was full of rage, because there wasn't not one piece of furniture in his two bedroom apartment. And tells me what he plans to do, which sounded wild to me. He had already told me about his past, which was very violent, especially with the cops. He explains to me, I'm going with him, and that I'll be driving his wide ford van. Telling me, I'll be the one to keep him calm, by not hurting anyone. Didn't think it would work, but it did, thank God it did. Well we arrived to his girlfriends's parents house, which was a big house in a nice area of Burbank, California. I stayed in the van, while he goes to the front door and knocks hard, with no response. So he knocks harder, and this time he sees someone walking up, but the woman noticed who it was, so she does an about face and started running. He noticed her run.

As this guy, my co-worker, noticed his girlfriend running, he wedges himself against a tree that was close to the front door, and pushes both of legs to open the door, as he did this, the door with part of the wall opened with the door, as it made a loud crushing noise, and it got the attention of the neighbors. As he ran after the woman, I yelled at him, hey dude don't hurt her, because the neighbors are watching, and they're going to call the cops. So he ran inside this house, and comes back out, with a jewelry box under his arm. He had a smile from ear to ear. And we take off in his wide ford van. And we cruised for a while, like driving in heaven. Nothing ever happened to either one of us. Another thank You God.

Another incident that I remember, with this guy. I had been stuck with this apartment with this woman I was living with, but I didn't have to sleep with her or stay around her. So this co-worker invites me to a St. Patrick's party, that one of his friends were throwing, and so I went. But all of a sudden, my buddy says to all of us. Wait here you guys, I've got some business to take care of. Everyone went back to what they were doing, but not me, I kept looking out the window, wondering what this guy is going to do. Remember what I told you about he, breaking down a very strong door to open it to get what he wanted. With success. But this time at the party, he steps outside and greets these guys, yelling at em, "what's up guys" as they see him with a four by four six foot long piece of wood, as he throws it at them, as they ran for their lives. They

ROBERT GARCIA

got in their car and took off, like a bat out of hell. I couldn't believe this guy. And thought some times, what am I doing over here with these people?

Another time of my life in Burbank, about a week before Christmas, on a weekend day, I decided to go to a competitive store of the company I was working for. Well I strolled on in this store, and lord and behold, I catch this purse from the corner of my eye. Now remember this the mid seventies. So as I strolled close to this purse, not noticing anyone around the purse. It sat among paint cans. Well hello, it was a paint store, what else would you find in a paint store. Paint cans. So as I sneak my hands slowly to the purse, I got into the purse and into the wallet, and I found five twenties. Thinking oh my god, all of a sudden I have a hundred dollars. I got into my car, and sat there thinking. What do I do, I go back into the same store I just found one hundred dollars, but I just had to go back into that store and look more into the purse. And I found three more twenties. And, man oh man, after all of this, I didn't get caught. And now, I now have one hundred and sixty dollars in my pocket. And I was broke, before this happened. My Christmas didn't turn out so bad after all. Going back to work, the following Monday, I felt anxious to tell my co-worker. He was amazed by the story. He kind of had suspicious looks on his face. I looked at him, and I said, hey buddy, you don't think I would pull some kind of thief in broad day light in the middle of the day, do you. All in all, everything financially worked out for me. But I still had that woman I was living with, and I had to figure it out how to tell her, why I was planning to leave her. And then I thought, why do I have to make this on myself. Just tell her I'm leaving, and don't procrastinate. Remember I was jumping around from hole to hole, like a jack rabbit. Because while I lived in Burbank, I would call the girl, my sister had introduced me to, if you remember my first meeting when I arrived from Nam.

What I'm about say, has nothing to do with pride, believe me. Because I don't know how I would've been able to support two women. As they both became pregnant almost at the same time. And get this, they both miscarriaged, and I would've had two sons. Unbelievable. Have always looked back at that. And thank God, because I don't know how that would've worked out. And there's nothing to be proud of, believe me. Looking back at that time of my life, I lived a very remarkable life. But was it a life? I don't think so, because of the way I live today.

Here comes the time I had to let go of this woman in Burbank, and at the time, it was a relief. When I finally mentally decided to say goodbye.

I had already left her a couple other times. So she didn't really believe me when I started the lines of goodbyes. And she knew I had been seeing another girl. But she thought she could keep me, regardless of this other one. And how I look at it now, neither one of them were any different than the other. But it has taken me a life time to figure it out. That has been one hell of a waist of time. You can say, I finally woke up from the dead. Because that's what it feels to me today. Who knows, maybe I had been psychologically dead until now, as to how I live today.

So when I looked at this girl in the eyes, she sensed something was going to happen. Asking me, what's wrong. Well I have to say good by to you. Of course all she could say was, why? Because I'm going back to Norwalk. Oh, she became undone and unhinged, and pissed off at me. Guess I couldn't blame her. But after a while, it becomes old. F**k, F**k, F**k. That's all it was. So I left one, the better of two evils. Like I said, all I've ever done was jump from hole to hole. That's all my life has always been. What can I say. Couldn't blame my mother, or my Dad. They didn't like any woman I would bring to their house.

During all of this time, there was this one woman from Spain. She told me she was forty two years old, and I was just twenty five. And she wanted to take me to Spain. And where did I meet this woman? Of course in that topless bar I always went to. Where else? Took out a few of those kind. Who knows where I'd be if I would've married one of those. I took out another one that wanted me to live with her and another man. She thought she could three some me. I thought I was bad, that one was worse. And where did that one live? Sharing a house with three bikers. And I actually spent the night with that woman, that claimed she was Cherokee. What a life and what a joke. What I figured out, from the time I was twenty my life. one until I was fifty eight years old. Can you imagine, that has been over thirty seven years of wasted time. Now I live a peaceful life with my current wife. I could have lived peacefully much sooner. But it is what it is.

How I see my life today, and how I lived before, has been a complete about face. My loving wife I'm married to today and I have talked about where would I be if I would have gone straight with my life. If I wouldn't have been a womanizer or if I wouldn't have done drugs, and gone in and out of jail, my wife and I wouldn't have met. I don't know what you think about that, but I find that's strange and quite odd. It's got to be God. He works into our lives, in a very mysterious way, whether you want to believe it or not. And the sooner we believe God will return, the better it will be for everyone. Like I've said, it's too bad we have to get old to realize, what happens after this life, and where are we going? You should all know this. God will return to judge the living and the dead. I'll try to explain my life's journey in simple words, but I don't have a large vocabulary, so I'll do the best I can. My life's ups and downs have been just that, ups and downs, but mostly downs. I believe my life started out with my first down, when I worked with my Dad in his waste business, when I was seven, I've opened that awful dangerous deathly experience to you before. And went to Vietnam, facing death again. And I really believe war tore me up psychologically, dying my second death. Now I'm experiencing my third death, as I write this. And I also believe I was much smarter when I was younger, just after that truck crash. Because as I've said, after that crash, I started receiving great grades. And I was okay up until I went to war. And then everything went f**ked up.

So I left that woman in Burbank, and as I leave that woman, she cussed me up and down. She was so pissed at me. Throwing things at me as I walked out the door. And I went back home to Norwalk, to continue my relationship with my first wife to be, because her and her family lived only a couple blocks away from my parents. Can't believe I'm saying that. Because little did I know what was about to happen, would start another disaster for my life.

Must have had a brain backlash. Have tried to remember how I continued this relationship with my first wife to be. I have to admit that was purely sexual. Because after I divorced this first wife of mine, figured it out, I felt cold for her. There was no love. So it had to be just sexual. With me, and this is just me. As I went out with this woman, it was just sex. Most of the time, we would go to a motel. We'd check in as husband and wife. So you tell me. And the more we went out, the more I wanted her. Sex was controlling my life, and as I look back at that time, it's a wonder she didn't kill me. Finding out in time, her parents had no control over her. Her Dad and her had gotten physical, he had to hit her, and never thought that was right. But she was out of control. And it would be all too soon before I find myself in the same situation, she would become also out of my control. Not that I tried to control her. I've never believed in controlling anyone. Have always believed in a relationship, by a couple compromising together. As I've heard other men talk about their past relationships. Hearing them say, how they tried to fix their ex wives or their ex girlfriends. Well guess what, I also tried to fix this woman. Finding out much to late, if your partner doesn't seem right from the beginning, you're not going to be able to fix them. I wish I would've known before hand.

Guess that's why, I tried talking to Dad a long time ago, when I was just about to start high school maybe just before puberty. As I tried asking Dad about girls he shrugged me away, telling me to go talk to my mother. Will never forget that Dad. How does a son talk to his mother about girls and sex? Does anyone know? Because I found out that Dad's response was humiliating. I just didn't know it back then. How many of us get treated the same way? Probably more than we would imagine. And of course it's never been right. How does a son come up to his mother, and ask her about girls? And that too, I never thought that was right either. How am I to find out about sex? Guessing, we just have to go by trial by error. As we make our mistakes along the way. Hasn't it been that way anyway? Trial by error? And how many kids have been born out of wedlock? Statistics have the answers.

Next, I'm going over to my first wife to be, to her parents house, looking for her. But she wasn't there, oh, I'll be darned. Surprise surprise. No I wasn't surprised. Her mom told me she was over her sister's house in Cudihey, which was a bad place to live. Didn't know it at the time, her sister was married to a drug addict. That was just a start of what I was to find out about this woman's family. It seemed at the time, the more I tried sweetening this relationship, the more sour it would become. Oh we would say the, "I love yous" So many times, in fact too many times. But it was only physical, just didn't know it then. Again I say, sex was good, but that's all it was, sex. What's bad about only having sex in a relationship, it soon runs dry. And then what do you have? Absolutely nothing, that's what. Absolutely nothing. What do we know about a good healthy relationship? Not much, if a couple doesn't communicate. Communicating was not the best thing to do with this girl. Because we never held hardly any kind of a conversation. She was a high school dropout, she didn't want to work. Most guys use common sense, but what did I know about common sense? When this girl was pretty, but dumb and stupid. And all she wanted was to drink and f**k. Her and sex, had me addicted. Didn't know which was worse, being a sex addict or being a drug addict, because my first addiction was sex. Came home from Vietnam, starving of women. And I lived in a neighborhood with kids that were just as bad as I was. My neighbor, a friend around the corner, guys across the street, guys blocks away. Thinking about back then, I had lived with whores and around whore mongers. So what kind of a life would I expect? This girl would become my first wife to be, when exactly, didn't know, because we would continue this falasco for five years.

We started dating when I arrived from Nam, and continued for about five years, and it was quite a journey. A terrible one. Thinking all along, love would blossom, but I was only dreaming. The more I was determined to pursue this relationship the worst it got. We'd go to the motel all the time, go to the drive in theaters on occasions, not to watch any movie, if that's what you think. Movies were the last thing we wanted to watch. I had a dodge van, so things were very convenient for sex, on the run. As I've said, was working all the time. Worked in the tank manufacturing company for about five years, until I got into local truck driving. And that didn't last long either. Through my years of misery, it would take me several years to be diagnosed with PTSD. Not having any support, no one to motivate me, and many times, not really having anyone to talk to. And not knowing I was developing an addiction, it's very obvious, that sex had become my addiction. And what did I expect, was with a woman that loved sex, maybe more than I did. And I thought about it when I wrote this, I believe she was the one that was worse than me. After all, she was dating more men than I ever realized, because I didn't know anything about it for years. Until I divorced her, oh my god, what a relief that was. Before that was to happen though, I would continue to struggle. As I've noticed around me through my life, have you people ever see bad possessed people, because there are people out there that are possessed. It should be without saying, be aware of those people, and stay away from them. You might be thinking, why am I bringing this up. Well because I think I was married to a possessed woman, that was very mentally sick. And she probably had me possessed to her sex addiction, and I never realized it before. I was just a blind fool. Sex starved, as she fed me sex. How perverted. I thought I was trying to help this woman, but I guess I wasn't helping her enough. Her disappearances continued. As I look at that part of my life, how disgusting. I felt I was always running around looking for that woman. How ridiculous my life was. But that was no ones fault but mine. No one ever told me to keep looking for that whore. But my mom was constantly feeling sorry for me. Couldn't blame her, being her only son.

After all of that confused life of mine, during the running around looking for her, and we're only dating, I still wanted to marry her. And get this, my parents paid for a beautiful wedding on the Queen Mary. Say what, that's right, that was a luxurious memory, and that would be my only good memory I'll ever have of that woman. My bad experience with a woman, I hope I would never meet another one like her.

So we got hitched. As I look back at that relationship, I wasn't married, I was hooked, and there's quite a difference believe me. As I experience my current wife and her love for me. This is a loving relationship. Which I've missed all of my life.

During all of this time, Dad was still struggling with his waste business, with a partnership with his brother. And both Dad and I agreed for me to help them out. What was my only position in my Dad's waste business, collect money from unpaid customers. Which became interesting, because I was collecting at an average of three to four hundred dollars per day, until we caught up, and no one owed anymore money. As wifey at home continued doing her alcoholism, and f**king around, and giving misery as a daily routine to our poor daughters. My poor babies. Well they're not babies anymore, they've been grown a long time now. And they continue to struggle with life as adults. As you can see, I've always burnt the candle from both ends. As a figure of speech, working around the clock. And again still no support at home. Because my mind would be in several places at once. Thinking what I was doing at first hand, and wondering what was happening at home. Life was so very hard to concentrate on. Worrying about our daughters, most of the time.

Now I had to worry about Mom and Dad's lively hood, because his waste business may be in jeopardy. And jeopardy it was. We didn't know it at the time, but Dad's brother and his wife were doing some sneaky shit. And years before that was to happen, I had already warned Dad about writing out some kind of a contract, and notarized with a lawyer. Which never happened. Dad's losing of his own business, was of nobody's fault but his own. Dad had always been the kind of guy that would trust anyone and everyone. When I've become the opposite. I've never trusted hardly anyone because of what I've seen what happened to my Dad, by his own brother, and later on I'll tell you what his own daughter did to him. Dad's way of thinking, if you're family, he'll trust you. Dad's brother and his daughter made it perfectly clear, that money is thicker than blood. Meanwhile back at the ranch, as the saying goes. This woman I called my wife was completely off her rocker, and completely off track. What I'll find out later about this woman, I called my wife, will become the shock of my life and leave me with a broken heart. Not so much for me, but for our own children. It was so sad for them, and very hard on me at the time.

Don't know if you see the problems I was going through. It should be obvious.

Because here I go back to helping Dad, on trying to make his waste business prosper. Which, by the way that never happened. Because corruption has always lingered on, in our family, when it comes to money. Dysfunction, greed, jealousy, and violence, and womanizing has always been my relations weaknesses. Oh did I mention drugs and alcohol, yeah that too.

Don't know if anyone that reads this would understand what it be like to own a waste business company today. If of course if you've paid any attention to any one company. Those kinds of businesses have become conglomerate in size, with many trucks strong. What I'm trying to say, if Dad would've listened to me when we were both very young, when I suggested to my Dad about creating a contract notarized by a lawyer. I believe we would've been multimillionaires, but that's long gone now. Dad's trusting his business without documents made him lose his business to his own brother. One more thing about these kinds of businesses, today they've become a utility. It's not any different than having to pay for your gas bill, water bill, or your electric bill. You would have to pay for your trash bill as well.

As I've said I was much smarter as a boy and as a teenager and going into the Marines, but once I returned from Nam, war had f**ked me up. Came home with anger, nightmare after nightmare, and the funny thing was, I didn't know what was wrong. I was psychologically and mentally unstable, and didn't know it. Ain't that weird. And trying to get myself straight seemed impossible. Needed help and didn't know how to ask for it. It all seemed like my whole like was a nightmare. And coming home to see Dad in the same position, drinking and drinking again. Had enlisted in the Marine Corp to get away from Dad, thinking I wouldn't come home alive. But I was wrong. Came home, watching Dad, that he wasn't prospering in the waste business he started in the late nineteen fifties, and here I come home in nineteen sixty nine. I couldn't understand that. And I felt sorry for him. Working so hard, and still the same. I just had to find out why.

And as I tried helping Dad with his business, I'm having trouble with a dysfunctional wife. Drinking her life away around our daughters.

At eighteen this woman was already an alcoholic, I should've known better than to marry that.

A life of stress had become my misery when I returned home from Nam. And looking for a woman like the one I married, would eventually bring me down, all the way down. I sometimes thought when I married that first wife of mine, maybe I should've divorced her right away, and re-enlist in the Marine Corp and go back to war. And get my life over with, and be done with it. At least I wouldn't have been stressed out. Because this woman was very nerve racking. And I still had the gull to have her bare my children, and put them through hell with me. But I didn't think that way then, and that was unfortunate for my children and I.

While I tried to progress in life, doing different jobs, and support that wife and children, to give them happiness. This wife would do the opposite, and disappear with our children, and no one seemed to know where they were. Sending our children to school was difficult for me. I sometimes felt I was raising three children instead of the only two we actually had. I'd go to work, our daughters would go to school, at least I think they went to school, and God only knew where my wife would go and do. With this wife, it was a mystery almost every day. There was this one day, coming home and finding a shot gun gone from my garage. And this woman would tell me, she didn't have a clue why it wasn't around. Again this other time, we had a television in the living room of course, and coming home from work and it's not there. And again this woman not knowing what happened to it. Without saying, I was getting suspicious with this wife. As I continued with this miserable wifey of mine totally disappearing for a spell, and again no one knowing where she was. So our kids have a break away from this woman they call mama. And my older daughter informs me how my shot gun and our television disappeared, telling me their mother pawned them for money to buy beer. Really irritating with this bad example for a mother. Our daughter tells me to please don't tell her mom, because she'll beat her up. You would think that would be it. No not with this woman. Because since she was gone about a week, my daughter also informed me that, again please don't tell mom, because she ended up in jail. I kind of yelled, what? My daughter next tells me why, their mother is in jail. Dad we went to this house, and mom broke into the house, and

I thought she was trying to steal something so she could buy her beer. It's statistically been a proven fact, that drug addicts and alcoholics, in order to support their problem, they have to lie, steal and cheat. Later on in my life's writings, it'll be a sad tale to tell you how I ended up in a deep dark hole of my life. Not only sad, but very emotional for those who loved me. But that's later on in my life. Right now in this what I'm writing, I'm still twenty five to thirty years too early to open that part.

Because I'm still lost in this upside down world with this woman, and crying on the inside for my daughters.

She was such a flirtatious woman, that she would flirt with any man right in front of me. Of course it would totally piss me off, and what man wouldn't get pissed off, seeing a wife flirt with another man, and without shame. All you had to do with this woman I was married to, is buy her a few beers and she'll be yours in a minute. That's all it took. Cheap, cheap, cheap. That's what I married, someone so very cheap.

Here I was working my ass off for her and our daughters, and what would she do, f**k around, with any Tom, Dick, or Harry.

And then back with Dad and his problem, which would become his brother taking Dad's business legally away from Dad. It seemed to me at the time, I was more in hell as a civilian than I was, when I was at war, in Vietnam.

At least I knew who to shoot at. So as you can see, I'm literally being pulled apart, or in other words, being crushed to pieces.

Having whatever I had after coming home from Vietnam, which would be years later to be diagnosed with PTSD, agent orange, and a list of other ailments I had.

Having a sister play cupid, introducing me to a whore. When she threw a coming home party. What did I expect, and I didn't know it back then, that this sister was a whore as well. Wow oh wow. It's kind of hard as I wrote this, to realize what kind of a life I went through. Because it was not a life at all. I was actually living a nightmare. While I had nightmares from the combat I had experienced in Nam. As I wrote this, it's no wonder I'm not in some psychiatric ward.

And as I wrote about my crazy life. Maybe the tattoo on my arm cursed me. I've had on my arm since I was eighteen, and now I'm in my seventies. (MI VIDA LOCA)

When Dad, my uncle and I agreed that I would come into the waste business, for starters, collect pass due costumers for what they owed. The entering in the company would prove to be a catastrophic disaster for Dad. And oftentimes thought, how long Dad would have continued before he would find out what his brother was doing against him. By me coming in, I think things expedited for Dad, Mom and I to find out what his own untrustworthy brother and his wife were planning on doing. But I will forever hold Dad accountable and responsible for losing a would be multimillion dollar business for Dad and his family. I think I did my part. I'll remember how I tried to warn Dad from his evil brother and that evil sister in law of his. And for Dad not taking this serious, have always thought, Dad you're a fool.

Can still remember when I was just sixteen, yeah, that's right, just a young teenager. Standing in Dad's living room as I tried to advise Dad to write out a contract with his brother and have it notarized with an attorney. And what did he do, he laughed at me and thought I was crazy. Yelling at me, "What are you saying, you think my own brother would take my business away from me, get away, you don't know what you're talking about, while he held a can of beer. No, I don't think my uncle will try taking your business away, but his wife and his kids will. And it was incredible, because thirteen years later, Dad was still receiving the same amount of money per month as he has for three years. He was always coming home bragging about getting new customers, but the money he was receiving wasn't showing that. Dad worked like a slave, and didn't know it, was blinded by his brother. Because he was literally working as a slave against himself. While his brother and family were abusing the money. Unbelievable, because It was really hard for me to believe what he had been doing against his brother, my Dad

And as I came into this business, collecting monies customers owed, I didn't have a problem with that. As I gave the monies I had collected to the book keeper. But one day out of the blue, the businesses' book keeper started talking to me about how hard my Dad worked and how he was such an honest man. Then she tells me. Now get a load of this, this book keeper is my uncle's wife sister. Because the next thing she tells me, "It's too bad my sister and your uncle isn't as honest as your Dad." That was a confession indirectly coming from the sister of the wife of my uncle. What a betrayal. Because this lying brother of my Dad, would go on everyday like nothing was wrong. Drinking with Dad and I, after a hard days work, laughing and talking like we were the best of uncle and brother and nephew. What a farce. Like it was the devil, not laughing with you, but laughing behind Dad's back.

Here's the information this book keeper gives me. After she tells me how hard Dad worked, and what a honest man Dad was, and how bad my uncle and her sister was not as honest. Mentally that threw me into a loop, with anger and outrage against this brother of my Dad and dad's so called sister in law. I could only imagine, how much they laughed behind Dad's back, while my poor Dad would work, not just this waste business, but he also had a full time job at Mcdonald Douglas, which was a airline assembly company. So Dad was always working his ass off. He was always tired. And for who and for what.

Let me remind all of you, while all of this is going on with Dad and his corrupt brother, about to lose his business threw deceit and corruption. I'm still in a f**ked up world with this woman I call wife, and our children living with her. Could only imagine what kind of living hell these little girls, our daughters, were going through.

Coming back to what this book keeper had informed me, about Dad's brother and his brother's wife not being as honest as my Dad. When I questioned this book keeper about what did she mean about my uncle and his wife not being as honest as my Dad. She informed me one hell of a hurricane with some rotten informed. This is what she said, "my sister collects the money, buys new cars for her children, or anything they want. And if they want another car, she'll buy them another one" When this book keeper was done giving me this one big bag of garbage of information, I was too pissed to say anything. In fact it gave me a headache. Do you follow me, if you're reading this, and paying any attention.

ROBERT GARCIA

Well it's without saying, I go back to Mom and Dad's house to inform them of what I was told about this business corruption, Dad had been building, which was not for him, but for that corrupt brother and brother's wife and children. For too many years. Because we're talking about, since nineteen fifty five until nineteen seventy seven. Just in case you can't count, that's twenty two years of my Dad thinking he was an owner of a waste business, when his own brother corruptly put every document in their names. Crooked, I'll say, but that's an understatement. And when I informed my mom and Dad, they couldn't talk. Dad asked me, what should we do. I replied, let's go talk to them. What do you mean, what should we do. As I've grown up, and I'm now an old man, I've noticed Dad, never able to defend himself. That's just a fact. And Dad has always been too vulnerable and to easy for evil relatives, like his brothers. I have never trusted any of our relatives. Especially once we all grew up and gotten old. No way. That's just the way our ancestry has been, through generations.

So now, Dad and I are off to Yorba Linda to meet up with Dad's brother and his wife, and I expected for the whole family to be there. And they were. And everybody should be there, because this was going to be a very serious meeting. Not much for them, but for Dad's future, hanging by a limb, as to how long he'll be in his own business. They had already made plans, before this day, before this was to happen.

So we arrived at Dad's brother's house, and I suggested this meeting to commence. And this wife of my uncle, asked, what was this all about. I looked at her straight in the eyes, and asked her, you don't know. I think you do. She replies, no I don't. Tell me what's this all about. I began "Well I have been told by your sister where a lot of money has been going. And we think you have some explaining to do. Because your sister says that you take out money for whatever reason you see fit. That you have been doing this for quite a while. That you buy your kids whatever they want. Whether it be a car, or if they want another one after they crash one, is that right? Of course she denied it, and instead of explaining anything as to what her sister told me. She started ordering us off the property.

By saying "Ok I need both of you to get off our property and you and your Dad are no longer permitted on this property. This is our company by all legal documents, this has been our business for a while." Of course, Dad and I were both caught by complete surprise. Especially Dad, he looked so heart broken, and speechless. Not a word was ever said. As we walked off the property as we were told, getting closer to our car, Dad broke down in tears, poor Dad. I almost broke down with him. Felt so sorry for him. But I had warned him years ago. It was, like I knew this was going to happen. As Dad cried, he tells me, "Now what am I going to do"? I'm already getting too old to get hired anywhere. I had to tell him, we'll figure it out at home. Didn't want this corrupt brother and his wife to see Dad crying. That probably would've given them more satisfaction.

Remember "I DIED THREE TIMES LIVED ONCE"

Now at this particular moment, I felt very alone and lonesome. Because now I had to figure out how to find a way to support two families. My parents and my wife and my two daughters. And did I ever get any supportive assistance from my two sisters, hell no. It was a terrible situation to be in. Dad had said as we were leaving his corrupt brother's house, now what am I going to do, I'm too old for anyone to hire me. But now, what the hell am I going to do.

But not knowing it at the time, God has always been my supportive assistance, but have always been too damn blind to see him. Here's what happens next. After thinking that maybe I won't be able to help my parents, all of a sudden, I come up with an idea. So all of a sudden, I tell mom and Dad, let's start a janitorial maintenance business. Mom and Dad looked at me, and asked, how? I tell them, buying some vacuum cleaners, a couple of mops, a bucket, and I'll go hustle the accounts. They just starred at me, as mom said, I'll be praying for us. Because at that very moment, we needed what God could give us. I mentioned earlier that I didn't get any supportive assistance from my sisters, much less from my wife. It seemed that the more I needed help, the more of a pain of the ass she became. She was too far gone into being an alcoholic and being a whore. She couldn't help herself, much less able to help me.

But my biggest focus was, to keep my parents on their feet, financially. And I was able to do that. They didn't lose their home. And that's what my mom and Dad were afraid of. Losing their home. And I was going to do my most I could do, so they wouldn't lose their home, not if I could help it. God helped us. God is good and God is Love. But boy, was I always tired. After all, I was burning the candle from both ends. If you know what I mean.

From starting this janitorial business, things went well for a while. From my high school days I had become pretty good with public relations, so I didn't have any problems in getting accounts. Was able to get accounts like about three per week at an average. I was always tired, but I was also proud that I was able to help mom and Dad stay on their feet. As for myself and my wife and daughters, that was another story. This woman I called my wife, had me mentally stressed out. And I was physically deteriorating away. Not eating well, losing a lot of weight. As I said, was able to get accounts pretty steady. I had five super markets in my list of accounts. That was good, but it was also a lot of work, because I didn't just do super markets, I also had about thirty offices also to clean. Does anyone know janitorial work? For me it wasn't so much about cleaning the offices and retail accounts I had. It was the part I had to clean them and go out during the day and try and get more accounts. And not getting any support from this woman I called wife. This was around the clock business. I had to be at many places at once.

Burning the candle from both ends. Have any of you ever done that? Because I've done it a couple of times in my life. A couple of times too many. Once to save lives, and another time to save mom and Dad from financial disaster. When Dad's business was taken away from him by his brother, that was not healthy for mom and Dad. That was a very crucial time of their lives, where they could have landed in financial stress., and in the hospital. And it was complete evil on that brother of his to do, to a loving man and brother that helped out that evil man to move out from Arizona and to relocate him to California when time of need to help him in his waste business. So how could I just leave my parents in a very sad, and bad situation. I didn't, I tried staying as strong as I could. But I never did this alone, believe me. I hired a few kids, I had to. I had to be bonded. I had a hundred thousand dollar bond to insure no merchandise would be missing in any one of my accounts. A hundred thousand dollar bond was proof of my guarantee nothing would be missing in any one building I was responsible for. Thank God I never came across any theives, in my company.

As I've said, was not happy at home, with this mistake, by marrying a woman that didn't give a shit about no one but herself. Drinking, and then she started doing drugs. And going out to see where she can go steal, which is burglary, and if they catch you too many times, you're going to prison for ex amount of years. I was walking a very straight tight rope in my business. Didn't say I was walking a perfect one, said I was walking a tight one. But I felt like I was in my own world. Which literally I was in my own world. So I didn't know how long I'd be in this business, with an alcoholic cheating wife at home, with small children to support. As you can all see, I was slowly spiraling down the toilet bowl, with all the shit that comes with it, what this kind of a woman can give a man. It's beyond me how I've survived all the obstacles I had to jump over and crawl under, and run around, because I don't know. But I have to say this. He's been there for me all along. Which is, and has been God there for me all of my life. And as of yet, have never broken a bone in my body. Oh, but how I've come close.

After I started slowly drifting away from this maniac alcoholic cheating woman who I was married to, I started wondering, I better do the right thing. Or I won't be any better or different than her. The reason I say this, because I started drinking as well, but I was in a small corner of any bar. With my own stressful self. All of you know, depression and stress will kill you, like it did my mother. And it was a slow death. And I'm surprised all to hell, why I haven't come down with any serious nerve racking disease. Mom was forever telling me to divorce that woman. And it was very easy for her to say, but it was hard to do that, because now I have children, with her. So now what, now what do I do? I once confronted mom, and asked her, if I was to divorce this woman, would she baby sit my daughters. Unbelievable, she immediately told me no. And I told Mom, in a rough way of speaking, "you want me to divorce her, but you won't baby sit your granddaughters, what do you want me to do, take my kids to work with me, sorry mama they won't let me do that. "So what do you want me to do mama, quit my job to watch over my kids, and how am I going to feed them"? Mom quickly responded, ok ok ok, I'll take care of them for a while. And she did, and so did that sister that introduced me to that, that was giving me a major pain in the ass. The mother to our children. It was nerve wracking, and heartbreaking. Nerve wracking for me and heartbreaking for our daughters. And that's the way I lived, if you call it living. The way I look at now, looking at it back then, I felt I was dying.

Will forever never forget my mama, how her and Dad would come over just to see if this woman was home. And she knew she wouldn't be home. It would be on one of my days off from work. Just my daughters and myself at home, and as I wrote this, it's was so disgusting to be married to that, to call her the mother of my daughters. It was so shameful for them us. Every woman that has children, is or supposed to be with their children, am I right people? At least that's the way my mother was, always with us, her children.

With my life, as an old man today, recently one of my daughters asked me, if there was any time while being with their mother, if I could remember any good times with her. I found it very hard to answer that big question, because I didn't know how to answer my daughter. Both of my daughters were very young when this catastrophe was happening to all of us. Because that's what it was, catastrophe, destroying all of us. And it did, my daughters are still suffering from not having a mother at a very young age. In fact my daughters never really had a mother.

Later on, I'll paint you another ugly terrible disaster, for mostly my daughters.

It makes me very emotional to recall those sad memories for my daughters.

When I tried to answer that big question, when one of my daughters asked, if I could remember anything good about their mother. All I could say, I'm so sorry my daughter, I can't remember anything good. Which was the truth. What could I say? I wasn't going to make up stories about someone that was no good. Because this is my life story and I'm not gonna creat something that didn't happen, just what did.

Have always loved my daughters, and always will. I will say, we three had our fun times. As I'm recalling those beautiful times together, they were so cute. I wasn't going to moan and groan when we were together, while we went to Disneyland, Knots Berry Farm, the San Diego zoo, the Los Angeles Zoo, the Griffith Park observatory. Took them to carnivals. Oh my God, I took them where I had never been, as a little boy. My mom and Dad never took their kids to where I took mine. That's all the more reason why I wanted to take my daughters to places their grandparents never took their children. But it is what it is, or for my story, it was how it was. And I was concerned about my daughters's safety so very much.

Remember telling them, and reminding them constantly, when they would walk to school, do not trust no one, and I would stare in their eyes to both of them and ask them to repeat what I was saying. As I told them, when you're walking either to school or from school, don't trust anyone trying to get close to you, by trying to walk close, or trying to get either one of you into their car. For me, it was very important they understood that. Then I tell them, so when they try to get close, and maybe get closer, yell as loud as you can and run to a close by house, yelling for daddy daddy. And I'd ask them, my daughters, this is very important you remember that. So do you understand me? And they would. And guess what, that very message of safety I delivered to my daughters, it happened to them. My oldest daughter told me, "you know what Daddy, there was this guy in this car, he was trying to get us to talk to him" thinking to myself, why that son of a bitch. Asking them and what did you do. We did what you told us to do. We ran up to a house and yelled out daddy daddy. Asking, and what did that guy do. My daughter, says, he took off quickly. Sex maniacs have always made me sick. Thought about that, oh thank you lord. God has always been sweet and loving to me.

At this part of my life, our loving God will continue to bless me, while I still had many more obstacles to climb.

Have never been very good at dodging any obstacles coming at me, don't know about you guys. Maybe you've been better at it than me. More power to you. But I've found out, now that I'm old, better

ROBERT GARCIA

late than never, that it's not so much the obstacles we have to watch, it's the trials and tribulations, God puts us through, to tests us during anytime of our lives. I've been through it, you've been through it, and sooner or later we all go through it, until our end of this physical world is over, we all will face our Lord. And by the way, I'm still going through my trials and tribulations. Until my end of this physical world. Don't know about how you feel, but I'm so fearful of my second life, praying everyday I'll be in our God's loving arms in heaven. So as I've tried to be a good person, I was always falling short, as a young boy and as a young man. I think I still fall short at times. But we're just children of God. I've always had too much anger in me.

And also at this part of my life, I'm slowly killing myself, because I didn't really know what was happening to me, going through my third death. Remember "DIED THREE TIMES LIVED ONCE" My first two experiences with death, were quick and had gone by me too quickly, but I'm still alive, and partly sane. My first two psychologically deaths were not even close as to what I'll experience on my last psychologically death. It will take me completely down under. In other words, I will hit rock bottom, as the saying goes. And it's not a joke to hit rock bottom. If of course any of you know what that is. Because I didn't know what it was either, for a long time, until it happened to me. Always thought it was a myth, yeah right pilgrim.

Without any Godly connections, at any part of our lives, before we leave this physical world, we must wake up before it's too late, because the way I interpret the Bible, if we don't wake up, and we die two deaths, the physical and the spiritual, we're doomed for eternity. And that my brothers and sisters scares me to death. Spiritually speaking of course. I guess what I'm trying to say, you can lose your mind, but don't by all means lose your spirit. And if we can follow our spirit with our physical body, we might have a clue as to where we will be for evermore through eternity. And that my friends is hard. But I'm going to try anyway. Nothing will ever be wrong if we try. Because it's real, I don't care how you look at it. God is on his way. No we'll never get to perfection, but we can try being better than we used to be. I know with my cursing and my anger, I fall short of being better than I used to be. And it can be so very hard for me.

But as long as I've looked for bad or evil things in my life, what kind of life do I expect. It's like an obese person pushing away food from his mouth, almost impossible right? Well, try pushing away evil bad things away from your lifestyle. Again impossible right? I know it's been almost impossible for me.

On my first experience with my first death, when many people thought we should've died and didn't. I wanted to ride on top of the truck's over head, to look at some nude pictures of women, as Dad told me no, I couldn't ride up there, and I was so upset. And then we crashed. Almost killing us. And then I went on my R.R. (rest&recuperation) to Hong Kong of my deployment of Nam, what did I want to do, like so many of us young guys want to do with women. You know what I'm talking about. I don't need to paint you the whole message. You know exactly what I mean. It's nothing new. Many of us, and of course I'm one of those, want good things to happen in our lives, when we spend most of our lives, and for some, we spend all our lives looking for evil without realizing it. Am I right? And like I've said before, it's too bad for the majority of us, we have to get old before we realize what we're doing.

For those of us that are lost in life, we're like dogs chasing our tails, until we realize, if we're lucky to realize what we're doing with our lives.

So as I continue this fiasco of this life of mine with this marriage I'm in with this betraying, alcoholic, woman I married, at a daily basis, for not just myself, but the two daughters we had. These two poor daughters of ours were the most delicate ones that suffered the most. Because they were first born to a woman that should've never been a mother, and then their Dad betrayed them as well. Because I had become no better than their mother. But that will be later on in my life's writings to tell on myself.

As three of us, my two daughters and I, would go have a great day or so, only on my days off from work, and not to focus so much on the reality of things. Which was mighty sad for all of us. I had become literally my two daughters's, their mother and father. I as their Dad, was missing my counter part, our daughters's mother. Because even when she was with us, she'd be drunk. She was a full blown alcoholic, and couldn't help herself. Sad huh? So I had to do the best I could, which was not easy. Especially when I didn't get any support from my mother, nor my sisters. And then one of them decided to help me out. So thank you very much sister. And then later that sister of mine, wanted to try to adopt my daughters from me. Say what? I didn't find that out for quite a while, until my oldest daughter told me about it, much later of course. As corrupt as this sister was and still is, with her pissant husband of hers, I wouldn't put it past them. Now remember this is the same sister that played cupid, by introducing me to this alcoholic woman I'm married to. And so I put trust in that sister, when I didn't know what she was trying to do, until much later. Thank God that never happened. They had already had a boy and a girl, that were adopted from some adoption agency, and they got along good for a while, until I heard that sister say something to Mom. That her cowardly husband of hers had molested the girl, and she decided to leave, without pressing charges. Can you people believe that? Of course there was never any proof. So it went untouched. I've always had a few choice words for those kinds of scum bags.

In this situation and in this point of this time of my life, trying to handle two birds with one stone. Impossible, because it's got nothing to do with birds and stones. And it's much more important than a stone and couple of birds. What I'm saying, it was really becoming very difficult for me. To do the janitorial labor at one end, and then go during the day to add new accounts to our company. It sounds impossible right? But I was doing it for almost five years. At the same time trying to raise my daughters. Maybe it wasn't impossible for me at the time, but I was getting burned out. And that's putting it lightly. I needed to help Mom and Dad stay financially stable. Like I said, it worked for a while. But I started running out of gas. But all along I never lost any of my janitorial accounts. In fact I would receive compliments, by keeping public relations with my accounts, with a simple phone calls, just to make sure of our cleaning service was to par. Don't know if this has ever happened to any of you. But check this. Because as I was getting burned out, I was starting to lose my brain power. What I mean is, I was physically getting tired and my mind was starting to burn out. Has that ever happened to you guys. Realizing when I wrote this, that happened to me twice in my life. But in this particular time, I couldn't believe what was happening to me, which was, my mind was starting to blank out. And it will get much worse before anything will get better. And my life will not get better until I reach my fifty eighth year of my life.

And by the grace of God, I've made it to where I'm at now. As I said, when I wrote this, I was in my seventies. And this has been far more and beyond than what I expected, believe me it's been a very very difficult journey for myself and for those I love dearly. Yeah I repeat, it has been a very difficult and dangerous journey for me. And that's too easily said, because being difficult, is an understatement. Because words will never describe the road or should I say thee roads I've traveled to get where I'm at today. I'm just trying to paint the worlds I've been in and out of to you is all. I'm not a writer by all means, but all I'm trying to do is relate a message to anyone that will read this, if in case this happened to you, or if it came close. Then we have something in common. Have never thought I was alone in the things that happened to me. But there are, of course, unique things in all of us, that are very different in treacherous ways of our lives. That naturally made feel very lonely. That's how I believe how evil wants you to feel. That's simply not true. But because people like myself go through negative experiences throughout our lives, we tend to feel, it's only happening to us, like I thought, it was happening just to me. But there's always positive outlooks in anyone's life, if we look for it, and reach out for help. If we want to, but a lot of times, we just want to give up. And that's what I ended up doing, I just gave up on myself and everyone that I loved. Which was very sad for everyone involved. That's was a very sad part of my life. And it still makes me emotional just the thought of that time of my life. That will forever stay as a scar in my heart.

I've heard people say, that life is like the game of dominoes. Once a part of your life starts to crumble, and if we don't try to fix what has fallen, you're whole rest of your life will follow to crumble like the game of dominoes. I know that happened to me. Statically speaking it's happened to many of us. Society doesn't care about anyone or anything

ROBERT GARCIA

that happens to anyone. And why should they? When we start to fall, we should seek help before we fall completely. I think I'm right, am I? But I didn't know where to seek help. So I continued to fall, and fall deep I will. But just not in this part of my life, as of yet.

When I started blanking out and burning out with fatigue, couldn't find a way out. So what did I start doing? Drinking!!! What an answer to my problems. That was a very cowardly thing to do. To just quit.

So, irresponsible me starts hiding, and where at. In a bar. Just not in a topless bar anymore. Had thought after having daughters, should stay out of nude bars, so I have since my younger days. To be respectable.

There was this neighborhood bar, where everyone I grew up with went to. It was the same bar, where I've caught my alcoholic wife with another man drinking together, in hugs and in arms. No shame that woman, with our children at the entrance door way. But now here I am, in that same bar with my own problems. Feeling sorry for myself. And who walks in, my dear old Dad. With a disgusting look on his face. Couldn't blame him. When I'm supposed to go and take care of business. Instead of being responsible, I'm in a bar, drinking. What a sad case of chicken. Because that's what I was, just plain chicken. As Dad asks me, "What are you doing in here, when we're supposed to go to work and take care of our business" I couldn't answer him, because I didn't know what to say. The next thing he says "You know I'm thinking of joining your sister and her husband with their business" which was the same kind of business we had, janitorial maintenance. I couldn't blame him. All I said, ok, go ahead. I'll go look for a job.

It was amazing, how within a few months, Dad and his son in law lost every account I had hustled, when I first started, about five years earlier. Now all of them are gone. Unbelievable

This was one of my lucky times of my life, out of so very few. I went job hunting and found this ad for retail management. I called, made an appointment to be interviewed. I arrive to my interview appointment, and I see about ten to twelve others waiting in line to be interviewed.

And all this time I'm still struggling with that dysfunctional wife of mine. Can you believe it? Because I know there's many guys that would've gotten rid that woman in a minute, if not sooner. Oh, but this guy (me). As I go back and forth from different things that I recall through my whole life, from the beginning to my present. It's been interesting how I been slow in many things and fast in so many other things. But I know this, I wonder why did I waste so much time with wrong women. Maybe being so naive, or maybe just plain young and stupid. I think that's it. Probably many of you won't admit it, but I have to. And by writing this, it relieves my spiritual being. Maybe that sounds funny to many of you. I say this, because there's been a few times in my life, people have told me, I have a strong spirit. The first time someone told me that, I wondered why he told me that for a long time. I'm sure you've met those few with strong spirits too. Have also had people tell me, I'm a unique guy, unusual but pleasant to be around. I liked when I heard the word, pleasant, because it was a very attractive woman that said I was very pleasant. Of course it was a topless dancer. Never the less it was a pretty young woman.

Because I'm writing my life story, I'm spilling my whole life on some paper, and we have the right to write about ourselves, right? Whether we like what we write or we don't like what we write. How I feel, as long it's the truth, the good, bad and the ugly. Besides, as I've said, there have been some people I've come across, that have advised me to write a book about myself. And now, better late than never, at my age, I'm writing my story. As much as you have the right to write about your life. But I think my life is more interesting, because I should be dead. But came oh so close. All three times I keep saying, "DIED THREE TIMES LIVED ONCE" I don't think I'm alone, each time I had death stare at me straight into to my eyes, and they were three times as I have kept repeating, I've come out a different person. Does anyone believe me? Doesn't matter who believes me, because it happens, and not just with me.

At this part of my life, I felt I was going through hell, torture and agony. An alcoholic wife, Dad losing his waste business to his brother, that could've been prevented, if he would've listened to his son (me), and didn't. Started a janitorial maintenance, business, which Mom and Dad totally relied completely on me. Having to look for cleaning

ROBERT GARCIA

accounts during the day and then having to clean them at night. How did I do that?

After five years, and my Dad came looking for me in that bar, was heaven sent. Now that I flash back to that time. Thought to myself at that time, and thinking about it now, I would've died for sure. I also thought, Dad didn't show any gratitude. After I saved mom and dad from financial burden, from maybe losing their house. Just after Dad's brother stealing Dad's business from him. How quickly people forget, and they can even be your own parents. But what could Dad do, after finding his son in a bar, when we were supposed to go on a janitorial cleaning route. I would be the one driving, and was half drunk. Maybe I could have crashed or get pulled over by some cop. That would've been just beautiful. For me to get thrown into jail, instead of doing my job.

All this time, didn't know where my alcoholic wife and our daughters were at the time. What an upside down world I was living in.

What a complete different world I could've been in, if, and just if. And this would've been financially beautiful for our whole family. If maybe Dad would've listened to me, years earlier. And at the same time, this woman I called my wife wouldn't have been an alcoholic.

But that's only when we live in a perfect world. With these people, my Dad, and my wife absolutely impossible. Looking back at it back then, lights on, and no ones home, people have always said. But then I wouldn't be where I'm at right now. Living in Las Vegas for the past eleven years. And married to a very nice lady. But it will take a long time to come. Too long. But that's how I think. And that's my selfish way, and not God's will or way.

Can't help but think back, when I was sixteen years old, and I remember it vividly, because Dad's ways of thinking, and running a business, was not the way to run a business. It was so easy for evil to take possession of Dad's brother's soul to think of taking a million dollar business from his brother, my Dad. Because Dad was just too nice of a guy. Evil people have always been able to see Dad's easiness, and vulnerability. You hear it, you read it, Dad has always been too vulnerable, I know it, because I was one of those, that took advantage of Dad's vulnerability. Sad huh? Yes I think so. Sad but true.

But Dad wouldn't listen to his only son (me), which really hurt Dad and Mom, financially, and it deeply hurt me, emotionally.

As I've written it, over and over again, when I was just a boy, and as I reached my teenage years, Dad and I had never been connected as a father and son should've been. That has always hurt me, but I just didn't know how to hurt at the time. I knew how to run from Dad, and that's why I enlisted into the Marines.

Let me write you this one. Most young people, that want to succeed in life, start out, by going to school, naturally, and some just barely graduate high school. And there are those few that continue going forward, and become successful with a great career. Whether it be in a medical field career, a law enforcement career, a communications career, an engineering career, or a major airline employee. Those are the smart ones. Have always respected every person that had a mind to succeed in life. And may God Bless those few. Later in my life, I will tell on myself, to tell you all, how far I fell. And lost a beautiful career that I could've had. Because of my stupidity. I'm not hiding anything, and I'm not leaving anything out. Because this is my story. And I'm not gonna build myself up, because I'm not proud. But there's only one thing I should be proud about, but I'll never brag. I'll only write it down. And every veteran should be proud, that they honorably served our country. But at this point of my life, it's all behind me. I've got way more important issues at hand. Mother and Father, my daughters and I hate admitting it, my alcoholic wife as well. And believe me people, I have to admit, and because we had two daughters, I loved that alcoholic wife. But I was so lost, and confused, with the idea that I wanted to keep our marriage together because of our children. So maybe just because I wanted the marriage together, but I had lost love for her and getting real tired of her alcoholism. Which was true, and after so much time, who wouldn't get tired of that kind of life. I had become physically and emotionally tired of that alcoholic, and not just for me, but for what our daughters had gone through, which was unacceptable for any little girls to go through. Because finding out much later, our daughters had experienced traumatic incidents. Being exposed to perversion, while I was at work, the mother of my daughters, would have men come over, lock up our daughters in another bedroom, and have sex with more than one man. And for me never to know about it, until I finally was divorced from that woman.

Can you f**king believe that. I not knowing what was happening behind my back. Oh I had my suspicions, but that's all I had, suspicions. But that outrage, and the gull of this mother of my kids, exposing little girls perverted filth.

And who knows how long that was going on. My daughters were just little girls my God. Always thought and wondered, what kind of a woman or even a man would think of doing indecencies. Our, or I should say, my daughters were able to sir-com difficult traumatic experiences at so young of an age.

I personally have had my times with alcohol, but have never once take it to my head, to touch any little girl, and very much less my own daughters. I've had a heart of love for my kids and they're my loving daughters. They're my blood. And so, for someone or anyone to take advantage of, and to expose any child to pure evil is beyond my understanding, because there isn't any. It's just evil. And that evil comes from hell. And through time, my daughters have grown young responsible and respectable ladies. And I'm very proud of them.

Evil possessed people don't last long, and other people sees them as who they really are.

Well as time goes by, I ended that disaster of a life for both my daughters and I, by divorcing that hellacious woman. She just wouldn't stop, until her dying day. I didn't know when she died, my sister that originally introduced me to the woman I divorced, and then two years after I divorced her, she ended up in the hospital, and died from cirrhosis of the liver. But what I noticed a few years before I divorced her, I witnessed her vomiting pieces of her liver. You'd think she would learn and wake up and reach out for help. But she was too far gone. In other words, she was beyond help. Don't think I didn't try to help her, because I did try to help her, three different times. I took her to three different hospitals. And each time she was released from each hospital, she came out worse.

After divorcing that woman, and I had to still call her the mother of my daughters, because by all rights she still was. But she was also an unfit mother, and that's why I petitioned her for divorce, because she was far out and beyond abusing my daughters. I couldn't stand it any longer, for the sake of my daughters.

But little did I know at the time what this life was slowing doing to me, was eating my soul away and continued to confuse me, so it wouldn't let me try and live my life that I wanted. But here I go. We all hear it all the time, I, I, I, me, me, me. It's always about ourselves, with no regards, and consideration of the ones we say we love.

Thinking I started getting my life together, just after divorcing the mother of my daughters, meeting with a woman through a dating agency. To me, it's not any different than how couples meet up today, on the Internet. But I just didn't know it at the time. Naive again. Naive maybe, but I needed a mother figure for my kids, yeah my daughters. So I dated a few women through this agency. And I met a young lady, from a latin country. Telling me all along she would love to take care of me and my daughters. And at the beginning it seemed that way. We looked like a happy family. And I'll say it, like many have. Many things in life don't always seem like they appear on the surface. There's something hiding underneath all the time. So we make our promises, and we thought we fell in love. That was just another reminder of a song, promises, promises, are made to be broken. And they do get broken, just like this life with this woman will be. Broken. No she was not an alcoholic, but just another bad apple. I think, by looking at it from another perspective. I was moving too fast for another bad relationship. And I'm falling down another hole again. And again I didn't know it then.

I might be talking about many of us. But for myself, I was too easy to entangle up into another relationship, for two big reasons. The first one being, and I'll admit, to satisfy my sexual appetite, and the second one being, having a woman around for my daughters, as a mother figure. And I don't know if it was because I was young and perverted and wanted a woman around me. Probably so.

Remembering the day I met this second wife to be, but this day would just be a trial, because we didn't know if we would stay together. And the way I look at it now, I wish we never had met. She didn't seem like it at first, but this woman was materialistic.

I have found out about life in general, from a man's point of view, if you look for a good woman, we probably will never find her. But if we lean into God's blessings and have him choose a good woman for us men, then we probably will have a better chance. I can say that, presently speaking, because here I sit with my current life with my current wife. And very happily married. And maybe because I'm old now, and when I was young I loved the sexual excitement. But when I was married to my first wife, I loved her, and I didn't have any other woman. And this first wife of mine, always had someone on the side. I don't know how you see it, but to me, that's betrayal. Through my life, I have always felt, if you're married, there shouldn't be anyone else. But then again, we're talking about living in a perfect world, and we're far away from that peaceful life. The world has been and always will be corrupt. Until the second coming of Jesus, to end this world, it's in the Bible. Upon Jesus's second coming, he will judge the living and the dead. I can only imagine how many people don't believe that. That's probably why the world is corrupt.

Coming back as to how I met my second wife. As I recall that memory, it seems funny to me now. How did I expect to find someone good, if I'm looking for a woman in a dating agency? You don't find anyone good. Especially if they're from another country. As for naive as I was, this woman had a big plan up her sleeve. And I never saw it coming at me. Before I was planning to see this one, I'd already dated a couple other women. And lost them quickly, because I was too fast for them. I was too itchy for a woman, and they could sense it, so they declined to see me again. Which was okay with me, there are plenty more where they came from. Cheap way of thinking, huh, don't you think? Guess that's just how I felt about a woman in a dating agency. Any woman. The old saying, you get what you pay for.

Forgot to mention, my procedure in divorcing my first wife. It was difficult, because I was trying for custody of my daughters. And if you think that's easy, think again, because it was not easy. Don't know what the procedure is to divorce anyone today, it may be the same, I don't know, and I really don't want to know. Maybe because how I feel about divorcing anyone, if it gets down to that, it's probably going to end very sour. With a lot of regrets. At least that's how my two marriages ended up. Ended regretfully speaking.

Mom kept telling me to divorce that alcoholic wife of mine, but never paid any attention to her. Until I finally got tired of that alcoholic. Eighty five percent of the time she was drunk and missing, and I not knowing where my daughters were. Or I would pick my daughters up at their grandmas house (wife's mom), and no one knew where my wife was. Of course after that fiasco f**ked up life, my daughter told me much later.

Had been already working at my retail management position for a great company, for approximately three years when I finally decided to divorce this wreck of a wife.

And to serve her with the divorce papers, that was another story. Because first I had to get me a lawyer, and with what money. I had to get a loan, no two ways about it.

And I also had to serve her the divorce papers. And I don't know how they do it today, but I couldn't serve the papers to her by me, so I had to get someone to do it for me. And I did. A co-worker of mine. And what did that future divorced wife do to the divorced papers, she took one looked at them, and she tore them up. I thought it was funny, because I pictured her tearing pieces of paper, like a little girl mad at her paper dolls. But it didn't matter, she got served with divorce papers, and that's all that mattered. And when it came time for court, I thought it was going to be a fight for the custody of my daughters. And boy was I happily surprised. As the judge started court procedure. Asking me who was in the courtroom with me. I pointed out my parents and my attorney. The judge was amazed, asking me, and where's the other party. Responding back at him, "I have no idea your honor" asking me if I had a job and where were my kids. Telling him they were being taken care of at one of my sisters homes. There wasn't much to talk about. He telling me, that there wasn't anything to elaborate about. Next he's

ROBERT GARCIA

dismissing the case in my favor. He banged his judges hammer, and court is adjourned, giving me custody of my daughters. Thinking, hey that's great. And it was. But my problems are to be continued. And after court, I was very happy with the results of having custody of my daughters. And check this out, no one, and I say, no one showed up in court, from my divorced wife's family. We're talking about ten brothers and sisters and her mother and father, and no one showed up in court. Which to me, was amazing. Because here's what happens next. Like I said, I'm enjoying my time with my mom and Dad, and how I now have custody of my daughters. And so we're all enjoying our time together, when all of a sudden, there's a call while we're all talking and laughing. Dad answered the phone, and he looks at me, telling whoever was on the phone, saying yes he's here. So I take the phone, and this woman started yelling at me, telling me, I better take my daughters to her house. Can you believe that? Because I couldn't. So she spoke to me at such outrage. "You know what young man, you better bring my granddaughters to me right now if you know what's good for you." And she went on, on, on. And threw a bomb back at her. I yelled at the top of my lungs as I could manage. Telling her, "You know what you old woman, you have no damn right calling this number and demanding me or anyone anything. Where were all of you at, when I went to court, divorcing your daughter." "I'll bring my daughters to your house when I want and when I'm good and ready, did you hear me" It was like, she froze, not knowing what to say. Because she knew I was right. As I slammed the phone down on her. Mom and Dad hearing every word. As Dad said, "Wow" Telling them that, that woman doesn't have any right calling and yelling at anyone. So she got the message. And didn't hear from that part of the family for a long time.

That part of my dysfunctional life was over, only to begin another. And of course I was unaware. But that's life, right?

Coming up to my second wife, and how did that go. Like I said before, it went well for a while. But everything always starts good for a while. There are very few things that go right, and stay right, even our health doesn't stay right. And unhealthy relationships are not good for anybody's health. As my first wife wasn't healthy for me nor for herself. But I had warned her.

And now I'm starting this second relationship with this woman, coming from a foreign country, temporarily legal. And I didn't know that for a long time. But I will find out in due time. And when she wanted me to know, and not until then. Because my figuring it out, she needed an opportunity, when the time was right.

Entering that dating agency office was just a small tiny office. As the office woman greeted me with a warm welcome, how could she help me. And was I looking for a lady. Of course I replied that yes I was. That it came with a price. Asking her how much was it. And I never paid what I owed. So I paid the office woman, I guess you can say, I put a down payment for a relationship. To me writing this down today, sounds funny. And she proceeded by handing me phone numbers to women. She handed me about three numbers. I called one from Peru, and we went out, but that didn't work out, because she didn't like the way I was treating her. She told me I was going too fast, trying to get her drunk at a dancing drinking lounge. And guess what, she was right. What do most men want when we're out with a woman, when we're drinking and trying to get a woman drunk? It should be obvious, without saying. Well I did what she requested, without a comment from me, took her home. Waited a few days. Thought for a few days, this dating agency was not going to work for me. So I tried the last number the agency lady gave me to call. And I called and it rang for a little while, until someone answered. Asking for the woman that matched the number, she came on. Exchanged some small talk, and apparently we agreed with our ways to go out for a meal. And like I said, everything goes well for a while, and maybe even for a little while longer. But like I've also said, many things in life, aren't always what they seem on the surface.

She lived downtown Los Angeles, in a not so good of a area. But at this point in time, I'll probably be taking her out of this place. But I didn't know it then.

Have to admit, it started rough, because all she spoke was Spanish, and just because I'm a Mexican by blood, it doesn't mean we speak Spanish well, and I didn't, and I still don't. Have always said, people like us can't help we were born in America. It wasn't my fault. But I have to say, I'm damn proud I'm an American. A American Veteran American. Can you tell my pride for her, America that is. I'll always be proud of my country. One nation under God.

Going out with this one, seemed soft and gentle, as she seemed to like I treated her like a lady. And why shouldn't I, I didn't know her yet. I've always focused on good and respectable impressions. And what's wrong with being a gentleman, absolutely nothing.

Remembering another time with this second wife to be, like I said, I just didn't know, she would be my wife at that time. And there are so many things that makes me feel regretful towards that marriage. Maybe because I feel she used me. Just not the way my first wife did.

Here I go being scattered brain again. Because I forgot to mention a few important issues I had gone through with that first wife of mine. And they are very important. Between life and death important, that's how important. I guess I should say, I've been miraculous lucky during my entire life. There were times with that alcoholic wife, she could've killed me, and why she never tried, or succeed I don't know. Because there was this one time, I was asleep, as she was going through my pants pockets, of course she was looking for money, to support her alcoholism. Well I was awakened by the noise she was making and I caught her and I gave her a kick, enough to knock her down. She quickly got up and I got up behind her. As she commenced to running through the house, and running to the kitchen she did. As I ran from behind her, knowing I could have stopped her from what she was going to do. Whatever that was going to be. So I decided to follow her just to see why was she going to the kitchen. As we're running to the kitchen, couldn't believe it, as she approached the utensils drawer, suddenly she opened the drawer and pulled out a knife.

A knife, oh my god, didn't and couldn't believe it, but I had to react very quickly. And I did, because as I ran from behind her, I was in my stocking feet, exactly when she pulled out that knife from the utensil drawer, I jumped in the air and kicked it out of her hand. I could not, I repeat, I could not believe it, what just happened, as I yelled at her. "What were you going to do, stab me, why you bitch" as I slapped her across the face. When I kicked the knife out of her hand, it flew about three feet and stuck into the wall, it looked like a movie, I've seen many times in my life. This other incident with this drunken woman, that I had made a mistake in marrying, we had been drinking together almost all day, and we were sloppy to say the least. And it was getting late into the day, but she didn't think so, since she didn't have to work.

I've got to say, that when I was in this lusting, disgusting relationship, when we ran out of sex, didn't know what else was there. It was like I ran out of gas. And I couldn't go any further. This car (me) ran out of gas. It was such a shame. She was a school dropout, she didn't want to work, and she couldn't hold a conversation, if her life depended on it. Sad huh? Yes it was, for everyone involved.

This incident that I'm about to tell you. Like I said, we had been drinking all day. And she's a mess as I was. So I decided to stop drinking for the day. But she tells me to go get her some more beer. With a glare in her eye, and with pure hatefulness. So that made me feel humiliated and I had to yell at her and tell her that I wasn't going to get her any beer. Oh but she couldn't take no, for an answer. And she had one more beer left, and picked that beer and threw at me, trying to hit my face. And she almost hit me, but I caught it. It was a good thing I was paying attention, because she came close. And as she threw that beer, she yelled, "Go get me some more f**king beer I said" Aww all that did was make me furious with outrage, as I ran up to her, and gave her a hard slap across the face. She broke down crying, saying she gonna call her Mom and Dad, which wasn't going to happen, as I yanked the phone from the wall. They'd kill me if given the chance. As it was, I had already pulled a gun on her brother once already. I didn't want my ass kicked or I didn't want to shoot anyone, that's for sure.

Have never been proud of what I had to do to that woman. But what was I to do, let her slap me, or let her hit me with anything she saw fit. And I would only hit her with one blow, and with a open hand. Never with a closed fist. Never never hit any woman with a closed fist.

I'm not going to keep on dragging this one nightmare on and on. I felt completely free when I finally built enough courage to divorce her. And after just two years after I divorced her, she was dead. And that was it. Only for me to start another disgusting life with another woman, my second wife to be.

As I started dating the second one, there was this time, when my ex mother in law came by to ask me, when would I bring my daughters so she could see them. Telling her, I didn't know. She had nerve, because I had another woman at the house. And the woman became scared, telling me that they could kill her. Telling her, don't worry, we'll be moving out soon. And we did. To San Bernardino, here we come. There were people had already warned me against San Bernardino, but I wouldn't listen. So we moved to San Bernardino anyway. Only to be a complete disaster. But I can't blame San Bernardino, or anyone else. It was my mistake from the beginning. I'm not going to sit here and play the blame game. Because it wasn't a game, when hearts were broken.

Since my first facing of death, when I was seven years old, and then going off to war in Vietnam and facing my second death, at nineteen, It's no wonder I have insomnia and had nightmares for a hell of a long time. Now pills help me out sometimes., but they haven't worked all the time. Anyone ever wonder how we get insomnia. Well I don't know about you out there, but my life has been pretty well f**ked up since my beginning of my life. And I didn't help myself out, meeting up with whores and bad influences. Because that's what I did, dig myself a grave, and now at this point in time of my life, I'm trying to stay above ground. Does anyone know how hard that is. Because it took me a long long time to figure it out. Even though I'm having a hard time forgiving myself, for the things I've done. And I know God has forgiven me, by giving me the life I live now, that I have never had even dreamed of. Because I never had these kind of dreams in my life. At my age, I feel more alive than ever.

And so as we continued on this fantasy I called love. It was all just a fantasy, and didn't know it. We'd go out. Still working at my retail management position, which I cherished very much. Aww those were the days I could be trusted. Trusted? Yes they could. Well I had already been trusted, when I started the janitorial company. Different accounts gave me keys to their buildings, and trusted me with hundreds of thousands of dollars merchandise. And now I'v been working with a company that trusted me with thousands of dollars per day. I'd say that's trusting me very much. And I felt good about it.

On my days off, my daughters and this woman I just met, and I, would all go out to a family restaurant and then go to a movie. Those were such peaceful days of my life with my daughters, and thinking this would be a right choice for a mother figure, but I'll find out otherwise to be wrong. Because she had children of her own, and in her mind, her plan was to immigrate her kids to the States. And to use me was part of the plan. And it will come sooner than I thought. To have me petition her with her children, because she wasn't a permanent American citizen as of yet. That would come with the immigrating with her kids, in due time, when she saw her advantage to kick in to use me.

Of course we had a sexual relationship, what couples don't? For a man, it's always delightful to have sex, right guys? Sexual satisfaction has always played a big perverted roll in my life. Finding out through my life, we can always find sex, but it's never been easy to find love. True love that is. We get what we pay for. And that's what I got what I paid for. And paid dearly, at my daughters expense.

Thinking at the time, I really loved this woman, and I would do anything for her. And I did. She worked in downtown Los Angeles at some leather company, doing piece work. Thinking, I couldn't believe they still did that. Working wage, getting paid for how many pieces you can put together? Outrageous, also I'm going to have to get her out of that working environment, since I thought I loved her.

I don't know how women feel about what I'm about to say. But from a man's point of view, men think they're in love, when they're really in love with sex. How many fools get betrayed, yeah I know, women get fooled as well. But I'm speaking for myself, because when I thought I was in love, the woman I thought I was in love with, was f**king someone else.

I can't say this second wife of mine, was betraying me for another man, but she betrayed me in another way.

So I proceeded to try to help get this second wife out from working for piece work. From downtown Los Angeles. And I did. But it was a lot of trouble. Because I thought I was in love. Imagine this, because she would take the bus from Whittier to Los Angeles, everyday she went to work. And how would I stop her from doing that. Oh, it took a lot of time, a lot of planning, and a lot of money. A fool right? Huh, huh. I guess that's why they came up songs, like "Fools Rush In" and here's another one, "Why Do Fools Fall In Love"

Question for many of you. Have any of you ever fall in Love by yourself. Because that's what happened to me, when I loved a woman, had finally figured out, I was in love by myself.

And everyone has their own definition of love, don't we? And when you think you can change someone, think again, because you can't and you won't. I know I tried with my two marriages, and I failed. But that's life, isn't it the way it goes. Of course.

Thinking I'm a much happier married man than I was with my first wife. With my first wife, that was not a marriage, and that was not a woman, that was an alcoholic. Now here I am with this one. No she was not an alcoholic, nor was she a drug addict. Good right? Of course I thought she was a good woman. But time will tell. She always promised she would love my daughters as if they were hers, and would always love me till the end. And little would I know, till the end, would become the end of a very sour relationship. She always said, if we would part one day, she would always be my friend. Yeah right.

So I continue on my dark tunnel with this woman, thinking all along, and believing her she loved my daughters. They all looked happy, we all thought we were happy. But looks were deceiving, and especially for my daughters. They would end up suffering the most. It's always been the kids that suffer the most. Through bad relationships. You seldom hear of good relationships that children grow up happily with mom and Dad. Very few.

Thinking I grew up happy with my parents. Not so much, because here again 'I had an alcoholic Dad. And Mom suffered, and she didn't deserve it.

We had our fun times, that second wife and my daughters, for a while anyway. But that now seems like a long time ago now.

And so as time goes by. And all this time, Dad had issues with me, as to why I never called their home. Well, since he didn't know, I became very busy with this second wife and my kids. I was very focused on supporting this woman. I was soo naive. Neglecting mom and dad, so terribly bad. I'm telling ya, that relationship with that second wife was just a continuation of my dark tunnel of my life.

She started talking about my mother, can you believe that? That started to really aggravate me. For anyone to talk about my mother.

One fine day, we're all having a beautiful day off together with my kids, and we get a knock at the door, thinking who could that be. There was this man, soliciting from door to door. Wanting to enroll anyone that wanted to become a Certified Nursing Assistant. I tell the man, please let me find out about my wife, maybe she would. I ask him to please wait, while I find out if by chance my wife would like to do that. And we talked about it for a little while, as the man patiently waiting outside the door. And oh my god, she said she would. And so that started a good career for her. Now remember, and just so you know, she's no longer working in Los Angeles. I had convinced her to quit that terrible job.

Now I'm the only one working, and that was okay, for a while, I could handle that. And now I had to support her even more, because nothing's free, as we all know. And to think this woman later started talking about my mama. So I started forking out the money with a down payment to start. And you still should remember, her kids are still in Central America with their grandma. She had a son and a daughter.

When we started dating, before we got married, I was working at a retail store chain as a store manager. Making good wages, and I was happy working there. But after five years, I thought I could buy and run my own store. At least that's what I told my district manager, where I managed one of his stores. And that was the biggest flop at this part of my life. Mom and Dad were going to lease a building to start a retail store, preferably a liquor store. But that fell down very deep. And it was very disappointing. Because it could have been a very prosperous location. But mom and dad didn't want to. Mom and Dad could not visualize making a profit at a location that would prosper, because all they saw was the rent we were going to have to pay. They looked more into the expense, than the profit.

Being it be as it was, my hands were tied. So I had to leave my parents with their own burden. Leasing a building in the most drug infested part of Los Angeles. When we had a beautiful chance at a brand new area, a brand new shopping mall.

So at that time of my life, I couldn't afford to marry anyone. So I had to put my romance on pause. Oh, I was still dating my future wife to be, we just didn't know when we would marry. So she waited for me, and I thought that was nice of her.

When the time came for my parents and I to talk about what was going to happen. No one was happy. I was very upset with them and they with me. And they wondered what were they going to do with that store in the ugly part of Los Angeles. I told them to sell it. Poor Dad, I actually left him alone to run a store, he didn't know anything about. Maybe because I was more interested in my life's future and maybe I thought they didn't care about that. I'll never know, there were so many mixed feelings.

Feeling at the time, mom and Dad couldn't see what I wanted, or maybe needed for my life. And what did I do, I ran from them. Leaving Dad alone in L.A. That was a very betrayal thing for me to do to them. But how could I help it. They leased a building in very bad place, where there were prostitutes, heavy drug addiction, alcoholism, and they were not going to approve anymore liquor licenses. So what kind of future would there be for us.

Mom and Dad were more afraid of what the expenses would be then the pending profit, and that was too bad for all of us. I should have known from the beginning, my parents were not business savvy. I also should have known, Dad losing a waste business to his own brother. Dad didn't even know, when I advised him to draw up a contract. And what happened, his own brother took the business away from Dad. And what he do, cry. When he didn't have to.

So I had to do something to keep supporting my daughters and the woman I thought I loved. Just another day of my life. I'm surprised I've never had a nervous break down. Because most people would have shot themselves. And that thought would come to me, much later in my life.

Anyone ever wonder how many things don't go the way we want them to go? Well guess what, I've oftentimes wondered as well. Until I finally thought I figured it out. And only if you believe in God, and only then. And you have to believe it that it's on God's time and will. Not on ours as we think it is. Sooner or later we would be much better off and much happier if we let go and let God. I've heard that phrase so many times, and I figured it out what it means. If we let go of the things that stresses us out and makes us worry, and let God handle it, we could be much better and much happier.

I've had to learn from the things that tried to pull me down, and the people that had tried to kill me. And even from the people that tried to make me cry. We have to, because if we don't, we'll live a miserable life, and you might end your life too short. And I've also had to learn from my relationships. I've always thought the women I married before my current wife, were wrong, and maybe I was wrong as well. I never thought I was wrong, because I didn't have time to do wrong. I was always working, supporting this wife or that wife.

All I've ever tried to do is do good. And I guess that's been my problem.

And this second wife of mine, thought I was a push over, and I probably was. Because it was easy for her to talk me into petitioning her and her children to immigrate them to the States. All she had to do was draw up the paperwork with the immigration department, and I would finance it. I didn't know what she was doing, and I didn't know what I was doing. She spoke Spanish with Spanish speaking agents. I assumed she was doing the right thing. And maybe she didn't do the right thing. That wouldn't have surprised me. It's been the story of my life. Trusting women, that I thought loved me. But as I've said, love is in the eyes of the beholder. Or maybe I was just in la, la, land, and dreaming.

And now this second wife started school as a certified nursing assistant student, receiving a white uniform and her instructions, where to start her classes, and how long it was going to take. I think it was six months, and by the way, I was also going to find out how much it was going to cost me. I think when she quit her Los Angeles piece work job, I can only imagine how happy she was on that day. So of course she's going to try to show more love than she has before that day. Normal right? Starting her new training at a nursing school, must had been an enormous plus for her and her family.

But before all of that was to happened, we would have to do some suffering first. Suffering, not real bad. Because I had to work two security positions. Which wasn't any fun. And she of course took the bus back and forth, from Whittier to Los Angeles, every day she worked. We dated for about two years before we got married. Thinking all along this was going to work out. As you can see, by writing this, that marriage didn't last, unfortunately for everyone involved, it was disappointing. A lot of her, and a lot of me was at fault.

Don't get me wrong, we started out on beautiful relationship. But they all do don't they?

But something had to change for the better, for a brighter future for all of us. And change will do. And I thank God when that happened.

I don't know why I've often thought about what I'm about to write. Just the other day I told my wife wouldn't it be nice if we could die for a night time of perfect rest, and perfect sleep. That would do wonders, and it would be great rest for guys like me, that has to take sleeping pills to go to sleep. It would surly relieve a lot of stress and pain. Wouldn't it? I know, that's a far fetched dream of weirdness.

I must had worked at a lot of security companies for too long. Until I finally got a break. One day, just happened to have to go to a cleaners to pick up some garments, and I see this lady with a hanger with a, it looked like a highway patrol uniform. So, me, with a inquisitive mind, asked, are you a highway patrol? She seemed so delighted and proud to tell me. "No I am not, I'm a Correctional Officer for the women's state prison in Chino, California. And she was very eager to inform me, "And you could become a Correctional Officer as well, if you want. Because I've been able to buy a house, and support my family very well." And I asked, "where do I apply, and what will I have to do" She responded, "First you mustn't have any felonies on your record, for the past ten years" "And they're hiring at state level and county level right now", and you can apply at any government office "I was so grateful, that woman giving me all of that information. Running home and telling this next wife of mine the great news. And she also informed me, I would have to pass a physical and pass an academy.

And she also told me, I would have to pass a ten year background check.

I felt I was hired already, because at the time I didn't have any felonies and although I was short in stature, I have been told, I carried myself very well. And that was true, because I've pretty much had been able to take care of myself.

Did some research on what was the difference between a state Correctional Officer and a county Correctional Officer. And found out there were big differences. Finding out on my research, a state Correctional Officer, I have always thought, they're all a bunch of babysitters. On the other hand, a county Correctional Officer, works in a county jail. A state Correctional Officer, mingles among prison inmates, in close contact. Now I thought why would I want to mingle among prison inmates. Almost all of them don't have anything to lose. And if I was a state guard walking around these idiot losers, and just in case one of them wouldn't like me for some reason, I could all of a sudden have an accident, and never see the next day or night. That part of being a state Correctional Officer, turned me off.

I guess I've never been too keen with killers given a life sentence to go to prison, when they've taken lives. I'm old fashioned. I believe if you take a life, they should take your life. America is too lenient, when it comes to high profile criminals. We see it everyday, an evil basturd is born every day, years later they're out there doing evil stupidity. To me, I've always believed, an eye for an eye, a tooth for a tooth. But not America. They'll drag out a long ass investigation, with evidence pointing right to the asshole, and finally take it to court, and if the victim's family are lucky, they'll find the asshole guilty, and sentence him or her to hundreds of years to prison. I have always thought that was a mockery to the innocent people, and the victims family. What do you think? We've all seen it time and time again. Society believes that by killing a convicted criminal, by whatever there might be, whether it be hanging, the electric chair, lethal injection, that we're not any different than the convicted murderers. Well it's so easy for people say this and that. Since the poor victim has been killed, he can't defend himself.

It might be very obvious which way I went. I decided to apply for the county position. I applied for county sheriffs, Correctional Officer position. Had gone to a government office, and requested an application, and went home. As you all know the county doesn't hire anyone just like that, it took about six months, from the time I applied until the time they hired me.

Meanwhile I'd been researching the benefits if they would hire me. Unbelievable, yes I prayed the county of Riverside would hire me. Great retirement.

Meanwhile we were living in an apartment, and not in a very good area. A bunch of hoodlums, gangsters, and thugs. As this woman I had planned to marry, was still working in downtown L.A., and I continued working security work. My daughters and this woman and I lived together, living pay check to pay check. Sending my kids to school and so forth. I even got hired at Universal Studios. That was a short worked job. It was nice, but there wasn't any future in it. It was quite a hassle trying to be patient waiting for the county to call me. And I was starting to think they weren't going to call me. But I kept on waiting, what else could I do. And then I worked at a Greyhound bus station, as security. Boring. Imagine you're working as security at a Greyhound bus station, and your job description is to run off any homeless people or any one disturbing bus customers. I didn't like it. But that's what I had to do, to feed my family.

Like I said, it took at least six months. Waiting all of that time, seemed too damn long.

I guess who I was really feeling sorry about was the woman I wanted to marry, and my two daughters. It was depressing watching my family suffer.

But in the meantime, I started doing exercises. Running miles at a nearby school, seven miles per day. I've always been a runner, at school, and in the Marines. Finally all of that stress and misery paid off. Because, by the blessings of God, I received a call from the county office, telling me I needed to report to their office at a certain time and at a certain place. Agreeing with anything they wanted me to do.

And I reported to the Riverside county office before my appointment time, and dressed up and ready to be interviewed. Have always known, to make a good impression, always dress for success, was my motto. And it always worked. Because they would always hire me.

At this point in my life, has anyone noticed how my life had started to shoot straight up, where the sky was limit for a wonderful and beautiful career. Now I haven't gotten hired yet, but I'm well on my way.

Haven't spoken to my mom and Dad too much lately, but at this point I decided to call them, because I had become too busy with two jobs. Told them I wanted to come by and talk to them. And drove over to their home the next day. They lived in Norwalk and we were living in San Bernardino. Telling them that I could get hired by the Riverside County Sheriff. And I told them, I wasn't sure, but the process was looking very good into my favor. And I should know in a couple of weeks. And I would let them know, when and if that happens. Th

At this time of my life, I was starting to feel, I was on cloud nine. Or maybe cloud ninety nine. Whichever I felt I was on of the better of the two fantasies. Because this fantasy would all end up, just being a fantasied nightmare. I had a dream on my lap, for it to all fall, as I threw it all away. And how did that happen, people would ask. But that will come in due time.

Right at this point, I still haven't gotten hired yet, with the Riverside County Sheriffs department because I'm still going through the process. Finding out, this will be my most intense interview in my life. For obvious reasons, it's a law enforcement position. After all, they never want to hire ex-cons. But we've all heard the ugly stories of some law enforcement agencies have done just that. I never in my life have ever had any problems with the law. That's my honest word, as God as my witness. But haven't we heard that all our lives. There are prison inmates that they'll tell you, they're innocent, right? I've heard that same guilty innocent story, and you have too.

Some more good news came my way again. And for the life of me, I just couldn't believe it. I received a call from the Riverside county internal affairs, informing me that my hiring process was looking very good. It blew my mind. I just about put the telephone in my mouth, I was so happy. Of course I was happy. Happy is a understated word, at that very moment of time of my life. The man on the other end of the phone, tells me that the hiring process is looking very good, and that they would like for me to be at their office at a certain time. Asking me if I could be there, I tell him, of course I'll be there, you can bet on it. I was so excited I must told everyone I knew. Oh my parents were so happy for me.

A few days went by, and I got to my county Sheriffs appointment an hour early. And why not, I wanted that career position so bad, I could taste it. And soon enough I'll be eating my career to hell, that's right, something drastic is coming at me so heavy, it'll feel like shit burying me alive, and didn't even see it coming. But the good things are coming at me first.

As I arrived to my appointment, I wasn't surprised to see many applicants waiting for their name to be called. Thinking, wow, it might get more competitive than what I thought. Because if we're hired, it can be a career of a lifetime. Retiring from a law enforcement agency, whether it be a county sheriff, a federal agent, from any law enforcement, it will be rewarding. Well, my name was called, was I nervous? A little, but I soon got over it. I put it in my mind, we're all just men, and we all put on our pants the same way. But there are those few men that think they are better than everyone.

As this interviewer greeted me, he started with asking a bunch of questions, which is common. And still is. Started by asking, if I had ever worked for the county before. And, am I working right now. Am I married. Do I have any children. Then came the heavy questions. Have I ever been arrested. Have I ever done drugs. Do I do drugs now. Do I drink. Did I drink before I came to the interview. Of course, the answers were all no. He made me feel like he was better than me, until he asked me if I ever been in the military. And when I told him I had been in the military, his attitude changed. Asking me, what branch of the military was I in. Telling him I was in the Marines, and had served in Vietnam. He completely became humble. He asked what did

I do in Vietnam. Telling him, I was in the front lines, in the infantry, for thirteen months, in Vietnam. As this interview came to a halt, he informed me, my answers were very impressive, and that all that I had said, will be investigated on. And if all that I had said was true, they would be calling me for another extensive interview. Do you guys know how I felt, when he told me that? You have no idea. I was super excited, I felt I was walking on clouds. Walking oh so lightly. You guys ever feel like that? I know I'm not the only one, whoever felt like that.

Returned home, ever so happy, everything around me, just looked so beautiful. Nothing could bother me. Telling my kids, telling my wife to be how my interview went, and that they would be calling me again for an extensive interview. Everyone in the home had a smile. Of course my daughters were very young then. Didn't understand what I was talking about, when I told them how excited I was, for this career I was seeking.

Well the time came when internal affairs of Riverside county called me, setting me up for my extensive interview with a psychiatrist. Now that was going to be very interesting.

And interesting it became. In that time of my life, had never been psychologically interviewed. Because this psychiatrist was very strange. He didn't greet me with any smile, or friendliness, like many people do. Just stares at you, as he asks questions. Now I thought, if I just concentrate on his questions and think about answering him the best way I know how, I might pass. But I wasn't sure, if I would or would not. So I did the best I could. But that's all we have, right guys? We give it the best shot we can, in facing life's obstacles. And some obstacles can be far out, and above and beyond. At least that's how we all think how life will be. Until we discover how God has been so close all along. I know I thought I was lost three quarters of my life, until I opened the door of my heart to the knocking of Jesus Christ. But I will not know how to open that door, until in my life's writings. I was very skeptical and confused, throughout most of my life. And I don't think I'm alone with that scenario either.

Lord and behold, I didn't know how I did in that interview until maybe a week later.

ROBERT GARCIA

Receiving a call later from the Riverside county internal affairs, just gave me an amazing feeling, telling me, you've been hired, and to report to the office for instructions, on what would be my next step in where to report to.

Everyone that reads this, should know what my reaction was. That's without having to write it down. I thought I was dreaming. But I'm glad I wasn't. It was actually happening to me.

And during all of this time, I still wasn't married to my second wife. I couldn't afford to get married. Things will change financially after I complete my whole hiring process with the Riverside county Sheriff's department. Our lives were on a merry go round of love, at least we were at the time. And that will change dramatically as well, at the end of my life's writings, going into my last deathly experience. "DIED THREE TIMES LIVED ONCE"

This second wife to become, was still struggling working in downtown L.A., and I was just making it with bills I had to pay, up until the Riverside county called me. It's always been a miracle to me, how God has never been in a hurry but he's always been on time. On his time, not on ours. We're such a imperfect being, we're confused more than half the time. Many of us confess, and promise they're going to do the right thing and then completely do the opposite. I've confessed, I've promised, and I've cheated. I've got nothing to hide I've got nothing to lose, not anymore anyway. I did before. Before I surrendered to our lord, I had a lot to lose. But since I found Jesus, and accepted him, as my lord and savior, my life made a one hundred and eighty degrees turn around. Anyone lost and confused as I was, you need to seek help, before you lose your life. Before you lose your second life, spiritually speaking, because that's the most important life we have to save. I of course started my athletic training long before the sheriff's department told me I'll be starting the academy with others, male and female alike. That didn't matter to me, as long we all did what we were told, and pass each phase of our training academy, we'd all be fine. This life's writings of my time, being hired by the Riverside county Sheriff's department had given me prestige and dignity, and class, with a lot of confidence.

And why wouldn't it, it made me feel like I was on top of the world. It made me feel so positive about myself.

I was so motivated and inclined to do what I had to do, to pass the academy. Running, and running, push ups, sit ups, and whatever else it took. I was as serious as when I was in Vietnam, saving lives. The Riverside county hiring me, made me feel proud of myself. And who wouldn't be. But I never felt better than anyone, because no one should feel better than anyone, simply because we're not. I just felt better than myself, feeling better than I was before.

So the first day of the academy began, and we were all eager to start. I knew I was. I have been ready since they told me I was going to start my Riverside County Sheriffs academy. We all had a hotel voucher, about fifty of us, to stay at a La Quinta Hotel, free. This voucher served us for the room and for meals. We were at that academy training for two months, for classroom and physical training. It was very intense, as I expected it would be. I wasn't worried about the physical training process of the academy. And neither was I worried about the classroom part of it. I had a lot of confidence and self discipline back then.

It was practically like going through boot camp. But now I was older, but still in shape. And we were getting paid for it at the start of training. Unbelievable, who could ask for more. Competing against one another. The best of the fifty would stay hired and continue on our probation working instruction, for ninety days with our trainer. Oh, I'm not gonna say it wasn't hard, of course it was hard

Waking up at six in the morning everyday, until noontime, and knock off for lunch, and back and hit it again, until four or five, depending on what part of the phase we were in. Have weekends off, for two months. Wow, I loved it.

And all is calm at home. Beautiful, those were my days of happiness, when I started the Riverside Academy training. And the woman I had planned to marry had given her job L.A a two week notice that she was quit that slaved warehouse she had worked for maybe four years, until I met her. Things were starting to look up for the good. No issues with my daughters and this wife to be, yet. And that word, YET, will be crumbling down within a few years, it will be unfortunately sad for the loved ones involved. Which will be my lovely three daughters. Very sad for all of them. But it will be devastating for the woman I had planned to marry. I've heard it said, and so have you. The facts of life has never been how it seems. It looked good, it looked very promising. But it will fall, all of it. My whole beautiful world will come crumbling down, along with my career, family, and myself included. That's right, everything that I ever wished and dreamed of will wither away, like it never happened.

But it will be strange as to how this all means to me at the end. Because still in my present life, I still don't understand, and probably never will. That's the same thing as saying, I don't understand God. Does anyone? But I've come up a certain conclusion, I don't think God wants us to understand him, but just love him, have faith in him, and with all of that, have hope.

As I've mentioned before. Almost everyone that wants a successful future, focuses on education or a trade of some kind. And what I've seen what people do they become successful, no doubt about it, right? Currently married to a lady, that has five children and are all successful, two retired police officers, two work for two major airlines, and the last one, is married to a retired police captain, after thirty years of honorable service.

Anyone can do it, if you want to. I've always said, the sky is the limit.

Well, here I was at my civilian boot camp, the Riverside County Sheriff's academy, after twenty one years of my return from Vietnam. And I felt pretty good about it. And I will be passing through this academy, with flying colors.

In classroom scenarios were terrific. Most of my school days were all on my side. And I would be passing this academy very well.

Back into a uniform, wow, as a Correctional Office, soon, but not yet. Because I'm still in my academy training. But I was already seeing myself in the nearby future, in a uniform, of a Riverside County Sheriffs Correctional Officer. Was I proud, I should say so. All the rights to be. Wouldn't you be? Come on, you know you would be too.

While going through the academy, it never fails, there was jealousy and racism. As I've said before, as long as man exists, there will always be prejudice and racism, that's just the way the facts of life has always been. There will never be future modernization, while there's barbaric people in the future modernization. Barbaric people do not know how to accept equality. There is just too much evil in the world, there has always been, and it exists today. Not much has changed since three hundred years ago up to now, when it comes to racism. It's the old will, evil people believe in. And they have the evilness to call it Christian. But we all have to some way, work with it, try to move beyond it. And it's always going to be hard to do.

Until the day of our Lords return, evil bad people will be here.

You hear me talking about this woman that is about to become my second wife, like If she was nothing to me. Well no, I'll try not to be so negative about her. Because I actually fell in love with her, and we both have a daughter from our former marriage. I'll always regret how we drifted apart, having a sad ending by divorce. You would probably feel a little negative as well, if you were writing your life's writings, about people that broke your heart too. But my life has been full of heartbreaks. There has been days I didn't know what to do with myself. I have realized that most people don't care about no one. So with that in mind, we have to care about ourselves. And I found out the hard way, we have to love ourselves before anyone can love us. I didn't say, to fall in love with ourselves, but just love and respect ourselves and love and respect others.

So when my second wife and I met. It seemed like a fantasy, and of course we won't find out if we were meant for each other, until much later.

I took her out the first time to the Disneyland restaurant, classy huh? We thought so, and I had a few drinks to myself, by talking her into going to bed with me. And why not, we weren't youngsters, and we weren't old people. But I think I approached her wrong. Because as we came back to the car, as we sat, and as we spoke, I pointed out the car back window, and I asked her if she would like to go to a hotel that was just across the street of Disneyland. And if you could have seen the look on this woman's face, I wanted to bite my tongue. She immediately told me to take her home. Man oh man, I regretted that night, trying my sneaky way of trying to get her in bed. After all we're just men and a man like me, I like women. It took me a while to take her out again. In fact I didn't think I would ever take her out again. But she must have liked me, or she would never want to see me again. Or our baby daughter wouldn't be here today. Baby daughter? She's now in her early thirties. As all old people approach our years, we all say, where have all the years gone? No one realizes it in the beginning, that time flies so fast. And then we're all of a sudden old and in pain. With me, I've had neck pain since I was in that disastrous truck accident when I was only seven years old. The first time I died.

As I said, didn't think she would allow me to take her out again, because I called looking for her, I'd say three times, without results. She had been living with her cousin and her husband, until I came into her life. And we both probably would have been much better off if we would have never met. Didn't realize it then, but she was too materialistic, as I was to find out later.

Oh, we had our good times, her and I, with my daughters. But I would find out, her pretending to play mother to my daughters, would become deceiving for my kids and I. Looking back at the time, she seemed so honest to me. And so I believed every word she would say to me. Why would I not believe her. The vulnerable victims are the easiest ones that believe anyone and everyone. Dad has always been the weakest victim in our family, to believe his biggest liars in his life. His own brother and the daughter, he claimed to love the most. Next to Dad, would be his son, me. I had been the number one target for my first wife, that had taken my love for her, and abuse it against me. And this woman that would become my second wife, would be the next one to abuse me, by taking my love for her, and abuse it against me, but in a much different way.

To this day, can't come up with as to who was more abusive, that second wife or myself. This is why I say, we would have been much better off if we would have never met in the first place. My youngest daughter was the result of my second marriage, and to this day, we don't talk. I can't blame my baby daughter, she didn't ask to come into this corrupt world. And she grew up without her Dad. Me

And I will reveal that part of my life in due time, in my later part of my life's writings.

Because there's so much in between that will happen, from this page to my last page, of my life's writings.

And we were having such a great time together, having a great time until I helped her immigrate her and her son and daughter. And I'm not blaming her kids, neither one is at fault as of yet. How sweet it was when my daughters were loving this second wife of mine, at least it looked that way for a while. With ages, we're talking, my daughters, eight and six years old the wife, forty years. That's a long time ago now.

Back up, while all of this was gonna happen, I've started my Riverside County Sheriffs academy training.

As I married this second wife, and commit to our "I Do's. Should have been, "We don't" Those were days I will cherish dearly forever within my heart and soul. For my daughters that is, because they're the ones that suffered the most, by their alcoholic mother and by this woman that became their step mother. Felt so sad for these little girls of mine.

Do any of you out there relate with me, in a similar way of life I've lived compared to yours. If it's even close, then you know very well what we've been through, right?

And how were you raised? Were you neglected and ignored like the many times my Dad neglected and ignored me. It's like a chain reaction. From one generation to another. Dad was abused by his Dad, then he abuses me, and then I ended up abandoning my daughters. In time that will happen in my life, when I became blindfolded by evil. That's what that is, pure evil. Simple bad choices and wrong decisions.

For me personally, choosing a wrong woman to have my first two daughters was a bad choice. Because it was just sex, we both were focused on, and that's when I should have stopped, and move on with my life. Asking myself, was I wrong in falling in love with a sexually motivated woman, because I'm not gonna lie and say I didn't like it. Looking at it at my stand point, now as a old man, I was starving for an American woman, coming back home from Vietnam, after seeing combat for over a year. As I experienced my second death. As I wrote this, I feel like I've been dying all of my life. Until living my life now, and experiencing a life, I've often thought I don't deserve. Because of my guilty feelings of my addictive past. And I have also wondered, could it had happened, with that truck accident, maybe knocked my head into a euphoria kind of world. Or did I completely get confused, what is right or wrong for me. I had no clue. And I, like Dad, tried the best we could, with no guidance.

You as I ever wonder where'd you be, if you had made better choices. I know I've oftentimes wondered. My current wife tells me her loving opinion. Respectfully telling me, if she had been my wife, before those other two, I would have been a successful man today. That's God's truth, because if she wouldn't have had a stroke, she would have stayed in her import/export business. And she has come from a successful family. On the completely other hand, if she wouldn't have had a stroke, we would have never met. Life is strange, when it comes with God's time, and his will. And I've stopped trying to understand God, because all it does is confuse me. If you out there, believe in God, and believe like I do, in the afterlife, and I didn't believe near as I as I do today. But as old as I am today, I feel like I've only just begun. Because I feel, as long as anyone lives, there will always be room for improvement. No one knows it all. No one. And for me, the more I learn about myself, and what God wants me to do, I'll always try and listen to him from within my heart. Because I can't hear him with my ears. I feel I see God around him, just by observing his creation.

All along, as I married my second wife, and I started well into my Correctional Officer position in Riverside county, thinking I had the world by the tail. My new wife and I thought we would last forever. Not when I had thoughts of actually thinking I was better than anyone. I'm telling ya, it must have been something in that truck accident and my Vietnam deathly experiences that had me well into my way towards my third deathly experience. Can't say for sure. And my wife started out her Certified Nursing Assistant school, which would last two months. I couldn't believe it, she could hardly speak English, and she's going to be a nurse. That's what I thought she would be someday. A regular nurse. It's sad, that after twenty five years, I've heard through the family grapevine, that, that ex-wife is still a Certified Nursing Assistant. Thinking after all of these years, she stayed stuck at the bottom of the totum pole. She's now an old woman. Sad. Also thinking, that If it wouldn't have been for me, she wouldn't have gone to that Certified Nursing Assistant school in the first place. Because at the time, I was working at my Correctional Officer position, I financed the school my ex wife went to. What I'm getting at, that without me in her life, she might have stayed stuck deeper in that leather belt piece sweat warehouse job, in L.A. when I met her. Well, here we are, a four member family, wife, my two daughters and I. We really thought we were happy, we looked and seemed happy. Well, you've heard it before as well as I have. Looks can be deceiving.

I've heard people say, that when a person is happily married, there shouldn't be any deceitful betrayal thoughts from neither spouse, while either spouse is at anyone place. Whether we go to the store, even just going to a gas station. Even when we go to our work place. Neither member of a married couple should not be flirting. That should be well understood, when we committed our promises, right in front of the alter, promising each other with our vows, and our "I Do's" Thinking that I could get away with anything, and maybe even go out with any woman behind my wife's back. And all of was starting to happen, when my wife started acting funny, since I promised I would help her petition her and her son and daughter, to become legal United States citizens. She had me fooled and convinced.

A couple of times I had seen this wife crying in the bedroom, and of course I wondered why. You see, I promised I would first help, by giving her money to send to her mother in her foreign country for her kids. That went well for a while, until she found out, when her daughter wrote to her, that her mother was not using the money like she was supposed to. So she broke down crying. As a man, like I'm supposed to be, help his wife, right? She responded to her daughter, that we have a plan, and we'll get back to her. Well I advised my wife, that why don't we have her kids move to the States. She immediately became very

ROBERT GARCIA

happy. With a smile from ear to ear. She grabs me and kisses me. And out came tears of happiness.

So now we have a plan. To process my wife and her son and daughter to the States. We continued sending them some money until they caught the flight to California. Everyone was excited, including my daughters, and it was exciting, because I felt loved by my wife. Well, I didn't know it at the time, that would all fall apart. All of that paperwork I didn't understand, only that wife did, for all I knew, she could have been doing something that would be against my better judgement. I'll never know what or how she processed the immigration papers for her kids. All I know what she told me what was going to happen. She did this all in Spanish.

Now we waited for the day her kids would arrive to our home. I was really looking forward to it. Aww, but the day would come I would regret everything.

Have always wondered what did it mean, love is blind. Through the years I would find out, my own definition of "Love is Blind" When you fall in love with someone, thinking they love you back. That's a hell of a assumption, right? Well that's exactly what I assumed, that this second wife of mine, loved me. Well I would soon find out, I was wrong. As like my first wife, likewise with my second wife. But I wouldn't know it, until much later.

Just like my first wife, there was so much shit going on behind my back, and her family not telling me a damn thing. That was so aggravating, and the less her family told me, the more I would get pissed off. And now this second one, but at this very moment of my life, didn't know crap. To put it lightly. I guess that's why they say, love is blind. Not only was I blind, I was naive and stupid. Fools and stupid, and naive people always seemed to fall so easy, during my time, since I lived during that time, I'll admit it, I fell into that trap more than once. Thank God, I wasn't always like that. Only when it came with women. Does that sound familiar guys? I know it's hard for you guys to admit your stupidity, like I used to. But this is my life and this is my life I'm writing about. You'll have your turn, when you write about yours.

As I said from the beginning, my second wife and I, got along great, including my daughters, they loved her. You notice how I say, "They loved her. Past tense right? Because that second wife, not only betrayed me, she betrayed my daughters as well. No, thank God, she wasn't a drug addict or a alcoholic, but she was a opportunist. For vulnerable people like Dad, they can't recognize opportunistic women. And I used to be vulnerable as well. So this second wife and I and daughters, were all living like we were meant to be.

While all was well at home, at least at that time it was, I was well into my career as a Riverside County Sheriffs Correctional Officer. Well maybe not all into it. Actually I had just begun. Because after our academy, we still had to go through a ninety day probation training, with a trainer, right by our side at all times. Oh that was very interesting, because my trainer was tough. And I'll never forget him, because he made me feel confident that I could pass my training all the way. Does everyone know what a Correctional Officer is, and what he does? I don't think all of you do. I'll try to be as job descriptive as possible. It won't be easy, but I'll do my best. Let me ask another question, does anyone know why they call prisons, "DEPARTMENT OF CORRECTIONS" because that facility title, doesn't fit the institution, criminals are sent to. The way I've seen it through my life, most criminals that are sent to prison, come out much worse than when they first went in. And I don't understand the justice system, when a murderer is found guilty, with overwhelming evidence, why do they give them life in prison, when they took lives. I guess I'm just old fashioned. I just believe in the old tradition, an eye for an eye, or a tooth for a tooth. Is that so hard to understand. It's always seemed to me, that the victims have no say so, and neither do the victim's families. I will always feel sorry for the victims and the victims families. I'll try to understand why America has abolished the death penalty. Because we're supposed to be a Christian government, and we're not to kill criminals, even if they took lives. Because then this country wouldn't be any different than a murderer. And even child molesters are given rights, now that one is hard to swallow. Because I have daughters, that's why. It's hard for people like me, to forgive murderers and child molesters.

Don't know why I took so long to apply for a law enforcement position. I've never really known what I ever wanted for my life, through my life. Life has been hard for me.

Maybe I'm crying from the inside. How I think life could've been for me, if I would have met a good hearted woman, instead of going with the first one that wants to f**k me, after just meeting the night before. That's been pretty much the story of my life. Until now, I'm writing my real story, what really happened to me. Oh, I guess life could've been worse, like a lot of other guys, that landed in prison for life, or even dead somewhere, maybe in some street, or gotten killed in prison. Or maybe something even worse, I could've been like anyone of my sisters. Oh my God!!! Oh, thank You my dear God. I cherish three blessed parts of my life, the first, being God being there for me all of my life, when I never knew he's been there all along. The second blessing, my lord sending me a lady, I've never thought I deserved. The third blessing of my life, is having Dad as my friend, because we've never been close when we were young. Thank you Lord.

But the bad is still coming at me real quick and strong, with this second wife, at this part of my life. The three blessings will come into my finally, climax of my life. Just writing this, and having a piece of mind that I never knew I would have. Is so overwhelming and satisfying.

As I continued on my end of my probation training, working in the Riverside county Sheriff's department, at the jail, had become challenging aggressive for me. I loved everything about it. And why wouldn't I like it. It was a well paid position. My God, it was a career with great benefits, medical and great retirement. What else could anyone want.

And as I worked at the county jail, my wife had started out on her new nursing position. Which all looked all well and good, nothing to bitch about, as of yet anyway.

Coming back to my county position in the jail. Being a Riverside County Correctional Officer was a great prestigious career. So what does one do as a prestigious uniformed law enforcement officer?

Like I said, after for filling my academy training, we all still have to be on hand training, what they call, a probation period, of approximately ninety days. At this point, it is the real thing, with face to face with inmates. Which almost all of them are pending trial. I was trained by a man, that had been a correctional officer for about fifteen years. Everyone seemed to know him. Even the inmates knew him. The repeat offenders that is. We're all talking about the nineties, when I had worked for the county of Riverside.

My wife is just about to graduate from her nursing school, because she wanted this real bad. And that was good, because she could start as a Certified Nursing Assistant for now, and continue going to school. At least that's what the plan was, at the time. And it wasn't a bad plan, if it would've materialized, how awesome that would've been. We would have been in a upper class financial world. Could have bought a house, send our kids to school. We had a lot of dreams. So many dreams could have become true, if disruptions wouldn't have come into our path. I'm talking about evil deceitful disruptions.

Just about finished with my ninety day probation, and it was working out just great.

My wife just about finished with her school, and I'm finishing my probation training, and looking good. In fact both my wife and I, were looking great for our planned future. At least that's what it looked like on top of the surface.

There's one thing that never changed with this wife, she could never drive. I tried sending her to a driving school, but she just couldn't get the hang of it. Even the drivers instructor told me, this wife of yours is impossible. When I tell her to step on the brake pedal, she steps on the gas pedal or when I tell her to step on the gas pedal, she steps on the brake pedal. And she doesn't learn, she continues to make the same mistakes.

At first he sounded and looked funny when he first told me, because he seemed so disappointed. Well it disappointed me too, because now I'm going to have to pick her up from her job, or take her to her job. That was very inconvenient for me. And inconvenient for her as well, because I could only be her ride on my days off from work. And she would have to take the bus to and from work. But I continued to stay married to her, thinking that this will all blow over.

Well, her son and daughter are coming to the States. We received a letter from her daughter, that they were on their way to California. At the time I was excited and looking forward in meeting her children. Yeah I really wanted to meet her children. After all it was only right, she was treating my daughters like she was their mother. At the time her son was, if I can remember, he was fifteen and her daughter was I think she was thirteen.

This is funny, as I wrote this part, I started thinking, I never once asked her, how long she had been in the States, nor did she ever have the respect to tell me. And I also never knew, how long was she looking for a man, before we met. Who knows. I sure in the hell didn't. Maybe she had been with who knows how many guys. Until she met with this fool (me). As I look back at that time of my life, I realize now, what a fool I was. That's another good example, of "Love is Blind" I know I've always been blind, I say, all of the time, I've been blindly in love with women. But aren't most of us? Some guys are just smarter than us dummies. Looking back, that's just how I look at it, and how should I look at it, I had been used and abused.

I have always been the kind of guy, that had to impress and please the woman I'm with. Does that sound familiar you guys out there? Because I know I'm not the only fool, that has gone through bullshit from women. But who's fault is that, because we let ourselves get fooled. Just because we always want to take a woman to bed, right? Now that I'm old, I look at myself, as a complete young pervert. Very blunt and to the point, as I've always liked putting it.

Don't beat around the bush, tell it how it is, that's how I've liked it.

So we got married downtown L.A., and she becomes the first step mother of my daughters, since their biological mother couldn't at least try being their mother, because of her alcoholism. That will always be a very sad part of our lives, my first two daughters and I.

I tried helping my first wife from her alcoholic disease, with no prevail, and I tried helping my second wife, become a American citizen, including her kids. And I was successful, and prevailed. And when her kids arrived at California, it was a very special day for all of us. I felt it was a holiday, so I took the day off from work. I've always thought I have been quite fair to the people that have known me. I've also been quite fair to my siblings, my two sisters. They in turn, as America and see it the way it really is, instead of what they read. And for the countries like where this woman came from, they don't know what freedom is. Because they don't have freedom. What those countries from where she came from, they have too much violence, and too much corruption, within their own government. Whereas here in this great America has always had law and order, and If you read her history, America has the reputation of fighting for freedom for the past, close to two hundred and fifty years. At the cost hundreds of thousands of lives. You don't know it, read her history.

Only in America can anyone come from any part of the world, as long as a person is legal, can go to school, and become what you want to be. Whether It be to study law, to study medicine, nowadays, study for computer technology. And if you can afford it, you can buy your own house. Anyone out there, tell me where else can we do that.

Don't know why I've noticed, and maybe some of you have too. I've noticed people that come from other countries, take advantage of the opportunities we have here in America. And most people that are born here are confused, and If not, they become confused through their lives. A lot through drugs and alcohol. What I'm saying, and I've even spoken with many immigrants. The foreigners will work hard to get to America, and then work extra hard to go to a college to focus on a career. And asked many times, I wonder why is that. Until I became one of those lost ones. It's such a waste people.

I thought I would have been one of those, that would take advantage of my youth, focusing on a well benefited career. Remembering my second wife saying, that America has too much freedom. Through the years, I've noticed that to be true. Never wanted to admit to it, because it would make me feel like a hypocrite. We're sent to war, to fight against communism, all for the price of freedom, with the cost of lives, defending freedom. And here I meet a woman whom I ended up marring, and for her to tell me, America has too much freedom. And as I was writing this, I thought it out very closely, that's not it at all. It's not that America has too much freedom. It's the government, the

ROBERT GARCIA

laws we do have, are not strict enough. There are far too many holes in our law system. America's laws have too many loopholes, making them controversial. Within some laws, in part of the wording, during through any particular law, it'll completely change, and end up contradictory. Having two meanings, in two paragraphs, within the same law. Did that make any sense, probably not. America's laws can be confusing, and very hypocritical, and left wide open to be picked apart. Maybe that's why, the very ones that write up the laws, can walk through the laws they write, because of too many loopholes. And even illegals can come over here, break a law, and their attorneys can literally pick a law apart, and a criminal go free, including committing murder, and the suspect get acquitted. I don't know about you, but that has always outraged me, to the point, that when I watch a vigilante movie, it satisfies me. Because I think there are too many bad people get away with too much crime.

And why is that, anyone wonder why young kids start off being a criminal. Here we go, too much freedom. Like I said, it's not the freedom, it's the laws that are not strict enough. Because there are those that will break the same law over and over again.

And looking back at what that ex wife said, saying that America has too much freedom. That offends people like me, because I'm a veteran, when we veterans fight for freedom, and believe me people, freedom is not free. This woman is just an example, as to how many people come to drug addicts, and repeated alcoholic offenders. That was a very interesting career that I had for a short time of my life. It was like baby sitting grown men, that never grew up. Mentally that is. Oh there were those few inmates that didn't belong in jail, they belonged in a insane asylum. And the new inmates that had been investigated for months and sometimes years. Having been in prison, and coming in on a new charge. They were veteran inmates. Joke right? Not really. Because life is never a joke.

A new charge, but I think the charge has been all the same, and all along. Guilty of our own selfishness and self centered. Because for many of us, we've been locked up, in our own lives for breaking man's laws and most of all, breaking God's laws. I've been guilty for denying God oh for so very long, too long. But Love, Faith, and Hope, has always been there for not only myself but for all of us. But I didn't find that out until only twenty years ago.

I'll repeat what I've said, like I have anyway. There are a few things I've done in my life, that I'm not proud of. But the biggest part of my life which I am proud of, is when I volunteered to fight in Vietnam, enlisting into the Marines. No you won't find me at some corner, or among people, bragging what I've done, but I think I have the right to write it down, since this is my life's writings. You can do the research, seventy percent of those that volunteered to fight in Vietnam, were killed. Proud, yes I am, because that's the only thing I'm proud of.

Coming back to this second wife, telling me, there is too much freedom in America. After she told me that ridiculous comment, I've often wondered, if what she says is true, then why is she here in the first place, and if it wouldn't have been for me, she would have stayed working in L.A. working her leather piece work job. Maybe it's because I never paid attention to what she said.

I helped this woman get out of that sweatshop she was working in and paid for her nursing school, and paid for her and her kids citizenship to become permanent U.S. citizens. Am I bragging, yes I am, because like I said, there aren't many things I'm proud of. Of course it didn't happen over night, but it happened, to their advantage. As I wrote this, I realized there are many people in the world, that look for opportunities, by using people. And they can be right in your own back yard. There's where my first wife came in. Now I'm married to this one. Another woman, never realizing back then, she used me for an opportunity. As I look back at my life, I can't compare to Dad, because he's much worse. No my, Dad was only married once, to my loving Mom, but Dad had a corrupt brother, and a very corrupt daughter. I'll describe the best I can how it all happened.

Right now I'm traveling through obstacles and difficulties in this part of my life. But don't we all have obstacles and difficulties throughout life. I'm sure we all do, but I've come a long way and it's taken me too long to write my painful experiences. And I'm sure many go through painful experiences, but I ask, why did I have to start so young, and why am I still alive?

But God has his own reasons and purposes for each one of us. On his own will and time. Not ours. At this point of my life when I started working at the Riverside county jail, continued on my probation training, and doing very well, as what my trainer had told me.

I was now working the career I had dreamed of, and working out very well for the wife and kids, her kids and mine. Here's when I was proud, that I've never been in jail, because as I worked there, I saw some pretty bad individuals. Murderers and what have you. Rapers, bank robbers, we've become old, have become dysfunctional, and disconnected with reality. Remember, I said, when I wrote this, my Dad was still alive, at ninety seven years old. And his daughters have treated him like he was already dead. Especially when I tell you what his youngest daughter did, her being his favorite child. But that will come later in my life's writings.

And on we go with this second marriage of mine, as her kids arrive in California from their foreign country. And everyone is happy, as we were all supposed to be. But I could already see through her son. Couldn't put my finger on it yet, but I'll figure it out soon enough. Something just wasn't right. Remember her telling me when we first met, that her ex husband had been an alcoholic. So we started with something in common. My ex and her ex were alcoholics. And my end of this life's writings of mine, is still afar, because I end up falling very deep.

Better late than never, as they say. The most important thing that had to happen to me, was a miracle. And a miracle did happen. I opened God's knocking at the door of my heart. And now as an old man, I have so much peace in my life, with the wife I'm now currently married to. God gave me this beautiful lady, and to this day, I feel I don't deserve. But that was God's choice, and my decision to marry her. I fell in love

So, until we give our lives and our heart to Jesus, we'll be locked up in our own prison. I don't know about you, but I'd rather give my life and my heart up to our Lord, than to have to give myself up to a warrant by breaking man's law.

I've seen guys actually laugh about what they were involved in, even as evil as taking someone's life. Can you imagine? The way I've always believed in, that if you take a life, man should take your life. And if by chance you beg God for forgiveness, you might have a chance, you won't die the second death. Although, in the Marine Corp, we're all trained to kill. While we're in the military, we're trained to kill the enemy, not take a life when we're civilians, unless you're defending yourself. Now, you and I know that's a complete different story.

Coming back to Love, Faith, and Hope. No one has to believe me about how I believe this, that should be obvious. I'm just writing these things that I believe is all.

LOVE, if I speak in the tongues of men and of angels, but have not love, I am only a resounding gong or a clanging cymbal. If I have the gift of prophecy and can fathom all mysteries and all knowledge, and if I have a faith that can move mountains, but have not love, I am nothing. If I give all I possess to the poor and surrender my body to the flames, but have not love, I gain nothing. Faith, now Faith is the substance of things hoped for, evidence of things not seen.

Hope, is what love and faith is all about, because without any three of them, you won't exist. It's like believing in God, but you don't believe in Jesus his son, and don't believe there's a spirit. You are a lost soul, and you could fall so easily.

As I worked my position as Correctional Officer in Riverside county Sheriffs department, it was a prestigious employment with dignity, and presented command presence in the most part when performing my duties. Had made quite a reputation for myself when I was there. That's been a long time behind me now. That's a long time ago.

While working at Riverside county, I sometimes reminisced of times of my life, how I have almost shot and killed four men, long before I applied for the Sheriffs position.

I'll always remind myself why I'm right where God wants me to be.

Going back to that topless bar, when a bouncer threw me out of that bar, and how angry I got. Because when he threw me out, I almost hit my face on the parking lot black top. And because he did his job, my anger controlled me and provoked me to almost do something I would've regretted for my whole life. When I jumped up and ran to my car and drove myself to my house to pick up my .357 mm revolver, with all the intent to go shoot that bouncer. Can anyone imagine what that would've meant for me and my future. Not much of anything, much less a future. No one really knows the future of anyone. But to commit a horrendous crime as murder, well no need to elaborate what could've happened to me, because we all know. And to think I almost killed four men, or at least almost shot them, just the thought has always haunted me. Only when I think about it.

And to land a career employed by the Riverside county Sheriffs correctional officer position, blew my mind, when they hired me.

Often times thought how many people get charged for murder, when all you were doing, was defending yourself from a big man (bully), when you had to use a gun. Maybe that's why I don't have a gun anymore. It's like being stuck between a rock and a hard spot. Sound familiar? A lot of us have been there and done that.

Thank God for good people, that have to babysit grown idiotic men, because that's the place I was working at, where good people work. And during the short time I was employed there, found it very interesting who worked beside me.

My co-working correctional officers were, for the most part, were interesting intelligent people men and women.

There are a few that stood out more than others. One would be, this young lady, that went through the academy with myself and forty others. Couldn't believe when she opened up to a few of us, how she said all of a sudden, she almost shot her husband. We all know we get provoked into evil temptations and can get caught in a huge spider web. I know I have gotten caught into too many black widows webs too many times for more than one life time. Because I feel like I've lived three life times. So this fellow co-worker female officer, goes on about her husband being an alcoholic, and tells us, how and why she stayed with him, she couldn't understand. But here comes the meat of her story. She later informs us, that she found their daughter crying way too much. And she had to dig it out of her, as to why was she crying about. Oh wow, her daughter finally told her, that her own Dad raped her. And Dad didn't know that the mother found out about it. So, we all have to sleep, even the alcoholics. Well she goes on, when her husband fell asleep, she pulled out the gun they kept in a bedroom drawer, and comes up to him while he was sleeping, with the gun at his head and how she almost pulled the trigger. And she says, "And I'm sure glad I didn't pull the trigger." And we as friends and co-workers of hers, all of us, said in harmony, "AND WE ARE GLAD TOO" As we all thought, what goes inside anyone, to go and molest your own child, evil and damn stupid. And it's against the law, and you should be hung. Just wishful thinking. Speaking of child molestation.

Believe me, I'm not proud about mentioning this cousin, that comes from my mothers side of the family. When he was young, I have to admit he was a very good looking man. He had women that wanted to crawl all over him. And I kind of envied him. But what was there to envy, after I tell you what he did. He started out on the right side of life, but he will soon fall. Like many of us do, but he fell much deeper than most. He had a beautiful family. He had a son and a daughter, and a very flirtatious wife. That was unfortunate for him. From what I heard through the family's grapevine of gossip, that he and his family, were all going to meet at a nice restaurant, whereas he and his son and daughter would be at the restaurant first, and his wife would be along later. But later would never arrive, because as they were waiting for his wife, suddenly their son had forgotten something at home, and he had to rush off to go get whatever he forgot. This is how I heard the story, as their son arrived home to get what he forgot, he was very surprised, when he heard moaning coming from his parents bedroom.

I can only imagine, wondering who was more surprised the son or his mother. What a terrible scenario. When he heard the moaning, he goes sneaking to the bedroom door, slowly opening the door, and what did he see. A shocking view of his mother getting pumped. Their eighteen year old son catching his mother in bed with another man. Wow, when I first heard that, I was so hurt for my cousin. But life goes on, because time doesn't wait for no one. Well needless to say, my cousin divorced that cheating woman. And I can only imagine, after their son catching mother in bed with another man, what kind of a relationship they had, if they even had a mother and son relationship after that.

ROBERT GARCIA

You would think, after that awful experience, with a cheating wife, he would be a much better man. But the chips don't always fall the way you and I would expect. And they didn't fall in any way close for my cousin. Because he made it worse. You may ask, how did he make it worse. Well like I mentioned, he was going towards the right direction, but I think something evil caught him in his tracks of life. He had young women, very attracted to him, and a woman, half his age caught his eye. Half his age, would be. You do the math, if he was sixty when he met this young woman, she was only thirty years old. But evil is lurking near by, to tempt him. And when he fell in love with this half his age woman, she had a little daughter, which also caught his eye. Didn't ever know when this happened. But the fact of the matter was that it did happen, and that was the tragic story. He molested the little daughter of the young woman half his age, whom he married. That was really something bad when I heard that awful story, and when Mom first heard about it, she would not believe one word of it. She was close to my aunt, this cousin's mother, so naturally she wouldn't accept any bad stories about her sister's children. And this one was the oldest of seven children. I didn't even believe it when I first heard about it. It was one of my sisters that first told me about it. As I told her, no, no, no, he didn't do anything, someone is just jealous of him, so they're making up stories. As this sister of mine tells me, no brother, he did do this, and he's in prison for molesting another woman's little girl. I yelled out, "No way, he not only did it once but did it again."? "What is wrong with this cousin of ours" So now he's in prison. What a terrible crime to be in prison for. Because anyone with a crime mark beside your name, like child molestation, will stay with you for the rest of your life. And no one wants anything to do with you. Can't blame society, that's just the way it is. Who wants to be friendly to weirdos. Because something is seriously mentally wrong with those kinds of people. They've probably needed help long time before they committed this horrendous crime. I have never seen this cousin ever again in my life. And I probably won't ever want to. Not even his family want to know him anymore. The last time I heard about what he did and where he was, fast forward, about twenty years ago. He's probably dead by now. I think I'd rather be dead than alive, if I would come to my senses and realized what I had done. Although I'll probably never see or hear about this cousin again, I'll always feel so sadly sorry for him. He was once a very happily married man.

I will always wonder what happened to that cousin of mine. What made him do, what he did, to go down so low.

But this cousin is just a fraction of society, of what kind of people are out there. Especially people that don't have a spiritual connection with God. And I've only come to realize that God has always been right beside me all of my life. Physically is one thing, but spiritually and mentally beside me my whole life is completely another thing. And I've never knew it before.

And just talking about this cousin of mine, was an example of the types of people that ended up in jail, like the one I worked in, in Riverside. Just people, just like anyone else, like you and me. But it all depends on our influences and our weaknesses. And we all have one of them or both of them. And some of us have either one of them to much to the extreme. Weaknesses, and that is what I'm talking about. We all have them.

I'll later expose myself as to how I fell into my own hole, even though I worked for a county sheriff. It doesn't matter who we work for, or what our plans are. If we want to do things our way, then plans are probably not going to happen. Or not in the way we think they are. As I've said, for many of us, we get caught in our crimes, within our own selves, and get locked up, way before the law catches us. Because of the way we think. We're not alone people, there's a super power watching all the time, whether we want to believe and accept it or not. I call that super power, and he has a name, our lord our God.

Going back to where I worked, the county jail in Riverside. There was this other co-worker, he had a secret to tell me. Have always wondered, why do people want to tell me their secrets. Some of those people have told me, I don't know why I'm telling you this. And have been told more than once. In fact more than six times.

This coworker told me, that it was a secret, and for me please don't tell anyone. And so I promised not to tell anybody. So the time came, when we were in a private secluded place to talk, secretly. And this guy started rattling off about some girl next door neighbor, coming over to his house, on his days off and while his wife is at work. Thought right away, what a double crosser. Trying to make me feel sorry for him, and I wasn't buying it. Because it didn't sound any different than the story about my cousin. But this guy thought he could get away, by having sex with an underage girl, while his wife and kids are gone. Can you f**king believe it, because I don't.

And he's exactly the people that I told you about, but for the most of us, we get tangled up within our own entanglement of lies and corruption. Come on, you know who you are. Just remember one big thing, temptations are always out there. But so are angels of God.

And that was pretty much how my life went for awhile. As I listened to this guy, telling me how this fourteen year old girl would come over his house, just to f**k him, and would make this poor fool keep f**king her, or get rattled on to the authorities. I never saw him again, and it was a good thing.

That was such a foolish thing to do from the start. Having children and a wife. Thank God I've never fallen in that hole. Because I have fallen in a hole just not in that kind of one. I believe if you fall that deep, you're chances of climbing out of that are too slim. I also believe if you get caught in a dark world, like committing murder, child molestation, terrorism, and on and on, because I can't list them all.

So going on with my short career with the county Sheriffs department, and believe me, five years short. But after all, it was part of my life, and in those short five years, I learned a lot about myself, that I did it, but I also threw it away.

Had built a good reputation while I was there. Lieutenants, sergeants, and fellow correctional officers gave me friendship and respect. And that's all I ever wanted. Wherever I've worked, you didn't have to like me nor dislike me, just respect me and I'll respect you.

Moving on with my everyday responsibilities, at my county correctional position. As I've mentioned, after my ninety day probation, and was given the lead way to work wherever they assigned me in the Riverside county jail. And even the inmates respected me. Oh there were those few that didn't respect themselves much less respect anyone else.

And like anywhere I've worked, I learned we have to earn respect. And I did, as long as I was on the right track, and on the right side of the law.

My first days being a jail officer, were challenging, but I passed my challenges with flying colors. I had a few run ins with a couple of self centered, selfish idiots, dressed in a Sheriffs uniform, just like I was. Not one officer was any different than anyone. But you'll always have those others that think they're better than anyone else. And if you knew me, you'd know, I've never taken any shit from anyone. And I still don't, in my old age.

We all wore the same uniform style as anyone. The patrol officers would have to train first in the jail for five years, while us correctional officers would work the jail until we retired.

Remembering times of my life working there. A sour apple, that I had to work with, was trying to abuse his experience working there against me. And it didn't work. It backed fired on him. Since one is a rookie, as I was at the time, this one, more or less wanted to push me around. And I didn't let him. And I told him what I thought. Told him to get off my back more or less. Don't know how they run that jail anymore, but back during the time I worked there, there were assigned runners to give fifteen minute breaks and lunch breaks and even transfer paperwork to the business office, coming from other jails or even prisons, information about inmates, and so forth. It was one hell of a short career. Which I'll will always cherish within my heart.

We became friends this one coworker that wanted to abuse his experience working there. We actually started talking about our lives before we started working for the county Sheriff. One time he invited me to go one weekend with him to go bunjee jumping. At the time I didn't know what that was. He tells me, well why don't you go with me and find out. Some laughs went on, and he explained to me, you tie a rope around your waste, while the other end of the rope is tied to a sort of a rock, and then you jump off. Thought immediately, this guy is crazy. I tell him, hell no, I'm not jumping from no rock. He thought that was hilarious.

I practically told him to go jump in a lake. Have never known why they allow dangerous sports, like bungee jumping, sports? To me that's a death wish, of committing suicide, and the public allow it. Well that was one coworker, that as time went on, he started disappearing, and wondered what ever happened to him.

What about the new books, when arrested in the streets, for being out of control in public. Or the inmates awaiting trial. Oh my God, the gangsters, of all kinds, mostly hispanic and black gangsters. I'm not being racist, because I'm hispanic, and I'm telling it how I saw it.

Working intake in that county jail, was the most exciting part of my career, working there. Anyone get arrested out there in the streets, came in handcuffed. And when they were uncooperative, good luck criminals. They wanted to swing and fight cops, they would get hogtied. And the laughter was on. They would look so funny. They would yell and scream obscenities, and how they would yell and tell us to get screwed, and how they're going to sue us. I personally would actually get into physical fights with a few during my time there. And during my time there, I didn't mind it at all. And being bilingual, it was to my advantage to speak to any hispanic, that couldn't speak English. Some times I would be assigned in the print room. Don't believe they use ink to print new inmates anymore. But when we did, it was so messy. Especially when assholes wouldn't cooperate. And what about the combative stupid ones, stuck in a cell, when they wanted to cuss and yell and spit. Well those were the special ones and would get treated special. Oh yeah, very special. Strapped to a chair in a cell, mouth covered with a catchers face guard. It was all well and good, because what officer wants to get spitted on. It could be sickening, if an inmate had a decease. I remember I used to be so gunho to go with a few other officers to harass an asshole, that thought he could yell and scream obscenities, and thought he could get away with it. And every once in while we would do that. It would take care of any miseries I was having at home. And working in the clothing department, where newly booked inmates would have to dress out of their street clothes, shower out, and we would have to check them as they showered, for drugs, they could be hiding up their ass, and make them cough it out. Sometimes we would be so lucky and something would come out their asshole. Grossed out. But people would do anything to sneak in drugs, it's done all the time. Smuggling must be as old as prostitution, two of the oldest trades in history. This one guy, was having a bad day, when he came in our jail. He thought he could yell at me and I let him have it. Working in classification was another very interesting station to work at. Classing newly booked inmates was an important to do with everybody to know everything about them. If they could be trusted with general public, or if they were racist, violent, gay, or if they had a criminal record in another part of the country. Everything mattered to know about everyone that was in our jail. But there was always those few that snuck through, and end up with general public and get themselves killed. Especially gangsters. We wouldn't cell different gangsters together, that would've been a murderous disaster for both gangsters. Two rival gangster members together in one cell. That was insane.

Just looking back at my life, and watching a bunch of war movies, movies could never replace the realities, and tragedies of actual war, and unless you've been in a war zone of any kind, then you'll never know. And the miracles of God, saved my life, and not just from the Vietnam war, but the awful tragic truck crash, my Dad, and uncle and I, could've died in, is wordless to describe my gratitude.

I think I'm at liberty to say that all combat veterans have their own stories of their experiences of the battlefields we were in. And have felt death brush by them, so close, as if you could see the angel of death wiggling his finger to get closer and then you'd be gone. Because that's what I felt, if you comrades get my drift, in a figure of speech, speaking. But that's now a long time ago. But the memories linger on for the rest of your life, like my memories of my war experiences will linger on through my life. They're called nightmares. Like you have yours, I have mine.

I'll never know the difference between the nightmares of my truck crash, we were in, when I was just a little boy, or the nightmares of the combat I was in, at Vietnam. You'd think one would have enough deathly experiences in one lifetime, and I know I'm not alone. There's a few others out there. Right guys? I know you're out there.

Thinking once I returned home to meet a beautiful girl to marry and have children, I would have a back to normal life. Not knowing the outcome, I wouldn't see normal for still two more life times, and I never thought I would see a normal peaceful loving life. With my current wife. I love her very much. She'll never know how much.

I even have a close friend that has been divorced twice with one woman, and has been married three times, twice with the woman he divorced, and happily married to his last wife, until she passed. My friend and I grew up together and have known each other as a friendship connection for over sixty years. I have been married three times, and divorced twice. So lovingly connected with my, like I said, my current wife.

We've all heard couples say to each other, I love you, I love you, I love you. But do they really? A lot of people use a bunch of words, no action. I know I was married to two women that always said, that they loved me, but it was a heart break to find out they didn't. It was fun while it lasted.

It's been a long time coming. Because as I have gotten older, I've become happier. Which brings me to a question, how many people can ask themselves, are you happy being older? And I'm not talking about physical pain, because you'll tell me, that's not happiness. But I'm not talking about physical pain, I'm talking about spiritual happiness. Another question, do you believe in spiritual happiness? Do you have spiritual happiness? It's amazing to me, when I wrote this, how God was actually writing this for me. And then it hit me along side of my head. Hey dude this is you. And that's true, I am happier than I have ever been, because of spirituality, spiritual happiness. Maybe because of my mother, I don't know, but it's a possibility, because she was always praying for all of us, especially for her oldest child, her only son, that's me, and I thank God so very much, because I was born my mother's son. With that statement, there's a message underneath.

But way before I would reach this happiness, I have opened a very bad part of my life, showing you the evil bad person I was. But I'll always have room for improvement. Because I'll always need improvement, that's a natural thing, because I'm a sinner.

During my trials and tribulations, and of course my obstacles of my life, I use to wonder why did God choose me. But I've stopped wondering and have stopped trying to understand God. The only thing I understand, that God Loves me and I love God. Because remember, "DIED THREE TIMES LIVED ONCE"

With a flash back of Dad, when I was on one of my escapades, at age fifty, can you imagine, fifty years old. I was totally corrupt, when Dad yelled at me, telling me, "You don't love your mother, you don't love your father, you don't even love yourself", and that stuck in my heart, since then, and that's been at least over twenty years ago. And what amazed me with what he told me then, is, that he never really understood why his own father never told him he loved him.

So why did God choose me, I don't know why!!

For people that don't believe in God, and think that you only die by leaving this physical world, boy are you lost, just like I was. And the reasoning for my life's writings titled "DIED THREE TIMES LIVED ONCE" Because it's no dramatic fictional story, to write about myself to make any money. It's just a self satisfaction, for when and if my daughters ever read about their Dad's life, from his perspective. What happened to him and where can they learn from it.

Physically, no, I didn't die three times, and when I wrote about this life of mine, as you know, I haven't died not even once. But mentally, and psychologically I did die. Three times.

Many people should know or already know, that life isn't guaranteed to anyone, from the time we're born. There's no guarantee of waking up, when we lay down to sleep, that's a fact, if some of you don't know that. And when I was young, didn't know much, and know very little now. I only know what I know, through experiences. But I've never been dumb as I look. I've done some stupid things, and some of us are in that boat together. One time or another we get caught up in the cross roads, and take the wrong turn at the fork for our lives and unless we're able to get back on track, those poor fools will pay dearly.

There are those poor fools, that know they're taking the wrong turn, but still keep going, and fall flat on their ass, in prison, or dead. I have to admit, I wasn't far from that.

But for a short while I was heading down the right track. And observed many criminals when I worked for the county sheriff, as a correctional officer. Thinking at the time I would never end up in jail. And I was proud of that. Maybe too proud. But I wasn't the only one with too much pride up my ass, because it's the same thing knowing someone that walks through life with their head up their ass. Funny huh, not really, because it becomes a tragedy.

I once spoke to a Riverside county jail inmate. I had a few of them up against the wall, about to escort them all to the old jail. Didn't know why I asked him, but I decided to ask him, that he looked like he'd been in jail before. And then he tells me, he'd been in and out of jail since he was twelve. He had already informed me that he was fifty two years old. And to me he looked like sixty two. Thought to myself, hey dude you look older than fifty two.

Can't even imagine how I would feel, to end up at a tragic end of the road, to be found guilty of murder, to either end up behind prison walls, or on death row. Well maybe I can't imagine it, but the fact is, I almost ended up going straight down the road to hell. But God grabbed me by the hand and caught me in mid air. Oh, I still have my nightmares once in a while. But my body pains are taking over my nightmares, so you can say, my nightmares are subsiding from having pain. But I've also been able to manage pain. I've often wondered how many people know how to manage pain. Don't think there are many that know how.

When I worked the county jail, remember being assigned to the second floor, where all of the suspected murderers were being held. I still remember the looks and expressions these guys had on their faces. The imprisoned looks on their faces. Some looked like they've been locked up for a long time. We've all seen them, either in the movies or on the news. Serial killers that have probably been running from themselves, all of their lives. Many people become locked up way before they get caught.

Every generation has their gang of corrupt wild ones. We want to blame the young generation, but we've all been the same. There are just more of them, because there are more people today. I really think that we as men, when we're first born, we're all given the chance to mature, but unfortunately for some guys, their body grows, but the brain doesn't. I'm a very different individual, at least I think I am. I'll explain why I think I'm different later on in my life's writings. I may think I'm different, but I don't think I'm the only one.

Working the county jail in Riverside, watching guys brought in for all sorts of crimes. Once our shift would begin, after a short briefing from the shift sergeant, the first thing I would do, is look up every inmate in the computer. Especially new inmates that were brought in before my shift, that was always important. Wanting to know who was I baby sitting. Because that's what it felt like, baby sitting big grown men, that never mature That's in every generation, immaturity that is. It's the facts of life in all walks of society. But I think, that most people will always have a little boy or a little girl in everyone. A child is in everyone, no matter how old we get, that I have noticed through my life. But there are those that are just a little too childish. We've all seen and probably been there.

HOPE, FAITH, and LOVE

And they must be all together, it's like God the father, God the son, and God the holy spirit. They're inseparable, like my current wife and I are today. Peace of mind I have in the life I have today. Through my time, I've been lost as most have. And when I was lost, came confusion, and so disoriented. Do any of you know what that feels like? I'm sure some of you know exactly what I'm talking about.

I'll start with HOPE, because a lot of us lose the sense of hope, when it's always been there, you just have to grasp it. Because it's always there. And because God is Hope.

But we have to take advantage of the time we all have in this physical world, because this physical life we live, is too short. Many people have an advantage, but waste their time away so easily. While others let the chance of asking for forgiveness slip right through their lives. I mention this, because it almost happened to me, but I still don't

ROBERT GARCIA

know how I will be judged. No one knows, until judgement day comes. That's why I continue praying and keep my hope with God. And I'm sure many of us have our own definition of hope, and so this is mine. And there's always hope with the love from God. You either believe it or you don't. Because when we leave this physical world, without the belief of not having any hope, you've lived your life for nothing. It would be living your life for nothing, sounds sad, doesn't it? I'm saying that, just because I was there. Feeling hopelessness, not having faith, and losing all love for myself and my family.

All what I'm saying, brings me to the thought of a close relative, in fact she's my sister. Really do feel sorry for her, because she became involved with an atheist, and married him. Have always wondered, what kind of a life would anyone have, having an empty world, of not believing in our lord and savior. Just believing in their possessions. Wow, what an empty hole. Do you ever ask yourselves what a empty hole in life feels like. Well for me, I was just existing, like living on life support of some kind. If you have any idea what I'm talking about. And when we have that feeling of hopelessness, we're vulnerable to evil, and it's ready to grab us. And again I tell you this, because it happened to me.

When working at the county jail, of course we find some of our peers as friends, since they're our coworkers. And I was becoming chummy with this one guy, when at first, we didn't like each other at all. But that friendship didn't last long. Pretty soon I don't see him around anymore. So naturally I ask, like we all would. The grapevine tells me all kinds of stories. The truth does come out eventually. He got himself fired from the Riverside county sheriff. Thinking, wow, what the hell did he do? Well that comes out, loud and clear. Got caught doing drugs. What?? Flash back on his personality. Which wasn't much. Arrogant as hell, and very violent, especially with the inmates. Now it all made sense to me.

I Remember this one rookie deputy, just a young kid about twenty five, and just big and naive. He would work intake with fellow officers, as I would work either the fingerprint room or classification. Where it was always fun and exciting, and I always looked forward to work there as much as possible. This rookie was very obnoxious, new bookees would be brought in through big sliding doors from the rear part of the jail, where all police personnel would bring in their perpetrators, either arrested at their home or out on the streets. Handcuffed of course, that was another story. Some guys wouldn't know how to cooperate, so they would be brought in hogtied.

Brought in to a greeting table, ordered to put their hands on this table, and leave them there, while they would be searched.

But there's always those who don't, either listen or don't pay attention. And this young deputy just loved to beat the hell out of those who came in drunk and didn't listen nor pay attention, and he seemed too proud of that. He would yell at them, and slam their heads on this steel table. The new bookees would scream and cry with pain. And this young deputy, would laugh. Thinking that was funny. Well one day we were working at a station together. And I didn't know why he wanted my opinion. So he says to me, "hey buddy, remember the other day when we were working intake?" "Did you see how I beat that asshole up, what did you think of that"? There were four of us working together, and he shouldn't have asked me what I thought. Because now the stage is mine. So I let him have it. I say, "Well I think you're an asshole, while all the others around us laughed at him, as I continued, because one day you might be out on patrol as a patrolling deputy, and you won't remember him, but that guy will probably never forget you, and God forbid if he thinks of doing anything to you. You see young man, I don't care about those people in the streets, it's you I'm thinking about, I'm looking for your well being." And the look on his face, seemed to me, like he got the message. Because the response was, "I appreciate that, that's good advice thank you "We're all human beings, good or bad, and it's too bad, but there's more bad people than there are good. That's just a fact of life. There are more corruptions than there are love connections between man, and that's a fact, ever since Cane killed Able.

We never spoke again, the young deputy and I. We just got along, and that was good enough for me. We respected one another, and that's what I always wanted, wherever I worked. That relationship with a fellow coworker Sheriffs deputy trainee, was an incident I have never forgotten. And there were others, like this one other.

My shift had ended for the day, and I was being relieved by a Sheriffs deputy trainee, and I forgotten a book, so I turned to go back to the station I had worked, but this deputy opened the door, having my book in his hand, and says to me, "Hey did you forget this?" As he threw it on the hallway floor. I just froze, as I saw my book fly in the air. Thinking to myself, now why couldn't this idiot just hand my book to me like a man. I didn't say a word to him, but I thought, I will see who I can talk to about this simpleton. So I waited for a day or so, and I run into a sergeant of the day, and I ask him, "sarge can I talk to you about something that's bothering me"? Sarge responds "sure Officer what's on your mind?" I tell him, "I'm not the kind of man to go around tattling as a little boy on anyone, but we're all men that work here." "But this deputy joe the other day, as I had forgotten a book, just as I was approaching the station I had worked, he opened the door and he tells me if that was mine, as he threw it on the hallway floor. The sergeant answered, "Aww, that's not right, I'm gonna talk to him, don't worry about it, I'll take care of it" And he did, a good job done. So another few days go by, and this deputy that had thrown my book like I was, some dog, looks at me, and all of a sudden, he's asking me how am I. And I immediately thought alright, I knew right away, the sergeant had spoken to this fool. That was another happy ending.

As I remember a lot of incidents of my life working for the county sheriff, they're memories of my life, as to who I was then, and it wasn't the Sheriffs employment that made me lose it, it was my private life that blew up in my face. I just didn't realize it back then.

There were those few times, at my correctional officer position, when I would see these guys dressed like wild dudes, bring in drug pushers, by the van full. That would be quite a sight. Undercover police officers, maybe they were the DEA. (drug enforcement agency) for those that don't know. These DEA agents looked like pushers as well as the real ones. You could hardly tell the difference. Long haired, bearded, earrings, tattooed and bushy tailed. When they would bring in the criminals, the only way I could tell the difference, when they would brandish their badge. That looked so cool. But it just had to be dangerous, no joke. I'm sure some would get killed, no doubt about it. We're talking, disrupting a cartel operation, or a gangster raid. So of course the undercover agents have to look the same. The same went with prostitution. Knowing a couple of female deputies, get dressed as prostitutes and go stand at some hot corner and catch a guy trying to pick up a prostitute, and it would back fire on any solicitor, make a money transaction, then it's a bust. Off to jail they would go. I could never imagine doing that. Just being a regular police officer is dangerous, much worse an undercover one.

In today's world, there's not much respect for law enforcement. Society have always blamed all police officers, for one or two bad apples. I've always found that to be wrong. Because there's bad in every bureaucratic agency. Just working for a county sheriff, I experienced some bad apples, in the personnel I worked with.

I've got a question for everyone, what would happen, God forbid, if there weren't any police? It should be very obvious to all of us. America would become an apocalypse country. Can anyone picture that? It would be a sight for sore eyes. Police officers are people like all of us. And I personally have always respected them. And I know, there are those few that don't show respect in return. Just because they wear a badge and a gun. And these guys should never apply to become police officers, just because they get to wear a badge and a gun. That should be wrong in everyone's book. That doesn't sound any different than a regular criminal to me.

In the history of America, there has been criminals of all sorts, including crime being committed by people wearing a police uniform. So, when a crime is created in a mind of a person that wears a police uniform, that should be without saying, it becomes a dangerous situation. Back in the sixties and even before then, there were some people wanting to be police officers to show racism against other nationalities. I think all that came from nazism, just after World War Two. It should have always been a civil country and should be a civil country as I write this today. God created all of us to be equal, and it shouldn't have anything to do with religions believing otherwise. They had interpreted

Christianity to their hatred towards others that had a different skin color. Throughout the world, there are people with different skin color, with different cultures, but no one is better than anyone. Especially being an American. How I've studied our history, America became a land of the brave and an opportunity for everyone, and not just for one race, for every legal immigrant Now let me take you back to another incident that happened at my county jail employment facility. As I've said, there are criminals in all walks of life, and like I've also said, that includes criminals among people that wear a police uniform. Now this one that I'm about to paint you is to me a one of a kind.

Like some stories, there are those few, that are one in a million. Like this one story, but the thing is, this is true. And like all walks of life, there was this one young deputy trainee. And like this young deputy, maybe a thirty year old, and maybe a little younger. But in this story, age had nothing to do with it. Because he could've been any age. A criminal is a criminal, no matter how old we are. Right? Do we agree with that? And I bring him up, is because I worked with this guy. So when we found out what this crazy one was doing after he would work his shift, it sounded scary. As myself having a weapon at home, like this guy probably did, that's why I say those kind are scary. And on top of everything, this deputy trainee had a judge for a Dad. Here comes the part what this crazy cop did right after work. And how long did he do this, no one knew. But there were mom and pop stores that were reporting that they were being robbed at gun point. And that's the scary point number one.

He always seemed self reserved, and kept to himself. And from my life's observations, those kinds of people, are sneaky. We never know what the hell they're thinking. That's just what I've seen in people I've come across. And just because this guy had a Father that was a judge, what, did he think he could get away with crime.

While we all worked together, all in uniform, he sneakily would change into his street clothes, like we all did. Like I also said about this sneaky snake, never said much to anyone, in what would be cooking in his corrupt mind. Because I don't know how you see this, but law enforcement officers are supposed to be serving the public, with dignity and honesty. But that's not how this individual thought. He could've been on drugs, who knows. He was receiving a good starting salary, like we all did.

If you can just use your imagination just for a second.

You and your partner own a Mom and Pop store, or another name they use, convenience store. You owners have had this small store for lets say, about ten years. And all of a sudden, this monster comes in with a gun in hand, with a disguise I'm sure, because he's not coming in dressed as a cop. And he demands your money. And just by chance, one of you owners have a gun underneath the counter, and he or she gets tempted to pull out the gun to shoot the armed robber, and he shoots you or your partner first. Now what. And that's scary point number two. And one of you end up dead. So now it's not just armed robbery, it's now been escalated to murder. Wow, and he got caught. Some one was able to identify him, and he left tracks following to his place of residence, but he never shot anyone, thank God for miracles. Apparently something went wrong with this fool's operation. It's obvious, because, one morning a briefing sergeant is informing us, just before our day shift began. As the sergeant gives a harsh and strong verbal, "may I have all of your attention please" and it was a strong voice, because he almost yelled. You could have heard a pin drop. As he tells us, "We had a bad apple amongst us. And he doesn't work here anymore, and he's being detained in another detention center. And his Dad is a judge" "He's been accused of robbing Mom and Pop stores" "He would work here, and after work he would go out and disguise himself, go in these small stores, with a gun and demand their money

I'm gonna talk about a very mysterious part of the human body. I'm sure some of you have heard about it. Because for some of you, it's not so mysterious, but it is to me. The mind, the upper muscle, called the brain. And there are some people that act like they lack that most powerful part of our bodies. It's very unfortunate for those. Because when we don't know how to use one of our most important muscle, we're bound for hell. Corrupt minds will destroy us, and lead us to do things that ordinarily we wouldn't do. We've seen those people all around us, or we don't, because they're either in a hospital, in a prison for life or awaiting death row, or they're dead.

The mind can work either with you or against you, and it can make a lot of difference how many marbles we have connected, to find out who are we, and who we will become. But what I've known with some people I've come across, they're ready to play the blame game. What do I mean by that, some of you might ask. What I mean, and you know what I mean. Things have gone wrong with part of your life, or most of your life, and you want to blame things that have gone wrong, on your Dad, or your grandpa, or someone other than yourself. If you do, your a coward. Grow up. It's very easy to blame bad things that have happened to you on someone else, to me that's stupid. They'll cry, as they sit in prison, or in a mental hospital. Can you imagine, there's fools out there, that are anywhere from twenty one to sixty, and want to blame their evil doings on Mama or Daddy. That's always sounded so childish to me. We hear it all the time, or we see it on television, the defending attorneys want to sympathize with the perpetrators, and these crazy fools, either they put mama in the hospital, or they killed Dad. Excuse me, but I think that's wrong. There's no justification for murder. Now if you kill someone, merely because they want to hurt you, or take your life, or want to hurt your spouse, by breaking and entering into your residence, and you kill them, that should be self defense. That's completely different. As I've said, the brain is a very mysterious muscle of our body. But unfortunately, for some, that muscle is a weak muscle, because they end up on the wrong side of life. I'm not saying I have a strong mind, because I've done some pretty dumb things in my life.

In each one of us, our lives will always have obstacles and difficulties down our own roads. And our minds will become difficult to put it in for good use. I wrote it down earlier, that Dad and I didn't have a close relationship, for many years as a boy and as a teenager, but I could have done what most guys do. And blame Dad. But I didn't, I've been responsible for my own actions, and bad choices. Let's talk common sense, do you have any common sense? Some times it's hard to say, right? We've all seen those, that lack common sense, and it's sad, because they've probably spent a great part of their time going to school, graduating from high school graduating from a university. And after all of that, they still don't have a clue. And why, because some will have some chip on their shoulders, and think they're better than anyone, just because they graduated from a university. Now does that make sense, not to me it doesn't.

I remember Dad telling me a long time ago, and I've shared with you about this, if you recall. Dad told me he had been hired by a huge company called McDonald Douglas, and Dad only had a fourth grade education. He was so proud of himself, and so were we, but he's never known how proud I've been of him. But after Dad had been working there for a while, his supervisor came up to him, to introduce a couple of young men, freshly university graduates.

Wow, when I first heard about that, I couldn't believe it, Dad being in charge of newly university graduates? Who wouldn't be proud? Although in those days, it wasn't about how much education anyone had to get hired, it was only about experience. And these guys didn't have experience, Dad did. This is why I say, the mind will always be very interesting and very mysterious, because no one knows where our minds will take us through our lives. I'd like to think I know where I'm going through my life and where will I end my journey and settle in my destination. But I don't. Just like we never know we'll wake up in the morning, because it's a miracle everyday we make it to the next day. And many times our wrong choices and decisions will lead us to our death. It happens all the time, we hear about all the time. Remember: **DIED THREE TIMES LIVED ONCE** ill repeat it.

Waking up after a truck crash, and a doctor telling me, we should have been killed. Was an astonishing statement for me to comprehend at my age then, seven years old. Having nightmares of falling, and falling, but never hitting the ground, stayed with me for a long time. You would think that would be enough, but no I'm on my way to my next deathly experience. Vietnam

All this time, working at the county sheriff detention center, I'm starting to have marital problems. As I've said, it wasn't my employment I was having problems with. It was my personal life, and my marriage that was starting to go under. And under it went. And it's my second

ROBERT GARCIA

marriage. And started wondering who's fault was it. And at that time, being a Sheriffs employee, I thought the woman I married was wrong. A chip on my shoulder, probably so. And then at the same time, on this particular day, my oldest daughter tells me, and I'm about to head off to work, and she says. "Dad what would you think if I told you I was writing to a prison inmate" When I heard her say that, it seemed like my heart stopped. And through the years, she regretted that, because she parted away from that guy. Thank God.

A lot of changes were going through my life married to this woman. Maybe because the way she started treating my daughters, and how she would talk about my mother. And anything I would try to say to her, wasn't registering in her mind. And without saying, our marriage was starting to deteriorate. The old saying is, there's a fine line of love and hate. And at that time, I really believed that. And now in my current time, it's true. Here we go again about the mind. This muscle upstairs in our head, can really play tricks on us, especially if you have no connection with God. You're fighting a losing battle, no matter how well you think you can solve the problem. You can never find the answer, no matter who you think can help you, unless you reach out for help. And my strong helper was and is my Lord and savior.

Naw, I never used to talk like this before, much less write like this. Could it be because we get old, maybe. Let me remind you all, I wrote this when Dad was still alive at now ninety seven, and I, in my seventies. Let me play the mind game again. Dad was always saying, "Leave it all up to the Lord" I would respond, "ok that's true, but why did God give us all a mind" believing he gave us all a brain to give us all freedom to choose the road to eternity. As I bring up eternity, that's a long time. But with a short life. Because time has flown, and time does not wait for anyone, as we find ourselves wondering where did time go. This is why we have no time to waste.

Can you imagine and just think about it, people, for a minute, the crazies that decide to take a life. I know, why do I keep bringing up these out of their mind monsters. And why do I call them monsters. Mostly because, a normal person doesn't kill anyone, and monsters do. And people that act like monsters, should not exist, because when they decide to take a life, their life should be taken as well. Have you ever looked at a monster criminal in the eye, they have that far away look, so far that they don't really know where they're at. But was born with hate for life, it's like a bad omen. Remember, I worked in a county jail, and I looked at a couple of serial killers in my time I had the privilege to work there. Have to admit, it was different and exciting, and challenging. And it was for the most part, challenging. One day I stopped at a gas station, pumping my car, and this idiot is walking by, and just wanting to demand money from me, and he caught me at a bad time, as he demanded harshly for money, by threatening me, that he's going to kick my ass, and I jumped towards him, telling him, with my gas pump in my hand, and a lighter in the other, I'm going to light him up like a Christmas tree. He realized I was serious, so he ran like a chicken. He was no joke, running down the street, like a bat out of hell. Thinking to myself, what gives a dumb stupid, the nerve to demand money, when we're pumping gas? Gotta be really dumb. See how the mind deceives some of those kind of people, that don't think. It can get you killed, or can get you put away in prison for a long time., for the rest of your life.

Coming back, when I told you about a daughter of mine, asking me, what would I think, if I found out she was writing to a prison inmate. I have never forgotten about that statement, like I said it made my heart want to stop. Why would she think of doing that, I have never understood. Because she almost paid dearly for her life. This guy, later on my daughter ended up being with him, having two children with him, after he was released from prison, had been sentenced for three years. And I had the unfortunate opportunity to meet this ex-con, that had done prison time for manslaughter. I don't know about you, but that sounded pretty scary for me, for my daughter. When I met him, when both my daughter and this ex-con, and their baby son, now my twenty six year old grandson, wanting to meet me. Never knowing why would he want to meet me. Later on, telling me the reason why he was in prison. Try to picture this scenario, this guy, and thank God he became my daughter's ex boyfriend. This guy, an ex-con, thanking God, he became my daughter's ex boyfriend. And thank God for miracles. Back when he wanted to meet me, and that day finally arrived. And here comes his justification for killing someone. He informed me, he was in a gang, and he was having a physical problem with a rival gang member, and that other gang rival attacked him and all he was doing was defending himself. And here I'm sizing this guy, my daughter's boyfriend at the time, standing six foot two inches, weighing about two hundred and fifty pounds, and he was telling me he was defending himself. And he did admit he killed that other guy, and wasn't trying to, but he tells me he had no choice, but to defend himself. And he asked me if I believed him. Telling him, since he put it that way, I would believe him. And he felt good about that meeting of ours ever since. Because as time flew by, and my daughter and him fell apart, my daughter had told me a few times that he liked me for good reasons. He has respected me, and I've respected him.

Here's this story about a man that was in the jail I worked, and I remember reading the charge he was facing, which was murder.

As I think of all my flash backs, and haunting memories of where I could have been instead of where I am. I'll never forget the things I've done, and how God has forgiven me. And that has always been hard for me to understand, but then who are we to try and understand God, that is not our place and it's not our time to understand him. My daughters have told me, Dad has told me, and my best friend has told me, that God has forgiven me of all my sins. But what's really hard, is, it is so hard for me to forgive myself. Maybe I will one day, but maybe I never will.

And I'm probably jumping the gun in my life's writings.

Like I was telling you about this guy that was charged for murder, and I working at the county jail. And things can get pretty hairy if we were in a different setting. This day like any other day, just got out of work, from the county jail I was working at, and decided to stop by a little store to buy me a beer, and all of a sudden this guy pops up out of nowhere. And says to me, "Hey deputy how are you doing" All I could do is stare at him, and think to myself, what the hell, where did this guy come from. And so he goes on and on, about why he was arrested for suspected of murder. I ask, and so what happened. He continues telling, I don't know if you have ever gotten into an argument with any one, and get real mad, as the guy you're mad at runs away and as he's running, you yell at him, "You know what, I'm going to kill you" and then this guy says, and then he ends up dead somewhere in the street. And someone saw his face when he yelled that out. "And the next thing I know, the cops are at my door, ready to take me in to jail. And to jail he went. He continued on, "And now I needed a lawyer to prove my innocence", "and thank God they found me innocent" "I was so scared I was going to get blamed for something I didn't do. Yes that would be a big disaster **for** anyone, getting convicted for murder when you didn't kill anyone. I know we've all wondered, at least the innocent bystanders have, how many people get arrested, and they get pointed out as being the perpetrator, get indicted, and get detained and await a jury trial, and the jury finds some poor fool, guilty for murder, when he probably didn't even know the deceased, and maybe wasn't even around when it happened. My drunken wife brought her drunken brother one late night, to my parents house, that asshole and we never liked each other as it was. So now by being with his sister, he thought it was reason enough to kick my ass. At least he thought he could, and he would have, if I would have let him. He being a foot taller than me, gave him a bigger reason to want to hurt me real bad. Since he underestimated me by sizing me up giving him motivation to fight me. Like I said if I would have let him. Well I didn't let him, because during our scuffle, when he's the one that grabbed my arm and started twisting it, and threatening me, "You know what you little mother**, one day I'm gonna see you in the street, and I'm going to kick your ass" And I surprised the both of us, because during the scuffle was in process, I had a small, 25 semi automatic gun in my top left hand pocket of my jacket, which I was able to slip out, as that drunken brother of my wife, and he saw the gun, he got off of me, and started yelling at me, as he ran across the street, practically begging me not to shoot him. "Don't shoot me man" And thank God for second thoughts, because my first thought was to shoot the basturd, and I wouldn't have cared. Because he was in my book just another motherf**king bully, and wouldn't have mattered. But I stopped and only shot by his leg. That scared him enough to whine all the way home, and into bed, and try being a good little boy. And that scenario has always reminded me of a song "I Ran All The Way Home Just To Say I'm Sorry"

Life can be a nightmare, when you're in with people that don't have love. I know, that's the only kind of people I've been with. Because once we leave the nest, there's no guarantee we'll make it to the next day, much less, try to make it to another year. Many of us make plans, and maybe a lot of plans won't surface. We can only try. Right?

No I was never close to my alcoholic wife and her family, hell no. A bunch of alcoholics and drug addicts. As if I was so much better. Yeah right. I might have been a little better then, but later on I'll let you know what happens.

Well that's the first man that I almost shot, pulled a gun, but didn't intend to shoot, but temptation was very close in shooting him, because he threatened me. My first wife the alcoholic, her brother. I guess what kind of made me disgusted with this brother of my alcoholic wife, had heard he was dating a fourteen year old girl, and he's as old as me. He's always been weird. If he's dead or alive, I could care less. Victim number two, that I almost shot. And again it's because I hung out with wrong people.

While I was dating my first wife, I was dating another girl, and that girl had a baby, and an ex boyfriend. Thinking everything was okay, she wasn't with anyone anymore, so I thought it was good to be with this girl, so we moved in together. Well that will soon turn out to be a dangerous situation to be in, for all involved. And this girl and I thought we were in love. Soon to find out, she wasn't any better nor diffident than my alcoholic wife to be. Just like my first wife, this other girl, also very flirtatious. And a whore as well. Anyway, as time went on, like I said this girl had a ex boyfriend, and he didn't much care for me, and I didn't like him. And here again, this is a gigantic kid, of about twenty years old, and I was maybe twenty five. As you already know, had been to Vietnam and back home, four years. And I knew guns pretty well. And that big bully of a boy, was only waiting for a good excuse to get me in some corner to beat the shit out of me, because he could, and here again, if I would let him. Well the day snuck up on us one day. This big boy, standing over six feet, came roaring to our apartment, where his ex girlfriend, now living with me were living together. And he looked really furious, like he could kill anyone that stood in his way. And I've never ran from any man, and I wasn't going to run from this bully either. Because that's probably the first thing these guys think, that everyone will run from them. I don't know, but maybe I'm one of those few that don't run from bullies. And I have gotten my ass kicked, but I've also challenged bullies, with aggression.

That day that he came roaring in our apartment, looking at me, well I met him at the door, and we stared at each other, as he continued at me, and grabbed me by the shirt and literally picks me up and giving me a message that he wants to throw me over the second story railing. And as he picked me up, we stared eye to eye, and I told him, if and when you throw me over, make sure I'm dead, because if I'm not, I'll be back. Well, thank God for all of his miracles through my life. This giant of a guy put me down and left me there. And I didn't have time to feel relieved, because all of a sudden I hear this "shh shh" there was this guy peaking just a little of face out the door. And he tells me, "hey man I heard what was going on out there, hey, and I heard what you said, that guy is too big, if he throws you over, you can end up paralyzed and end up in a wheelchair" As I tried to absorb what he was saying.

He hands me a gun, and tells me, "listen man, take this gun, you have to defend yourself, he's gonna hurt you real bad, and if you do use this gun, don't bring it back to me, throw it away somewhere" As I thought what he was saying, I take this .32 semi automatic pistol, and put it in my waist part of my pants. And it wasn't even a few minutes, when this giant guy comes back, as he was coming at me, as he offered an apology, "Hey man I want to apologize to you" and I didn't let him get close, as I say, "Don't get any closer, he responds, "What"? I repeat to him, "Don't get any closer I said" And he didn't, what a miraculous God, saving me again. All he did was walk away. Never felt so good of the outcome of that situation. Just as he was leaving, the girl I was living with, the ex girlfriend of who I was about to shoot, looked amazed, as she asked me, "What did you have in the inside part of your pants" I didn't respond, all I could do was just look at her. As she screamed out,

"Oh my god, you were gonna shoot him" I said "Well what did you want me to do, just let him beat me"

Thank God, that wasn't victim number two.

And time moves on, I was drinking my ass off one day, in at the time, one of my best bars, the topless bar I always went to. Terrible place, that's how I look at it today. Back then, it was a beautiful place to go see naked women. But this particular day, at this bar, I had become out of hand. Had been drinking there all day, and should have left a long time ago. But no I was obsessed with this one woman that caught my attention in many evil ways. Because it could have gotten someone killed. As bars have bouncers, there was this one, that had already warned everyone last call for alcohol, but I didn't want to listen, and I didn't want to leave. And as far as I was concerned I wasn't. Well the bouncer comes back to me and tells me, you have to leave and right now. I just looked at him, and tell him, to get f**ked. Well that didn't go very well with him, because the next thing, he's grabbing me and dragging me out of the bar, and throws me out. And that didn't go too well with me, because the next I'm doing, I'm jumping and running to my car and speeding home, just a couple minutes away. Grabbed this .357 revolver pistol and drove back to across the street from the bar, and just waiting for the bouncer. And I waited and waited. And he never came out. Another miracle incident for two men.

See how the mind works. Either good, or very very bad. Of course the next morning I'm thinking, what the hell happened last night.

As I've said, not proud about of any of this. I'm just writing about my life, is all.

As I worked at the county jail, looking at all of those inmates that were in jail for shooting someone. And thinking, wow, I could have been in any jail for doing something stupid, and looking at myself.

But I have done some things in my life, that haven't been too smart.

It seems to me after I enlisted into the Marines, and made it back home safe, everything backfired into my face. Listening to my sister, when she wrote to me, about some woman she wanted me to meet. That woman could've killed me.

Now writing about this part of my life while I was working for the county, and married to this other woman. Another mistake, because like I said, she was starting to treat my daughters second best, and talking crap about my mother. I pretty much hung up my gloves with this bull shit, in other words, I got tired of this marriage too.

I was talking about my first wife when I said, she could've killed me, that's for real. She had a serious problem with alcohol. I mean, what do you think, she pawned off two guns of mine, and one late night, I caught her going through my pants pockets, when she thought I was asleep. Obviously she was looking for money, as I kicked her down on our carpet floor, she quickly got up, running for the kitchen. Didn't want to grab her right away, because I was curious as to what was she going to the kitchen for. And lord and behold, as she ran right up to the utensils drawer, she pulls it open, and grabs a knife and picked it up, and my reflexes kicked in, I kicked the knife out of her hand, knife flew and it stuck to the wall, it looked like a episode of kung fu. And all in one motion, I slapped her. Yelling at her, "What were you going to do stab me" She didn't say a word. As you can tell, I've never forgotten about that. Who would? Now you tell me, is that a serious alcohol problem? I should say so. After all I had to put up with it. And after three hospitals in taking this alcohol wife, there was this nurse, that had the damn nerve to tell me, that it was my fault that this woman was a alcoholic. Couldn't believe this nosy nurse, telling me it was my fault for this alcoholic wife of mine, for being how she is. Well I let that nosy nurse have it, "You know what woman, you don't have a clue as to what you're talking about, and you better get back inside to your hospital, before I talk to your supervisor" Well needless to say, that nurse was quickly out of our sight.

Why did I waste my time with that one and this one, the second one was my the current one then, that also used me for an opportunity to get her kids and herself, legal citizenship. And that's not what bothered me, it's the way she changed her attitude about things. How she bad mouthed my mom and Dad, and how she started treating my daughters, very different than she did before.

My county employment wasn't my problem, it was my personal life that was falling apart, and I let it tear me down. Because this is what happens next. I started womanizing, to the point, I started picking up prostitutes, right after clocking out from the county jail I was working at. For some of you, it might seem shocking, and it was. Here I was working at a facility, like all jails, housing inmates, criminals that commit crimes. And here I am picking up prostitutes, right after work. Something was starting to fall apart. Maybe someone was falling apart, I can only see that's falling completely off his rocker, was me. It doesn't take a genius to figure it out. I was losing the whole concept of being normal. Normal, there was nothing normal about what was happening to me, and what I was doing to my family. Family, being, my daughters. That was being self centered and selfish on my part. Even a blind man could see that. The only one that couldn't see that was me. Maybe because I was in denial.

As I look at that person, who I was then, it's hard to imagine what I did, but I have to admit it, I did it.

Do you know of any psychopaths, you probably don't, or you wouldn't say you do, but I'm sure you've heard of them, like we all have. Another question, do you have any psychopaths in your family? I wasn't hiding anything when I wrote this., I tell it how it is. I have a few weirdos in my relations. Remember I'm talking about the mind, how mysterious it is. And how people can use the mind, only for their advantage, and only for their disastrous life styles.

For many of us that have been blessed by God to have children, it's always been an amazing experience through life to have children, isn't it people? And then there are those that can't have children, and they feel left out from God. I don't believe God leaves anyone out at all.

Its people that leave God out of their lives. And God has a reason for everything and for everyone. I speak this way, I guess because of the life I've lived.

1. My first attempted shooting: a man wanting to throw me over a 2 story balcony, he lifted me up, and then put me down after I told him, when he throws me over make sure I'm dead. Then

he came back, I now have a gun, and I was going to pull it out and shoot him..32 automatic

2. My second attempted shooting: A brother in law threatened me, he would kick my ass if he ever saw me in the street, I had a gun in my top left hand pocket, and I pulled it out, ejected a round in the chamber to shoot him as he was running away from me. .25 mm automatic

3. My third attempted shooting: Drunk in a bar, didn't want to leave the bar, so the bouncer grabbed me and dragged me and threw me out of the bar. Almost hurting me. Im pissed, I drove my car to my house to grab my pistol and waited for him. .357 caliber revolver

And there was another time I almost pulled out a gun, but I might have had just cause to shoot, because a member of a gang demanded alcohol after hours, while Dad and I were about to clean the facility.

At this point of my life's writings, I don't have any words to describe how I feel about myself, and how grateful I am I never shot anyone. Are you kidding, it's beyond any kind of words to express, as to why I'm here alive and not in some slammer.

As I said, my second marriage was falling apart, and the whole thing was, I didn't give a damn. And it didn't just start falling apart, it had been falling down for quite awhile

And of all of those times I attempted shooting, that time I was with my first wife. So there was no violence with my second wife. My second marriage had no violence. It was my infidelity that was out of control. Too much perversion, because I blamed it on the wife wasn't giving me any attention. Oh poor baby, now that I look at it, maybe she wasn't giving me any attention, but I didn't have to go into the far end. Way out of line. Way out of control. Mindly thinking, my mind was out of my control. I was overwhelming myself and everyone that loved me. Of course my daughters couldn't believe the change in me. Because with the change I was going through, picking up prostitutes, and actually taking anyone of them out for a meal. Can you guys believe that? All I wanted was communication with a female. Because I wasn't f**king all of them, if that's what you all think. All I wanted was some kind of understanding. Does that make sense? Because I'm trying to understand this as I wrote it. I would imagine I was taking out my wife, and just having a normal conversation, which wasn't normal at all. It was completely psychotic, because I was committing a crime. While I worked for the county sheriff, I'm out looking for whores. Weird huh? I think it was now. And every prostitute I picked up, always wanted me to do drugs with them. Of course I wouldn't let them know I was a cop in a detention center. They'd freak out.

So that went on for a while, and I enjoyed every time I got a chance. I was literally pushing more and more away from a marriage I didn't want anymore. All of that time I did that, picking up women and taking them to a motel, I wouldn't get home until late night. The wife always asking me where I would be. Always telling her, I had to work overtime. She would believe that for a while, but then that lie became very old.

The wife was starting to have doubts, and what woman wouldn't have doubts? Because she was starting to realize I was lying. And I was. And like I said, I didn't care anymore. And I was always daring myself, while married to this woman. Can't put my finger on it, but I would venture to say, that I started building a resentment against her, all because she was talking about my mother and putting my daughters second, she promised she would love my daughters and she would treat them like her own. Here's a whopper of a womanizing life I was living but the thing is, nothing I've told you has been a whopper. It's all been the truth. I've never been into reading fiction, and this life's writings of mine has nothing but the truth to it.

Here's the thing I wanted to say. After divorcing my first wife, nothing was ever right about anything. Guess what I'm trying to say, everyone that gets married, marry for love, right? Well mentally in my mind, those two women I married, married me for convenience, the way I see it now as I reminisced about those times of mine. I think I was just looking for an excuse to womanize, to make up a reason to talk to and be with other women. Come on guys, there's always temptations out there. If you've said "I DO" like I have three times, somewhere along the line, it's gotta be for love, like it's happened to me, this third time married. But if you continue to go through life on a marry-go-round, and don't marry for love, you're probably going to fall deep like I once did. But I was so damn lucky, no let me put it to you this way, luck had nothing to do with it. Like a song I know, "WHATS LOVE GOT TO DO WITH IT", because all of my relationships in the past, had nothing to do with love. But it's few and far between, as an old saying goes. What that means to me, there are those few people that love will find them, and that's a blessing from God. Found out when we look for love in all the wrong places, you're not going to find love, because I have. Better late than never. Have also found out a while back, I have been a late bloomer more than once in my life. I think I've seen that in movies, it's always been the victims to find out the truth, about the liars. A wife lying to a husband or husband lying to a wife. That's what makes the world go around. But I think I've done some pretty harsh things to this second wife, and how she never found out. She suspected, but never knew what I had done behind her back. It's no wonder God cursed me, in his own way.

What I've done for this second wife, I don't think many other men would have done. Writing this down, I start thinking of the time we met. It was so easy for the both of us, her looking for an opportunity, to hook a man to process her and her kids to become American citizens and me looking for an opening when can I put this woman in bed. I don't think other men would have treated her any different than I did. And that goes for the both of my first two marriages.

The way I see it, in my old age, you get treated in the way you carry and portray yourself. She advertising herself in a dating agency. The first wife, wanting to f**k all of the time. And not just me. I think by the time I woke up, it was too late.

Remember this one time, after my first divorce, my second wife would go off to work, taking the bus and be gone all day, and while she would be gone, I would go looking for women to come over and you know it, everyone knows what happens when a man and a woman cling to each other. They're stuck for a minute. But not in it for love, unfortunately that is true. After our parent's times, love wasn't the same anymore. During those times of the forties and the fifties, love meant something to a man and a woman. But those days are long gone. There's nothing true anymore.

Yes, the good old American way of living of love, when there use to be a one man, woman, and a one woman, man. What this means people, The American style of loving today, a man has to have a mistress, even though he's married and has one or ten children. And a woman has to have a boyfriend on the side, so just in case the marriage doesn't work out. Ain't that ridiculous. The good old ways are gone. The generation they called, (THE GREAT GENERATION) had more love, than any generation I've noticed. And just to be clear of what I said, it wasn't just this one day, it was every chance I got, to call any call girl, a prostitute to come to our house, and have sex. How terrible!!! I mean just because I was falling out of love for this second wife, I shouldn't have betrayed her in such a perverted way. That was filthy on my part. And I admit, I enjoyed it. Because it was this one prostitute that I was starting to fall for. So she would come to the house from L.A. and stay with me for a couple of hours. No shame I'm telling you. But someone is always looking from the outside. Because we had this next door neighbor, lurking around, and putting his nose over the fence. And we've had our bad looks a few times. So you can say, we didn't like each other at all. And putting his nose at just the right time he did. One day the second wife started telling me that this neighbor of ours was talking about me and saying things like I had a woman coming by while she went to work. Of course I shove it off to the side, and act like I didn't know what he was talking about. Telling my wife, "Well he's going to say anything bad about me, because we don't like each other" and then I tell her that one day I caught him beating up his wife in the back yard. And he saw me looking, and told me an obscenity word. Because he yelled at me, as he told me to mind my own business. So I proceeded telling her, so you can believe him or believe me, because I wasn't having anyone coming over to the house. Telling her he was just making up stories against me, so we could get mad, to get me in trouble with her.

Things with our relationship kind of settled down, because she believed me over our neighbor, but it didn't stop me from continuing having that same prostitute come over. In fact I started going over her house, and met up with her father, can you believe what I'm talking about. Completely off track from reality. Because I was married and acting like I was a single man. And all because, this second wife of mine didn't like my mother and treated my daughters bad. Did I take advantage of the situation, you could say that, and I probably did, to feed my sexual appetite. You probably think I was a sex pervert. It might look like that, but I was not a molester, nor a rapist of any kind. Looked for grown women. And I know, it still didn't make it right.

As we moved to a different place and different county, and applied for the county sheriff position, I settled down some what. But I've said it before, temptations are always around. You and all of us, know it is. Womanizing continued on after I was hired in Riverside county, after I started receiving a good income. Starting to throw more money on more prostitutes. Oh I thought my second wife and I could reconcile, but it didn't last too long. Because Mom would tell me things, like maybe this second wife was some kind of witch. And mom convinced me that maybe this woman was a witch. I'll never forget how this woman came out of one of our back bedrooms, coming up to Mom and scolding Mom, lecturing her on why mom didn't like her. Boy that completely destroyed any love I might have had for this woman. She turned me off.

There was this other time, I would get off work, and instead of going home, I would drive out from Riverside to San Bernardino, to go look for women in the streets. They were always out there. In those days, hitch hiking, always hitch hiking. And of course I'd picked any one of them that looked good to me. And then it happened to me again, I was falling for another hooker. As I wrote this, wondering what kind of a life was I living. Now as I look at it, I was in my own hell.

Falling for a another hooker, was easy for me, because she would listen to me, also because, we could laugh and I would make her cry, and the both of us would talk about old times. I spoke about how this second wife of mine was treating me, and the hooker acted like she understood, and would sympathize with me. I would invite her out for lunch or breakfast or even dinner, whatever the time of day it would be. That was my world guys, can any of you relate, I know this must sound familiar with anybody out there, and maybe not. It doesn't matter to me if it relates or not, this was the kind of life I lived, and I just couldn't help it. I had to admit, there were some nice looking women in the streets, and then there were those that I couldn't understand how any man would pick up some losers. And stink too. And for a long time not one did I tell what kind of work I would do, for a long time, I kept my Sheriffs employment away from my sex life. And there were two women that were sisters, and they both liked me, and they even fought over me. Now there's a sight I had anyone do for me, actually argue over me. I wouldn't let them get out of hand. I would tell these sisters, if you two are going to act stupid, then I'm not coming around anymore. Then they would change their attitude, as I would tell them, we could all act like grown up men and women.

Life is good if you know how to respect yourself and others. But when we start disrespecting ourselves, and others, by not showing any class, and act demoralizing, people will find you uncomfortable to be with. I'm talking about normal people that lose themselves to communicate with society. That can take a whole toll on people like myself, that get nervous and tongue tied, or even stutter. Now that's way out there, not knowing how to communicate with common people. But I'm no better nor different than anyone. I'm not trying to get that impression when I wrote this, we all have a lot of learning to do. And some learned before others, that doesn't mean they're smarter nor better than you. Coming back to size, there are so many things in life, that size doesn't matter. It's never mattered to me. And I've even had to prove it, that the stature of anybody is not important. To me, as long as you get the job done, is all that counts. But I wasn't getting anything done, as I slowly crawled into a hole. Because that's what I had become. I was actually wallowing in with a bunch of pigs. Terrible but true. I'll continue with this wild attitude of mine, because it wasn't just wild, it was pathetic. I was in a hell of a world of my own, and it was gonna get much worse before it would get better. And believe me you that read this, I'm not a boaster by any means. Because since I wasn't receiving much attention from my wife at home, these women from the streets were giving me a whole lot more than just attention. And of course they were giving me more attention, because I was paying them, for sex and attention. I've always wondered, have I been the only one, that things like this happen. Have always thought so. But maybe things happened much worse to others. I wish I could believe that. I can only focus on things that were happening to me, and no one else. It's understandable nature. People like me, are self centered selfish cowards that just decide to quit on ourselves. We see them all the time, homeless people. And they'll tell ya, it's because of this and that. Their daddy or mommy has never been there for them. Which is absolute bullshit, I know it, and you should know it. Some people go through their entire lives blaming others, when they're the ones to blame, no one else. With many people, it's always been easier to blame other people than themselves, that's called, denial.

Here in my life's writings, I want to blame bad things that happened to me on my relationships with my two previous wives. If anyone is wrong, it would be this idiot called me. Because my life wasn't going to get any better if I can't find my inter-self, and that's what's wrong with most people that lose themselves, like I did.

I thought I had the world by it's tail. I'm sure you all have heard that cliche before. No, no one ever has anything by any tail. Remember "DIED THREE TIMES LIVED ONCE"

Earlier did I say Daring? Yes I did. This is how daring I was, as I mentioned before, I would call women to come to my house while my wife would go to work, and my neighbor started telling on me to the wife. Things got a little close, so I kind of cooled it for a while.

And then when we moved out of L.A. county to relocate to San Bernardino, everything was still kind of okay. Mostly because I couldn't afford any hooker.

Well as time goes by, we've been relocated to our new place in another county, good old San Bernardino, and I found out later, there wasn't anything good about San Bernardino. But I wouldn't know anything about it, until everything starts crumbling down, and crumbling it will. I was doomed for damnation, because I couldn't stay away from evil thoughts.

ROBERT GARCIA

Going back to where I am in my writings. And all of this time, I still have never been in jail. I never thought I would. Thinking all along, I'm too good for jail.

At this part of my life, remember I'm working for a county sheriff, I can't go to jail. I'm too good for that. Excuse me asshole, I used to call myself. No one is too good. Finding out, when people walk around amongst us and think they're better than anyone else, and think everything is funny, they walk around with their head up there ass. And guess who am I talking about. I also found out about some law enforcement officers, that I've once worked with, they can really think they are something else better than anyone.

And I started thinking the same way, just after I was hired by the county of Riverside. I was much younger then, and the way it looks as to what I'm writing, I was lots dumber. Here we go, about the mind, no I'm not talking about book smart, I'm talking about common sense. And as I, there's a hell of a lot of people that lack just that, common sense.

And I'm just as guilty as the next guy that lacks something so simple as common sense

I was really happy when I was working with the county, because it was all about the money. And who wouldn't be, right? At least I thought I was happy.

And the excitement continues at my county jail employment, and I have to say, it was the greatest career employment I had ever worked at. Yeah, before I had worked for a big retail management position, and that was also a great job to be trusted, to handle thousands of dollars of someone else's money. That felt good for my ego.

Even one of my daughters asked me, why would I ruin a beautiful career, like this county Sheriffs law enforcement officer position. I will never be able to explain it, as to what gotten into me, to do something so wrong. But I'm starting to get ahead of myself.

Things of the times I had gotten into fights with a few inmates. Did that make me feel good, I think so at the time. Because the most biggest crimes I despised the most, were murderers, baby killers, rapers, and the most that I hated the most, were child molesters. I'm sorry, but

I could never forgive any evil asshole that molests children. I'm sorry, but I just can't.

Would I be the only one that thinks that way. If any of my readers have children, I should say so. Just like society hates alcoholics and drug addicts, drug pushers, murderers, and child molesters fall in the same category of evil people. But I strongly believe that convicted murderers should be sentenced to death. I'm old fashioned, the old book, an eye for an eye, tooth for a tooth. Someone takes a life, the authorities should take his or her life. What saddens me and pisses me off the most, the victim and the victim's families never seem to have any say when the victim is murdered, on how the perpetrator should be sentenced. Guess you can think I'm barbaric. So be it, because I speak for the ones that are killed senselessly. It's sad they can't speak for themselves, because they were killed.

But there are those kinds of people that are just a step down the ladder that are not liked very well either. Burglars, that have the f**king nerve to break into any home they choose to steal anyone's possessions and could even kill anyone in their house. Ain't that something, anyone minding their own business, and some asshole breaks into your home, to steal and maybe kill someone in the process. But if anyone is able to catch the burglar before he hurts you or kills you, or even your spouse and you kill him or her first, now you'll be detained pending investigation. To much bullshit, is how I see it. There are far too many loopholes in the laws and in the judicial system.

Later on in my life, I'll open up to write you what happened to my Dad, and what his youngest daughter did to him. And there should be a law against that too, for anyone to do what she did to any other parent. That, I'll always remember what a shameful thing that adult child did to her own Dad.

Updating on my writings on what's going on with my second marriage. Only to say, it's only getting worse. And getting worse on a daily basis it was. And because this wife at the time, was starting to get on my nerves. And mom and dad were noticing things about her, which I was too blind to see. I would arrive from work, and have to cook my meals, and when I would cook, Mom would notice this woman's son would eat like a dog, and hardly leave anything for anyone else. And that was true, because there were times I did notice him eat like there was no tomorrow. He would put away the food like nobody's business. And his mother wouldn't say a damn thing, for regards to her husband, me. She wouldn't greet me, after a days work, and show any affection like most wives do. That would've been nice. But that never happened. It's funny how I look at it now, all what Mom told me were true, but I seemed to be on this wife's side.

Having flash backs on how Mom took care of her kids and her husband. Those were the good old fashioned days, of yesteryears. You'll probably never see that in this day and age. Mom would be the one to tell me how hard it was in the old days, and to see her son be with women that didn't care about anyone else but themselves, was breaking her heart.

And to see this kid to abuse his freedom, it didn't matter to his mother, because she wouldn't say shit. And that was starting to, as I said, starting to get on my nerves. And that was definitely pushing me away from that marriage. And that is why I started whore mongering around the streets. No, I'm not saying that was right, because two wrongs didn't make it right.

Somewhere along the line, something was going to blow up, or should I say, someone was about to blow a gasket, and the results were going to be devastating, for those involved. Well, it doesn't take a rocket scientist to figure that out.

The good times were fading away from my second marriage, for so many reasons, maybe because love was deteriorating and becoming invisible, as if it was never there. Wow, that didn't take long, it seemed not too long ago, we were madly in love. But at this time of my life, hate was brewing, and steam had blown over.

I wasn't coming straight home from work anymore. I was taking detours to the streets. And asking for more trouble than I could handle, but I didn't have a clue at the time. But isn't that what happens to most people that get all tangled in the devil's web, because that's exactly where he wants us. Picking up dirty prostitutes from off the streets. Now doesn't that sound really outrageous, coming from as a Sheriffs county worker. Taking sluts out for a meal. Now, how filthy can one get. But once I lost love for this woman, I became lost into another world. A world of lust. I'm not kidding, because I look at it today, I didn't even know where I was. But the law will catch up with you, or in this case, catch up with me. Oh, it sure will in more ways than I wish I didn't have to write it down. But down deep I had to write this, to show many out there, that there is Faith, Hope, and Love, for everyone.

And going to work, like nothing was wrong. And during my work shift, whether it be day, or night, I'd play Mr. Law man, and after work, I go play whore monger. It was sure far from playing superman, Mr. reporter, during the day, and play Superman, when crime was close by. No, it wasn't funny. Like I'm trying to play it off. There was nothing to play off, because none of my ridiculous behavior made any sense, because I wasn't showing gratitude for a beautiful career I could have had. I'll soon show you, how I threw it all away. Not only was I starting to throw a beautiful career, I was also slowly throwing away my life, and what will hurt my precious ones the most, my daughters and my momma and father. It will break my daughters and my mother's hearts. You'd think I would stop there, are you kidding, not even close. I should have, but my evil side and my evil self, enjoyed every minute of it.

Have come up with an explanation about how the body reacts, when we think we're having fun. It's not fun, and it's not healthy, it's a slow death, and slowly eats you alive, and by the time we realize it, it's practically too late.

Here's another sneaky shit I pulled while my second wife would go to work, and had pulled this bullshit sneakiness more than once. I was always looking for more excitement, with either a regular hooker, or a new one. I thought I had tried enough whoring, but no, I came up with another one. Like I said, when this wife went off to work, while our kids were in the either in the living room or did whatever they did in their bedrooms. We had a walk way, between our house and the neighbor, and a door to the master bedroom. I had the nerve to bring in a hooker into my wife's and I bedroom. And of course f**k our brains out. And would do that a few times, without shame. That's right, had no remorse, because I didn't give a shit about what I did.

ROBERT GARCIA

And then the wife and I lay in that same bed, can you people believe this, because when I wrote this, it started to make me gag. I really needed someone to stop me, because I didn't know how, because I didn't want to. I'm sure any woman that will read this, will think, what a pig I was, wallowing in a can of worms. That's what it looked like to me, from my stand point of life today.

Man has always thought, and it doesn't matter who we are, we think we're alone, and no one's watching, think again, because you're wrong, and I found out I've been wrong about a lot of things. Especially about thinking that no one's watching, and I'm not alone, because this has been going on since man was created. Do you people know who I'm talking about, probably not, at least those of you that don't believe in God. Every generation has its millions of non believers, and becoming lost within their own lives, and wondered how we ever got that way. No I'm not saying, I understand God, I'm not saying that at all. But we're not suppose to understand God, but that's my belief. What I do know, is, I have faith, and I have hope, and I love my God. And I was very lost, and he found me, just when I thought, I didn't have anyone to turn to. And I was wrong about that as well. But at this part of my life, the part of being married to my second wife, and can't say if my first wife or my second wife, on which one was the worst. My first was an alcoholic and my second was an opportunist. I might want to ask you, which one would you think was the worst one. Neither one showed any gratitude, and I'm not blaming them for my disastrous down fall, as I did before. As I see clearly now, and how it was so easy to blame everyone else about my downfall. I've heard many others blame everyone else, about why there're in prison, or why they were in and out of jail. We all have different avenues, and different options to choose a better way of life, instead of following the cowardly way. But I had to fall, and recover to realize who's fault it really was. And, don't think I knew how all of this was going to end. But I really think now, I could've died numerous times, and why I'm not, I haven't a clue. As I wrote this, I feel like I was on a roller coaster ride, and I could have been thrown off anytime, but I wasn't. The only part I can say, and vaguely remember, where I was thrown, is when we were in that truck crash. Having nightmares after that tragedy was so scary, and then what happened, I'm sent to Vietnam, just to have more nightmares, and why I never committed suicide, well that's where my loving God came into my life. With Hope, with Faith, and with Love. And he's been here with me since then. But actually he's always been there, I just never opened the door to my heart, until seventeen years ago. No I'm far away from perfect, but I'm a hell of a far cry better than who I was before.

I'll continue on my outrageous life, when I was married to my second woman of marriage. How I had the gall to bring hookers to our house while I was still married to this woman, is beyond me, and do what I did to these women, in the same bed, where my second wife and I slept in. And how I was never caught, was a miracle. I should've divorced this second wife, instead of doing those devious things to our marriage. And how I could just go about my business like nothing was wrong. I would go pick up the wife from her job, and I'd bring her home, and act like nothing was wrong, I must have come out from some hole out of hell, to possess me to do the things I did. Even after writing this made me feel like throwing up. No one is supposed to get away with that kind of evil. And I didn't get away with anything, because my forward writings will reveal where I ended up, instead of dead.

We all have different roads, and different options to choose from, but I made very bad choices, and I paid dearly for them. But at this point, I haven't learned my lesson yet. Oh, but I will. We all do. Those were the days of being possessed by evil, and now I'm possessed by God. Because things have happened to me, that I would never have dreamed of.

Through my life, have found out that we have many choices, but our biggest choice we have, could be the deadliest choice of a life time. Because for most of us, it will take all of our lives to make the right and best choice to save ourselves. And it's very important for all of us, or at least for those that want to live eternally, that's right. Because if we don't pay attention to God's Ten Commandments, and obey them, we're doomed spiritually. For those of you, you might think I talk like this, because I'm old. You can think that all you want. Because like I said, for most of us, it might take a life time to realize to prepare ourselves for a eternal life with God.

What I do now, I read the Bible, and I pray, and live a peaceful loving life with my current wife. And I have often wondered how I deserved this life of forgiveness. Until I felt the love from God, and when I felt his love, then I started having hope and faith. And unless you know and feel what I'm trying to say, then you won't know what I'm talking about. I know back in my time, when I would hear people talk about God, as I do today, I didn't have a clue of what they were talking about either. It's weird, now that my ninety seven year old Dad, and I pray on the phone together, I feel more of God's forgiveness, than I did before. I really believe that it cleanses the soul, after Dad and I pray our daily prayer. And believe me, for too long of a time, Dad and I were not the closest father and son relationship. We were far too distant from each other. And I've wrote it down, and I told him something terrible, "Dad I'll always love you for being my Dad, but I'll never like you as a friend." I can only imagine, how terrible that would have sounded to me, if my son would have told me that. After years of remembrance, years later, I thought about that, what I had told Dad, thought to myself, what kind of a jerk am I. Like I said, we've come a long way, we talk on the phone everyday, and we pray everyday. He did mention to me, "Son that was a beautiful idea you came up with, to pray to God with each other on a daily basis." I told him, that it wasn't me that put that prayer daily in my head, I told Dad that it was our God who we pray to. That's who gave me the idea. And it felt good, and it still feels good, because I feel God touched my heart to talk to both of my Fathers, my biological father and pray to my Heavenly Father.

Continuing on my road with this second wife of mine, and at the same time, working at the Riverside county jail. As I look back, working at the county jail, and being married to this woman, was like living two separate lives. At my job, I would be a well respected employee, looking as though I was a perfect deputy, all uniformed, with a big shiny badge, and after work, I'd go out looking for trash. And never make it home until the wee hours, and when I felt good and ready. Don't know about you, but those kinds of people, are dangerous, and I was one of them.

The paragraph where I said I love both of my fathers. That's true, but I haven't arrived to that part of my life yet. The fact of the matter is, I do arrive when my God has forgiven me. But my judgement time will come, when God comes to judge the living and the dead.

So as I told you before, I wouldn't come home until I felt like it. And that my friends, wasn't being devoted to my wife, regardless of falling out of love for her. The old saying was, if you don't love your wife anymore, then divorce her, don't betray your marriage. Because that puts a bad reflection on yourself, and it did, it did put a very bad reflection on me. Because it doesn't make me better, by going out to the streets, looking for hookers. Those my friends, are just some of the sins I committed, as God as my witness. And not just that, also bringing prostitute women to our home, and in our bed, wow. And as I wrote this, it hit me hard, like a fat punch to my heart, and leaving a scarred spirit. Because as I read this, it brightened my eyes, with amazement.

And it's got a lot to do with how I look at life today, and how I feel about those days of mine, and how disrespectful I was with people and myself.

Disrespectful, now that's a big word. And it can make us look like idiots, if we lose all sense of reality, and it can also make us lose the respect of our children, and I almost did, but two of my children, forgave me. Looking back as to what I was, and who I was before, and having my daughters forgive me, has been and will always be a feeling of hopefulness and gave me a whole lot of faith in God.

But at the time I had developed a huge problem and started losing all hope and despair within myself. And that also my friends, can and it will make you feel like you're on the edge of your world, and very negative about yourself.

And during my time in this marriage and my employment with the county, had given me a feeling of too much pride. Observing the inmates, and how low class they all were. Thinking all along I could and would never fall that low. And also the fact of the matter was and still is, don't play with your spirit, and definitely don't play with God's love because God is watching your physical actions and staring at our spiritual side of us. Because when we fall, it's going to be deep. Called hitting rock bottom. And I will, like most of us do, and have, since man was created. But I'm not gonna talk about everyone else. This is my life's writings, about my three deaths throughout my life time, and how I survived, by God's reaching out to my need of forgiveness, and I have to admit, that's the part I will never understand about God's forgiveness. But as I wrote, I don't have to understand God, all I know, that God loves me and I love God. And I have faith and hope in him.

As my wife and I continued to try to reconcile our marriage, because she started having suspicions about my whereabouts on me, when I didn't come straight home from work. And who wouldn't have suspicions, if you're in your right mind. And she did have many suspicions, and would always ask me where have I been, and my lies would be, I'd work overtime.

I had started out on a journey of destruction and I was too blind to see it. Because I was deceived by the devil, making me think I could do whatever I wanted to do. Because this is my life, and I'm a veteran. And then I thought I could do things to this woman, because she didn't like my mother and mistreated my daughters. And so one day, wifey decided she and I should talk about our disconnected relationship. Telling me, that if something was to happen to us, and we end up divorced, that she would always be my friend. But as I thought about what she said, I never thought that to be possible, because once you wrong me, it's over. Just it was over with my first wife, this one is coming to a screeching halt.

With my whoring around out in the streets, and liking my regular hookers, them knowing me and I knowing them. It seemed at the time, I was on a road straight to hell, and not seeing any hope. Because once I started falling, it felt as though I couldn't get a hold of anything or anyone to help me. Does that sound familiar, to anyone out there.

And after that little talk we had, second wife and I, all of a sudden, she tells me she's pregnant. Thought to myself, wow, after all of that, she still wanted to have my baby. Thought to myself, that didn't make any sense, because I became worse. Started staying out away from home more often. My losing of myself and my loved ones, just didn't seem to matter to me. So, so, sad, but true.

And still to this day, wondering what made me do the things I did. Because I can't come up with any normal reason why. But I keep coming up with a rational thought to my mind, that if someone hurts my what little ego I had, I'm going to try to hurt your feelings in an emotional way. If that makes any sense. I just couldn't come straight home, I guess maybe it was the excitement of daring myself of getting caught with another woman, by my wife. But she never did.

One day I took a big chance of getting caught. I actually took my daughters with me, to go out with a prostitute and her daughter, can you believe that, because it's really hard for me get that. We went out, all five of us, and I can't remember where exactly we went to. Because I just can't swallow down the psychotic reasoning behind a man with his daughters, go out with a hooker and her daughter. Wow, something has got to be completely wrong with a man like that. Im telling ya, I was wrong, so wrong.

So as I continued on my escapade, because that's what it was, a daring evil act of deception on my part. Working in an environment, at a county jail, and then go out and commit crime of lust. And caught twice and almost got caught a third time. But lying to a police officer, and he believing my lie, I was able to escape by a close call. But the first two times I did get caught. and the police officer warned me that if he caught me again, he would report me to my supervisors, and I would lose my county employment for sure. Close call? Yes it was.

Another close call during my whore monger days, why I never caught V. D., is a miracle. I'm telling ya, God has always been with me, on every evil roller coaster ride in my life, but always thought I was alone. Our lord will always be there for you, even when you think he's not. That was me then, but how I realize it now, is amazing to me. But I'll never try to understand God. As I've said, I don't think we're supposed to understand him.

Back to my sour second marriage, because that's what it had become, because I was losing everything, and I didn't care anymore. And that to me, was very selfish, having daughters, that showed not caring about them, when I should have. In fact, I married this second woman, as she promised me, she would take care and love my daughters, and

ROBERT GARCIA

treat them like her own daughters and had become quite the opposite. Everything came down on my poor loving daughters, because they were my first kids, from my previous marriage, the alcoholic wife. Psychologically they were beat up by their biological mother, and now by this woman, called step mother. I can't even come close to imagine how my daughters felt about that tormented life they lived, at such a young age. We're talking eight and six years of age, my two daughters going through a hell of a life, with both their own mother and then this step mother. And then you would think it would stop there, no their Dad had to become an idiot. Not any better than those two women. When I wrote this, I got very emotional, maybe because my daughters never stopped loving me, and forgave me for what I was back then.

Now let's find out what kind of children this woman had, that promised me, she would love and take care of mine. Well, not so much her daughter, she wasn't a bad person, she showed respect, but that brother of hers, I would've loved to ship him back to where he came from. Somewhere in Central America. Won't mention it, because then it's getting too personal.

All this time, I'm still working as a correctional officer, with the county sheriff.

One day, don't know what got into me, but I just about let this kid have it. For being such a lazy boy. He was already nineteen or twenty, and he wasn't going to school, and he didn't want to work.

What would anyone do with a lazy kid, I ask you. Well like I said, I had just about enough of him. On a couple of days off from work, my oldest daughter and I went visiting my parents, daughter's grandparents of course. Had a few beers in my system, with Dad at that time. And on our way back home, I had this resentment about my wife's son. So I arrived home, and thought everything was okay, but my head was about to explode, when I found out this kid is no where to be found. But I knew he was home, and looking for him, only to find out he's locked up in one of the bedrooms, with his girlfriend, and locked up he was. Because when I knocked on the door, he wasn't answering, and I call to him to open the door, but he wasn't budging. And it really started to get on my nerves, pissed off was more like it. And numerous times I ordered him to open the door, and he just wouldn't. That's when I told him to open the f**king door before I break it open. Because he had the door wedged locked with a two by four piece of wood. Thinking to myself, this kid has nerve, so I yelled at him again, open the door, before I break it down. And I almost did, when he finally opened it. But instead of beating this kid up, I think I better call the police on myself. To report myself, that I've been drinking and to please send a police officer to my residence, before I hurt this step son of mine. They didn't take any time, an officer was out to our house in minutes. Looking out our window, as the police car arrived, I immediately came out to greet the police officer, as he started asking me as to what was wrong. "Sorry Officer, But I've been drinking, and I got home on my day off from work, from visiting my folks, and I find this step son locked up in his bedroom with his girlfriend, and I just got tired of it. He's always at home, and never looking for a job. And I think it was about time I said something about it." The cop was fair with me, he seemed understandable, because as he sighed, he asked if he could speak to this lazy kid. As I called the boy out to talk to the police, his mother finally decided to ask me, why did I call the police, I tell her, I didn't call the cops on him, I called the cops on myself. She still didn't understand, so I say to her, its either call the cops, or I was gonna hurt your son. And she still doesn't get it, asking me why. Because I'm tired of your son always home and never looking for a job of some kind. To help me out. I was getting burned out, with me working two jobs, and this son of hers can't even get one job. I was supporting my two daughters her son and her daughter and the wife. I figured if her son could eat like there's no tomorrow, then he should help me out by supporting himself. She seemed all bewildered, like as if I was picking on her little boy.

I started feeling I had married an opportunist. Thinking she might of had a problem with this boy of hers. And now it's my problem. And I learned this son of this woman, had a molestation problem, he liked underage girls. Never realizing before, but he could have had plans with my daughters, wow, now that would have outraged me to a point of no return. Something similar of this female coworker, another correctional officer, that almost shot her husband, after finding out, he actually raped their daughter. That would outrage anyone, I think. And that my friends, would have outrage me as well, if this son of this woman I married, would have put his hands on one of my daughters. Oh man, I hate to think what I would have done to him.

When I impregnated my second wife, and now I'm going to have another mouth to feed. Burned out will start by burning the candle from both ends. And that was the next thing I started doing.

A true story can have a lot of fun loving memories, but it can also have a sad ending, especially for the kids. And that's exactly what happened to my baby daughter, at the end of my story.

This part of my life, is one of my sad parts, in losing all connections of a father and daughter relationship, with my youngest daughter, especially when you leave them at toddler age. Four years old, is when we were in each others presence. That's a long time ago now.

My baby daughter, will probably never know the truth, why I couldn't come back to her, and why I left her in the first place. What this young lady, my youngest daughter, doesn't know, is, without me petitioning her mother, and making her an American citizen, our daughter would have never been born.

But things got complicated for me, but no one had never cared, not my second wife, not her kids. I having to work two full time jobs. And never having any time for myself, always burned out, and feeling completely drained. Almost falling asleep behind the drivers steering wheel, from going from one job and going to the next. It was a bitch, I tell ya.

You'd think, I would be happy having a new baby in the family. But the old saying, when you play, you pay. If I would have had any sense, and if I would have known my child would be in the cross fire, maybe I wouldn't have done what I did.

This, like I said, will be a very hard part of my life's writings. Mostly because I'm going to have to admit what a coward I was, in falling behind my responsibilities as a father. But it's the truth, what can I say. And where do I start, I'll start by saying, I'm not blaming anyone, because it's all my fault. Oh, I could say, it was that woman I married. And maybe it was a little of her fault. But a lot of it was mine.

As a boy, had always wanted to be a cop, so where's the best way to start, security guard. But as I've said, have always been a little slow in doing anything in my life. Have tried to look at it in a positive way, but it's a little hard to look at it that way, at my age now. I'll admit it, just slow in mind. Sometimes I would think backwards. Ain't no joke, but I have survived. Because some, had not survived, because they thought they were geniuses. I would rather be a slow live thinker than a dead genius. There are so many in prison, because they thought they were smarter than the law, and they thought they would never get caught. I've come up with an evaluation, that anyone living past sixty, everyday is a reward. I know it's been quite rewarding for me, in my old age, in my seventies when I wrote this.

I even went to detective school, now that was interesting. A lot of sir-valence. I couldn't take it though, it was too much just sitting in one place. Waiting for anything to happen, and many times nothing happened. Boring? Hell ya. And did a lot of security work, roaming security, just stand guard, and then got hired by the county, as a correctional officer, and when the new born came into the family, I had to take on another full time job. Tired, all the time, tired was an underestimated word. Burned out more like it. Like I said earlier, burning the candle from both ends. And there's where I think, that second wife, took advantage of that. Never having any time for the love of life. Dad kept calling me, wondering about me, mama worried sick. And this second wife not telling me my parents have been calling me. Dad would yell in my ear, telling me, what kind of a woman is that, that doesn't tell you, your mom and dad wants to talk to you. Dad said, that woman is too much. I'm losing peace of mind, and falling out of love for this woman. I was slowly falling out of reality for life.

Question to all of you while you read this, especially you, that was once in love, and start falling out of love for the woman you married and said you loved at the alter. How does that feel? I'll admit, the love I lost for this woman, didn't bother me, in fact nothing bothered me at all. Terrible? I'll say it was. Because I had three daughters, that should have bothered me tremendously, but it didn't, and I will pay for that. And, at the end of our lives, we all have the biggest payment to pay, and that my dear friends, will be judgement day. When I lost love for everything and everyone, I lost myself into another world.

I think I'll never know who my baby daughter is, and that started when I left her, when she was just four years old. And she is now in her thirties. You tell me.

Life at the time of this second marriage, had become to exhausting for me. I couldn't breathe, there was absolutely no time for me in my own life. Can we relate you guys? But I think I tried, and tried I did, until I just about collapsed.

What was so exhausting, some people might ask.

As I said I was working two full time jobs, sometimes I'd work a full eight hours at my day job, and then go running to my other job, which was my county sheriff, for another eight hours. It was a very tiring life I was living. But I had to do it, to support the family I had. My wife, her two children, and my two daughters and myself. Oh, and now the newly born baby girl. For obvious reasons, the wife couldn't work, because she had to stay at home, to take care of the baby. And where was I? In the streets, working my ass off. And there were times, I wouldn't get a day off for months. And when I would get a day off, would spend it sleeping. What else? Can't remember how long I did that. The way my body felt, way too long.

And now I didn't have any time for hookers, how could I, there's only twenty four hours in a day. All of that whoring around, when I wasn't working two jobs. But now those days were over. In a way it was best, because sooner or later, I was bound to catch a sexual disease. Why I never did, was just another miracle for me. Oh, but those days were coming back, because the new baby had entered into her new world. And little did she know, what a hell of a life she will have.

So now what, well the baby was born, and I went back to my escapade, looking for women in the streets. And started doing it again, staying away from the home, sometimes over night and sometimes for a few days. Wow. What a horrible life I was living. Well it's all true, because I'm not holding anything back. If I would have thought a normal way of thinking, I would have been more grateful, for the county hiring me in the first place, right? If I would have thought a normal way of thinking. And how could I do that, if I wasn't living a normal life in the first place. There were times, I had self pity, opening up, and talking to some women, about how bad I was being treated at home. Some of these women, would respond by telling me, divorce that woman of yours, and I'll marry you. Thought to myself, oh yeah, right, and what kind of a life would I be falling into. I can only imagine. Like I said, why I never caught a sexual disease is beyond me, because there were many times I never used any protection from having intercourse. Say what!!! That's right, and I'm still alive today. And I'm so relieved and so grateful for God's forgiveness and blessings. There aren't enough words to express my love for my God. That's just the way my life has been, since I made peace within myself, and God.

I guess I was having self pity, and maybe I wasn't, because there were so many things in my life, that have been going on, and it didn't just start with this marriage, it's been going on for a long, long time. Dad and I still have our differences, and our issues and that will be that way, probably for the rest of our lives. And maybe our father and son relationship started way back then, and all it did was escalate from there. But I've made my amends to Dad, many times over, and over. Have learned that as a son, we have to follow and obey God's commandments. Did I say it was easy, did I say that, no I didn't. In the Bible, just in case some of you don't know, there are Ten Commandments, and the fifth one is, "HONOR THY FATHER AND THY MOTHER", and in my younger years, I failed to do that. And maybe many of you have failed as well. But what I'm only focused on, is what I've done against my Dad and my Heavenly Father, during my life.

So as I continue my confused life, because I was very confused.

My bad choices and my wrong turns of direction, as to where I was headed to, really started when I arrived from Nam. Does that sound familiar, I'm pointing at you, my fellow comrades, my fellow Vietnam veterans. So in the long run, it wasn't my first wife and it wasn't my second wife, that were at fault, it was I that chose to marry them. I didn't have to marry neither one of them, but that I did, those were two very bad choices of my life, that I paid dearly. And paid dearly I did. And that probably wouldn't have been so bad, if my daughters wouldn't to had suffer for my mistakes. Because I've always known that it's the Dad that is supposed to be supportive and responsible for his kids to help them out to succeed in life for their future. But I was not there for them. Because I couldn't even be supportive for myself, so how could I be there for them.

Not too long ago, I've gotten to know my son in law, a little at time everyday, and it's blossoming to a close relationship, not only for my daughter, but for the both of us as well.

He wasn't shy to let me know, that he didn't have a Dad to speak of. When he first mentioned that to me, it kind of hit my heart sideways, like oh my god, how sad for him. And I'll continue that part of my life's writings later.

Right now I want to update you, as to where was I going with my county employment position. It started to fall slowly into a spiral up side down pancake, if you know what I mean. And it didn't taste good to anyone involved.

I'm in a car, that's being driven by a maniac and going straight to hell, and all this time I thought I was doing well. Now let's be honest with myself, I knew exactly what I was doing, and just pretended to everyone that it was everybody's else's fault.

And just about this time I met up with a Puerto Rican prostitute and have to say, she was an attractive woman, but still a hooker, and getting to know each other very well. And she had two very bad habits, the first one being a prostitute and the second one, being an addict. A crack head. Nasty habits!! But what do they say, don't knock it until you've tried it. And trying them I wasn't going to do. At least I thought I wasn't. And the more I dated that woman, the more I will fall in my own hell. If I would have just stayed away from that girl. Then it wouldn't have been so bad. But the chips fall where they will lay. I mean, here I was treating this woman, like she was my wife, driving my truck, she picking me up from work, taking me to work. And then we would go back to our room, and I would stay with her nights at a time. Without shame. And my real wife, not having a clue as to what is really going on. And then what happened, one night we're in our room, motel room that is, she went out to pick up some crack cocaine, and she got caught and taken to jail, and I didn't know she had been on parole, so she went back to prison.

Thinking, oh my god, now how long will she be in prison, and why would I worry about that. Now, how did I look, here I was working for a county sheriff, keeping criminals locked up, right? And here I was dating and practically living with a crack cocaine addict. Say what? Oh yes I was, practically living with a parolee, actually I was living with her part of the time, and she had already done time in prison, and out on parole, for drugs. Now ain't I the hypocrite. That's exactly what I was, a hypocrite. And what did she do, while she's again in prison she wrote me a letter to my house. I was a jack of all trades, and a master of none. Ain't that a joke, but the joke was on me. She even called my house. For a while, wondered, now how in the hell did she get all that, address, phone number, and knowing I'm married. But I had discussed all my lost love for my wife. This is why she felt writing to me wouldn't matter to me. But it did matter to me, because it would start a scuffle of trouble with this already weak marriage, and how would I explain this to my wife. But then it would explain a lot of shit, as to why I was always gone, and hardly ever coming straight home from work. And she only wrote one letter, well how many times did I expect. And get this, when her letter arrived at my home, while my wife read it, when I was getting ready for work. She yells out to me, I come from the bedroom and she showed me the letter from a woman's prison, with a woman's name, with a lipstick kiss at the bottom of the letter. With big words, saying "I LOVE YOU" I thought, oh my god, this bitch really has nerve. And the next thing I'm doing, I'm visiting this woman in prison, and bringing my baby daughter with me. Crazy? I'll say. I was a real asshole. I was lost in my own world of hell, to say the least. Although I admit what kind of a life I was living, and although it looks like hell, I'm sure I'm not alone. In fact there are those that are far more worse than me. I would never have gone so low as to rape or molest my own child. Oh my god, that's got to be the lowest thing to do to your own flesh and blood. No, I'm not proud of some things I've done in my life, but I'm sure glad I've never stooped down lower than I have. Thank God. This woman even wanted me to help her get out of prison, like bail her out,

I couldn't believe it, but it was happening. I guess she thought because I worked for a law enforcement agency, I could easily bail her out. But it was impossible for me, ain't no way I was going to bail her out. First of all, I didn't want to, and second of all, she violated her parole. And besides she wrote to my house, and that my friends, she should have never done. That totally pissed me off. Thinking the next time I see that hooker, gonna let her know.

Let's go fast backwards, because I forgot to mention that something terrible has happened to me. Yes, what I'm about to tell you all, is a very shameful thing.

Now remember, I've already been down my own death row twice in my life. And remember this, "DIED THREE TIMES LIVED ONCE" and now I'm about to walk the aisle of my third death row., drugs. And I was always preaching against drug addicts, and how I would never go to jail for anything stupid. And what happened, you may ask.

Like I've said I was practically living with this Puerto Rican prostitute, and she was always trying to talk me into smoking crack cocaine, and I was constantly pushing it away. Until it happened, and she won the fight, of me pushing crack away from me. And I don't remember how it happened, but the fact of the matter it did happen. I crossed the point of no return. I became a criminal. And that's the bottom line of my non-innocence.

And I'm still employed at the Riverside county Sheriffs department, now that was quite down under, and double crossing for me to go against a future with the county. And I would lose a perfect opportunity. And I did lose it, and I'll explain it the best way I can. Was I stupid, you better believe it, that was the most stupidest thing I had ever done in my life. And how old was I when I fell in stuck on stupid. In my late forties, I should have known better, but it is what it is. And it happened how it happened.

As I said in my previous life's writings, I enlisted into the Marines at the age of nineteen, and that was my smartest thing I've ever done, and now in not even thirty years later, I've enlisted into the world of addiction, and this was my dumbest thing I ever did. Looking back at that, it's just has to be God's biggest miracle given to me. Because

I wouldn't be where I am today, if I hadn't joined the Marines, in my golden age of nineteen.

Thinking I was having a time of my life, with this Puerto Rican girl. I had already told her all about my personal life, and my personal love life, and my problem with my wife, and how she tried to talk me into divorcing this second wife of mine, just so she could marry me. What a catastrophe that would have been, married to a Puerto Rican hooker, now imagine that, because I can't and I didn't. And she also did some singing. She would sing in Spanish, and she sounded pretty good. She really did. But I was still going to work, and doing my duties as a deputy correctional officer was supposed to do, and things have not gone wrong as of yet. Here me out, not yet, I haven't fallen, and have not let this hooker bring me down yet. This was quite an experience for me, because the way I look at it today, that girl would dress up with a red dress and high heels, and then go to the bathroom and strip down, and stand at the door way, naked, but just her high heels on. Smiling an evil smile, like the devil himself. She was already possessed by evil and just looking to see who she could take with her.

We were driving around like we were husband and wife, she would take me to work, and later come and pick me up from work. Like I said, it was an empty experience. I would go home, to shower down, change clothes. And that went for a good while. Did I say a good while, yes I did, because I was having fun. But I was too blind to see the reality of my real life, with the cost of my daughters lives. Yes, unfortunately for them, they're still suffering because my selfish, self center attitude. And I'm starting to wear myself out, by letting this evil possession engulf me, like a piece of shit that I was.

And what do you think my wife was thinking about this that's going on. She was disgusted, how would any wife react? Now to me, looking back at that, why didn't she divorce me, is beyond me. Maybe somewhere along the line, she might have thought, I was disgusted with our marriage. But she never gave me any signs, on what was going on inside her mind. And maybe she thought, she just didn't know what to do with me.

ROBERT GARCIA

Here we go, help me, I'm falling off my life, and my realities of my life, as I fall into a fantasy world. Yes, I fell, and very deep into disaster.

I must had been very stressed out, when I finally decided to go way down. And through out my entire life, before this incident, I had been able to shake any drug off. How wrong was I? Dead wrong. That's how wrong.

When I was interviewed for the correctional officer position, they asked if I had ever done drugs, and I answered, with a yes, but I've never done jail time for any drug, and no matter how you answer, they check up on you anyway. That's just a formality, of serious employment, I should say so, law enforcement. But to be already hired and working for the county, and having time under your belt, as a figure of speech, and then start doing drugs, that's a completely different story, and that's a slap in the face to who hired me, in the first place. In fact, that's an insult to the county. Because they've always treated me very well. And I can't give any reasonable answer, or excuse for why I did what I did. Having a flash back about a coworker, that saw me with that hooker, he didn't actually know what she was, but he could smell something wasn't right.

And so one night, as all other nights with this girl, in a motel room, and as other nights, she pulled out her crack pipe along with her crack and started smoking and offered me a hit, but this time it was different, I decided to take a puff of her pipe. Thinking all along, I've done a lot of drugs in my time, and so this one won't be any different, at least that's what I thought. And oh shit, I couldn't comprehend what was happening, I wanted to start flying, and at the same time, I felt like I was floating in air. The next thing I'm doing, I jumped out of the chair I was seating in, and I literally ran out of the motel room, but running real fast. Can anyone believe that, because I don't know about anyone that has experienced that kind of feeling, after just your first hit of crack. But that's what I felt, and realizing now, how fast my heart was beating, and how dangerous that was for me, and for anyone else that smokes that shit, because people, that's what that is, shit. Some other guy was with us, when I ran like a bat out of hell, and he ran out after me, to tell me, hey man, what's wrong with you, you're going to draw attention to us, and someone is going to call the cops. And after that day, that complete change on my look at life. And it ruined me disastrously to the point, that all I wanted was more and more of crack cocaine.

After a while, my life depended on crack cocaine, I just couldn't control that feeling. It was a terrible thing to go through. And I've only just begun, with this controlled substance, and worse was yet to come. I shit you not. When I started this drug, I was getting paid well from the county, so I was able to get credit from crack houses. These crack houses were giving me two to three hundred dollars of credit of crack. They never knew where I worked, and it was better that way.

And when this Puerto Rican woman was busted and had to go back to prison, and then when she wrote me a letter to my house, I felt right then I didn't need to be around that woman anymore. Because she pissed me off. And when we saw each other again, it wasn't a friendly encounter, because I roughly told her, I didn't want her around me anymore. And as she kept talking, I just drove off. And never saw each other again, and I felt good about it. And one last time I did see that hooker, she had been arrested and was being put in the back seat of a police car. And little did I know then, I'll be riding in the back seat of police cars, only it'll be in a different county.

Anyway, I continued on my way to hell, slowly but surely. In the beginning it was a slow process, a slow transitioning, so to speak. From a beautiful start of a life's career to a dark world of loneliness of drugs. But I haven't lost my county employment as of yet. But soon is yet to come. Just give it some time, it's coming.

Although I hadn't lost my short career yet, but I was starting to call off from work. Slowly slipping into hell, and I just couldn't stop my fall, mostly because I loved the feeling what crack cocaine gave me.

My whole situation was like a cancer eating me alive, and I had no cure for it, and out of control. Because mentally I was brain washed, with the sensational joy crack gave me. My body was starting to crave it, the more I smoked it. And the more I smoked it, I did. And I had no plans on quitting anytime soon. Satan had started to wash me away from the face of the earth, to guide me to the pit, where he has taken many. Little did I know, God was waiting for me to open up the door of my heart. I just didn't know when that was going to happen. And did know that then, hell no, I didn't even know where and who I was anymore.

This next episode of my beginnings of my cocaine addiction, starts to get very deep, as if I'm falling, and falling, and crying and crying. But no one can hear me, because no one's listening and no body cares.

It's funny how life is, isn't it, in the reality sense of it. We're all ready to ridicule those we call alcoholics, oh my god, drug addicts, drug pushers, only in that line of crime. All the others that have fallen completely lost into a world of loneliness, with those alike. We all know whom I speaking of, don't we. Those lost in a world of murderers, rapers, and so forth. No need getting into details, it'll just piss me off and others as well. But coming back to the world I'm falling into. And that drug world, will send me into an orbit into a completely different planet.

At work, I had already found out about an ex coworker, the one that thought he was better than most. Heard he had gotten caught doing drugs, say what, how could he. And I was on my way in following him, it just hasn't happened yet. Give it time, it's bound to happen.

When I found out about this ex coworker getting fired, I just thought, wow, I hope that doesn't happen to me.

Speaking of coworkers, for the most part, I was pretty much respected by most, and admired by a few. That was well to be expected. And I often thought, that maybe that guy, wasn't well liked, because of his attitude. Through my life, I was a kind of guy, that anyone could come up to, and ask me anything, and ask for advise, I've always been ready to help, if you asked me, respectfully. So maybe that was a plus for me in the long run. Because the way I was treated, in the short time I was at the county Sheriffs department.

Go ahead and ask me, why did I do the things I did? Do I have a simple answer for my ridiculous behavior, no I don't. Because it's not all that simple. My life was and had been very complicated. But it was nobody's fault but mine.

As I've said, my most intelligent choice I ever made for myself, in my entire life, was enlist into the Marines, and deployed to Vietnam, in the infantry, as I thought I wouldn't come back alive. But I did come back home, physically that is, but psychologically wounded. Can you combat veterans relate with me? I know you're out there, and maybe worse than I. Only you know, and maybe you don't want to talk about it. But I'm not talking about it, I'm writing about it. And there's a big difference. I'm not at some corner of a street, yelling like some fool, what I did, or where I've been. Because nobody cares. We'd like to think that our loved ones, love us. But I have a couple of blood relatives, called sisters, that don't give a damn about anyone, but themselves, to the point of manipulating our old ninety seven year old Dad, by talking him and our mother into signing their home over to her, and then later selling the house, and never giving any money to our Dad. But that part of my life, I will write later.

So here I'm still working at the county jail, and started doing drugs and, and hanging out with a hooker. But something has got to be wrong with this picture. Let me get this straight. A county Sheriffs correctional officer, doing drugs with a hooker. Do you all see the picture I see, because looking at it many years later, that's a very ugly picture of anything that supposed to make sense. Because that doesn't make any sense at all.

During the time of that horrible setting of my life, I couldn't wait to be with that woman, and be with her in bed, and do drugs with her. Now wasn't that a crying shame. Shameful for who, shameful for me or shameful for the county I worked for? For the both of us, the way I see it. All of you must be or got to be asking yourselves, what kind of a stupid idiot does that? No I can't understand it at all, about who I was at that horrible part of my life. But I'm not proud, and I'm not making this up, just to write about my life.

Well, that was the way I was living, living, now that's a badly stated word for me, because I surly wasn't living by no means. I was actually falling into a lost dark pit, and I didn't know when it would be before I would hit rock bottom. As I look at it today, that's exactly what happened to me. Lustfully practically living with a Puerto Rican prostitute, and doing drugs with her. There were many times I would call off from work, just to be with this woman, and believe me, I did that, more times than I would like to mention. As I wrote this, and reread it, it gave me flash backs of a man I once was. And who I am today. Two completely different people. And that guy died as far as I'm concerned.

I was getting so obsessed with wanting to be with this woman and do drugs with her. But when she wrote a letter to my house, something turned me off, why did she write such a letter. So I broke it off with her. I had to, or I would've ended up with her incarcerated much earlier than when I did. But when I stopped seeing her, what I should've done at the same time, was quit doing drugs as well. But I didn't want to. What was really happening in my mind, it was starting to get too expensive for me, doing drugs and being with this woman at the same time. I couldn't afford doing both of them anymore. All I did was prolong myself from going into jail, because that's not too far from my freedom.

And freedom was starting to leave me on a daily basis, but by no one's doing but my own. One day I called off sick from work, telling them, that I had passed out in my home. Now, that became a bad call, because the next thing I see, is two deputy police cars pull up in front of my house. With a sergeant, I recognized, with two deputies. Knocked on my door, asking me if everything was okay, what could I say, but tell them, I was getting better. But as I found out later, all of that was just part of their investigation, because they had started investigating on me. And as to why, I was calling off from work, too often, and my physical appearance was changing terribly. You would think, with all of this happening to me, I would seek help, help, that's another badly stated word. During this one time on duty, at my work at the county jail, this one deputy comes up to me, and asked if he could check my eyes, because he was doing a study on drug addicts. So he checked my eyes, and he looked very disturbed about what my eyes looked like. By this time, I guess you're thinking, would I dare do drugs at my job, at the county jail, no, I wouldn't have the nerve, or would I. Yeah, you're right, I did dare anyone to catch me doing drugs, in a county jail setting. But the most important thing was, I never got caught, because if I would have, they would have thrown me in jail, immediately, no questions asked. But I look at it, from my present day, looking back then, what a waste of time and money, for them to investigate on someone, and send me to an academy. That's a slap in the face to the county. And a slap in the face to me as well.

It might have been a slap in the face for both the county and myself, but I don't regret it not one bit.

You people probably think, now why would I say such things, that I don't regret what I did with my life, because if I would have done what I was supposed to do, my life wouldn't be where it is with my current wife, peacefully living in Las Vegas, purchasing a home. But if I would have continued that life of drugs, I would probably be dead, or in prison. So on a hairline of a decision I had to make, with God as my guide, and I didn't know what I was doing. I could only feel that I had to change my way of thinking and living, or I'm going down under, I'm gonna sink my ship. I just couldn't breathe, as I lost my momentum to live.

Remember I've started doing drugs at law enforcement at a detention center. Something is completely wrong in doing that, I know that, and I couldn't stop it. And only as God as my witness, I never got caught. Have you all noticed how far I've gone, off the far end?

I was bringing crack cocaine to my place of work, and actually smoking it while I worked at the county jail. Now, if I would have heard someone else doing that, I would have said, put him in jail or through him in prison I'm no different, that's exactly what they could've done to me. But since God has been with me from the beginning, things were quite different than most.

And I kept up with that life for too long, and something was about to change, and something just had to happen. Well, as I continued with that horrible life, didn't know it, but I was being followed, after every shift, every day of working at the county jail. And the investigation was about to Pop my bubble. Thinking I'm so smart, I can do what I want, and when I want to do it. But I should have known better, because that's not how reality works. Reality is, drugs was wrong in doing them anywhere, much less at jail environment, where I worked as an officer.

For those of us, that fall as deep as I have, or for those of you that fall deeper, and don't quit your addiction, your bound to die, or end up locked up in prison, for a long time. But the question is, will you pay attention, and realize what we're all doing with our lives. For the most of us, probably not. But I didn't want to be a statistic, then all I would be is a number, like many others.

So I continue on my road of no return, because I won't be returning to finish my retirement. To most people would say, oh my god, why not, and as everyone thinks, it's a career of a life time. Then I'll present to all of you, another retirement, and where I retired at. And how my Marine enlistment paid off for me in the long run.

The most powerful thing that we all lack, and we can't see it, like so many other things we can't see, is knowledge. Because no body knows our fate, and no one knows where we're headed, as much as the next person. Because I surely don't, do you? But one big thing I do know, is that God knows our fate and where we're headed, if we don't turn to him for help, we'll end up in a dark world, and at a point of no return. I thought I was doomed.

Well the time came, when I had called off from work just once too often, and I had lost too much weight. On this particular day, I was coming into work, as I got on to the elevator to report for work, there was this sergeant, going up like I was, as I say, "Good morning sarge" we made eye contact, and here I am, with my eyes, as big as tomatoes, he didn't just return my good morning, he just stopped and stared at me, with eyes that could kill, as he stared and said, "Good morning" and he didn't look at all very happy. Couldn't blame him at all. That same day, he called out for me, on the walkie talkie, to report to the sergeant's office.

If you could have only imagine how nervous I became, the instant the Sargent called me on the walkie talkie, thought to myself, this has got to be it, get fired and maybe even go to jail, but only if they caught me red handed. And as I arrived to the sergeant's office, sarge informs me that I won't be needing this walkie talkie where I'm going. And then he's telling me to follow those people as he pointed to a man and a woman, dressed up in business attire, with badges, as they tell me to follow them to the Internal Affairs office. To tell you, that if I was scared, would be an understatement word, I was nervous and petrified, as what was going to happen to me. That wasn't the size of it. They were very nice people,

Imagine this, I had the f**king nerve to take crack cocaine to my work environment, which, and what am I talking about, I work for a county sheriff by god, and here I was taking drugs to my county jail, where I actually work. They've should've caught me, because I would have deserved it, and they almost did. Especially at night, working in a pod, have all the inmates go into their cells, and then I would be alone, and do whatever I wanted to do. Pretty daring, and pretty stupid, and if I would have gotten caught, I would've deserved it all the way. And thrown in jail. Because now I'm looking at it, there was no reason for myself or anyone to be doing drugs, inside a government building, where they keep inmates. It was like an inmate running the jail. But only this inmate has a uniform on

This wife of mine, wasn't the greatest supporter in the world. In fact she didn't support me at all, she acted like she didn't know what was going on. In fact, the less she knew about it, the better off she was about it. Forgetting to say, I had two insupportable wives. Had to think for the both, in separate occasions. The first one, an alcoholic, the second one, an opportunist. You guys know what that is I hope. It's when a person sees an opportunity, and takes advantage of it, at the first opportunity. Then you have vulnerable people like myself and who else, you got it, my dear old Dad. In so many ways, I'm not any different than him. I could've chose to not marry neither one of these women. But when you're young and stupid, like I was, we make drastic mistakes, at least I did.

People say don't compare, well I'm going to compare anyway.

Which is worse, a man making bad choices, in picking the wrong women to mother his children, or a man losing a multimillion dollar business, by trusting his brother, by not writing up a contract, and trusting his most loving child, she taking his house, and selling it, and Dad never receiving a penny. Although I'm the one that suffered, in my life, but thank God for miracles, I've recovered and I've survived. Excuse

ROBERT GARCIA

me for saying, but I think Dad suffered the most. Wouldn't listen to his own son, at such a young age, which I was only sixteen, and tried to talk some sense in Dad, into writing up some kind of a contract, with an attorney, and having it notarized. But Dad thought I was crazy, will never forget that, he thinking that I was crazy. But I'm not the one that lost a multimillion business, so who's crazy. All I've ever tried to do for Dad, was help him. But I can only admit to my mistakes, no one else's. But in the long run, Dads mistakes made his whole family suffer. And who am I to talk, wait until I tell you about what happened to my whole family, when I finally went way down under, and hit rock bottom.

But that's another time of my life, that I'll have plenty of time to reveal my last deathly experience. Remember I died three times and lived once. That's the damn truth. What do they say, you live and learn. We're supposed to get better as we get older. But there are those that never learn, and I almost winded up in the statistical world.

Anyway back at the ranch, with my second wife, and all hell is breaking loose. Because she found out about my bad interview with Internal affairs, with the county I was working for. Apparently they called her and told her what was happening with me. And she didn't like it. Neither one of us knew it at the time, but this was just the beginning of the end of being together. The end was on its way, inevitable, and at the end of no turning back.

Although the county internal affairs officers gave me a fair chance to get back on my feet, in a sort of speaking, and although it looked like to them I was really going to do my damndest to do that, I was just putting up a show. Because I was not paying attention to what they were saying. I was already too far gone into my addiction. They tried convincing me to register into a drug recovery program, and that after a year of recovery, and coming back clean and sober, I would still have my correctional officer's job. Like nothing ever happened. I couldn't believe my ears what I was listening to. But like I said, I was too far gone into my cocaine world. As they spoke, the words went in one ear and came out the other. Internal officers telling me I would receive an early retirement check and to move along, as they wished me good luck. As they escorted me out of the detention center, it was sure embarrassing, to say the least. Being escorted was a weird experience, because while I was being escorted, I was still in uniform, and there was a dressed officer on each side of me, escorting me out of the jail, while all of my peers watched on. People I worked with, and some of them became close friends. But all they were doing at this very moment, was staring at me, like I was some kind of a criminal. Embarrassing? Oh yes it was. I had set myself up into a situation that I'll never get out of, so I thought at the time. Well at the time, I could hardly wait to get my hands on that retirement check. At that very moment, I was pathetic, although I had worked along side these people, I could care less what they were thinking of me. All I wanted was that little two bit check, cash it, and go buy drugs. Was I really embarrassed, I don't think so. All I did was act like I was. Because if I had been really embarrassed, I would have focused on getting my addiction clean off my head and out of my system. But that was my least of my thoughts. I just wanted to pick up that little thirteen thousand dollar check, cash it and be on my way. How cheap huh? But that's how drugs started to make me feel. I wasn't thinking at all those lines, in fact I wasn't thinking at all. My mind was looking forward in getting high. Wow, as I reminisce that time of my life, my visual of myself, makes me want to gag, and vomit, because I was pretty disgusting. Disgusting, at that moment in time of my life, disgusting was so far away in my mind, to feel reality. But reality is going to soak in soon enough, and grab me by the balls. Because I wasn't taking my life serious, and at forty five, that was pretty naive, and immature.

So on with the escort, these internal affairs officers, escorted me out of the jail, and the male sergeant, in his suit, informed me that I was to go home, and that he would follow me home, so he could collect the rest of my uniforms and my badge. My badge, I tell the man, I bought that badge, he didn't care, he wanted it, anyway. I had no choice, but to give him the badge. If I would have kept that badge, it would have been my only remembrance of the county I once worked for. I was at a time and a place, that should have never happened, but it did happen, because of my negligence. I had become a full blown rock cocaine addict. And I fell, and I didn't know how to get up. And felt no one wanted to help

ROBERT GARCIA

me. And like I've said but I didn't know it then, society hates alcoholics, drug addicts, bank robbers, baby rapers, and the list goes on. People just hates our kind of people.

And I started getting that hate from home, from the wife I was married to then. Although I didn't get fired, because I was given an ultimatum, and a confidential promise, that if I was to register myself into a drug recovery service, I would still have my employment waiting for me, with a certificate to prove I actually did and completed the recovery service I attended. And they gave me a time period of one year, which was fair enough.

So when I arrived at the apartment we were living in, with the internal affairs officer right on my back, he waited outside, so I wouldn't be more embarrassed. We had already lost the home we were once going to buy, under a lease with option to buy contract, due to the fact, I wasn't paying rent, because I was using the money for drugs. It's no genius thing to figure out. It all amounts to one big mistake I made with myself and those I loved dearly. Because once you're either an alcoholic or an addict on any drug, it involves those that love you. I hurt the whole family, when I did what I did, and I haven't been incarcerated as of yet, at this point in time of my life. But don't hold your breath, that time is coming after me. Because after all, to do illegal drugs, it's still a crime. No matter how we look at it. The way I look at, in my current life, thank God, drugs are still against the law. Can anyone imagine what this world be like if the world went wild, and drugs were not against the law. If you can read between the lines of my writings, you may have already figured me out. At part of my life, as a kid, we were almost killed in a truck crash, and then I almost shot three different men three different times, and then I worked as a jail deputy, and now at this point in time, I've become an addict. It's not hard to figure people like myself. Just complete idiots is what people like myself become, right after you start using. And that's what I had become. But at the time I started using rock cocaine, I was in complete denial. Telling myself and others, I was not an addict of any kind. And that's also the evil part of it.

Evil has always been around, and for me at the time, evil was there using me, and abusing me as well. So now what do I do, and where do

I go from here. Didn't have a clue, because now I didn't want to work. Say what, so now I want to be a lazy f**k. Well that wasn't going to fly too well with this woman I was married to. And I couldn't blame her what soever. Before she started working, and let me say at this point, it's because of my helping her getting the job, she probably still has. I don't know, because I don't know her anymore. But if it wouldn't have been for me, she and her children would have never become U.S, citizens. I thought I would throw that in, after all it's the truth. And then she started treating me like dirt. So now she's been treating my daughters like cinderellas, and me like dirt. How dare her. Gratitude was not in this woman's mind. After all I had done for her and her children.

Remembering a time she found out she was pregnant, and going to have my youngest daughter, she had asked me, why was it I was treating her like this. But I didn't have an answer for her. She just cried and cried. But through the years I had to look at how this wife had treated my daughters and what little gratitude she showed for me, after all I did for her and her children. I even lost respect for her. Because one morning, she's getting ready for work, and we got into a dispute of some kind, and she yelled at me and called me a stupid ass, and I threw back a yell, calling her a whore. And from that moment on, we drifted far more away from our marriage.

For me, the only thing I had left, was to look for employment of some kind.

And I found an ad, a truck driving ad, an ad, stating this trucking company were looking for people with some truck driving experience. Oh my, oh god. Thinking right away, hey that's for me. Just so I keep you on track, I still haven't been arrested yet, and I say, as of yet. Or they wouldn't have looked at me twice. So my record is still clean. I'm looking for a job, and I'm going to get it. And I did, they hired me right away, no problem. There were probably about twenty of us, that applied for ten positions that were open. A cross country driving, making deliveries from state to state. Thinking, this is going to be interesting, because now I get to stay away from that ungrateful woman. Here I go, being selfish again, where does that leave my daughters? All alone with this what I called wife. I came around once in a while to visit. And that went well for a little while. Because now I thought, I was through with drugs. And I was, and I was going places. First had to go through a driving school for a certain time. All along this school is going to cost me a few grand. And I never paid that. Fortunately for being a combat veteran. There were two education school loans, which I owed for a long time. And I never knew they could have them waived, but only when I would file a claim for compensation from the V.A., which would be much later in my life.

The good thing about this part of my life, is, I wasn't doing drugs, for a little while anyway. And only for a little while. Nothing was for sure until I really quit.

At this trucking school, they were very basic, all about the Diesel engine, and don't ever, ever put gasoline in a Diesel engine, or you will burn it up. Some guys laughed, but the instructor didn't think that was funny. By saying, "Some of you think that's funny, but it's no joke, because it has happened, and then you get fired". "Now laugh" no one made a sound. And that went well for a while, and then we were all going to be tested for what was taught. And some of us will pass and some will just have to move along to their next phase on what they're going to do with their lives. At that time, I really thought I was going to drive cross country for the rest of your life. Yeah right, such thoughts, I was only dreaming. Because I never took life very serious. And that's a damn shame.

When it came for my examination, I was very confident, in fact others called me Mr confidence. Imagine that, me, Mr confidence. I felt good about how people thought about me. Because most of my time, I had little confidence in myself. Not having much support by anyone, because everyone needs a little support from either a parent or a spouse. And I had neither, so I had to build my own self confidence and my own self discipline. And I once had self discipline, when I was in the Marines, because that's what they did to me, they trained me to have self discipline. But at this point in time, I had lost a lot of things, my self respect, credibility and my self discipline. But most of all, I had lost my loving connection with God. And when I lost my loving connection with God, I lost everything else. And that my friends, as God as my witness, that's my honest truth.

Being assigned to a dispatcher, and he dispatching us on our first delivery, but I had to first be assigned to extended training with another instructor, and bad luck started with a female instructor. And she thought she was God's gift to men. She thought she was really a sight for sore eyes. And she gave me a sore alright, but it wasn't my eyes. In fact she literally pissed me off. She showed absolutely no respect for me or herself. She was an absolute bitch. But she didn't think so.

This first day with this female trainer, must had been my worst part of my life, while preparing to drive long haul. In fact I actually quit the trucking company, as I had told her one day. And she acted so surprised, like she didn't do anything. She was constantly using the f**k word, in fact if I would have counted the times she used that word, it must had been, thousands of times. Thinking the whole time, what gives this woman the right to cuss me out to train me. I had never been in any work environment and have a trainer cuss me out. That was so low class on her part.

She was driving the truck one day, and she had to back up the trailer at some dock, so I thought I would get behind the trailer and guide her, to let her know how much room she had, until she reached the dock. And she's got the gull, to jump out of the truck, and started cussing me up and down. As I was trying to guide her, she jumps out of the truck, and started yelling at me "What the f**k are you doing back there, do you know I can accidentally slip the clutch, and I could smash you up against the trailer" as she yelled from the top of her lungs. All of this was, while she yelled at me, like I was some little boy, and while people were looking and listening, that was so humiliating, and I'll never forget that. So the first chance I got, I went to a pay phone and called my dispatcher, and I could hardly wait to tell him, that I was quitting this bullshit. As I told him, he interrupts me, saying, "What are saying, you're going to quit, what for" I telling him, what gives this woman the right to cuss me, in everything I try to help her out. While she thinks she can just cuss me out, using the f**k word, every time she yells at me. And I don't call that right. As I continued telling him, so I quit and I'm coming back to the office, to pick up my last check. But he wouldn't hear it, he was very forthcoming by telling me, you don't have to quit, I'll just assign you to another instructor, and I'll deal with her.

The next morning came around, and she was acting like nothing was wrong, as she asked me, "so how was your night" "did you sleep well" and I respond, "no I didn't, because I'm quitting" and she acting like she couldn't believe her ears. "What, But why" I tell her, just take me to the nearest greyhound bus station, if you want to. The dispatcher already knows I'm coming in. And again she used the f**k word as she says "oh f**k" just one last time with me, thinking, good riddance bitch. And I hopped off the truck, with my little bag of my only belongings, as I rode the bus to the trucking company office. Feeling so good about myself, I felt like I accomplished something. And I felt like I really did accomplish something, letting that woman figure out what she had done.

When my dispatcher told me he would deal with her later, maybe he did, and maybe he didn't, I could care less about whatever happened to that thing they called truck driving instructor. Why they would have an arrogant bitch teaching people how to drive trucks, is something I have never figured out. And so what, but now I'm home free. My dispatcher was assigning me to another instructor, and a better chance, and had talked me out of quitting the company.

When I arrived at the trucking office, another instructor was waiting for me. What a relief it was, because meeting with a normal human being made me feel, that there were good people in the world, sometimes. Unfortunately there is more evil in the world than there is good. And maybe I'm wrong, or maybe because I've been at the wrong places at the wrong times. I'll say it again and again, if we don't have a loving connection with God, then how do we expect our lives are going to be.

All my whole life has been, since arriving home from Vietnam, had been full of mistakes and disappointments. And have always wondered why, why me. But don't we all say those things, when our lives don't go the way we want it. I've seen it, and I've heard it, as well as you all have. It's no surprise. We get stuck on we, we, we, or how about, me, me, me, or another one, I, I, I. We get stuck on our selfish selves. With no consideration of God's love or not considering God's forgiveness. Somewhere along the line, I had to change my selfish ways, or nothing is going to change, and nothing good is going to happen. But I just couldn't figure it out. But little did I know, my time is coming, thank God for miracles. My life with our miraculous God will change my life, entirely, and forever.

Have any of you ever wonder, what happens to a brain, when it gets banged around inside a vehicle, for me it was a truck. Being in a truck crash. Well it gets scrambled like scrambled eggs. If you can just imagine, your in a vehicle, and you're literally being tossed around, and your head is getting banged around like a couple of eggs. And that is what happened to me.

And also, have any of you ever wonder, that it's a miracle for every baby that is born. There are good miracles born and bad miracles born everyday, unfortunately it's the truth. It's no surprise to see the world as to where it's going. And it's not a question, if the world is going to end, it's the question as to when. It will be an absolute disaster, and an unfortunate ending for those that didn't take the advantage, while we had the short time in the physical world, to choose, where we want to go for eternity. Doesn't it sound beautiful, you've accepted the lord and savior to be your God, and we follow his Ten Commandments, and we might go to heaven. It's our choice, only if we believe. And I didn't say anything about it being easy, because it's not. Just try being a good person just one day. One whole day. And see if you can do it. And I know there are those few that are good.

Just like the life I live now, was it easy for me to get to where I live. No way, and hell no. I'm in my seventies right now, and I've only been clean and sober for seventeen years, that my friends, to me, is not very long time ago, compared to how old I am. And although people say that if you ask for forgiveness from God, you will go to heaven. I know in my heart, it sounds great, but I'm sure having a rough time forgiving myself. I guess because it was very shameful, for the things I've done to my daughters and to my Dad. I abandoned my daughters and stole my Dad's private things and took them to a pawn shop, just to get money to go buy drugs. And I didn't do it just once, I did it numerous times. And he caught me all of the time. It's unfortunate that it takes people like myself too long of a time to realize what we're doing to our lives, and what we're doing to the people that love us. It was for the thrill of a evil amazing feeling, we feel from getting high on any drug. At least that's how it was for me.

When we're not looking for good things to do, and your mind is in a corrupt mode, and looking for something to do that will give you a thrill, guess what, that's pure evil. It's not that hard to figure out. If we never wake up out of ourselves, in the kind of dark world we're lost in, we're going to fall into the pit.

But in my first part of my life, when I was almost killed in that truck crash, I really do believe, that started my first spiral of falling into the pit. And things didn't get any better, when I went to Vietnam, and fought in the front lines against the enemy.

I never knew and I never understood what people meant, about calling others, that he or she is a bad seed. But now I do know what that means.

Although I'm not the best son that Dad could've had but I'm his only son, he's experienced some pretty harsh times with all of his children. At the end of my story, we will have become the best of friends, Dad and I.

During my trucking experience with this certain company, and after that ridiculous female instructor experience, as I said, my dispatcher had assigned me to, not a instructor, but just a co driver, which was quite a change. Because it was a normal person. What do I mean by normal. He was a good guy to get along with. Married, had children as I did. Pretty normal to me, right? But normal will be disappearing soon, because, although he seemed pretty normal, but he loved to be a womanizer, and he also did drugs. So if it ain't one thing it's another, so there was nothing normal about this co driver. Because after we had done some deliveries together, we would have a pause from delivering to any state, and what would we do, go look for drugs. And we almost got caught. Can you imagine what that would've been like to get caught being high on some drug, while driving a semi truck. I probably wouldn't be driving anything today. Because let me tell ya what I did while I was under a controlled substance. Both my co driver and I were driving radical, in and out small streets in downtown L.A., and why we weren't caught, is unbelievable, but it was I that was behind the wheel, not my co driver. It would've been me that would've been prosecuted. How crazy that day was for me, we were out of control. I almost took out a telephone pole, can you imagine that. I could've taken out a pedestrian, as crazy as I was driving, a tractor and fifty three foot trailer. This is just another part of my life that haunts me today, only when I think about it. So in and out of neighborhood streets I drove. Going to whore houses, with this company truck. Wow, as I think about that, it amazes me, and it scares me to think, what could've happened to us, but especially me. I was living on the edge of my life, about to fall into hell for the rest of my life.

Now you know why I keep saying, God has been there for me all of my life, taking very good care of me. And why, I don't have a clue. I keep thinking it was because of my mother and her prayers. Because she was always praying for us, but especially for her son.

But my driving continued with this company. We had another lay over, which both my co driver and I had a couple of days off, and I took the truck home, when I wasn't supposed to, but leave it to me, I've always done things against rules and regulations. My dispatcher had already told me not to be taking the company truck to my house, but I kept doing it anyway. And one day my dispatcher had enough, so knowing where the truck was, using satellite, he called a truck towing company to come to where my assigned truck was to have it taken away from me. I couldn't believe it, as I heard this loud roar coming down my mom and dads street, and I wondered, what the hell. I go up to the tow truck driver, and asked him, what's going on. He informed me, that he came to pick up the truck I was assigned to. I immediately got on the phone, calling my dispatcher, asking him, what's going on man. And he's upset with me, telling me, that he had already warned me about taking their truck to a neighborhood, and this was my last warning. Asking him, now what do I do, he informed me, to come to the trucking yard and he was going to assign me another truck, and to go pick up a trailer, and I'd be on my way, with a delivery.

Thinking all along, I've got to quit this company and look for another company to drive for.

And now I'm well on my way delivering all over the country, again, and still with my co driver, which means every load we deliver, we have to share the money. Which by the way, is the part I never liked. When other drivers, driving for otter companies, drive solo and get paid double the money. And that's what I wanted to do, because I've had an excellent driving record. Regardless what I was telling you about how radical I was driving, because I never got caught driving crazy. And thank God for that. So I thought I could be hired by a better company, and get paid more, doing the same thing. Coming back about driving crazy, which I've seen my share of crazy drivers, I think I have anyway. Let me tell you how crazy, long haul drivers can get. A few times when I would deliver loads, state to state, and when winter came around, snow everywhere, there would be those few guys that would drive anywhere in any weather. And you better not get in there way, because they will run you over, when there honking at you to get out of there way. There was this one crazy, I was looking for a place to stop, because it was snowing really bad, oh but not this guy, he comes right on my butt, honking to get my ass out of the way. And he wouldn't stop honking until I got out of his way. And when I did get out of his way, he goes barreling by, and flips me the bird. Thought to myself, well f**k you too. But get this, miles down the road, I see highway patrolmen all around, and had part of the road blocked off, and what did I see next, I see that truck and the driver that was honking at me, and now he's off the road, all wrecked and he's crawling out of his truck. Thought, that's what you get asshole. And what I also thought, I wonder how long I'll be driving, noticing maniacs driving crazy around the country.

Found out later, trucking companies will hire anyone, which means, they'll hire even ex convicts. If you think about it, that's pretty scary, to say the least. And it can even be dangerous.

I was once driving with this one co driver, that thought he was better than most. He must had been about twelve years older than me, but he was arrogant, and that he sure was. In fact he was very vulgar. And he couldn't back a trailer for shit, and I humiliated him once, by being able to back up a trailer better than he could. He was so pissed. All I was doing, I was trying to get the job done, and he was holding us up, by not being able to back up a trailer full of the merchandise the guys at the dock were waiting for. And I was doing, my job, and when I showed him how it was to back up a trailer, he blew it, by cussing up a storm. And when we finally got out of there, he drove, and as he making a wide turn, he took out part of a chain linked fence. He was out of line, and I'll never know to this day, how he ever got hired. So the next thing I'm doing, I'm putting in for a request to change my co driver for somebody different. Within a week my request was honored with a different co driver, and a much more respectable guy than who I had before. He didn't have his head up his ass, like the other guy. But most of the time, I spoke about wanting to apply for another company that I could drive solo, which meant I would get paid more money. And we both agreed. Eventually we would be going our separate ways. But on one of our deliveries, there was this one stop in Tennessee, when I was really hungry, so we stopped to get a bite to eat, and you should had seen the people staring at us, just because I was hispanic and my co driver was African American, it was an all white restaurant, but I was too busy being hungry, so I wasn't paying any attention. This co driver of mine, was scared shitless, and he was over six feet tall, and me, well you know by now, I've always been a little shit, but don't ever underestimate me, because then I'm not short anymore, because now I'm exactly your size.

So this co driver and I were well on our way of going our separate ways, in our own driving careers, because we each wanted to drive solo. But to tell you the truth, wasn't quite sure if I wanted to drive my life away, because I would have to devote my entire life on the road. And that was a big decision to make. Yeah, that would be a nice way of seeing the country, if you call that traveling, always on the run. Hardly any time at home with your family. And you wouldn't know what you might meet out there. But then again, I just screwed up a beautiful career with a county sheriff, as a correctional officer, so now what, what's out there, to really give me a prosperous future. I'm losing ground, by f**king up my life, when I had it right in the palm of my hand. I was lost, and started getting more confused. Why would I all of a sudden, start worrying about family, those were just excuses I was making. Non valid excuses.

So what were my credentials, almost getting killed in a truck crash, went to Vietnam, watched my comrades get killed, the enemy just missed me by a hair, and why I didn't get shot, it's a miracle. But my life has been filled with miracles.

Coming home, working whatever was out there. Desperate more like it. But I had to eat, and I didn't want to stay living with my mom and dad, after being twenty one. And now I'm pushing fifty. I was going backwards with my life. And didn't know it then, but I'll be well on my way back home to my parents home, and then they wouldn't know what the hell happened to me. But the damage had been done. Evil had engulfed me, and I was completely out of control. I just didn't know what to do, because my body was just craving rock cocaine.

This is why illegal drugs are called, controlled substance, or when anyone uses illegal drugs, the mind has been altered. It makes sense to me. Because that's exactly what happened to me.

So I'm still trucking at this point of my life, and wondering when will I get the chance to apply for another trucking company, that are hiring for solo drivers, and pay much more, and they have always been out there. I just had to make the time to apply soon. And eventually I will. But people like myself doesn't seem to get the message, when I was using rock cocaine. I thought I was smarter than the average person, that didn't use drugs, and I thinking I could outsmart the system. How stupid I was using that logic, because no one outsmarts anyone when we're on drugs. And all I did was become completely idiotic, because I wasn't making any sense with my behavior. This is what I thought I could get away with. The day came when I applied for a very good paying truck driving company. I was too sure of myself. The application was simple, because they hired me immediately. That wasn't the problem, the problem was, immediately hiring me, and for me to request, if I could start working on a Monday, after the weekend. Well is a deep subject. So much for nonsense. Because nonsense is how I was living, and because on how I was thinking. And during the weekend, I decided to smoke my idiotic crack cocaine, and thought I would party, and have a good time. When the weekend was over, and reporting to the trucking yard that hired me, arriving early, and they, under a mandatory policy, inform me, that I was to undergo a drug test. If you could only imagine what went through my mind, I wanted to scream bloody murder, because I knew I was gonna test dirty. The testing was simple as usual, just urinate in a cup and hand over the cup to the company doctor and he'll examine it for the results. Don't have to tell you what, but I will, my drug test came back positive.

And boy was the company doctor pissed, and he let me know what he thought of me. He didn't hold anything back. As the doctor was examining my urine, for drugs, I'm waiting in the company office lobby, and the front desk operator received a call, and the other end of the line was the doctor, wanting to talk to me. And he could hardly wait to cuss me out, and cuss me out he did. When I took the phone, and I saying hello, he responded by telling me, "Get the f**k off our yard, you're an insult to the company, you asshole", Although I'm only five foot eight, I felt like I shrunk to two foot two inches. I felt real small and real bad. How could I blame them.

Have any of you ever wonder, that a split second decision can make a big impact on your life or death. And another thing, how many people do you know, that have made bad decisions and still come out successful, and I'm only talking about myself. Because that's what happened to me. If I would have stayed with my correctional officer career, I wouldn't be where I am now. I don't know about you guys, but that sounds weird to me. But our lives will always have surprises and disappointments, if we want to call it weird, so be it. And life will always have its twists and it's turns through our journey to our destination. I've almost gotten killed, and some have been killed, at a very young age. It's no surprise by all means, proof tells it all, on how many people have made their mistakes, as I have, and still prosper. Oh, I'm not a millionaire at all, but I'm wealthier than most millionaires. God, is my heavenly father that has given me more than any money, that I have ever earned. That's my hearts truth. And I'm very happy and blessed with the life I live now, because I'm at peace. This is why I speak of the hairline split decisions we make during our life's journey to peace. And it sure has been a journey for me.

And during my time in the Vietnam war, was not a joke, but I did what every Marine is trained to do. But it's unfortunate not all Marines would challenge the enemy as I did. And that was only because I didn't want to come back home, alive that is. Because I really didn't think I was coming back alive. Maybe that sounds cold to you all, but that's war, and war is hell. Love and glory, so they say. And that was my second death, and now through this addictive life I'm going through, at this point of my life. I didn't know how not to stop punishing myself, I just didn't know how.

So back at the ranch, so my story goes, as I continued to fall within my own dark self, In my own chaotic world. Now, what was I going to do without a job. And guess what, this trucking company decided to call my wife, that I got fired before I started driving their truck across country. I could only imagine what this woman I called wife was thinking. Pissed for sure at me. Couldn't blame her whatsoever. First burning a great opportunity with the county, as a correctional officer, and now this, being fired from a great trucking company, before I actually began. And when I called her, she told me not to come home, because she already knew what had happened, and she tells me, don't come home, or I'll call the cops. Thinking, wow, what an ungrateful bitch. She had already called the cops on me once, and now she's threatening to call the cops again. After all I've done for her and her children, making her and her children legal U.S. citizens. Now, she doesn't want me near her, or she'll call the cops. Wow. I couldn't believe it. I made another mistake picking a woman, to become my second wife, and helping her and her kids, to become legal citizens, and this is what I received in return. That for me, was a test of love, failed. So I had to move on, and so I called the best people I had left. Mom and Dad. And they rescued me from being literally homeless.

Living in the streets, I was theoretically homeless, and if it wasn't for my parents, I probably would've died out in the streets, no doubt about it. And just the thought of that, was so shameful, so embarrassing, at my age. But true mothers and fathers will always love their children, no matter how old they are.

Of course I didn't dare tell my parents about what happened at the trucking company that was going to hire me, they would've been very broken hearted, especially Mom. You all know how moms are. At least I know mine, she was always sentimental. Was always crying about me. In fact my current wife reminds me of my mother. My most loving ladies I've ever had the pleasure to love, because they loved me.

I made up some story about, I didn't know why this trucking didn't hire me, and that this second wife, wasn't letting me come home, unless I had a job. They were outraged to hear that about how this woman was treating me. Dad telling me, what kind of a woman is that, she doesn't love you, but your mom and dad does, come over here, to who loves you son.

So now I'm on my way, in becoming my mother and father's worst nightmare. And they didn't know what was coming at them. Poor mom and dad. Just the thought of that time, makes me emotional. I wouldn't be alive today, if it wasn't for my loving mom and dad. Can you people see what I'm saying. Here I was pushing fifty years old, and my parents were in their late sixties, and if they wouldn't have been alive, who would have been there for me. Absolutely no one, that's who. But did I care about that, hell no. I was too far gone into my nightmare of crack cocaine, and that was a pity for all that loved me. And I had lost the whole concept of what love was to me, and for me. I had ridiculed my own parents, and I didn't care what I was doing. All I cared about was getting high. That was a shameful and ridiculous behavior on my part. Just the thought of who and what I was pisses me off, just writing this, and taking me back to that horrible time of my life.

There are many people that wouldn't have put up with the kind of attitude I gave my parents, and people are in prison, because not so loving parents would just leave my kind of son go to jail or prison, or to hell.

But not me, I was very fortunate in having two beautiful loving parents, and what did I do, I took advantage of them. In every way I could. I was no joke. I was abusive to the core. Mom and Dad blamed to who I was married to, instead of who I was.

I guess you can say, in the long run, of the kind of life I had, and with who I had married, and just making all the wrong choices. But before I got drug hooked, I worked and worked my ass off. Sometimes working two jobs. But no one seemed to care. But Mom and Dad didn't know about that, because I just didn't want to tell them. I didn't want them thinking bad about this second woman I had married. Ain't that something, just because I didn't want them thinking bad about this second wife of mine, because I had made a bad choice with my first wife, and by then she was already dead. I told you, she passed away from alcoholism, I'll say that was a bad choice, from the beginning with that one. And now making another bad choice with my second wife. I was always such a fool for any woman, during my time as a teenager, and then coming home from war, meeting a typical whore, and taking all the bullshit, from that one and her family. And then when I divorced my first wife, and then going out looking for a mother figure for my daughters, thinking at the time, what was wrong with that.

But it was wrong of me and then on the other hand, it wasn't wrong. Because I was stuck between a rock and a hard spot. After divorcing my alcoholic wife, I needed someone to look after my daughters, and I had brought that to Mom, and she didn't want to, at the beginning. So what was I to do, I had a job to do, and that was retail management, and I was very focused on that career I thought I was going to have. So I went looking for a woman, to look after my daughters and maybe marry. But definitely needed help. My daughters were suffering from their education, from moving around too often. And I just couldn't keep still, moving from one place to another. That would hurt any child, if you ask me. So who's asking, because no one really cares.

Since this woman actually kicked me out of the house, and now I'm moving in with my old folks. As I wrote this, thinking to myself, I was such a little boy at what age, I was forty eight years old, can you believe that. What an imbecile I had become. Imbecile I might have been, but I guess I was just tired and burned out with my life's happenings, because nothing was happening right, and for no one. But I wasn't paying attention what was happening to my daughters, they were going down on a downfall as I was. But I was only focusing what was happening to me. Self centered idiot Dad that I was.

When Dad told me to come home and him and my mom would help me out. That sounded so good, but that was the beginning of their vulnerability, because they were very vulnerable. But that's how parents are right? They didn't care how vulnerable they were, to them, it was love for their son. And love for their son, is what I took advantage of. Thinking from the beginning, this is going to be easy for me. And it was easy for a while, until Mom and Dad caught on to me. Aww, it had taken a little while, but sooner or later they found out who and what I was. Remembering my Dad telling me, you've always been able to find a job, so you just come home and look for a job around here. Thought to myself, yeah right. I wasn't going to go look for a job, like I said, I was too far gone, rock cocaine had me in control. Hell, from the first day I got settled in my old folks home, I started making plans on how I was going get my drugs. This is such a terrible true story, it makes me sick to my stomach, because this is a story about me, remember? But I just had to write it, guess you can say, it's more of a testimony, and so it's my whole life's long testimony. Well then, that's how it's gonna be.

The way I look at it today, there will never really be an excuse to become a coward, and just quit living a normal life, and turn to doing drugs, like I did. And I always thought, that I could never get hooked on anything. But I was wrong, as you will see. I had pushed everything out of my way, to support my addiction. Shit, I'm sure glad I never became a bank robber, or burglar, or even worse, a killer. Wow, I wouldn't be here, in the comfort of my own home writing you this. I'd be long gone and in prison a long time ago. I'll repeat it, if it wasn't for my lord's grace, blessing and love, I'd be long gone, and I would be dead, and would end up just another statistic, yea, just another number, like all of them others.

Speaking of numbers, living in this side of life, maybe we are just numbers, but when we leave this physical world, and God takes us with him, we won't be numbers, the way I believe it, our God has our name on his list., and it's not a very big list. And he will be coming back to

ROBERT GARCIA

judge the living and the dead, that's no lie people. Wake up, before it's too late. Don't stay asleep with the devil, because he wants us to snooze, and if you snooze, you lose.

I can't imagine how many people won't pay attention to that, because most people don't believe in God. And it's too bad, because they will be left behind and swallowed up by the evil one. I feel I just about got swallowed up, and consumed by pure evil. And it was our heavenly father that pulled me out of that awful world I was lost in. Talking about snooze and you lose. We only have just a short time in this life we have, to choose which way we want to go for eternity. And I know I wasted a good part of my life by playing with God's love, and believe me, he's not to be played with. And don't dare think that God is not watching, because you would be completely wrong. And we all start that way, I didn't think anyone was watching, and I paid dearly for thinking that way. Because just when you think no one is watching, guess who is. The almighty father is watching every move we all make. And I found out the hard way. But isn't life full of surprises, and there are more bad surprises than there are good ones, I don't know about you, but I don't like surprises. But if I'm gonna have any surprises, I would rather have God surprise me, by taking me with him. But I shouldn't be surprised, because I haven't been a good person through my life, I'm sorry to say. All I have is prayer, to beg my Heavenly Father to forgive me for what I have done. When I still had my Dad, he being ninety seven years old, and I was in my seventies, we prayed everyday, was a good thing to do, so we could both talk to God, and both my Dad and I could become friends, because we haven't been friendly to each other for a hell of a long time. It seems like a life time since we were in good terms. And as I wrote earlier, Dad and I, always had issues with one another. And I have felt bad about that, practically all of my life.

So as I start to fall apart, living with Mom and Dad, and lying and manipulating them, each and every day I was there, doing drugs. As I said earlier, I had seen other families, when I noticed other father and son love connections, and had grown to envy that, because I missed that closeness with Dad. And as I wrote this, came to think that, that was a big factor of me falling under the spell of addiction. As you see, there were many reasons why I fell apart. My life had become in shambles. Was it my fault, yes it was. Because I was a grown man, and I should have handled it a different way. And don't blame others for my crime. Because the law doesn't look at it that way at all.

The very first day I started lying to my parents, had become my first day of disobeying of one of God's Commandments. "HONOR THY FATHER AND THY MOTHER" and I didn't do that, because I think I was possessed, and evil had control of my actions. There shouldn't be any excuses, nor reasons for dishonoring our parents. But in the matter of speaking, unless of course, either one of our parents are incompetent. Like my first wife was completely incompetent, because she was lost behind alcoholism. And that was unfortunate for our daughters, and for me. And that might have had a big significance in my life, to make it an issue of my fallen apart from myself, and my daughters and reality. And am I my making up excuses, no, because those are facts of my life. And it started back when I was psychologically killed in the truck crash, and then went to the Vietnam war. I was still suffering from my earlier trauma, when I was sent to the front lines at war. Do I regret going to war, not at all. Because after all, I enlisted, I was not drafted like most were. And coming back from Vietnam, I was so disoriented, and fascinated with any American woman I could put my arms around. Now, is that normal or was that perverted?

I'm thinking it was normal to want to meet an American woman, even if my sister introduced me to a whore. Because the girl was pretty, so at the time, I thought it was okay. And also at the time, I didn't know she was a whore, and maybe I didn't care, because if she was a whore, that would be okay with me as long as she would be my whore. Unfortunately for me, that's not what happened, but what really happened, was the beginning of an upside down world for me, and our daughters. I'll never know, who suffered the most under a incompetent woman I married, or for her to become an incompetent mother for my daughters. Because we all three went through hell. Now I'm an old man, and my daughters are young ladies, and they are still suffering from that trauma, but they won't admit it, as to who's fault it was, either their mother or their father.

Although this story of mine, may sound traumatic and disastrous, but you won't hear anything about imaginary, because it's all true as I wrote it.

But back to the time I was abusing my old folks, according to them, I was a good boy. But the way I see it today, looking at myself from my present perspective, I was a rotten apple and a complete asshole. From the first day living with my parents, at age forty eight years old, was a continuous life of lies, and for a long time they believed me. Until Dad finally got sick and tired of my shit.

When Dad found out that my wife wasn't letting me come home, because I didn't have a job, he let me come home to their house to live with them. Looking back at that, that was Dad's mistake, and I became their worst nightmare. And as I lived with them, everyday, there was always something new I did to them. To this day, I can not come close to describing the kind of parents I had, and I still to this day, have a loving Dad, but when my mother was still alive, she was my mentor, she was my defender, she was my loving mother. No matter how much I broke her heart and no matter how much I made her cry, she never broke the love she had for me. As I wrote this, and if I keep reading this, it will always make me cry.

I was an addict, what can I say, but I wouldn't admit it, at the time, I was outside of the person I once was. The person I once was, I was an honest person, I had never been in jail, no record with the law. I was always clean. And one day and one hit of rock cocaine, changed my whole life, because I wanted more and more of the feeling, crack gave me. Can we relate, you recovered addicts as I am, we all know who we are. As long as we've recovered, that's all that really matters. I know I don't miss that horrible way, I once lived, as a crack cocaine addict. It's amazing to me how I've recovered, and the way I live today, it's a beautiful life with my current wife. She's the only person, that knows everything about me. From the beginning we met, I've been the mother of my youngest, told me I was not allowed to come home, and our daughter was only four years old. And now she's in her thirties.

To get high. To be high was my way of life, and that's pretty typical for an addict, isn't it? But just being an addict, is not all, it comes with making you a liar, a thief, a cheater, a burglerer, a bank robber, and it can also turn you into a murderer. There's absolutely nothing good about being an addict of any kind.

On top of always asking mom and dad for gas money, I would go out to different places of any shopping centers and ask people for gas money. Always scamming people for money. Terrible person that I was. And people would give me money, because there's always nice people around, that believe liars, and would give me money, and I would run off to my drug connection.

But before I forget about this one, I just gotta tell ya, when my folks had me living with them, they bought me a car, wow they were so loving to me, and all I did was abuse them continuously. Well, since I didn't know any drug connections in Los Angeles county, I would drive to San Bernardino, to go and buy drugs out there. Although every day I was an addict was stupid, but I can't even imagine what would've happened if I would gotten busted, simple right? I'd just go to jail in San Bernardino, anyone could figure that out. And on one trip out there, I had become very sleepy, and as I'm changing freeways, I almost flipped the car. But if I would have flipped the car, then my folks would have known where I ended up. Dead. Then I wouldn't be here, telling you of this, and my folks would've lost their son, the monster. Well that didn't happen, and thank God I didn't fall asleep, because I guess God had other plans for me. God's later plans for me, turned out to be true, because my life today, has given me, a tremendous gift from God, I can't begin to describe, simply because it's indescribable. I don't have enough words to tell you, what a beautiful life I have. But I had to do, what I did to end up where I am, if that makes any sense. It makes sense to me, and I don't know who can share with me or others, to compare, and come close, to say they had a similar life as mine.

It's far too bad, that I had to lose, to win. And to think and to know, I had to go to hell and back to live the life I'm living today.

Here I am with mom and dad, making their lives miserable, but before that, I had to lose a beautiful career with the county sheriff, as a correctional officer, but beyond that, I have lost a relationship with my baby daughter, as a result of my addiction. That will be the saddest part of my life, having lost, what we could have had. To this very day, both my youngest daughter and I, don't speak at all. But, it's unfortunate, like I said, I had to lose for me to win. And that's a big scar on both of our hearts, maybe she may not think so, but I do. During her mother and I, when I lost my county employment in law enforcement, she really didn't want anything to do with me anymore. She showed hate for my mother and my daughters, from my first marriage. So when I went out of control, she showed hate for me. Giving me a message, that she was materialistic. That told me, she didn't love me for who I was, but for what I was. A man making good money. And that's all she saw in me. And I ended up losing complete control of myself. I guess you can say, I had to lose to win, and there had to be some collateral damage. Sad but true. I hate myself for what I caused, but in the long run, I had to survive, or I would be dead today. Also sad but true. One more thing, I had left the home, since trying to be really nice to me, asking me how have I been, and bullshit, bullshit. And she pops a question, telling me, that they're all at a restaurant, and she thought, if I wouldn't mind to come and join her and them. As she did to me, I didn't hesitate to answer her, telling her, no I don't think so. And she responded with, a surprise in her voice. She says, no. I replied, no thank you, and hung up the phone. Anyway by that time, I had been arrested for the first time, so by then, how could she help me. She was out of time and too late. So I didn't pursue anything with that woman anymore, and thank God, for his blessings. Because in the long run, looking at it now, I'm sure glad I went to jail, than to go back to her. And that makes me laugh today, because who knows what would've happened in that life with that woman. When she refused to help me, she did me a big favor, or I wouldn't be where I am today.

Have you people ever heard, that God is never in a hurry but he's always on time. I heard that about twenty years ago, and I didn't really understand what that meant, back then, but I do now. If by chance, anyone will read my life's writings, and understand what I've been trying to say, you might understand the kind of life I lived. Which was very shallow. I was like a dog running around chasing his tail, and I could never catch it, Is that funny, maybe to most people, but I'm not trying to be funny, because my wrong decisions, almost took my life, three times. This is as serious as life or death, and I'm trying to relay a message to anyone that might have been in my shoes.

Well, from the time my second ex wife refused to help me, and then later wanting to see me, and I refused to see her, I was well on my way in becoming a full blown crack cocaine addict. And although this might sound funny and crazy to most of you, I feel I had made the right decision. Because in the long run, I was much better off going in and out of jail, than going back to that woman, I called wife. I didn't think about that back then, but I think about it now. And boy was that a hell of a way to live, because I was literally homeless. And when I first started doing drugs, it was in San Bernardino, and that's where I became a lost soul. I just couldn't believe what was happening to me. Before my addiction, I had convinced myself, I would never be a drug addict. What do they say, don't ever say never. And I was too confident, and I had developed an ego, just another man with a chip on his shoulder. Have any of you, ever known a man to work as a correctional officer, and then wind up behind the jail bars. How pathetic I had become. It was a damn shame, and I had insulted my character. And Insulting my character, is not even close to what I had done to my mother, my father, and most of all my daughters. Can't really care about that woman, anyway, she had become too snobbish for me.

Like I've tried to describe to you, in this whole life's writings of my whole life, and not one part of it has been fun whatsoever. I'm sure you can understand why. There aren't too many differences between Dad and I. I guess I could see something happening to Dad, before it would happen. Call it what you like, before it happened was probably a premonition. At sixteen years old that I was, I could see, in my mind, that Dad's brother would end up taking Dad's business away from him.

That's now a long time ago, and my daughter and I have never gained a father and daughter relationship. I never knew what collateral damage was, until this happened. But what I've also said, I had to lose so very much, to win where I am today.

So as I became familiar with Compton, California, which was a drug infested city. I couldn't go back and forth to San Bernardino, for too long, that just wasn't possible. At this point in my life, I still haven't gotten busted for drugs yet. You notice I said, I haven't gotten busted yet. Aww but I will, I'm bound to get busted, sooner or later.

All this time, I would tell my folks I was going to church, having a bible under my arm, giving them the impression I was really going to church. Such lies, using God as an excuse, to go get drugs. Driving all over different cities, scamming people for money, just to go to Compton, to buy crack. What a world of cheaters and liars I've entered, and I had become very good at lying I was so good, I even believed my lies. Have any of you ever been very good at lying, that you even believed your own lies? You know who you are, I know I'm no stranger living in the world of liars.

Dad was very good, and easy to lie to, I mean he believed his brother, when he cheated Dad out of his own business. Wow, that's another part of my life, I'll never forget. This family of mine, is full of corrupted people. Mom and dad were too good to end up with the three kids they had. Their oldest, me, their only son, becoming a drug addict, their first daughter, mentally unstable, and their youngest daughter, taking our parents out of their own home. Manipulating and lying to them, making them sign over their home to her and her husband, for her to sell it, and not giving any monies she promised our Dad, because by then, Mom had passed away. So, who and what am I? Well at the time, I wasn't any better than anyone. Just the thought of us, makes me want to vomit. I think that would make anyone sick to your stomach. And Dad still talks to that, what he calls daughter. In addition to my family being full of corruption, and evil. Dad had a uncle that actually shot and killed someone, a long time ago, and went to prison for killing a man.

So I continue on my rampage, as I continued abusing my poor folks, and yes I continued with my addiction, and It continues to break my heart, just the thought of it, and when I wrote this. But I'm trying not to let that bother me, because I have to keep writing my life's writings. I've given a short version of my life's testimony, face to face, with others similar to my kind, when I went to a recovery service.

I was once trying to save myself from going to jail, I really did. It was practically begging my wife to take me in, and help me out, like

I once helped her, by paying for her nursing school. Had explained to her, if she would help me finance a nursing school, and then we could reconcile, and possibly get back together. That turned out to be a joke. And Mom was witnessing my phone conversation with her. As this woman flat ass told me no. She didn't even hesitate or evaluate, she tells me, no, I've been living better without you. I was humiliated, I mean, I had petitioned her and her children, to become U.S. citizens, and now here I was asking her to help me, only to mock me and tell me no. And then get a load of this, it wasn't even a month later, she used her son-in-law, and calls me, and I immediate smelled shit, something was fishy about this phone call. Dad answered the phone, as he starred at me, and saying yes he's here. Telling me, that young man wants to talk to you. So I take the call.

And this kid, telling me how wonderful it was to talk to me, I thought right away, he's full of bullshit, knew right away, something was up. Telling me how nice it was to talk to me, and that now, she had become my ex wife, but he said, that she wanted to talk to me. Thinking, what the hell does she want, not even a month earlier, I had asked her to help me out, and now she wants to talk to me, what the hell for. She got on the phone, the most honest man I've never been.

I'm still revealing to you all, of the kind of monster I had become, under that controlling drug, crack cocaine, and taking advantage of my poor old folks. Aww and my sisters, oh my god, at first they also believed my manipulating lies, for a little while anyway. But not long, they were able to find me out. It wasn't hard.

And I was always asking for mom and dad for money, to put gas in the car, so I could go look for a job. And I was always coming home empty handed. Maybe because I was never looking for a job, because I didn't want to work. My thoughts were, if I would get a job, I'd have to work for at least two weeks before I got paid, and then I could go get high. right? That to me was too long to wait. I wanted the money now, not in two weeks.

In other words, my uncle with his wife, had the f**king nerve to sneakily, through the years, would put Dad's business, equipment, and accounts, under their names, without Dad ever knowing about it. But

ROBERT GARCIA

Dad had it coming, I tried warning him what his brother and his family could do, but Dad thought I was crazy, and that I didn't know what I was talking about. So when Dad finally found out what happened, he couldn't believe it, and I ended up telling him, "I told you so" Dad cried like a little baby. Walking beside him, telling him, Dad, I told you what was going to happen, but you wouldn't believe me.

So those kinds of happenings in my life, took a big toll on my life. Dad always taking my advices second, or just wouldn't listen to me at all. Like I was nothing to him. You don't think that would hurt any man, for his Dad not taking his own son seriously. That has always hurt me. But wouldn't that hurt anyone. I think so. Emotionally, Dad has hurt me, practically all of my life. That started way back when I was a little boy, I just I didn't realize it back then. Then that truck crash, which Dad, my uncle and I, were almost killed. And then years later going to Vietnam, getting into several gun fights with the north Vietnamese army. Then coming home, getting into a relationship with a woman, that becomes my first wife, becoming an alcoholic. And then after divorcing her, getting involved with an opportunist, from another country. And now in this part of my life, getting involved with drugs and losing my employment with a county sheriff, as a correctional officer. And finally getting caught with drugs, and going to jail. Wow, what an expedition, it seems like I've been to hell and back.

And the thought of me practically begging that second wife of mine, to save me from falling into the hands of the law. But she wouldn't have no part of it. I helped her and her children become legal U.S. citizens, that's all that mattered to her. She didn't give a damn about anyone else.

Do any of you see where I'm going with this? Maybe because I see it very clear, because it happened to me. Hello!!! But you know what, I can't believe I was the only person that drastic things happened. Looking at it in a different scenario. Maybe there were some other guy or anyone else, was involved in another vehicular crash, but he was killed, and I escaped death, he didn't. Or maybe someone else escaped death, but maybe he lost it mentally, and I continued on to a different and intensive intelligence, because I became better in school. That may be the only thing that I can write good about myself, other than

I enlisted in the Marine Corp. or another one scenario, when I looked for drugs in Compton, a man pulled out a gun, and took my money, but for someone else, he wasn't so fortunate, because he was shot for his money. What I'm describing is, how lucky and blessed I've had it, through my life. And others haven't had it as well as I have. And one other one of my scenarios. During the Vietnam war, there were over fifty eight thousand soldiers that died. And I faced death, face to face. Not one bullet had my name on it. God bless those heroes that didn't come home. And that goes for all wars, not just Vietnam. I'm not trying to make a long story short, because how can anyone make a life time, a short story, but it's real hard to put a lifetime into words on pieces of paper. And I've also have never written a book.

On one of my drug days, during the time living with my folks, went to a drug house, and sure enough, I got busted for my first time, at the age of fifty years old. I couldn't believe it, but I was surprised, that it didn't bother me. Here I started my in and out days of my jail adventure, and I didn't give a damn, and I didn't feel any shame. My first time of my jail experience, I was locked up for two days.

I acted like nothing was wrong, even when I did two days in jail. What the hell was wrong with me? Here I worked in a jail, and then I wind up in jail. Something had to be wrong with this picture. And nobody knew about it at the time. Not yet anyway. But my jail days have only just begun. Soon I'll paint you about my ugly self, how I was In-N-Out of jail for eight continuous years. Started to feel like a In-N-Out hamburger, being ground meat. Because believe me, for those of you that have never been in jail, you get humiliated, and the cops put you to shame. So my first two days of jail time, should have told me something, like for instance, stay out of jail. But I didn't get the message whatsoever, and didn't have a clue. Didn't know it back then, but drugs were making me do things that normally I wouldn't have done, if I wasn't on drugs. It's the same old story, that everyone has probably heard. But, it is what it is. But the facts are the facts, mentally, drug addiction and alcoholism is a disease of the mind. No matter how you look at it. It's been proven, that it is a disease. It's funny, but then again it's not funny at all, but a controlled substance can make you believe

ROBERT GARCIA

otherwise. What makes perfect common sense when your not high, does not make common sense when you are high. Does that make any sense? If I would have had any common sense at all, I should have done jail time, maybe a couple of times, when I was young, not when I started getting old. Because for me to start going to jail at fifty years old, didn't show any sense, it showed complete stupidity. Even the inmates when I was in jail with them, kind of wondered about me, like what's wrong with this guy. If I wasn't being ridiculed by the inmates, I was being ridiculed by the cops. But did I get the message at the time, no way, I was stuck on stupid, because I continued for eight f**king years, in and out of jail. Just writing this, when I wrote it, makes me feel stupid, was this me. But it was me. Can't believe how this looked to me, from the way I look at life, from my current perspective. But I was too far gone into my crack addiction, to know any better. My mind was way out of control, and the old saying was, you have to hit rock bottom. But when I was in complete denial, I didn't know what rock bottom meant. Because I was completely denying that I was an addict, much less knowing what the hell was hitting rock bottom meant.

Looking back at my life, at sixteen I wanted to cigarette smoke, because where I went to school, almost everybody smoked, so I thought I had to. Smoked a little pot, but never out of hand, just a little bit. I wouldn't let anything get in my way of my school studies. So that was a good thing right? School, when I was young, was a must for my future. But the Vietnam war got into my way of my life. You all might understand why I say, "I Died Three Times And Lived "Once". For my entire life, it's almost been like God resurrected my life each time I looked at death in the face. Does that sound funny to you all, maybe so, but that's how I feel. Because I just gotta tell ya, God has been right beside me all my life, not just when I faced death, he's been there, even when I made wrong choices and wrong decisions, or I wouldn't be alive or wouldn't be at peace as I am today. There's always been reasons why and what God does for all of us. And he's had his reasons for me, to lose everything, and to give me the life I live today, but I still don't understand why. And I've said, we're not supposed to understand God, his reasoning for what he does for all of us, is above and beyond our comprehension. So I don't dare to touch to try to understand God. All I know, that he loves us and I love him.

And that's all I need to understand. I mean what else is there? What I think, and only because I think so, there's a lot more to do, to see if God will take me with him to heaven, than just loving him.

Remembering one of many things, towards the end of our time in the physical world, Dad and I would pray everyday, which was a beautiful conversation with God, Dad and I. But what stuck to me the most, Dad would say, leave it to the Lord. He even said that, when there were things more drastic than leaving everything to the Lord. I guess because, yeah, God will always have the last word, no doubt about that. But aren't we supposed to do some things, to do our part? God gave us all a brain to use right? And I know, even if we use the brains, God gave us, we still don't know what is going to happen, because at the end, it is all up to God. I just think, that God gave us a brain to use, and to choose which way we decide we want to go, for eternity. And I've only just begun in thinking that way, because maybe of all the wrong choices and wrong turns I made with my life.

And now back to all my wrong choices and wrong turns in my life. Because when I did a two day stretch of jail time, thinking back how I thought then, those two days of interrupted freedom didn't seem to bother me. But I was released on O. R. Some may know what O. R. means, and maybe some of you don't know. Well just to clear the air what it actually means. O. R. (Own Recognizance) so when I was released on o.r., just as I was being released, I had to sign a ticket, like a promissory note, promising I would show up for court at a certain day and time. And guess what happened when I didn't show up in court. It doesn't take a genius to figure it out. Well, since I didn't show up in court, the judge issued a bench warrant for my arrest, the first chance a police officer catches me out in the streets. He'll be dragging me to jail, so now I have no choice but to show up to court, that is if I'm not caught with another stash of crack. Which was very likely I would, because that was my life, getting high, and I was always looking for another day of that shit. I was living a disastrous life, and I didn't want to stop.

ROBERT GARCIA

And sure enough, I got busted for a second time with a stash of crack, and with a warrant for my arrest. But only this time, I had to wait until the judge felt like seeing me, and for two weeks I had to wait to be called for court. My mental way was so weak, because jail time wasn't bothering me, when It should have. Looking at it today, two days didn't bother me, and now I have to do two weeks, and that didn't bother me either. Something, without saying, was completely wrong with my logic, maybe because I didn't have any logic. Nothing I was doing was logical. I thought I was weird, but I met with some strange guys, that had been in and out jail, way before I started. Asking them, what were they doing there, answering me, by an obvious answer. Doing the same crap I was doing. As I look at my past life, as a old man, what a waste, people do with their lives.

Immigration is full of people from all over the world, wanting to come to America, to live a better life. And then we have people that are born here, that throw their lives away, like I did. What a terrible shame. Regular Americans have it made, being born an American, and then we f**k our lives up. I don't think I'm the only one that sees this, for sure the immigrants see it very clear. This is why many legal immigrants come to America, and become doctors, lawyers, judges and so forth. I find those people, show more intelligence than many Americans. Maybe I say this, because I've been with the wrong people for too long.

As I continued on my yellow brick road of confusion, en route, with my head up my ass, walking backwards and headed the wrong way. Anyone ever know any body like that, I did, me. I can only think about myself, that screwed up my life, because I don't know anyone else that did. But, how do they say it, it's better late than never. Looking at that crazy self of me, I was one, out of a million. I think, for every million people that are born, there's one big dummy. And I had become one of them. But what happened to me next, after my escapade of course, was nothing else but a miracle, and that's an understatement, because my life has been full of miracles, I just didn't know it.

God had taken my soul, and pulled it from inside out to pulling it to right side in. Making me realize, what a dummy I was. How's that for humiliation. But I'm so blessed, and I'm so grateful, for God's love and forgiveness, but I'm not done with my journey until God says I am.

All of this past life of mine, trying to put it into words, has not been easy, but it has been the truth. I'm hoping and praying that for those who reads this life's writings of mine, will not only take it as a story, but as a message. Believing that the message, anyone can understand will be the most important. I'll put it to anyone of you, plain and simple, don't do alcohol and don't do drugs. Plain and simple? Yes it is, for most people it will be too plain and simple, because temptations will always be around. Curiosity and temptations walk hand in hand. How do you think I fell, because of evil temptations, and curiosity took me down to a dark world. I'm just one of a very few, that with the helping hand of God, he pulled me out of the air as I was falling into hell, before I actually died.

I'm sure for all of us, that have been incarcerated, putting it in a lighter word for jail, have seen some pretty sad individuals, and I started wondering, what's going to happen to me? Better question, what is happening to me? Have anyone notice, I haven't mentioned love, until God pulled me out of my hole. And that my friends, is love. And I had lost the whole comprehension of what I was doing and love.

Remembering this one other time I was in jail, receiving a letter from my oldest daughter. My poor loving daughters, but my oldest telling me in a few words, how she knew what I was doing, because of the change of my character, had gone from clean, loving, and a very hard worker, to my disappearances from family. Letting me know, I couldn't fool her. She just couldn't understand and believe why I did what I had done to our lives together. That letter from my daughter had been the only letter I had received from anyone. And it hit me hard, and I still remember it. She was probably crying when she wrote it. But that crack cocaine had a hold of me, and I just couldn't help it. I felt like I was in a pot of boiling water, and I was getting boiled alive. I had so many opportunities to quit what I was doing, but ignored them all. But the most emotional opportunity I ignored was the love I had from my mother, my father, and most of all, my daughters. It still makes me cry in my silent way, because I just couldn't get it, and I just couldn't grasp the love I once had for those that loved me, but I had broken their loving hearts.

Has anyone ever really know what love is when you lose it within ourselves. That's what happened to me, in case you haven't figured it out by now. I once loved my family, and I lost it, the very first day I took that first hit of rock cocaine. And I've regretted it ever since.

But still all this time, I'm still deaf and dumb, and I'm still brain dead. Absolutely had to be brain dead, because of that crack cocaine I was consuming. Very obvious right? Behind drug addiction, for others, it had become much worse. While in jail, I had met up with some characters, like burglarers, and bank robbers. Spoke with this one guy, asking him, what was he doing in jail. And tells me, for burglary's. It kind of got my attention, because I asked him, why man. He says, because I'm a drug addict, and I had gotten that far, to support my ugly habit. He advised me, to seek help or just quit completely. Thinking to myself at that time, now why would I take an advice from another addict, that's absolutely a no. And as I thought about it later, I'm sure thankful to God, it never entered my mind to break into other people's homes, I can't even imagine where I would be today, if I would have gone that far. Prison for sure, no doubt about that.

From the very first day I took that first hit of rock, what did I expect was going to happen? But isn't that the way most people think? But with me, I always thought I could do any drug, and never get addicted. Now we all know that became a big joke on me, and a time bomb exploded in my face. Because I was running out of time, sooner or later I was bound to fall with all the rest of the drug addicts. We all become just a statistical number, because there are too many people that give up on life. Needless to say, I had become one of them.

I like to think I've grown wiser since I've become old. But when I was young, like so many of us, we don't take advantage of the time as youngsters should, we just let time slip right through us, as if we're never going to get old. But I'm speaking for most people, and I've heard it soo too often, "Where has time gone" And I'm not the only one that thought I would ever get old. Everybody thinks the same when it comes to thinking, we're not ever going to get old. It's a dog gone shame so many of us waste our time away. Especially when people like myself waste our time and lives away on alcohol and drugs. But I never had a problem with alcohol, or cigarette smoking, and with any other drug, until I started smoking that crack cocaine. I'll never forget that part of my life, and how that took me down under.

And as long as I enjoyed smoking crack, I would continue to go to jail. That makes sense right? It's complete nonsense, because it's senseless to continuously abuse yourself, like I did, and like soo many others have and people will continue on that road, until they wake up as I did, one strange day. But there will always be people who will not pay attention to their life abusiveness. And what makes me so different. Well I've explained the spiritual awakening I went through, that too many people will not believe. And I didn't want to believe it either, but it was either believe it or I would die. It's not that hard to figure out. After all, if you believe in God, God is life. If you choose God, you might live a little longer. So guess what I did, I started going to church while incarcerated, and started listening to God within myself. I've been told, it's the spirit of God talking to your spirit. Believe it or not, it's true. When I did attend church while in jail, there were a couple of pastors, telling us, that they had been exactly the same jail bars, we were in, years before. We were told that we could continue living the life of addiction or just stop. And he told us, but we know it's not that easy.

As they would preach to us, I would have flash backs of how sick I would feel, when I wasn't high, and how good I felt when I was high. Is that sick? Yes, it's about as sick you can get, under an addiction under any drug of your choice.

But like too many of us, we would take those preachings in one ear and let it go out the other.

I keep thinking when I use to work for the county sheriff as a correctional officer, how I thought I was better than most and how I would never become an addict. That's all just an old worn out joke on me now.

Let me have your attention, those that were similar as the life I lived. Have any of you ever feel like a dog, chasing your tail, and can't seem to catch it. Well if you continue chasing that kind of life, you will never catch it. If you don't want to ask for help, and you don't want to help yourself, you'll be stuck in that up side down world, as I was. And if you never been in a dark world, why would you want to go there, unless you're weird, as I was, then that's another story completely. And that's why I'm writing mine. And all of you, can write your own life story.

Remember, "I DIED THREE TIMES AND LIVED ONCE"

Remember I mentioned losing my fatherly connection with my youngest daughter. The results have been very sad, because to my present day, I never receive any greetings, a call, nor a text. If I'm lucky, I might get a response, when I text her a birthday wish, or if I send her any money. Sad? Yes it is, but I don't think it's only sad for me, it's also sad for her. Because she had to grow up without a Dad. Is It my fault, I should say so. After all, I'm the one that chose to leave the house, when I became an addict. But then again I seem to recall, I asked her mother for help, before I became worse, but she refused my request. Does that still make it my fault? I look at it, it's not completely my fault. Her mother could have helped me out, but she decided against it.

Our lord knows everything, everywhere we go, and do, and of course he knows our hearts. When I was in my dark world, lost and confused, what little heart I did have, was ice cold. No one knows our destiny, but God, that should be, without saying. The day I decided to smoke crack, my heart and soul left me, and I lost all comprehension of what I was doing. You people that don't believe that, then you've never gone through the road I traveled. I lost every material thing I owned, cars, house, family, and myself, and I didn't care. Absolutely nuts? Of course I was nuts, what normal person does what I did? Well, I was not normal.

Remembering before I did what I did, my old Dad was proud of me, but when he noticed what I had become, he actually told me I was crazy. And looking back at that, what he called me, it was true, and I didn't feel like I had to respond. All I did was stare at him, like a disobedient dog, because I was too busy chasing my tail, actually I was too busy chasing crack cocaine, just to see how much more higher I could get. Ain't that some shit, I had become completely brain dead.

Thinking later, now why didn't that second wife of mine want to help me? Things are too obvious, don't you think. Looking at the person I was back then, I was a terrible person to live with, because I turned into a family thief. I would either steal my wife's jewelry or even pawn off the family t. v. And then when my parents took me in, all I did was continue where I left off, living with my second wife. Mom and dad didn't know it, but a monster was coming to live with them, their son. They thought their son was being abused by his second wife. When I was coming to live with my parents, they didn't know what I had become.

Even when I had been arrested for the second time, I made a collect call from the L.A. county jail, and right away my mother asked me, why are you in jail son. And of course I lied to her. Telling her, the police were confused with another person, that it wasn't me, they had me confused with someone else. Just remembering that person who I was, makes me sick. Just straight out lying to my own mother.

While incarcerated, remember this other time, I learned, never to double cross another inmate, you're going to give something to someone, when you get released, and then you don't follow through with your word. Because when I first arrived in this part of the jail, I had been given a very comfortable mattress, by a nice female deputy, and didn't have a clue why she did that. Anyway you should have seen all eyes on me and my mattress. It was probably about the middle of the night, but you should have heard the whispering, asking me, where did I get that mattress. Responding, hell, that deputy gave it to me, I don't know why. One inmate asking me, when I get released to give him that mattress, I didn't think much about it, all I said, ok, I'll do that. For those of you that have maybe never been in jail, your word is a must, when you promise something, you better hold yourself to that promise, because if you don't hold up to your word, your ass is on the line, or maybe even your life. But I had become very hungry, because when you're coming down off any drug, you become hungry, and I started asking for food, because some inmates receive money from family members, and they're able to buy regular food, and so this inmate tells me If he gave me some food, could I give him that mattress, and so we had an agreement. So this inmate gave me some food and I gave him the mattress. And boy you should have seen the looks I received from the inmate I told I was gonna give the mattress to. I got word, that he wanted to talk to me. As I went to talk to him, all of a sudden, I was surrounded, and this inmate tells me, you promised me that mattress, and you gave it to someone else. I tell him, well because he was gonna give me some food. He responded to me, no, no, man, while you're in jail, and you promise anything to anyone, your word is like gold, and if you cross anyone, you can get your ass kicked or you could get killed. But it didn't seem to phase me, because all I said was, come on you guys, get real, over a mattress, anyone of you would go to prison for killing someone for a mattress? They just looked at me, as I just walked away. But that was risky, because they could have beaten, me, and no one would have dared tell anyone. In my later times of my incarceration when I had gotten stuck again, I'd see inmates would corral the bunks, like a fence circled around a couple of inmates, so they wouldn't have any choice but to fight your opponent, by then it's either him or you, that comes out beaten, and needs to be hospitalized, or the one that is laughing.

Has anyone ever heard of the phrase, you can't bullshit a bullshitter, I'm sure many of you have. It's been around for a long time. Mostly because there's been bullshitting people, I believe ever since man was created. And I have a few of those in my family. And I was quite good at it myself.

But since I was lost, and God found me, I don't bullshit my life anymore, in fact I take my life very seriously. When I see or hear those kinds of people, all it does is remind me of who I was, a bullshitter. Oh, I was full of it, alright. We've all seen them, even if you're only half my age. We're surrounded with them, it's been a bullshitting world for too long. And when we're growing up, those types of people come at you like a stampede of bulls. And when we end up incarcerated, as I have, it's because we've been bullshitting ourselves, no one else. Not the law, and not our family. Like the only letter I received from my oldest daughter, telling me in so many words, she knew I was up to no good. That made me feel loved, and sad at the same time, because I didn't feel that from anyone else. But you would think I would change, right? I mentioned this before, if you don't seek help, and you don't want to help yourself, then you're gonna fall and fall, until you hit rock bottom. I say this, because, and you probably know by now, I'm falling and falling.

It took me ten years of my life, and eight years of in and out of jail time, because of my addiction. If you ask me, that's a hell of a long time for me to finally wake up out of my dark world.

But while I was lost, no body could convince me I was doing anything wrong, except God. That's right, it took our God's spirit to enter my heart, to awaken my spirit, to make me realize I had been blinded by evil. During my incarcerated years, I guess I had to find out who I really was. Does that sound weird and strange? Maybe for some, but as I flash back those years, I wasn't seeking help out side. I had to find it while locked up. It might have taken me a while, but at the end of my journey behind bars, something actually clicked. Something had to happen for me, I didn't know about anyone else, I had to concentrate on myself. And that was hard for me to do at first.

I kept seeing the same judge, she even got frustrated with me, seeing my same distorted face, month after month. This female judge could tell, I wasn't going anywhere, and she could see I was living blindfolded. We all just become numbers. Statistically speaking that is. Most of the people I had become, don't want to learn, because the evil feeling that drugs make you feel.

Have any of you ever see people that laugh, but always laughing about everything. To me, something is not right, a few screws loose. I've met people that were actually charismatic. And little did I know, they were tightly wound up. That's the difference between people being with screws loose or tightly wound. And I like to think I have been both. Some people have told me, I had a strong spirit, and someone told me I should have been a pastor. But that's been a long time ago now. I've become who I am today, because of God.

I've always had a problem understanding what D.O.C. meant. I mean I know what it stands for, Department Of Corrections. What I've seen through my life, many people end up in prison, but how many come out Corrected? I haven't heard of any, oh, maybe a few. But just a few. D.O.C. has always been misleading to me, thinking that people are actually going to come out of prison better than when they went to prison. But, since I was very young and now that I'm old, I haven't seen much of correctness, for the many I've heard, they went to prison. Especially in American prisons, I've always thought that our country's jail systems are too easy, and too weak. Look at all the other prisons around the world. They're torture chambers compared to ours. If you don't believe me or don't know, then not too many people pay attention.

I was so very close in ending in prison, I just woke up in the end. Good for me, God spiritually pulled me out of a living hell I was in. That's God's truth. When I I think of those days, of back then, it gives me the chills, where I could've ended up, instead of where I am today. It fascinates me just the thought of it. While giving mom and Dad a huge pain in the ass, all I did was continue on my rampage addiction, because evil is heartless. During my self medicating days, I continued acting like I was going to church everyday. I wouldn't go to church people, it was a lie to go out into the streets, and drive to many public places to ask strangers for money for gas, but I wouldn't use the money for gas, I would collect money for drugs. That makes sense right? Being an addict. Complete stupidity. Way out of control. Sometimes I'd collect recycling items, like bottles and aluminum cans to sell for drugs. Like I've said, when we're on a spiral downward falling out of a normal way of life, we become in-prisoned within our own selves, before the law catches up with us.

Way before the law throws us in jail. The big problem is, I/we become senseless behind a controlled substance. Today there are far more illegal drugs in the streets than back in my day. But what's the difference, illegal drugs are illegal drugs. Anything that makes your body feel good, when it comes to breaking the law, has got to be bad for you. I sure found out the hard way, but don't we all. Not all, because I started on my addiction to late in my life. In other words, I should've known better. Aww, I did a little bit of drugs, in my early teens, a little in Nam, and coming home from war, but nothing bad to make me addicted. But those days were long gone when I took my first hit of rock cocaine. That made me feel like flying, in a very evil way.

I felt like I was sicker than most, and became sick and tired of being sick and tired. As the old saying goes. So as I continued my road to hell, and as I kept running away from my true self, I had already been in jail twice, and it still didn't bother me. At age fifty. I tell ya, something had to be very wrong with me. How many people start going to jail at the age of fifty? In my day, not many.

Back in San Bernardino I had gotten a traffic ticket, for a traffic violation, not letting a pedestrian cross the street, right in front of a school. And never took care of that. But later on, it took me under, by having my drivers license suspended. And my mom and Dad never knew about that, as I drove Dad's car everywhere in L.A. county, to buy rock cocaine. I think by now, you know rock cocaine was my drug of choice. And it was one of my very bad choices in my life. It had become my worst choice of my life. But later I'll tell you how that worst choice of my life, would be the result of where I live today. I still find it amazing, how I wound up free from drugs and crime. I'm living a miracle. Most people don't live long after a miracle, but I'm living with my beautiful wife, and in God's arms.

But it will take me a few more years to get there. I still didn't know how to reach out for God's hands. A lot of people don't, or can't believe that God is always there. I didn't believe it, or I didn't want to, because the evil spirit will blind you every time. It did me. I might be an example for most of you. This is why, I say, I'm not just writing this as my life's writings, I'm also trying to reach out to those that have been confused as I was.

Anyone that ends up in jail, broke the law, it's no big secret. It happens to a lot of people, even for minor violations. It's not hard to figure it out, we break the law, we don't pay the fine, we go to jail. But people like myself don't make any sense. For me it was like a merry go round. Go buy drugs, get busted, go to jail, and then get released and go buy drugs, get busted and back in jail. I wasn't making any sense with my life.

If I wasn't using Dad's car to go buy drugs, I would go on a bike, that's right, I would go on a stupid bike, look for junk, cans, sell them, and then go buy drugs. What a low class of living. Can't believe I'm alive. Many things are for sure, but especially this one, I thank God I became an addict in America, because I wouldn't have survived anywhere else in the world. There's always help in America, only if you look for it.

Especially when you look for help in the United States Of America, because of one nation under God. There are very few fascinating things that happened to me, while under my addiction.

But this one, was bicycling. Because for approximately ten years, I was always on a bike. And get this, riding a bike on an average, twenty miles a day. A few times I'd ride the bike, since I'm a veteran, I would ride the bike to the V.A., which was about twenty miles, one way. And only one time, I rode it, to and from Los Angeles, to and from Norwalk. Crazy? Yeah, I sure was, now that I think about it. For sure I wasn't who I am today. Sometimes I'd go to the bus station, put the bike on the bus, pay a small fee, and go to my drug connection. What a world I was lost in. That should go without saying. This one time, I thought I was king shit, on a Mother's Day holiday, on my bike, had already gone on the bus to Compton, with my bike of course, and coming back home to Norwalk, and I just got off the bus, riding it to my parents house, and I was flirting with all women, I put my eyes on. Wishing all women, happy mother's day, as a Sheriffs deputy police car came right along side of me. As he yelled at me, "Get off the f**king bike" as I replied back at him, "Oh, just like that huh" he repeats, "I said get off the f**king bike", I guess I was, starting to piss him off, as I said, "Or what"? Then he tells me, "Or I'm gonna kick your ass" It had become quite a day, remembering that mother's day holiday. Because next thing I did, since I had in my possession, a small piece of rock cocaine in my pocket, and I threw it away from me. He asked me, "What was that" I tell him, nothing. He yells back, "You f**king liar", so he goes over to where I threw a little package, and picks it up, and then asks, "What's in here"? I came back, as a smart ass, "now what do you think" he tells me, you're really something. It was no doubt I was going to jail. But, as he was handcuffing me, I tell him, we can't just leave this bike laying here. He asked, so who's is it. That's my Dad's bike. I don't know if that was a good idea, because now we had to take the bike to the house, with the bike in a Sheriffs police cars trunk. In broad day light, with all neighbors out. And I had become a sight for sore eyes, on that particular

Mother's Day holiday. Wow!! Because, now the deputy driving down my neighborhood, made me feel so shameful. The deputy got off the police car, and goes walking to my parents door. As he knocked on the door, Dad came outside, and came walking with the cop, and pointed me out, as I laid on the police car back seat, and Dad looking at me, as he nodded his head at me, with so much shame of his only son. Oh yes, I didn't strike too many points with Mom and Dad that day, and it didn't stop there, because I'm still on my upside down rampaged world. That didn't stop that cop taking me to jail, but as he looked at me through the rear view mirror, he gets nosy with me. He chuckled a little, as he asked me, how old was I. Telling him I was, if I can remember, I think about fifty three years old. He continued to insult me, by telling me, you're getting a little old for that, don't you think. Not answering, I thought about it, and yes he was right. When would I stop that ridiculous life of mine. Good question, because evil is not prejudice, and addiction is not discriminating, it does not care, who you are, or how old you are. And one other thing, addictions of any kind, does not care if you're a veteran, a civilian, or what country you come from. Rich or poor. It'll take anyone down to hell, it'll even kill you, I know, because it almost killed me.

You know how I say almost killed me. I actually felt, when I would smoke crack, how many times I wanted it to kill me. Little did I know, but that Sheriffs deputy would not be the last police officer, that had told me, I was too old to be doing drugs. Because on my road to and from hell, there would be one last cop telling me, that I better quit before I die in the streets somewhere. I wish I would see that last one, I would've liked to thank him. Because there was something in the way he told me, that stuck in my head. Right in my own mom and dads house, because n the bathroom, smoking shit, and wanting it to kill me, can you believe that. Can't even imagine, how Mom, would've felt if she would've found her own son, dead in their bathroom. What a sight that would've been, because I would've died with my pants down. Just like celebrities have, that I've heard of. How the bad side of life, can get you so confused, and make you feel negative about yourself. All for the love of drugs. Ain't that something, those days of my addiction, how I loved drugs, but drugs hated me. Because it's all the devil's work. And I didn't know it, and if I did, rock cocaine, f**ked me up. For many people that have never done drugs, I'll plead with you, don't do it, you'll be sorry you did. Many people like myself have had great things going for us, until I/we destroyed a beautiful career, and I know I'm not alone. I thought I was, we're all just a bunch of statistical numbers. Another day of my life, while I was in my addiction, I always went to a certain rock house. And I always knew the same faces, but when I went up to the door of this same house, the people were different. They were just different, and the young man that answered the door, asked me, if I needed anything. Something inside of me, told me, something is not right. So I tell him, no I don't need anything. And just went on to another rock house, but as I go on to other rock houses, no one wants me around, and didn't have a clue as to why. A woman at a crack house, told me, to go home, because it was too hot with cruising police cars, and snooping around, wanting to bust any illegal drug sales. But I didn't want to take no for an answer, and just being stubborn and stupid, so I went back to my original, and regular crack house, I had originally went to. But my wrong decision to go back to the original crack house, will become detrimental for me. As I went back to the house I went to before, the same young man answered me, saying to me, "Well you're back, and so how can I help you" "did you want anything" I tell him, yes I do, and he let me in, as he continued asking me what did I want. I want some stuff. He asked me, how much. I tell him ten, as I lay a ten dollar bill in his hand, and at the same time, out of the blue, about three uniformed police officers came out of the bedrooms of the house. And I yelled out, "Why you motherf**kers, as they all laughed at me, like I was a kind of a clown. They arrested me, right there in the living room of the crack house, I was always buying crack. But this day, had become a day, where I was at the wrong place at the wrong time. But that's been my life, since I decided to go into the dark side of my life, because that's what rock cocaine made me feel, alone. And I didn't find out until much later, that the drug addiction life, will make you feel every way but good. It'll deceive you all the time, it did me. Why am I any different than other addicts, many of you may ask.

No, there isn't many differences, but it's made a great impact on my life, from the time I came home from Nam, and where I am today. That's the difference between many of you and I. Many veteran addicts, including but limited to, and regular citizen addicts, commit suicide. Don't think that didn't go through my mind. Of course it did. But I chickened out, thank God, I became a chicken, at the right time and at the right place. I can't imagine, what I would have missed, oh yes I can. I would have missed out of this life I'm living now. Because, in case you all don't realize, addicts or non-addicts, if you let the devil convince you in taking your life, you've become another kind of chicken. Those that have committed suicide, chickened out of facing up to Godly responsibilities. Like being a real man, to support your family, which I failed to do, under my addiction. That was a strange and weird feeling that went through my mind, when I thought about jumping off the Long Beach Freeway bridge in California. I just stood there with my bicycle beside me, looking at the bridge, and how to climb on the fence and just let go, and fall onto on coming traffic. But as I looked at it closer, and thought about it, started thinking, what if the jump didn't kill me, I would for sure end up in a wheelchair, there's no doubt about that. What a way to go, and what a waste of my life. I wouldn't be walking, I wouldn't be talking, and I probably would have needed a care giver.

And I know, God was with me all the way to convince me into not jumping off that bridge, like the devil wanted me to. God and I won that day.

I've always believed that there's a good side and a bad side to everyone. Like I used to watch cartoons, when I was a little kid, they would show an angel of a person on one shoulder and a devil of the same person on the other shoulder. And I believe that today. There's good and evil inside everyone. God only knows how evil I've been, but I don't know about anyone else, God does. Like he knows all of us. After that suicidal thought passed out of my mind, I started thinking, no one cares about no one, and if some people have a chance, they'll kill ya, for what we have, or just simply for jealousy. So I had to fight for my survival.

ROBERT GARCIA

There's a super being, and two people that really care and love us, and that's God, and our parents, most of the time.

It's too bad, for most of us, we don't open our hearts sooner than later to God. Can you imagine the world we would be living in, if there were more good people in the world.

There were so many things that happened to me, when I was in my lost world. It was down and dirty. More like filthy. I was a filthy drug addict.

Got beat up a couple of times, almost got shot about three times.

Four members of a gang, wanted to shoot me, because I owed them two hundred dollars, and one of them told me if they would have had their oozy, they would have shot me with it. Instead they beat the shit out of me, and left me with a swollen jaw. Was robbed of my seven dollars, when I was looking for some crack, and this guy wanted to shoot me for seven dollars. Imagine that. And this went on for ten f**king years. And it was going to end with my life, unless I wanted to change. But God interrupted my way of life, by throwing me in jail, constantly. Now that sounded funny to some guys. Because of course they didn't believe in God. But I figured it out, that God was throwing me in jail, instead of killing myself out in the streets. Once in a while someone would slap me around, threatened my life, some other times.

Guys would tell me, you don't know what you're talking about man, God is not throwing you in jail, it's you, you're throwing your own self in jail. I didn't agree with that. God was saving my life, and I didn't understand. Oh, it sometimes made me think, that maybe these guys were right, about throwing myself in jail, and not God. But that's how the devil would want you to think, that there is no God. I believed otherwise, that there's always been our all mighty God. Those people didn't go through things that I personally went through. Remember "DIED THREE TIMES LIVED ONCE" and from the incidents I've mentioned, while in and out of jail, and people threatening my life, something was about to happen, if I didn't end up in jail, and it was always on God's timing, I would just escape a deathly experience. Or perhaps get killed. We hear it all the time. People get killed everyday, for some stupid reason. And I came very close in becoming just another person that could've got killed. Especially women, if you're not working in the wee hours of night, or any time at night, you're looking for trouble. But I can understand prostitution, prostitutes are out in the streets, twenty four seven.

From the start of our lives, we really don't have any clues what the hell we're doing. We think we know what we're doing. Unless we're working, and going to school, and trying to go the right way to life. On the other hand, you have people like myself, a drug addict, looking for drugs, every day, and any time. Then we're on our own road of destruction, and anyone that gets in our way. Ain't that the truth.

When I first started my addiction, I didn't know it then, of course I didn't know it then. When you're an addict, we're stuck on stupid. Before I became that pain in the ass, for my loved ones, I used to say I would never become an addict. But I look at it this way today, if you have a weak soul, and we don't have a strong connection with God, you'll become wide open to evil. And that's basically what happened to me, no doubt. Although, I've had a dangerous life, from the truck crash, to being shot at in Vietnam, as I witnessed some of my comrades get killed. Then coming home disoriented from war, getting acquainted with the first woman that comes along, just because a sister introduced me to her, just to f**k. I divorced her, taking custody of my daughters, and having one hell of a time, but who is going to help me raise my daughters? Just two years after I divorced the mother of my daughters, she passes away, from alcoholism. Now who's going to help me raise my two daughters? Good question, because no one knew the answer. Mom was big, by telling me, to divorce my alcoholic wife. But when I needed help with my daughters, she didn't know if she could or not.

As I look at this today, I was psychologically being squashed, or how do they say it today, I was in between a rock and a hard spot. And I better find someone quick, because I still have to go to work, and my kids, still had to go to school. While Mom, and my so called sisters, talk about, if and how they're going to help me. So, I had to make my own decision, and it was just another wrong one again. I found an advertisement in some newspaper, how men could find a woman. Thinking, and wondered, how that could help my daughters and myself, but unfortunately, my journey explains for so many reasons, how and where I'm going to end up.

Sitting and thinking about my life as I wrote it, of course it makes me emotional, and who wouldn't be emotional. Now that I have true love and true feelings.

As I was horrendously going towards my last death, and I really thought I was going to die out there in the streets, probably somewhere between Compton and Norwalk. Just the thought of me out there in the streets, laying out there like a piece of crap. And the whole thing was, I didn't care.

So I still have to get arrested a few more times, before anything will come to light up my head, so I will wake up, and make sense to what's really going to happen to me. And I would be in another world, when I used to get high in my parents house, hiding in my bedroom, and then come out, and see my two old folks looking at me, and my poor oh mom crying. Dad just staring at me, as he tells me, "Your Mom is crying, you know why" Of course I responded, "why" as if I didn't know why. How stupid. "Your Mom is crying because we don't know what is going to happen to you" "Your fifty years old, and your living with us, something is wrong", and I didn't know what to say, so I would just walk away, and Dad would immediately tell me, "See how you treat us, you just walk away" What do you want me to do Dad? He would tell me, where are you going, I'd say, I don't know, just away from here. And off I would go again, just out of that house, I don't remember, maybe back to jail. As I've said, I didn't know what the hell I was doing. If you think I'm stupid, and just a dummy, try smoking crack, or methamphetamines, or even yet heroin. Today they have much more harsher illegal drugs. That will maybe kill ya quicker. Better yet, don't try any of that, because if it doesn't kill ya right away, it will kill ya later.

Life to me today, with my beautiful wife is much more glamorous and interesting, how nature can make me high in its own natural way.

People like myself, will always make our lives complicated, because we get bored, and boredom will either put you in prison forever or kill ya. And that's for real, that's no joke people.

I had to learn to grab life by the horns, and open my heart to God, or I wouldn't be writing this today. I can't even believe I'm writing this about myself, but my whole story is true.

Oh, some other times, I thought I was soo smart, I would actually sneak on my hands and knees to Dad's bedroom, in the middle of the night, and Dad is sound asleep, to sneak his car keys out of his pants pocket, can you believe this shit, just writing this, makes me sick, better believe it. Because I'm not that monster no more, but as I was writing, and remembered those things I used to do, and not have those evil thoughts, it makes me feel ashamed of myself. I'm glad I'm just writing this, and I hope people receive the message I'm trying to send, to tell you all, what drugs make you do, without love or feelings for your loved ones, especially your own mother and father. I hurt them so very much, it actually hurt me to write and re-read it. I would sneak out the front door, and push Dad's car out of the driveway, and continue pushing it, until I would start the car without any noise, and go down the road, to my drug connection. Pick up my rock cocaine and come back home, and lucky If I didn't get busted again. But surprise surprise, getting home, and walking in the house, with the lights on, and Mom and Dad looking at me as I walk in. Asking me, where did I go. And always having the nerve to lie to them, as I tell them, I went to go see a woman. I was just a lying bird dog, that's what I was. No, better yet, a lying piece of shit.

Now that I'm much older, I think about those rotten days of mine, I'll never have enough words to describe what I was. Because there aren't enough words to explain my dark world I was once in.

I ask again, why am I any different than most addicts? I'll tell you why, because I was going to kill myself if I didn't quit doing crack. Does that make me different. Not really. Because statistically speaking, there are so many addicts, that overdose. Well guess what, I wanted to do that. But it just wouldn't happen. Have people overdosed on crack cocaine? I would think they have.

Anyway back at that house where I got busted, when I handed a ten dollar bill to a undercover cop, and they snatched me, and hooked me up, as they took me to the back yard, and you should have seen the string of drug violators. There might have been about twenty or more people chained up, men and women. It looked funny, because it seemed like everyone knew each other, including the cops. A lot of people had smiles on their faces, even a undercover cop, said to me, hey buddy, how are you, didn't I just release you last week? That's getting really bad, when the police are starting to know you by your name. And off we went in two vans, chained. To me it looked like, we were chained up like dogs, going to the dog pound. Pretty much the same thing, don't you think. They arrested the whole shit and caboodle, meaning they took the drug sellers and anyone that came by wanting to buy drugs, and all the buyers had to do, was just make the move by putting the money in the hand of the undercover cop, and you're a goner. This was just another part of my life story. Nothing too exciting, because I really thought I was going to live that way for the rest of my life.

Have a question for you all. Have any of you, ever have the stupidity in trying to evade arrest. Well I think I did it twice. Every year, there are holiday sobriety check points, at different parts of populated areas to check for drunk drivers. And that's a good thing, as drunk driving has been responsible for many vehicular crash killings. So why not have sobriety check points.

My point being, on this particular holiday night, just a few days before Christmas, I just had to get off the freeway, onto a very busy highway, looking at what I'm coming up to, saying to myself, oh my god. Oh, how stupid of me. And I had to do something real quick. Like run, run quickly. So as I'm approaching the highway patrolman, and I noticed, he's all alone, and his motorcycle is about thirty to forty feet away from him. He instructed me to roll down the drivers window, and I tell him, sorry officer I can't roll it down, it's broken. And he seemed like a nice highway patrol man, as he says to me, that's no problem, just drive your car over there, across the street by my motorcycle, and I'll be with you in a few minutes. Then I started calculating the time it would take him to get to his bike, it would give me a very good chance to hit the road fast and hard, down the boulevard, and hitting the boulevard hard I did. As I took a glance at my rear view mirror, watching the cop that told me, he'd be with me in a few, jumping bloody murder, imagining him cussing me out. Oh yeah, he looked real pissed, but he never tried to hop onto his motorcycle. Without you, asking if I was scared, hell yes I was very scared. Because what if he would have called some other cops, because he might have taken my license plates. But he didn't, so I was home free. The only thing is, I wasn't home yet. I hid myself in a dark neighborhood for about twenty minutes, and then I still had the nerve to go pick up my crack cocaine. I couldn't let any cop pull me over, because I had a warrant for my arrest and a suspended license. I think if they would have caught me anyway, I don't think I would be driving today. I've never considered myself a crazy man, but I have done some crazy things, but I believe I'm not alone in that category either.

Am I? As I wrote this, I thought about all the times I had worked for the county, as a correctional officer. Now here I am, a street junky, running and evading arrest, just another drug addict. Have been beaten up, more times than I would like to mention. Remembering the times I would go with other coworkers, other correctional officers, and go harass inmates just for the hell of it. Now at this part of my life, I'm running on empty. But did I know what I was doing, absolutely not. When I say I was running on empty, I was running on a empty head. Ain't that the truth. Going round and round, in and out, and getting real dizzy with confusion. And the more drugs I did, the deeper the hole I was falling into.

Still on my road of confusion, and that's exactly how the devil wants you to feel, it's a hell of a feeling, I tell ya.

Remember writing you, my first evading of arrest, but I have wondered about that. How can I call it evading arrest, when the police officer never was able to identify who I was, but what I did was, when he instructed me to wait for him across a street and wait for him for a few minutes, and all I did was, drive off and I was never caught. So I don't believe that's evading arrest. Although if I would have obeyed the officer's request to wait for him across the street, and he found out I was driving on a suspended license and I had a warrant, and then I try to drive off and run from the officer, then I think I would be evading arrest. Now that would have been a whole new different story. The officer would have had a chance to identify who I was, and where I lived. And that never happened, and lucky for me, because that was a close call.

You would have thought, I would stop doing things like running away from the cops, right? Wrong, I'm too far gone into the dark world of drugs, and I wasn't quitting and stopping for no one. But I was wrong again, because the law was and will stop anyone breaking the law, and it shouldn't matter who we are.

Because I'm still on my own dark world of destruction, and when I was far too deep in a hole like I was, I wasn't listening to anyone or no one. For those of you that don't know, common sense is not making any sense. It's complete nonsense.

Let me open this other incident that happened, when I decided to run from the cops again. What, was I stupid or what? More like a complete idiot. Because I'm about to do it again. But this time I was on live television, but of course I didn't know it then.

Was a beautiful summer day, and once again I was at my regular crack house, but something came up. The man I always bought rock cocaine from, started asking me for a favor, and he convinced me into doing the favor by offering me more crack. So, what do you think, I'm not going to turn that offer down. At my level of being a rock cocaine addict, you'll almost do anything for more crack. I became used to living in a small world, because I felt bottled up, and that had become my whole life for ten f**king years.

My favorite crack house seller had a cousin at his house and his cousin didn't want to go home, driving without a license, made sense to me. So he asked if I could just follow behind her, as the other person who drove the car take her home. Sounded simple to me, but that won't last very long. Because as us two cars pulled out from the that crack house, just started heading down the road, and out of no where, this L.A. Sheriffs police car popped out right behind the car I started following.

Thinking and hoping that, that police car was just driving on, and not being suspicious. But lord and behold, I was completely wrong, when he was driving behind the car I was supposed to be following, and that police car right behind the car I was following, he gets into another lane, slows down and then gets right behind my car, and now started following me. Did I become paranoid, above and beyond, freaked out was how I was feeling. And what does that cop do next, he puts on his flashing red lights. This asshole is going to pull me over. At least that's what he thought. So we both stopped, as he gets out of his car, I pull up ahead a little bit, he goes back to his car, gets closer behind me, and he gets out of his car again, and I creep on forward, and he walks back to his car again, gets closer behind me once again. All this time we're by a freeway on-ramp, and I'm playing this cat and mouse game with this cop. And he didn't know it. By this time, as he started to get off his car, I let him start walking up to me, and what did I do, I slammed my car into drive, and hit the freeway on-ramp, and with my lights off. And I'm in and out traffic, on a busy evening, as usual, people coming from work. The usual bumper to bumper traffic you find in California. And I sure don't miss that California crowd anymore.

Anyway I'm in the fast lane, and then in the slow lane and then off the freeway, and probably about a mile away from the crack house, I always go to, and walking back to it, take off the baseball cap I was wearing. Dogs barking from everywhere, and then this great dane, as big as a pony, looking at me, thinking it was going to jump the small fence it was standing behind. Just growling at me. Oh my God, he scared the shit out of me. I wanted to run, but thought against it. He'd catch me, chew me up like a rag, shake me and spit me out. So I just creeped along, walking slowly, towards my crack pusher. Hoping I wouldn't forget where I parked the car, on my return. Because I would return with rock cocaine in my possession, and I could easily get busted with crack in my pocket and then figure out, it was me that ran from the deputy, when he was trying to pull me over, and then taking off onto a freeway on-ramp. I can't imagine what could've happened to me If I would have been caught anytime that evening of my life. But I have a very good idea, since I've been in and out of jail. I wouldn't be driving today, if I would have been caught running from a police officer, on foot or driving off onto a freeway on-ramp. It's not that hard to figure that out.

Oh, you should have seen the look on my crack connections face. He started going off, telling me, "What are you doing here man, you were on television, a police helicopter was after you, but they weren't able to see you, because you had your headlights off." I tell him, "Hell yeah I had my lights off, I just couldn't have them take me in". And yeah, if I would have gotten caught, who knows how long I would have spent in jail. But the bottom line was, I didn't get caught. But my connection tells me, you gotta get out of here. But I tell him, you have to give me some rock, because it was you that had me do you a favor, remember? He says "Oh, ok ok ok man, here" And he gives me a lot of rock, that was good, it turned out to be worth it, or was it. Not really, but I was able to survive another month, maybe.

Remembering when I was in San Bernardino, when I was still working for the county sheriff. I had owed two hundred dollars to another crack cocaine connection. Because this one had given me credit, because I was always buying two to three hundred dollars worth of rock cocaine, but when I lost my correctional officers job, I couldn't pay. But one night I'm out looking for that shit, and I stop at this house, and this girl, and she recognized me, and said hi really sweet, and as I was talking to her, she grabbed my ignition keys, and yells to the guys, who I owed the two hundred dollars to, and they came running out, and pulled me out of my car. And commenced to beating me up. It was easy, there were four of them, as they took turns. It reminded me, when I was beaten in the Marine Corp, also beaten by four guys.

Now here I was thirty one years later getting beat up in the streets as a drug addict, by drug pushers, in San Bernardino. I've always thought of assholes that think they're men and take advantage of anyone, and it only being just one, me. Well these assholes, beat me so bad, that my jaw swoll real big. And to top things even more, they stole my car. And when they beat the hell out of me, I had fallen out on the street, and one of them says to me, "You're lucky I don't have my oozy, I would have shot you" and as I'm laying on the street, I saw a police car roamed in and out of the neighborhood, and felt safe to tell these A-Holes, "You guys better watch it, there's a cop cruising around" and they took off with my car. Thought to myself, oh my god. Now what. I had to walk home, with a swollen jaw, with no car. But that was then. In San Bernardino county. And never got arrested in San Bernardino county or riverside county, sure glad that never happened. But once I'm in L.A. county, in and out of jail for eight years.

When I got home from a real bad beat up from four gangsters, with a swollen jaw with no car. And after that terrible experience, didn't know it then, but I'm not going to have a car for quite a while.

Have you all noticed, grown men, from the age of around twenty one to well into their fifties, riding around on bicycles. I bring this up, because I was there. Once in a while, Dad would let me drive his car, but like I said, once in a while. Don't know about you guys, but I think we all look pretty stupid, having our driving privileges taken away from us, for the dumb and stupid things we do. I tell ya, society does not like dangerous stupid people, so they have us locked up. Some idiots are locked up for keeps.

Whether I was in San Bernardino county, Riverside county, or L.A. county, I was facing danger every way you look at it. Anyone that lives the life I I lived, will live or have lived a miracle if by chance you live as long as I have. Because I speak and write, of the miraculous experiences, and incidents I've endured. And they've been quite traumatic. Just in case you haven't noticed, I've had P.T.S.D. before I was deployed to Nam, because of the truck crash we were in, when I was just a kid, at only seven years old.

So Mom and Dad taking me in, did it for the love for their son. That's of course right? Thank God I had loving parents, because if I wouldn't have had, I simply wouldn't be alive writing this. That's for sure. And if they would have kicked me out of their home, finding out what kind of a son they had living in their home, where would I be. Gone for sure.

As I continued on this upside down rampage life of mine, in and out of jail, and having to go see a probation officer constantly. I'm telling ya, I didn't have a life, and no one does, when you're on in a world of self destruction, as I had.

As I wake up everyday in my current life, have shared my past life and traumatic experiences with my current wife. Thank God, she's so understanding, because she can't believe that I was the man I once was, I guess because of my change of character.

As I continued on my numerous times I went in and out of jail, which had become way out of control. And it wasn't funny anymore, shit it never was.

When a man like myself go through our trials and tribulations, and obstacles we have to crawl under, jump over, and barely squeezing by, with our lives facing death right in our face. "DIED THREE TIMES LIVED ONCE" But what can I say, when you look for trouble, we're going to find it, in all the wrong places, we shouldn't be. And where was I, in all the wrong places at the wrong times, and I'm surprised I'm alive. That's become the story of my life, since I was a little boy, and looking for drugs as an old man, wow, what a journey. But I'm still not done, because I still haven't hit rock bottom. And for a long time I didn't know what that meant. It's too bad I had to find it out the hard way, and almost costing my life, throughout three quarters of my life. But believe it or not, I will finally wake up.

But right now in this part of my life, I'm still waking up, with a bunch of men around me, incarcerated, a glamorous word for jail. Or just being locked up. In the slammer. It's all the same, but I believe, I was locked up, long before I went to jail, because of my way of thinking. That pretty well goes for most, doesn't it people? Because again, I'm not alone, when I thought I was in a lonely world. Drugs will make you feel that way, lonely. As I speak to you, from the world I live now, I can tell you today, all drugs will make you feel lonely. And make you feel, you're the only one. Such bullshit, what evil has and will do, to all of us, when you do the things I've done.

It's in the Bible, it's the fifth commandment, "HONOR THY FATHER AND THY MOTHER" and I surely didn't do that, under my addiction, so shameful. And coming out of a family of five, with Mom and Dad and my two sisters. Witnessing all three of our parents's children, all three of us have disobeyed the fifth commandment. That's so sad for my Dad, since he's still the one still alive, when I wrote this, at ninety seven years old.

About a paragraph or two ago, I mentioned I will finally wake up. What I should have said, we better all wake up, before it's too late. And that's no joke people, just observe the way the world is going. Everyone is born and then we die, plain and simple. But it's not that simple. Not when we try to go the way our lord would want us to go. And if you call that simple, well bless your heart. But not simple for people like me. Try being a good person, and if you call that easy, like I said, bless your heart.

Look at this life I'm writing to you about, I was no where close, in thinking about God. But God has been right beside me all the time. This is why I've called it, as how I've experienced it, "DIED THREE TIMES LIVED ONCE" because I've lived through death three different times, and I'm now living a life, I've never thought I deserved. I'm writing to you, about my miraculous experiences.

But I'm still on my road to crazy. I'm surprised I'm alive and never had a nervous break down, and maybe I have, but didn't know it. Because a lot of things were happening to me, and I didn't know it, because I was truly very sick.

About the only thing good about being incarcerated at one of the times, they had made me a trusty, couldn't believe it, me a trusty. My own family couldn't even trust me. A deputy had put in charge of a cleaning crew to cleanup different cells, where new inmates would come in to be processed. People can be such pigs, but then again, who am I to say that.

I met some people, in and out of uniform, through my life time, that can be absolutely so damn mean. Why do I say that? You may wonder, well, remember I used to be a Sheriffs correctional officer in another jail, in another county in another time. That seems like so very long time ago now. Because it is a long time ago. It's just, that so many things happened to me, that I feel like I've lived numerous life times. Through and thick and thin, I've lived to write my life's writings. And I'll continue on in just a few. I like to reminisce a while, as I look back behind me. The person that destroyed my life, who I once was, has long been gone out of my life.

But I still had to fall a little more, before I knew how to stand and walk a straight line, and learn how to live a better life. And a better life I better focus on, or I'm doomed for sure.

Doomed for sure, I've never forgotten about that way of life. Doomed meaning dead.

As I continued on playing with death, by going back and forth to Compton, to buy drugs, from gangsters, it was so f**king dangerous, but I couldn't or wouldn't let that bother me. There were a couple of times there were guns drawn to rob me of whatever money I had to offer to buy drugs, and they would steal it from me, and I better keep my mouth shut, or they would have shot me. And you would think I would stop after that, no not stupid me, I just had to keep going, and maybe one day, get shot and killed. And that would be the end of me, and my problem. But as I've said, God has been right beside me all the time. I can only imagine how many people don't believe that. Just remember, there's no doubt we're going to die the first death, but I pray I don't die the second death, because if we die the second death, we're going to hell.

And I experienced three very close calls of deaths. The first one, not so scary, because I didn't know what happened, after a truck crash, but the second one very very scary, because I was at war, the Vietnam war, being shot at numerous times, but I was able to manage my fear, and that's only because of my Marine Corp training. Enlisting in the Marine Corp, every Marine is a trained killer. And my my, oh and my third close call to almost getting killed, or putting it much more clearer, wanting to commit suicide. I think that was my most scariest moment of my life, for my most biggest reason, because I didn't know what the hell I was doing, and I didn't care anymore about what was going to happen to me.

One night I rode my bike to a crack infested apartment complex, you don't have to guess where, you know it, in Compton, wanting to buy very little piece of rock, and all of a sudden, this guy pops out, with a gun, and tells me, to give him my money. I went ballistic, instant paranoid, but I still had to tell him what I thought. "You're going to shoot and kill me for seven dollars"? He kept telling me to shut up, as he just walked away from me. Thinking to myself, you crazy asshole, you're going to get yourself killed one day. I didn't know what I was doing people, going to a drug infested apartment, at night, would be like going to the front lines of the enemy. Because believe me, I've been there as well, in Vietnam.

I think every crack house in Compton, knew me.

Does anyone know the difference between being at war and being a drug addict? All you combat veterans should know. The answer, there is no difference. Because life out there, being at war or being a drug addict, is cheap. We all just became a statistical number.

I'll never forget, when I ran out of gas driving a old pick up truck, but I was always running out gas. I can imagine what I looked like, pushing a full size pick up truck, when I would run out of gas. And I always underestimated myself, like others would, pushing this truck. But this one particular time, ran completely out of gas, walked to a gas station, thank God it was close by, and then I started asking people for money to buy gas, and I approached this guy asked him for gas money, and I'll never know why he asked me, "You want money just for gas"? Of course I responded, "yes that's what I need money for" he immediately hit a temper button in me. And then he tells me, "you know I could give you much more money than just for gas." I tell him, "But I don't want any more money than just for gas" he looked bewildered, "are you sure" I tell him, yes I'm sure, so that was all he gave me, just enough money for gas. You see what I'm trying to say, here I was, no job, out of gas, a complete dirty stupid drug addict. Haven't taken a shower in weeks, just a pure stinky guy. And I refused this guy, that looked like he might have been well off, wearing a suit, driving a new Mercedes Benz, and I turned him down, for any money he claimed he could give me, he told me, just name the amount. Until this day, as I started remembering the parts of my life's writings, thinking to this day, why did I turn down that guy. Maybe it was the way he looked at me, he kind of reminded me of the devil.

My in and out of jail experiences, aren't nothing to brag about, let me tell ya. In fact anyone that winds up in jail, for anything, especially for drugs, should be ashamed of themselves. And do you think I was, no, not just no, hell no. During my addiction, I had become a shameful

ROBERT GARCIA

character. And maybe I couldn't blame the wife I was once married to, because of the things I was doing in our house. Like smoking crack in the bathroom. And at the time, my youngest daughter was only a toddler of two to four years old. My complaint about that second woman I was once married to, could have helped me, but she chose not to. And I thank she never accepted my request to help me, because who knows, where I would be. I wouldn't be where I am now, that's for sure.

Well as I continue to write you my sad and bad times, during my addiction years. It was embarrassing for my daughters and my mom and dad. But like I said, I was not embarrassed, and I didn't feel shame, as a matter of fact, I didn't feel a damn thing. When it came to normal. What I did feel, was E.S.P. I would hear and see things that weren't there. If you ask me now, I think that's pure bullshit. It was ridiculous.

I didn't want to listen to anyone, and I didn't want to listen to the law. And that's how most people end up in prison. Thank God, I didn't end up that far. Like I said, ninety five percent of the people that come out of prison, come out much worse than when they first went in. And that's always been a misleading term, D.O.C. (Department Of Corrections) to me. And after eight years of in and out of jail, I finally woke up from one hell of a evil world I was lost in. And I couldn't believe the way I was starting to think, that drugs would kill me one day. I don't know, something just clicked, or something just snapped, that I was going to have to change, or wind up homeless, like we've seen so many people out there. And we've also seen veteran homeless people as well. And if that would've happened to me, I would've disgraced myself.

But I've been disgracing, my Mom and Dad, and daughters, but most of all, myself, for a long time, the time in question, ten f**king years, It's no big secret, and it's no big surprise, by a long shot. Any intelligent person, can figure out dummies real easy. Speaking of dummies, I remember being with one of my brother in laws, at his work shop, and his work yard. I got off his car, and I started exploring the yard he worked at. I noticed his truck work yard, had nickel plates all over the yard, and I started picking them up, and putting them in his car. I happened to know a little bit about metals, so I already knew,

I could make money from those nickel plated plates. But I didn't get far, because my brother in law, asked me, "Hey dude, what are you doing?" I was caught red handed, and with shit in my mouth. Didn't know what to say to him. So I told him the truth. "I'm just picking up some metal plates" he responded, "Why are you doing that for"? Again I didn't know what to tell him, but the truth. "I just wanted to make some money" He was enraged, by saying, "I can't believe you're doing this, you're going to get me fired." All we did, was stare at each other. We're driving back home, to my mom's house, and we didn't say a word to each other. We were so quiet, so it was long drive home. But when we did get home, I'm trying to avoid him, and he followed me, and says to me, "What happened to you brother, you used to be so smart" You know that, I've never forgotten about that, and it hurt me, to hear that. And it's no wonder, no one could trust me, as far as you could throw me. So they say. Nothing was ever brought up again, about that incident, basically stealing metal plates from my brother in laws working yard. It was embarrassing for him, and shameful for me. But did I feel shameful? Hell no, you see, during my enraged addiction, I had lost everything. They say, when we lose our careers, our vehicles, our house, and family, and finally lose ourselves, the saying fails to acknowledge, about what else we lose. At least for me, when I lost all of the above, I lost all of my emotions, true feelings of my own self, my self discipline, and I also lost my self motivation, and dignity. At this point, what else did I have to lose? You tell me, because I can't think of anything else, because I literally lost it all. And unless anyone reading this, has been through a road of catastrophes, as I have, then no one can tell me, they know anything about me. I don't have any words to explain to anyone, why I did what I did. Oh, I've tried to explain it, but still, no one understands. Only God understands what, and why I did what I did. Because even to me, it just doesn't make any sense. I felt when I lost everything, I mean, everything, everything, anyone can possibly lose, I would never recover, but I did. That's right, I recovered. Most others, don't recover, maybe because they didn't want to, or didn't know how, or failed to ask for help. Because there is help out there. No, I didn't know it then, but I know it now. And I'm not talking about asking another person

ROBERT GARCIA

for help, I'm talking about asking God for help, as I did. Do you have enough courage to ask God for help. It was hard for me to ask him for help. But when I was falling down deep into my turbulence, felt I was hitting every obstacle on my down that dark scary hole. I didn't think I deserved God, much less ask him for help. Often times I would ask myself, would God forgive me, after betraying my mother and father. And would answer my own self, by thinking negative, no, I'm not good enough to ask God for any help. And I go back out and do something else again, and back to jail I'd end up. I'll tell ya again, I was on a merry go round, seeing the same bad things over and over, over again. And didn't know where or when to stop. Mostly because the body didn't want to.

To scare anyone, has never been my intention, however, being friendly has always been my focus, and with that, comes respect. Not saying because I'm bragging, because I've been told, that I have a pleasant to be around my type of person. At least that's how I used to be, a hell of a long time ago. But I've come back again. And I'm not a scary looking person. Just old.

But I'm still on my merry go round, in and out of jail days of my life.

There's always been a certainty in life, that tomorrow is not promised to no one. Do we agree with me, with that fact? Because it is a fact. Life isn't even promised even from the day we're born, can you believe that? Because that's another fact. We hear sometimes, babies being born still born. Born dead is the term. I've heard of a couple young kids, playing football, and all of a sudden, have a heart attack, and they're gone. Just like that.

So when people like myself gamble our lives away, by risking more than just natural mishaps, like vehicle crashes, and continue to go even against our lord, then nothing is for sure, for our well being. I can ask If anyone agrees, but I already know, most of you won't agree with me. And I wouldn't blame you, mostly because most of you are still in your infancy part of life. I'm not saying, you're an infant, I'm just saying, many of you are at a stage of not able to believe something or someone you can't see. For me, it hasn't been very long ago, but I've become more faithful, more hopeful, and more loving, with life. This is why, I praise God, and thank him everyday for my current life he's given me, as when I wrote this.

We can't see God, but he's always there. We can't see Faith, Hope, and Love, but their always there. And God gave me his love, when I finally gave myself to him.

The three lives I once lived, left me with, I'll say it this way, left me with nothing. Oh, as you can see, I was very much alive, when I wrote this. I'm not talking about physical death, I'm talking about psychologically and mentally killed. That's what I'm talking about. Is there anyone out there, know what I'm talking about? Because maybe there's a lot of people that don't know what I'm talking about. And I'll understand that. And being psychologically killed, each time, it gave me Post Traumatic Stress Disorder. Didn't ever know what the hell was P.T.S.D., until I returned home from Vietnam. Psychiatrists make up these diagnoses, the next thing we know, it's been around forever. Well I'm sure glad they've come up with something. Because then where would we be. I can't imagine how many World War Two veterans came home with just that, P.T.S.D., and doctors never knew, what it was.

As I've said, I had to change, and change I better, before it's too late. Because the law is going to catch up with me.

By this time, I've tried seeking help from the V.A. Not strong enough, but I'm trying.

It was one day, out of the blue, rode my bike, from Norwalk to the Long Beach V.A. In case you don't know how far that is. It's approximately twenty miles. To me at the time, that wasn't far for me to ride a bike. But to seek complete help from the V.A., was still too far for me to try as of yet. My heart and my mind wasn't into it yet. They had this very young girl at the receptionist desk, and she wanted to enroll me at the V.A., and to stay and work on my recovery. And I didn't want to. When she said I had to stay there, I told her, no I'm not gonna do that right now.

Looking back at that, I guess I just wasn't ready. When that receptionist told me, I could stay there at the V.A., and start recovering from my addiction, that didn't sound good to me, because I still wanted to go get high. You recovered addicts out there, you know who you are, when you feel that we're not ready to start recovery, we don't do it yet, the addiction still had me by the balls. So what did I go do, went out on my upside down world. And I probably went back to jail, by this time, it became a regular thing for me, in and out of jail, for eight years. They had already offered me out patient programs, and they weren't working for me at all. Constantly on probation, those probation officers constantly urine testing me for drugs, and I testing positive for crack cocaine, constantly. Just another statistic going no where, but down the drain, like many have. Can only imagine how many people have died from what I was doing to myself.

I really believe I was a disaster looking for a place to happen, to die that is. Just thinking of that life I barely lived, I could've died from a suicide, someone could've killed me, in or out of jail. The angel of death was always right beside me, no doubt about it, but God has always been right beside me as well. The angel of death, on one side of me, and God on the other side. With God's blessings, with his hands blocking the angel of death to kill me, when I was in that truck crash, when I was a little boy. And my God was beside me, when I was getting shot at in Vietnam, and he still protected me from the time I wanted to jump off a freeway bridge. So you tell me what have I been through.

I could've ended in prison, or when I was in and out of jail, and blame my Dad, or blame someone else other than myself. It was no one's fault but my own. I could've handled it much different and much better, than how I did it. But I'll repeat it again, if I would have gone down the straight road, I wouldn't be where I am today. Don't know about you, but I find that kind of weird and strange. Don't know anyone that has gone down a crooked road, and still end up successful. No I'm not a rich man by no means, but I'm living a beautiful peaceful life, which I would have never would have dreamed of.

My crooked way of living is getting closer to an end, which I didn't think would ever happen.

One of the times I was in jail, I remember that I was put on a release listing, just after I faced the judge. But with this certain deputy sheriff, he was too busy chaining everyone that he thought, had to go back to downtown twin towers of L.A. county jail. And I was trying to get his attention, that I was on a release listing. But he wouldn't hear me out, he yelled at me, "Get in line and shut up", but I insisted that I was right. And I tell him, "but deputy I'm telling ya, I'm supposed to be released today" and he's being an asshole, "I'm telling ya get your ass in line before I wrap this chain around your neck" now I'm looking at another female deputy, and she stares back at me, and came up to me, asking me for my name, and I gave my name, and she looked it up in the computer, and finds out I was right. She came out of the computer room, finding out I was right, and tells that asshole deputy to release me. And he did, with arrogance. He was such an asshole. And I was released, and I was so grateful and happy with that female deputy, I even told her how grateful I was. "Thank you so much ma'am" And all she did, was say, ok good by. What did I expect? That's just one of my many times and many experiences of being incarcerated. I think the most I've ever been locked up in one time, was seventy days, and one other time, was sixty days. And I don't know about you guys, but that's a hell of a long time. And I've never been able to understand how these sentenced lifers can take that. I would rather be sentenced to death, instead of being in prison for ever.

But if I didn't watch it, I could be looking at prison anyway you look at it, If I don't stop doing drugs. But stopping doing drugs was not my plan, because I had no plans on stopping my crack addiction any time soon. But the fork at the road, with the light at the end of the tunnel will become my most difficult and most smartest direction in my life. Just because I was getting real tired of going in and out of jail. But I'm still in my infancy of trying to be good. But I'm trying right? At least it's a start in the right direction for guys like me. Because so many guys like me, don't ever take advantage of a right choice we have to make, or we'll be lost forever. And I was at a hairline of falling into a spaghetti bowl of disastrous catastrophes, for a lifetime, like many have.

When the day came for me to make the biggest decision of my life, like I said, it wasn't easy. But nothing has ever been easy for me, when I thought it was, when we're trying to be good. It's easy to be a bad person, or a real bad man. For so many others, it's easy to just quit. And you know it, and I know it, I did quit, and I have a daughter that

ROBERT GARCIA

doesn't talk to me anymore, because I did quit, I quit being a man and I quit being a father for all of my daughters. Today, I like to think I went through a pause in life, during that part of my life. But my youngest daughter won't agree with me, and why should she, she's the one that grew up without a father. Because her mother wouldn't let me stay at home anymore, because I had become a crack cocaine addict. Does anyone get my drift, on where I'm going with this scenario? Well it's never been a good one, because I look at it every now and then, and it hurts me to look at it. Because my baby daughter, will always be my daughter, no matter what. And before anyone starts thinking bad things about me, don't start thinking I haven't tried to making it up to her, because God only knows how hard I've tried. But I can't be saying I'm sorry, over and over and over, for the rest of my life, after all, I have a life now, and I've moved on in life. But this youngest daughter of mine, the way I see it, she will always have resentments towards her father. To her, I'll always be the villain, the drug addict father, that left the house. But that's okay, I've had to move on with my life, or I would be living it sourly.

Remembering this one time, after I got released from another time I was in jail. There were a few of us inmates that were released after our time of our release date. And a few guys put a lawsuit together, and were able to receive a few thousand dollars, and one day I received a check for a little over two hundred dollars. Blew my mind, but I was lucky to get fifty dollars out of it. Mom reminded me, I've been living there free. So she took the rest, it was enough for me to go get some piece of the rock.

By this time, I've already been in and out of jail, too many times, and this particular judge is about to throw the book at me. She had been giving me programs after programs. And I guess she didn't understand that, those out patient programs were not working for me. I can only imagine how much money it was costing the county, for my stupid ass. To this very day, all of us problem makers have to be grateful, for the people that want to cure us.

The very last time I was in jail, I finally had to make a very big choice for my life, and thank God, it became the best choice, that I have ever made, or I would have been in prison. This was the time I told you about, being in jail seventy days, and this had to be the one, when I received two hundred dollars.

I remember this deputy, while in my last visit in jail, he noticed I had stayed more than my time, so he asked me, "You still here?" At the time, I didn't know what he was talking about. Until I received that two hundred dollar check.

And the day finally arrived for my release, oh my God, but something about this release, told me, that I must never go back. And I never have, thank you God. Because little did I know, this release out of jail, would prove to me, to be my utmost of myself being, and regain my self discipline and self respect, and trustworthiness. And also this release would be, not just release from jail, but it would be my release from the evil within me, that had controlled me for far too long, and had been trying to condemn me, and tried throwing my spirit and I into a hole forever. Like I've said before, something had to had happened to me while in my last time incarcerated.

And it became fun to be free from a controlled substance, but the good thing about this release, I've never looked back. Oh I think about it, every now and then, and who wouldn't, because it's been a loving blessing from God, and because it was God that released me.

On that release day, I really believe that God had prepared me for something far, above and beyond of my understanding, and to this day, I'm still trying to understand it. I have a very good idea, but I still don't quite understand how God has given me the life I now live. It's an amazing awesome life I now live, because now I have love in my life, that I've never had before. God's love is powerful and tremendous. Many of you, that don't believe, you might want to try it, it doesn't cost you anything, but your love to God. It's too bad I life.

I thought I had tried to recover, but it was very hard to start, and along with that comes weakness. If your mind and soul is not in it, then you probably won't recover, and you will die, or spend a whole lot of your life in prison. And that's the facts of life, death under an addiction. What I'm describing to you all, is my third deathly experience. Remember "DIED THREE TIMES LIVED ONCE"

ROBERT GARCIA

My first part of my life's writings, and my first experience of death, I was in a truck crash, when I was very young, and authorities said we should have died. And then I wrote to you all, how my second experience of death was, when I faced being shot at, and as I watched comrades get killed, while I was in Vietnam. Now here's my third deathly experience, under a killer addiction, that should have killed me, but it didn't. To be honest, I really wanted to die under that terrible addiction, mostly because I had broken my loved ones hearts. And it's been God, right by my side, all along. I'm an old man now, but because of God, is why I've reached my old age.

Crying to myself, oh mama, what happened, my mama. Felt so sorry for her. Because of my dumb ass stupidity, while I was in jail, I felt Dad didn't take care of my mother like her son did. And after that happened, I knew mama wasn't going to live too much longer. She was a diabetic that's why, and diabetics don't heal well, if they heal at all. And Mom never healed, she passed away, after being bedridden for four years. She had developed gangrene, from where she broke her foot, and it slowly crept up her leg, and it killed her. That was so so sad, and it still saddens me to think about it, to this day.

But during those four years, Mom was bedridden, Dad underwent testing to see how much Dad loved Mom. I guess you can say he loved her. But everyone has their own definition of love, I have mine, you all have yours, and Dad has his. Because during my mom's bedridden years, and as two years go by, Dad meets up with another woman, at a store down the street. So you tell me, what kind of a definition does Dad have for love. But I had to realize how Dad was raised. Because during the time Dad was growing up, he witnessed too much violence and corruption. Hardly any love at all. He couldn't even remember when his own Dad told him he loved him. I always found that amazing, if you can't remember when your Dad said he loved you, then he probably never told him. But the part that has always bothered me the most, was, he meeting another woman, just two years after Mom became bedridden. To me, I thought later, they were both making plans, so when Mom would pass away, he would have another woman to accompany him. But that's all gone now. Mom may be gone but not forgotten. Next to my current wife, Mom was the first lady that loved me. My wife is the second lady that loves me, and keeps me in peace and she keeps me in love.

So when Dad told me, Mom had broken her foot, I just had to do something about my addiction, but it wasn't going to happen, until about another year later. You would think, I would react immediately, no not me, not this stupid me. Hearing about Mom breaking her foot, just gave me a reason to get high. That's how stupid I was, and I didn't show any real love for Mom. Like I said, my recovery wasn't going to start for another year. And that's too bad for me and my loved ones, because all it did was shortened my love and my for a change. It felt like a long time coming.

Like this deputy told us to go to that van, that's exactly what I did, follow the deputy's rule. And I've tried to follow laws and regulations ever since, and it's not that hard to do, if you're in peace with yourself. Which I've become.

Don't suppose there are too many people that can say, they're happy getting old, well I'm one of them, that can say I've never been happier in my life. You'll feel much happier if you just accept the facts of life, of the things we can not change, than to feeling arrogant, being bad or sad, and you as well can find happiness. And I'll tell you why I'm happy being old, and happy to be getting older. Guess it's because I now see what God has been trying to tell me all along. And many of you, probably won't understand, or won't believe, I'm talking about being humble, and living peacefully in love.

Back to my telling you, when I was released from jail for my last time. But that day I was released for the last time from jail, you see, it wasn't just jail I had been released from. God released me from being possessed by evil, but that day I was released from being possessed from evil, I had accepted our lord, as my lord and savior, and that my friends, had become my happiest feeling of freedom. But it took me a while to get there, but for some, that's also another fact of life, because there are those that never see the message, until it's too late. Fortunately that's God's spiritual truth.

ROBERT GARCIA

When the day came for being released for the last time, I'm not going to say, I wasn't scared, I was scared to death. Because now I had to concentrate on being good, and not do drugs anymore. The times of going to church incarcerated had paid off. I had learned to become peaceful within myself, and I had also become peaceful with my spirit. I had met a few of those kinds of people, as pastors, while in jail, telling all of us, they had once been in the same place before. And now they're in peace with themselves. Thought to myself when I first heard that, that must be a beautiful feeling. And now I'm experiencing it.

When they yelled out my name, to roll it up, and for you innocent bystanders, that don't know what, roll it up means, and when you've been in and out of jail, like I have. You soon find out really quick what it means. It means you're being released. I still remember this L.A. county deputy sheriff, he was kind of funny, he acted like he was afraid to release us five inmates, he acted like we might make a run for it. The next thing he tells us, "when I open this door you're to go to that van over there, but if you decide to run, instead of going to that van, you will pay the price, and you'll be back in jail, it's all up to you" Well no one had to tell me anything but what I had already decided to do, and I went to that van like that deputy sheriff told us to go. I felt real good about myself, for the first time, I've started doing something right. But it's only just the beginning, and the beginning is a feeling like no other. I started feeling real good about being free. And it seemed like it took me too long to get there, after all, freedom is not free. If you guys could ever know how it felt to finally do the right thing, after being too long of being possessed, under an addiction. Many of ya, do know what I'm talking about, but for those of you that don't, you don't want to go down that dark road, because that's what it becomes, a very dark dangerous life, because you'll be sorry, like I've been for too long. I just couldn't get a grip of my life, but now I was finally getting a handle of things, to go right, had to find that out in jail, but the important thing is, I found out.

There's this real sad part of my time, while I was locked up, and it's about my mother, I'm sorry to say. Just knowing we're all getting old, from the time we're born. Every time Mom and Dad and I would go anywhere together, since we're all older now, I'd hold mom, right beside me, so she wouldn't fall. And this saddest day of my life came, when I was locked up, when I wasn't beside my mother, of course right? So one day I called home, a collect phone call to my parents's house, and Dad answered the phone. And the first thing Dad says to me, "You're in jail again, you're breaking your mother's heart, don't you know that" and the next thing he tells me, broke my heart. "You know what happened to your mother" of course I'm thinking, "What happened to Mom" What Dad tells me next, has echoed in my heart, even after she's been gone over thirteen years now. So Dad tells me, "your mom broke her foot". When Dad told me that, it literally tore me into pieces. And I tell him, "how did she break her foot" as he tells me "she slipped and fell and twisted her ankle, and her foot broke" and here is where both Dad and I got into a heated argument while on the phone, "And where were you" he responded, "well we were visiting your sister and brother in laws house, and she wanted to go her way and I went my way, and she went down on those stairs going down, and she slipped and broke her foot" and as he was telling me the sad incident, mom breaking her foot, I got mad, "and why weren't you with her going down those stairs, you should've known better than to let her go down those stairs alone" And he could tell I was mad at him, so he tells me, "oh you're the one in jail, but it's my fault" I tell him, "yeah, I'm in jail, but you're her husband, doesn't that mean anything" And he gets mad at me back, "Oh jeez" I tell him, oh shut up, and I hung up the phone. And I practically ran back to my bunk, and I silently cried into my pillow.

The driver to the van we all got in, was a nice lady, telling us where we were going, a couple of us would go to one house, and the rest of us would go to another house, each house being a house of recovery, to recover from alcohol and drugs. It was all brand new to me, because I've never lived with a bunch of men in one house. And it was a big house, a house of men and women. And soon as we arrived to this house, which was a very big house, sitting on a very big piece of property. And I was looking at a whole lot of chaos, because I saw men and women at this house, where I would start my first day of recovery. Thought to myself, wow, is this going to work for me, already having my doubts, oh my god, oh no dear God. That was not a good feeling, on my first day of release, and my first day of recovery. Thinking again about this situation, will I be able to do this? At a coed recovery service. Having doubts, was not a good thought, just being released from jail. But what could I do, I had to sit on myself, and swallow my thoughts, and endure the first day. And that's what I did, but being patient was never my best qualities in life. But I had to look for new qualities, or I'll lose it again. And I was determined to win this time, because I have lost too many times.

Got off the van, and walked up to the door, and someone immediately answered the door and letting me know, I had to report to a certain counselor, and he or she would then take my paperwork to the director, where, in this case, it was a male director. And it just happened to be a very arrogant asshole, and that's putting it mildly speaking. He seemed like a person, with his head up his ass. It was the way he spoke to people. He spoke to me and others, with so much arrogance. He spoke to me, like he was talking to some piece of shit. And he would wait if you would just take a jump at him, and you would go back to jail. And he would love that. It was another part of me, that I had to sit on. We all know, that are things in life, we hate following the rules and regulations, oh yeah, we have to also obey laws as well. And that's never a problem for me to do, obeying laws was easy for me to follow, all my life. Until I became a drug addict, and then I became a criminal. All of my life, I didn't have felonies on my record, until I became a drug addict. All of my life, I never had to register as a drug offender, until I became a drug addict.

So at this point of my life, I had to learn to correct the bad I had done with my life. So I had to start a new life, and it was like being reborn, and that's what happened to me. And I've never regretted it at all, because being a reborn again Christian, has been my best I've become, with God being beside me all along. And the first steps in this new life of mine, were a little difficult at first.

And becoming a new resident at this recovery house, was just an obstacle I had to climb, no matter how big an obstacle it would be, I just had to climb over it. And it was a matter of life or death for me. And God as my guidance, and I becoming one of God's warriors, I had become a fighter for my life, at last, after ten f**king years. Evil almost swallowed me up, as I reached out to my dear lord for help, and he grabbed me out of harms way, in the nick of time. I can't even come close in imagining what would've happened to me, if I didn't seek Jesus. That's always been a scary thought.

Starting my first day at this recovery house, I was still in my dirty rags, I had first got arrested in, now going over two months.

But I had arrived at this house, on a Wednesday, when everyone goes mandatory to church, in the evening, thinking to myself, that's beautiful, I can do that. And when I say mandatory, I mean it's a rule, we either go to church, and anyone that doesn't want to, goes back to jail. And everyone had to pile in two vans, thinking to myself, what a ride. So we arrive at this church, somewhere in Los Angeles. Not a big church, but a peaceful looking one. Not rich looking, like some Catholic Churches are. And as I sat myself off to the side, but about in the middle of the room. Church began with this pastor, with prayer, but something started happening, which to this day, has always been amazing to me, and to some others, that is if they believe me, and some have, and of course others have not. Didn't really care if anyone believed or not, because this amazement happened to me, and that's all that mattered. Because it's the truth. Something within me started talking to me. Don't know if that has ever happened to anyone else, and it has, because I've been told many stories in my time, I just never knew it would happen to me. But it was a good feeling, and it's helped me through my life ever since. God was there with me in that church, and I didn't know it, because of my blindness. And evil will always do that, in case you don't know.

The pastor started his sermon, and he started saying things, like everyday there's always someone that needs to be saved, and there's brothers and sisters that needs Jesus more than ever, right this very moment. As he continued on, right now, and you know who you are, come up here and ask Jesus for forgiveness. And he continued on, you out there, come right this minute, because you know you need help, and the only one that's going to help you, is our lord and savior. So come up right now. And all of a sudden, I started feeling something

ROBERT GARCIA

or someone touching me, and I couldn't believe it, it felt strong. Like a whisper, telling me, go up there, and like a huge feeling touching my back. Pushing me, and it kept pushing me and pushing me, I'm telling ya guys, it was a blessed feeling, and I have prayed and thanked God, that he saved me from more destruction of my life. And that very moment of walking up to the alter, I swear to you, it wasn't me walking up to the altar, it was the spirit pushing me. And it felt good, and it's been a feeling I keep within my heart and spirit. I haven't told this just to anyone, it's been a secret between God, myself and to the ones I love, for over seventeen years. It's been a long time coming, too long to be honest with you all.

And so after church, I started a brand new life, and it felt so relieving, and it's been quite a life, to be happy with the life I live now. But I still had more obstacles to climb, because as everyone should know, life doesn't go by at the snap of your fingers. Life goes by so fast, and yet it can go slow at times. It always depends on our situation. Having to go back to the house of recovery, was just my first day, and it had become the first day of my rest of my life. But like I said, I still have to climb a great big obstacle, because I had fallen so deep in the dark hole, I'm slowly climbing out of. But this place was so big, it had a huge back yard, chairs everywhere, adult swings as well. People talking about their alcoholic life or about their drug life. It was all the same, as we all know, alcohol is a drug too. And it's always seemed strange to me, how alcohol is legal, and how it will kill you as well as illegal drugs do. Society has and is, a very misunderstanding if we don't follow the rule of law. Although we live in a free country, nothing is free, because we all know, we have to work for a living.

I thought I was doing things right, but not if I've been doing things wrong for ten years. What made me think I was. After all I've been going the wrong direction for too long.

Get a load of this, while being at my first recovery service, as I've said, thinking I'm doing the right thing.

So one day, I tripped a little, when a woman that worked at this L.A. recovery service, she announced that if anyone would like to work, to follow her. And guess what, I along a few others followed her to a work force, just a block away. Not thinking anything was wrong, so another woman comes along and she's looking for people to work for her. She needed a group of people to work for her to clean up the Los Angeles allies. And she wanted to hire a special person to operate power tools. And I saw a great opportunity to work for her. So naturally she hired me and a few others. And for the first time in my life, I felt good about myself, after a shameful reputation of conniving my loved ones, my own parents and my daughters, so sad for them.

Little did this lady know, that hired me, she woke me up from being irresponsible to being responsible again. If anyone could understand how that made me feel, for the first time in ten years. And we worked for that lady for about three weeks, and I never got paid. Say what!!!! Do you understand, I, me, that's right, I never got paid. And why would I want to work, while at a rehab center, right? I got tired of smelling myself, I had the same clothes on for about three months. No matter how many times I took a shower, I still had the same clothes on. That is why I needed to work to buy some clothes. That's all!! But that turned out to be just another mistake, because when you're court ordered like I was, there's conditions and consequences. I was court ordered with a condition to not leave the premises at where my rehab center was, for sixty days, and I violated that. And I'm about to face the consequences. And I really thought I was going to face a big consequence, because wait until I show you what happens next.

Well, as you know I've been working three weeks, coming back to my rehab every day, like nothing was wrong. But something is going to pop my bubble big time. No joke people!! Does anyone relate with me? Because there's got to be someone else that's happened to me, that maybe happened to you.

And the time came. It was just another afternoon at my first recovery service, and someone was yelling for me, and I could barely hear her, because it was a girl yelling out my name. Coming up to her, what's going on, I asked. She lets me know, that the director wanted to talk to me, and he was very upset. Oh my God, thinking to myself, oh no. No one knows exactly what was going through my mind, but just the thought of going back to jail, was starting to give me paranoia.

There was no way around it, I had to face this man, no matter what he was going to do to me. I double timed to his office. As I'm waiting for my turn to speak to this guy, I overheard a loud mouth just grinding someone else. Literally cursing this poor guy. As he yells at him to get the hell out of his office, he sees me, and about to tear me apart, because I'm next. "You, get your ass in here" and boy that was some temptation to yell back at him. Flashback, remembering the time when a Marine lieutenant yelled and cursed me out, and how I reacted back at him. But I wasn't in the Marine Corps anymore. So I had to be very careful and stay calm and cool.

It was a whole new ball game for me, and I wasn't having any fun, because as he started to chew me out, as to where have I been, what have I been doing. And he's yelling at me, like as if I was deaf. "Where have you been and what have you been doing?" I repeated to, "What have I been doing?" I guess he thought I was mocking him, he asked again, "Yes what the hell have you been doing and where have you been?" So I say, "I've been working", he comes back at me, "You what" my God he was a loud mouth. As he was yelling at me, he showed me a piece of paper, telling me, you have no permission to leave the premises for sixty days, and you have violated your court order, and you are out of here, "Get the hell out of here, and you're going back to court tomorrow" What could I say, I yelled back at him, "With pleasure" as he stared at me for the last time. And it felt good to have the last word for a change.

So the next morning I'm in the court van, and my name wasn't on the list. We arrived at court, and there must have been about ten of us. We all filed out in order, as we all entered drug court. And the lady in charge must had been kind of curious, when she approached me, as to what my name was, and then says, you're not on the court list. Of course I had to explain to her, as to I've been kicked out of the director's recovery service I violated my court order. She wished me a lot of luck, "Oh my oh my, good luck sir" and I really thought I needed all the luck anyone could give me.

As the court room started dwindling down, the more I got nervous, because this female judge and I have seen each other under my drug problem for twelve years, and that my friends is one hell of a long time. And one hell of a long time to waste. And drugs will surely make you look old real quick. And the time for this judge to wonder, as to why was I doing in her court room.

And I started hearing her talking to her court personnel, and listening at what she was saying, like, "I can only imagine how many people spend their tax money on proposition thirty six, and still these drug addicts still don't get it" as she was looking at me as she was saying what she said. As I heard her say those words, I was going to do my damnedest to prove her wrong, at least for me personally.

So here it goes, as she stares at me, she calls out to me, "may I ask you sir what you're doing in my court?" "Please come up closer into my court" "Because I don't have your file, but I do remember who you are." And I started out by telling her how sorry I was for being there. "Well your honor, don't know where to start, so I'll start with the truth, I've been kicked out of my recovery service, because I broke a rule" she didn't understand, so she says, "you broke a rule, what rule did you break", I respond, "Your honor, I wasn't supposed to leave the premises for sixty days and I did" she says "ok, so where did you go", "I tell her, "I got a job so I started going to work" she responded, "and what kind of work were you doing" I say, "Well first of all your honor let me say, there was this lady at the recovery service that worked there, and she asked everyone that was interested in working, to follow her and there might have been about ten of us, and I was one of them, and she took us to a job fair, and I immediately got hired" she asked, and what kind of work was it" I answered, "we were hired to clean up L.A. city allies" she seemed interested as to what I was saying. And what were you going to do with the money." And I'm still in the same clothes I had on, since I'd been released from jail, which was already about two months. Dirty ugly stinky clothes on. "I needed to buy me some clothes, I still have these same dirty clothes since I've been released to jail" she said, "Well working isn't all that bad, but you left the premises, so let me think what I'm going to do, follow the public defender to her office, and I'll

ROBERT GARCIA

see you in a few minutes" I m thinking all this time, I'm going to jail for sure. So I followed the public defender to her office, she got on the phone not knowing who she was talking to. And then I figured it out, she was talking to the judge, who else.

As the public defender was talking to the judge, on the phone, I must have looked sad and depressed, because when she got off the phone, she asked, "Sir what is wrong" my answer was, "just wondering how long I have to go to jail for", and she instantly made me feel so much better, and brought me out of a very negative feeling. When she told me, "You're not going back to jail", trying to look as calm as could be, as I say, "Thank you very much for telling me that", And she continues to tell me, "The judge is going to give you an envelope, with an address of another recovery service, so let's go to the court room." I didn't know how to act, as I walked back to the court room, but my heart was full of gratitude, because of what I had expected, it turned out to be, the love of God. And the judge was sitting at her bench, waiting on me, as she tells me, "Sir I'm going to give you an envelope, with an address, and it will take you to San Pedro, do you know where San Pedro is"? As I answer, "Yes ma'am, I remember where San Pedro is", as she reminds me, "You're going to have a whole day to report to a counselor, and her name is Diana, I suggest you report on time" I could not believe myself, how I changed, in my way of thinking. Usually when I would get released from jail, I couldn't wait to go to Compton, to buy crack cocaine, and get high. Those thoughts, like they disappeared, I had no intention on going anywhere else, but to go straight to Mom and Dad's house, and sit on myself, and behave, until the next day.

So I called Dad, asked him, if he could pick me up from the Compton court, and says, I'll be there. He wanted to ask me, what happened, telling him, I'll explain when you pick me up. On the way home with Dad, obviously started asking about what's going to happen. And I tell him, I'm just going to have to wait for tomorrow, and report to San Pedro. And he asked, what's in San Pedro. Telling him, another recovery service!

Now, you brothers and sisters, that might be reading this, I'll remind you, I've been through three traumatic life's experiences, as a boy, in a truck crash, got deployed to a war in Vietnam, being shot at, and as I watched my comrades get killed, and now this addiction recovery, I'm now going through at this particular time of my life.

And I've tried to describe to all of you, just how traumatic it was for me, and each one of those traumatic experiences, changed me into a very different person. You all might be thinking, I'm exaggerating, like a V.A. psychiatrist has once told me. And that's okay, just like assholes, we all have an opinion. To say my life has been difficult, that doesn't explain half of it, but there are people out there, that have had a much worse life than I have, I really understand that, but I'm only writing my life story, not yours. Don't mean to be so blunt, but that's how I've become through my life. Guess it's because of my life's traumas. It will change anyone, like it's changed me, three different times.

Continuing on my recovery, and to say It's been easy to get to where I'm at, would be a lie. Who told you it was easy to do good, or to be a good person, let me tell ya, it's been one hell of a journey, and I still haven't reached my destination. Praying, God will make it easy and smooth, when and if he takes me with him.

As I said, I'm still going through my recovery, and as Dad and I were doing some serious talking, on our drive home. He just couldn't believe how differently I've changed, in the way I was talking to him. But as I told him, I had to change Dad or either face prison or die. Not that hard to figure out, I would be just another statistic, or to put it plain and simple, I would've been another number down the drain. Literally down the drain. We arrived home, and I couldn't wait to see Mom, as she has been Mom, all my life. Because of my wrong doing, never gave her a reason to change her love for me. She will always be my sacred lady of my life, my mama. I can't help myself about how I feel about myself, because although, God, Mom, Dad, and my daughters have forgiven me, I just can't forgive myself. I feel too guilty for the things

I've done to those I love the most. Because they have always loved me, unconditionally, and that my friends, is true love, like no other. Mom greeted me so lovingly, like all moms should, but unfortunately, I've seen some moms, can't and won't ever come close, in comparison to the lady my mother had been.

We enjoyed each other's company so beautifully, and Dad just couldn't believe I wasn't going anywhere, because I was going somewhere all the time. So, when he asked me, what was I going to do, I told him,,"I'm not going anywhere Dad"

And I'm not going to do anything, but stay with you and mom, and wait until I have to go to San Pedro, and arrive on time. I had to go there, even if my life depended on it. Mom and Dad were amazed, because I was always going somewhere, and it's no big secret, where would I go, my favorite places to pick up drugs, my rock cocaine. So, this was all new for all of us, especially for myself. The judges words kept echoing in my mind, "I suggest you arrive on time", I wanted to make a big change in my life, and with God as my witness, I was going to do that. And we have to do it, one day at a time. Ain't that the truth, no one can change what happened yesterday, no one knows what's going to happen tomorrow, and we barely know what's going to happen today. To be frank and honest, no one knows what's going to happen, but God, all mighty.

So I stayed home, where I still called home at that time with mom and Dad, until the next morning, and take the drive to San Pedro to start my new recovery service at nine A.M. sharp, in my Dad's Jeep. And I still remember what date that was, January seventh two thousand seven.

As I was about to start this brand new life of mine, I felt like I was floating into a realm of a miraculous life, that I would have never dreamed of. I'm telling ya people, it's still unbelievable to me. Especially after the three traumatic deaths, I went through, that I really didn't think I would survive. I really didn't.

And so I arrive at my new home, where I will call home for six months. San Pedro, oh my god, I haven't been to San Pedro, since I was only seventeen years old. When I arrived there, it seemed like a century ago. And now I'm there to recover from my drug addiction. Man, what a change of life, but I just had to do this. It beat going to prison for three years. Six months would be a hell of a lot better, than three years. But the question in my mind, what kind of people would be there. Other drug addicts, that would be for sure. Found out later, even the counselors and get a load of this, even the director had been a recovered addict.

Didn't have any problem finding the place.

Don't think I mentioned this before, but at the previous failed recovery service. My counselor at that place had given me permission, chaperoned of course, to go to downtown L.A. to apply for general relief. Don't know if they have that anymore, but that's not important to me anymore.

Both the chaperone and I took the bus to social security administration, to downtown Los Angeles. After I submitted my application, for general relief, (GR), we had to wait for quite a while, and wait and wait, we did. Then when I was finally called and approved, I couldn't believe my eyes and ears, what I saw and heard, what was on my approval paperwork. Although I wasn't approved for any money, but I was approved for eight hundred and fifty dollars worth of food stamps. And I showed this guy, the approved paperwork and how much I was approved for. His eyes popped out of his head, with his mouth wide open. We were both very impressed, and he advised me not to say anything to anyone, and we didn't, kept our mouths shut. Of course I had to give my EBT card to my counselor, as soon as we arrived back to the recovery house. Without letting the counselor know about the amount of the food stamps value. That would've been kind of stupid, to say the least. All the counselors of that recovery service would collect all EBT cards from everyone, so they could buy food for everyone, to feed us. And that place never found out about my card value. As a matter of fact, none of my recovery services ever found out. The one in L.A. nor San Pedro. And I'll never know what would've happened if they would have found out, not important anymore. They could have abused my EBT card, telling me, they would need it for the service, I don't know, and don't care, no how.

And my lucky day came, when I was kicked out of that recovery service in downtown L.A., and I've explained as to what happened, why I was kicked out, for working, because I wasn't supposed to leave the premises, as you recall, and now I'm going to start January seventh of two thousand seven, with this new recovery service, in San Pedro We will all see, how this recovery service, would become one of my luckiest decisions of my life. If you've noticed, seven, seven, seven, July seventh, two thousand seven. But we will arrive to that date as I write it. Remember, one day at a time.

And with this brand new recovery service, comes a brand new life, with my EBT card, of still around eight hundred dollar value.

Arriving on my first day of my rest of my life. In a Jeep, and I get out of the Jeep, and take out all of my belongings I collected from the previous recovery service, from clothing donations, a bike, and a cell phone.

That was all I had for my life, at the age, at that time, fifty eight years old. But it was a start, at least I was heading towards the positive, instead of walking backwards. Everyone like myself, coming out of a dark world, and we want to recover, we all have to start from a crawl, like a new born baby, at my age. It is what it is. The facts of life. And I was very serious at this point in time, so I walked into the San Pedro recovery service office, with a serious look on my face. I had to make this big decision, and treat it like it was the last thing I had to do for my life. Thank God for his miracles. Because that's what it was, because I finally decided to do something right.

As I approached the office, a counselor saw me, and asked to me to wait for a few minutes, and then tells me to come and sit at her desk. One of the things I noticed right away, at this recovery service, it was not a coed recovery service. And I felt good about that. And one of the things I've noticed about how I felt about coed recovery services, I didn't believe men and women should recover at a same residential house. Because, like I said, for me anyway, to recover from an addiction, we all have to start a brand new life, just like starting out as a baby. We have to crawl before we walk. This woman, I started talking to, I found out, she would be my counselor. She explained to me, what the rules were, and asking me, how did I get there. I told her, I drove myself to the place. She just about fell off her chair, she laughed so hard. And then she tells me, "no no no, Sir, you can not have a car at this recovery house. And I didn't think it was a big deal. So I say, ok. She explained to me, how everyone else had arrived to the recovery house, they were always brought by some police officer or a probation officer, she tells me, she had never heard of anyone ever driving themselves to this recovery house. She says, that is why she found that very funny. Telling me, listen sir, we're having a meeting in the garage, so just get yourself situated, and get to the meeting as soon as you can. I agreed, and I'm on my way to my first day, with this recovery service with a good reputation. Another step towards a positive life, for the rest of my life.

Arrived at my first meeting with this new recovery house meeting, which was in a garage, thinking to myself, oh well, I have to do this.

As I arrived to the meeting, my counselor tells me in front of the rest of the group, that I got there pretty quick, and to please introduce myself to the group. So I went on with the rules and regulations. Finding out, this was a spiritual recovery service program. I became very quickly to admire this program, because we prayed in the morning, and prayed

ROBERT GARCIA

out at night. I felt it as a blessing for all, but of course I felt that blessing for myself. How my dear God had planned this for me all along. I felt, God was answering my mother's prayers again, for her only son.

There must have been about forty in patients at this recovery service, I included, and there was someone graduating every now and then. I was now off and starting a program, that a interviewer had given me a choice, just before my last release from jail, to either go to prison for three years or choose this program, for six months. And I still remember, this woman, the interviewer, asking me, which way I wanted to go. Three years in prison or six months in a recovery service. It should be very obvious for most, but you'd be surprised how many guys, go sourly, and choose prison. When I was being interviewed, and while I was being asked as to which way I wanted to go, there were a few guys around me, luring me, to choose prison. I could sense the devil around us. With that feeling around me, and also feeling confused, I receive this yell. It was the interviewer yelling at me, "Hey, what do you want to do", I yelled back, "What" she repeats, "what do you want, prison or program". Well, thank God that's all behind me now. Decided the six months program.

Little would I know, I would become an example for many, that were near my age, and some much younger. And I was impressing the staff, and the director as well. Without letting it show, I was impressing myself. And strived for more impressive examples, not just for others, but most importantly for myself. Because, when it comes right down to it, nobody cares about anyone, but themselves. And sometimes they don't even care for themselves. Sad but true, just because I was there.

We went to meetings, almost everyday. On Sunday, the recovery service, would give us a choice, you could go to a meeting or go to church. And every Sunday a few of us went to church. And had thought many times, when I started going to church while incarcerated, and I thought, it really paid off.

And now here I am, in San Pedro, going to church as God and I would prefer it, every Sunday. And church going wasn't the only reason, while on my whole life's process, why I am, where I am today. There are many reasons, for starters, I'm not doing drugs anymore, ta. That's probably the biggest reason, and I've fallen in love, another big reason, right?

I've mentioned it a couple of times, if you've lost your self discipline, your self respect, your trustworthiness, that means you don't love yourself, and who is going to love you. So all of that had to happen to me, in order for someone to love me. With that goes with the memory of what Dad once told me, "You don't love your mother, you don't love your father, you don't even know how to love yourself." Boy, did he catch me off guard, and off balance. I didn't know what to say to him, because it was the truth, and until this day, it still echoes in my heart.

And, did I mention, that this recovery service, when we went to meetings, we would walk. Now, just for a second or two, take a picture of that, in your head, thirty to forty grown men walking down your neighborhood. What would you think, where are they going, or who are they going to kill. No, just kidding on that last comment.

I've often thought, that cities like San Pedro would have had to get some kind of an agreement with the residents of the city, to allow a whole lot of recovering addicts, because there might have been about a few hundred of us recovering addicts, and some would run. And of course, they would get caught and get thrown back in jail. And I don't really believe, many cities would approve that. But thank God for those few. And this city, San Pedro would receive donations from clothing stores, and food was also donated to this recovery service, remarkable right? I thought so.

So I was en route to a great start, to say the least, at a place, where the judge gave me a second chance, and assigned me to give it another try. And as God would have it, he helped me work my addiction out of my life. Oh yes he did. But as I've tried mentioning, that because of God, I was able to clean my life up. Oh, you should have heard a reaction from a brother in law of mine, telling me, that there is no such thing, and that there's no such thing of God. He even growled, like some beast, my reaction to him, oh, I should have known better than to even think of mentioning God to an atheist like you. All we did was stare evilly at one another. As my sister was trying to control us from going into obscene confrontations. That would've made it worse for both of us.

And she called that, her husband, what a shame that turned out to be. Don't know who was more shameful, Dad, or that woman, he calls his daughter, but she never showed any shame. Towards my end of my life's writings, I'll let you all know what those two did to her own father, our father. But we all have to face judgment day, whether we believe it or not. For those of you that believe that, you know exactly what I'm talking about.

So much for non believers, I don't want to know what is going to happen to those people. Because the thought of it, scares me.

I had to concentrate on myself, and anyone else that wanted to do the good thing. At this point of my life, I had to concentrate on my recovery, and I was doing just that. Thanking God, at that particular time, for the way I changed my way of thinking. While some thought I wouldn't make it, I prayed to God, to stay along side of me, to give the strength to do it.

And not everything at this recovery service, was good, there were good and bad things that happened, but I had to stick it out, no matter what, because it was better there, than spending time in prison, for three years. Oh my God, and when I was only there about forty days, it seemed like eternity, but the thought would hit me hard, where else did I want to be, dead or in prison. So I was just where I was supposed to be. Taking care of my well being. One big thing I've always noticed about myself, no matter what I ever did, whether I liked it or not, I would do my best. So here I am, in San Pedro, trying to clean my dirty life, and I was going to do my best, and I knew, it was going to take some hard work. And hard work I was going to do.

As I was there, saw some guys, run away from there, to get kicked out. Once this one guy, was caught stealing prescription drugs, I couldn't believe this guy, what he attempted to do. He snuck upstairs where all the these prescriptions were, he thinking no one was watching, but there's always someone watching, of all the people that aren't watching, God is always watching us. This guy was there when I arrived, and he talking about finishing this recovery, but somewhere along the line, he got tempted. That was too bad for him, because he had to face the judge, again.

And there was this other guy, he was an alcoholic, and he just couldn't keep still, because he was going to run, because he told me he was. I tried my best, in trying to talk him out of running away from this recovery service. But he wouldn't listen to me.

But I couldn't criticize anyone, because I could've said those guys were weak, they don't deserve to be there, but I couldn't say any of that, that just wouldn't be right for me to say. Being humble, you don't go criticizing anyone. And that's what I had become. Humble, as best of my ability. And at first, being humble was hard to be. Humility has to grow within you, it doesn't just happen. As I thought about it at the time, becoming humble, is part of being a Christian.

And becoming a Christian all started while I was incarcerated. And as I've said, going to church while incarcerated, paid off, it became to my advantage, for the cleanliness of my life. Thank you Lord.

Not once did I ever think of running away from that place. Running away from myself wouldn't have been very smart. It would prove, that out of all the work, I've tried to accomplish, it would end up for nothing. And wind up in prison for at least three years.

And so I had to continue on my recovery, and as the days flew by, each day had become easier for me. Because at the end of the tunnel, I could see light. God's light.

The Bible that I have today, I've had it since I was incarcerated. That's become a long time now. I've had this bible, at the last time I was incarcerated, and released, in two thousand six. And it's become a great part of my life, that I will cherish secretly in my heart. I have read it numerous times, and keep reading it to this day.

And during the time of this recovery service in San Pedro, I never left my bible just anywhere, it became part of me, everywhere I went.

As you have humble people like myself and others like me, you will always have people that don't believe, or they just don't want to hear about God at all. And I was very much criticized about me wanting to talk about God, and how I got to where I had arrived with them, but I even had a few cuss me out, for me, mentioning God. I couldn't believe how bad the devil had possessed those guys. But since this was a spiritual program, my counselor backed me up, by defending me for my believing in God. In fact she yelled one of them that cussed me, telling him, to quit yelling at me.

Recalling telling you all, there were times when it could get real boring. There were times we all go to meetings in the evening, and sometimes the meetings would last for two to three hours. A hell of a long time, especially when a talker that would be up front, talking and talking, and not say a damn thing. Anyone of you ever meet anyone like that. I'm sure you have. About the only thing that wasn't so boring, is when the meeting would take a ten minute break, and everyone would rush to the snack bar, for coffee and cake. Or just go outside and talk to a couple of women, which at the time, it was a hell of a lot better than listening to some boring fool.

But that's just the way it was, during my great experience while I attended this recovery service, because it stayed in my mind and soul for the seriousness of my life till now. And everyone that has been an in patient member of this recovery service, under proposition thirty six, or otherwise, should forever be blessed. God bless you all. I know I was blessed, and now live a freedom of joy, because of this great recovery service.

To say doing this recovery service was easy, would be a great big lie. And since I graduated from that recovery service, I've been a free man from a evil possession.

Since I was in my first recovery service in downtown L.A., and didn't follow instructions, of not leaving the premises for sixty days, now I had to stay a hundred and twenty days, four months of extreme self discipline, and trustworthiness, which I earned while at this good recovery program.

I had already asked my counselor if I could go look for work, before my four months were up. When I asked her, she laughed. Oh by the way, all the counselors at the program were female, and even the director was female.

Didn't ever hear the story, about the director's husband, also a recovered addict, was the original director. She cried when she told the story, about what happened to her husband, one day, and she couldn't understand why he did what he did. And that became a very sad ending for the original director.

Apparently, her husband decided to go out, and relapse, into doing heroine. The truth behind relapsing, if anyone decides to go back and do your drug of choice, and think you can do it, it'll become suicide.

And that's exactly what happened to the original director, as his wife was telling the story, she cried the whole time she told us what happened to her husband. I still remember that, as if I heard that story just yesterday. Not only did it sound sad, that story scared me, into never to relapse. And I never have again, and that's now sixteen years ago. But not all get the message, from any recovery service, unfortunately, that's the truth. I feel, I should have been offered this kind of service, years ago. But that's okay, it happened when it happened, I'm clean and sober today, and that's all that matters, and that's the bottom line. And never been happier since that hell of a life I lived, has been over, and I feel so great, and grateful about it. Thank you Lord.

After a couple of months, I couldn't believe it, I was starting to get used to this, and I was even getting used to the boredom. Say what, yeah, I looked at it this way, each day was another day to my freedom. And now I was taking this recovery service literally into my life. I even told everyone there, how I felt about my life, that I have to live a life of clean and sober, for the rest of my life, no matter what. And I have.

Thought I'd share what I thought about living with men, with these guys.

"I don't know about you guys, no offense, but I don't find living with a bunch of men, normal, being in jail, or being in prison, is living with men, and I don't find that normal"

"I would much rather either live alone or wake up with a woman sleeping in my bedroom, instead another man in my bedroom" No one said a word, it was so quiet, when I said what I said. Because it was true, in your right mind, what man likes living with another man, I know I don't.

After I had been there about two months, I mean there was always someone new coming into this recovery service, but there was this certain young guy, and he became a close friend, and I never thought that would happen. Always thought, who makes friends at a drug program. But this young man seemed too smart to be there, so we started talking, freely about how we ended up at this place. A common question, we all had to tell our story, about how we ended up in this recovery service anyway, I told him, I had been in and out of jail, and I wasn't getting anywhere, so I finally got court ordered, to either do this, or go to prison.

So of course I asked him, how many times did he go to jail. And I couldn't believe what his answer was, I mean I thought everyone that was at this recovery service had been to jail at least a half a dozen times, like I had. Or like others, had been to prison, a few times, and have been to a recovery service before, and they're back again. Or maybe the smarter ones, before they end up in jail or prison, or worst yet, lose their family, also like I had. Admit themselves to this recovery service through their insurance company, with the permission of their employer. I was long gone from that, ten years back, when I was employed for a county sheriff.

So this young man's answer, totally blew my mind, when he tells me "Dude, I've never been to jail" I say, what? And he continued, "You can believe me or not, but I've never been in jail" of course my response was, "You're super shitting me, are you kidding me man" he continues, "No I am not, like I said, I've never been to jail, and you don't have to believe me, why would I lie about that" And he was right, why would he lie about that. And he says, "Oh let me tell ya man, I came very close in getting caught, but they never caught me, but I've lived under many Los Angeles bridges, literally homeless, living out of my little suitcase" I couldn't believe this guy, but I did believe him, because of his sincerity in his voice.

As time went on, we became friends, but he became friends with many of the others. He seemed like a likable kind of guy. And I noticed he was also spiritual as I was, went to meetings, but he went to church every Sunday, as I did. There were very few of us that went to church,

ROBERT GARCIA

maybe five of us, out of forty, the rest would rather go see the recovering girls. I made it a point, not to get connected to any women, that were going through a drug rehabilitation, always thought, that would be too dangerous for my future. After going through the kind of life I've been through, the last thing I would need, is a woman going through a drug rehabilitation, as I was. Bad idea. And this young man thought the same. Smart kid, since he was about twenty years younger than I was.

Just to let any readers that I might attract, I'm not going to bore you with my whole visit at this recovery service, just writing you my highlights of the new life, God created for me, is all.

We both had the same counselor. So as far as our counselor was concerned, both this young friend of mine, and I, she seemed to draw attention to us, and that was a good thing.

Because the next thing, she's inviting us two to Downey, and for all three of us to give our testimony, at a small convention center, as to how we ended up in a drug rehabilitation program. And that was very interesting for all of us. And it was quite emotional, for each one of our testimonies.

Speaking of emotions, since I was starting to develop emotions, because most of of my times of my adult life, I had stopped crying, until I arrived to this recovery program.

This rehab place, with our counselor, she gave all new in patients, homework, say what, yes that's right, homework. Right away you might be thinking, like going back to school, no nothing like that, it turned out to be, quite more complicated than that. She gave us psychological homework. Interesting huh? I thought so. And that's how it got emotional for me. She wrote down a list of people, like our mother, our Dad, our wife, and our children, to write letters to each one of them, and for each one of them to write back letters. But they never really write back. We write what we think they would write. To tell you the truth, it was hard. No, the writing wasn't hard, it was the emotion that hit me, like a ton of bricks, hitting me in my heart. It really did, because when I sat down and wrote each letter, I literally cried like a baby. And I haven't cried like that, since I was a little boy. So it hurt badly, because of what I had done to my loved ones. Especially how I hurt my daughters and my Dad, when I became a monster of an addict. You might notice I don't mention my second wife, maybe because she kicked me out of her life, and my daughters and Mom and Dad never have. Till this day, we have a beautiful father and daughters relationship, and my Dad, we've become friends, and that I thought would never happen.

When we wrote letters to and from our loved ones, we also had to read them out loud in our group. In each group, were ten men, so, as a new comer, I had to read them, and that became emotional for all of us, because my life story with drugs, was quite a heart breaker.

I think the biggest person I had become for myself, was my trustworthiness, and not lying anymore, and to me, had made me feel like a brand new person. And that's putting it lightly.

Now get a load of this, after I had only been at this drug program, about two and a half months, all of a sudden I receive word, the director wants to see me. And that kind of scared me, why I don't know, maybe because I was still paranoid from the last rehabilitation center I was kicked out of, prior. On my way to the director's office, you think I wasn't thinking negative about myself, of course I was. But as I arrive in her office, she's real polite, and I'm wondering why, as she offers me a seat. Well sit down. Boy, do I have something wonderful to offer you. Now at this point, I'm bewildered, wondering, what is this woman talking about. As she continued to surprise me, I kept my mouth sealed shut. Not a f**king word. The next thing she says to me. I want you to prepare yourself for a flight to Sacramento. I'm thinking, what the hell. And do what, I continue to think. You're going to represent our group, and there's going to be thousands of people there. I just couldn't believe what I was hearing. You're going to take off on the eighteenth of

ROBERT GARCIA

April, you'll have your own expense account. I had to almost yell out, by saying, I can't go. She yelled back by asking me, why in the hell not. I say, because I have to be in court on that date. She couldn't believe her ears, when she says, oh my god, you would have been the number one person to do that, but oh well, I'll just have to find someone else. I tell her, I'm so sorry. I will never forget that beautiful opportunity, I had to turn down. But this proved to me, that I was at the right place at the right time. And that my friends, is why I'm clean and sober today.

All during the time I was at this drug rehabilitation center, I had found out so many things about myself, and who I had become. Another completely different person. Remember, "DIED THREE TIMES LIVED ONCE"

A big compliment my counselor had given me, you see, I had requested to extend my time there at the rehab center, and she asked me, why would I want to do that. "Sir, you were ready to do this program, the day you arrived, so go and live out your life, don't waste anymore time here" "Just remember what happened to you before you got here, and who you had become" Those were strong and heavy words coming from a professional. I experienced so many great changes for me, that as I wrote this, I'll keep it sacredly in my heart, and take it to my grave, a happy man.

At this rehab center, don't think I mentioned, there were bank robbers, guys who had committed burglaries, and drug pushers, and of course registered drug offenders like myself.

And a big thing I've noticed about so many people, like myself, it takes us too long for us to realize what we're doing to ourselves, that we think we're by ourselves, and we're the only ones we're hurting, boy don't we become blind. I know my God had truly opened my eyes.

There was this ex bank robber, when he graduated. Everyone that graduated from this rehab center, each day a person graduated, he had to go to each one of us, grab each ones hands, and say he about that person. And he got to me, he tells me out loud, brother, you scare me with your God. Thinking to myself back then, good for you. During that same time, I'm glad I found out to be a God fearing man. Because if you're not, and you don't become a man that doesn't fear our almighty, then you're going to have a big problem with your second death. And may God Bless you, because we need all the blessings, God can give us.

When I wrote this, I have noticed, and maybe you have too, how every generation gets further and further away from believing in God. Just look around us, from the politicians on down. It doesn't matter who we are.

And when I asked this friend of mine, asking him, what he was going to do, when he graduated from that place. Another surprising answer, when he said, he's going to be a lawyer. This guy was surprising me everyday. I am at liberty to say, mostly, as to how I noticed the class of men that were there. What I'm saying, I believe very strongly, my lawyer friend and I are probably the only ones that have survived all of these years, to stay clean and sober. I really believe that.

He becoming a lawyer and then obtaining his own law firm, this guy didn't have any support but God, and his own self disciplined motivation. And I'm also living a life of happiness, and it's because of God's love and blessings. You better believe it, because I do.

Two months before I graduated, I was finally given permission to go look for a job, can you believe that. I was finally going back to work.

Not far from the rehab, there was a Vons super market, maybe about a mile away, give or take a few blocks, and it seemed that everyone wanted to work there. I had written earlier in my life's writings, that I had worked retail management, but that's decades behind me now, but since I was given permission to look for work, I decided to apply there. But upon application, I had to drug test, and then I had to wait for the test results, which took about two weeks. But I didn't wait around, I went on looking, and I found another, and got hired. Working at a clothing cleaners, and the guy that hired me, hired me for management. It was all well and good, but it was a sweat shop. It would get really hot in a cleaners, because of the steam. And I didn't like it there for too long. The guy that hired me was way too picky, I wasn't allowed to talk to anyone. Because there were too many people that had worked there for a long time, and I was telling them, I will become a manager, and there were a few that didn't like that. So I quit I thought it was only fair for obvious reasons. I had been hired to be trained to become a manager one day, but that didn't last. The owner didn't inform his employees that he was going to hire a person for management, and he started getting a little salty with me, so I tell him I'm going to quit. And then I tell him, I want you to pay me right now. Oh, he acted like that was impossible. I don't care how impossible that seemed to him, but I wasn't leaving until I got paid. And guess what, in a couple of hours, the owner calls me into his office, and tells me, he's going to pay me. Yeyy. I didn't walk out of the building rich, but I didn't walk out of there broke either. I was a little disappointed, quitting the first job that hired me, and I thought, now what, just go with the flow, go back to the rehab group, and see what happens. And to see what happens, happened, because we went to Vons supermarket to shop for some things, and this employee that does the hiring and firing, saw me and calls me out, hey dude, been looking for you, have been calling you. And I ask him, "so what's up" he says, "You're hired" I couldn't believe it, I didn't think they were going to hire me. "I am, ok, good" he says, when do you want to start" I respond, "today, or tomorrow" he tells me, you can start tomorrow. Ok, and the show begins.

That's right, the show began for me, for the rest of my life, as I started to recover, and climb out of my dark hole I was stuck in for ten f**king years.

This guy, asked me, where do you want to work, stocking shelves at night, or work in the meat department in the day? Thought right away,

"I will work in the meat department" And I'm back in the working force. I was so happy, I felt like was going to become a millionaire, but that was okay, a job was still a job.

I've told all of you, how my life started, and how I've almost died three times. Now I'm living a life, I never thought I ever deserved. But that end of my life's writings is still a few miles away, and we'll get there, one day at a time.

But for now, I've only just begun. What a beautiful beginning. And not many men wanted to hear me say, that it was because of God, is why I survived my three mishaps, struggles, and difficulties. You'll never hear me say it was easy, hell no, because nothing is easy when you're trying to live. Life is a struggle from the time we're born. If you don't believe me, just read this.

So my first day on the job, and you won't hear me complain, other than never having enough hours to work. I was constantly complaining, I wanted more hours. But wherever anyone works in the world, we all have to prove our integrity and our credibility. And I did just that. If you don't believe me, ask the health department. Because I was always being scheduled to close the meat department, and clean it to health department's rules and regulations, and specifications.

I would have to wait on customers, while I had to clean the messy meat department, as to how the butchers left it. It was a messy job to do. Let me tell ya, hell ya it was. But what the hell, what was I going to do, cry? This job was not for boys, and we had a few boys working there, and I wasn't one of them. Because when I would clean up the meat department, and when the health department came by to inspect it, I would receive an A, for cleanliness. That didn't just happen once, it happened a few other times. Do you think I was proud? Hell ya I was proud, with a capital P. But you would never see or hear me brag about anything I've done in my life. I'll let the bragging speak for it self. But like I've wrote you before, I had done that kind of work decades before, so I had experience.

As days went by, one day at a time, my time at my rehab center was getting shorter. And it has proven to me, my biggest part of my life, and I will never forget the beginning of a normal beautiful life that recovery service, has given me.

And at one step at a time, because at this rehab center, it was not just a spiritual program, it was also a twelve step program as well.

Step 1: we admitted we were powerless over our addiction, that our lives had become unmanageable.

Step 2: We came to believe that a Power greater than ourselves could restore us to sanity.

Step 3: We made a decision to turn our will and our lives over to the care of God as we understood him.

Step 4: We made a searching and fearless moral inventory of ourselves.

Step 5: We admitted to God, to ourselves, and to another human being the exact nature of our wrongs.

Step 6: We were entirely ready to have God remove all these defects of character.

Step 7: We humbly asked him to remove our shortcomings.

Step 8: We made a list of all persons we had harmed, and became willing to make amends to them all.

Step 9: We made direct amends to such people wherever possible, except when to do so would injure them or others.

Step 10: We continued to take personal inventory and when we were wrong promptly admitted it.

Step 11: We sought through prayer and meditation to improve our conscious contact with God as we understood him, praying only for knowledge of his will for us and the power to carry that out.

Step 12: Having had a spiritual awakening as the result of these steps, we tried to carry this message to addicts, and to practice these principles in all our affairs.

As you can see, these were the twelve steps we as addicts, either had to follow, or fall back into our dark hole. And you better believe it, I've been following these twelve steps since then. And they have, and will keep me in peace with God's love and blessings.

To me, those N/A (Narcotics Anonymous) twelve steps, were my first baby steps of a brand new life. This is what happens, when we as addicts don't know how to live, and we get caught up in a world, we never knew how to get out of. So we have to ask for forgiveness, from a power much stronger than ourselves. My power stronger than myself is my God.

So as God and this rehab center, has saved my life, I strived for more, by reaching out to others that needed help and support.

Before I forget to mention the Serenity prayer, we prayed that prayer everyday, at least twice a day, as a group, once in the morning, just before we had breakfast and once at night, just before lights off.

So I continued on working at Vons, like I said, where so many recovering addicts, or alcoholics, wanted to work at. The reason I keep saying that, there was this one guy, much younger than I, got really upset with me, because Vons hired me, instead of him, like as if it was my fault they hired me over him. It was just a job, I couldn't make Vons my career, because of my age. An employee informed me of that, I was a liability to the company. I thought it was kind of cold, when he gave me that terrible truth, but it was what it was, the truth. But what no one knew, that I had applied for a claim for disability with social security and the V.A. But I always thought, it was no one's business, what I was doing with my life.

So the time came, when I was to graduate, now bare in mind, my mother has been bedridden for two years, when I finally seen the light. And woke up and crawled out of my dark world of my life.

I had already, through my time at this rehab center, had received visits from all three daughters, which was so loving. And I did some cooking for them. And my oldest daughter had asked me, when would I be graduating, and had told her, on the seventh of July, which was just a little ways yet. But time flys when we're having fun. And having fun at a rehab center, it was very important and it was also court ordered, so to say I had fun, would be a joke. And just so you know, being court ordered, I had no choice in the matter, it was either I did that rehabilitation program, or go to prison, just as simple as that. No big surprise, everybody does it, one way or the other. Many choose the evilest of two worlds, and that's too bad for those people, because like I said, many don't come out corrected, after being locked up, in the Department of Corrections (DOC)

I have always found that very misleading.

But what has never been misleading, during my life, is when I made the choice to rehabilitate myself, instead of falling even further, if I would have chosen (D.O.C.) I definitely don't believe I would have come out corrected.

At this rehab center, one day our counselor had ordered me, as to when I was to get out of work, that I was to head to a auditorium, that was just down the street from our rehab place. Because there was going to be a dance, and this was mandatory, and there were no exceptions.

Period!! And I hadn't danced in a very long time, and I didn't want to. Period!! But at this point, there were no exceptions. My counselor, had stared me down, telling me, you better be there. Don't disappoint me sir.

As I was about knock off from work, all of a sudden, I started thinking about the dance I was going to, and I have to say, of course right? Started thinking about what kind of girls were going to be there. It just had to be the ones, we've seen at the meetings. No surprised faces. But that's okay, girls, will be girls. And just the thought of living with men at the rehab place, made me feel better, to see women, for a change. The next thing was, to dance with any of these girls.

Can anyone see the colorless dark world I'm starting to crawl out of. And it's been quite a journey, to say the least.

Then came graduation day. Can't say, which one I had actually been was more exciting, graduating from high school, when I was eighteen, or graduating from a rehab center, when I was fifty eight. I'll tell you, without a doubt, neither one, because they're too different to compare. One of them for a diploma, and the other one for my life.

My graduation It was very unique, the date was 777, July seventh two thousand seven. How's that for a graduation date?

I have to hand it to my oldest daughter, although I would never tell none of my daughters, who's my best, because it just wouldn't be fair. But I can write it down can't I, she has been my best daughter. She may never know it, unless she will ever read this. one day. Her and her sister and I were very badly wounded, psychologically by their mother, my first wife, being an alcoholic.

As I said about my oldest daughter, when she says she is going to do something, or if she tells you she's going to be there, she'll be there.

And when she said she was coming to my graduation, that's exactly what she did, she came to my graduation. How time had flown by so quickly, and I had actually been through seven months, because of my breaking a rule at my first recovery service, and then got kicked out. And didn't know it then, but the director that kicked me out, did me a favor in the long run.

Now here I was, seven months later, finally graduating, and about to join the free world, and live life, as how God would want me to live it. Many of you people won't come close to imagine how I felt, when I was going to live life, peacefully, and stay grateful with God.

But I'm not out of the woods yet. Yeah I was still working at Vons, and I still had to do an extensive recovery, called sober living.

And when everyone graduated from the rehab center, each one had to give a last day testimony, to how we each arrived there, and what were our focuses for our well being as we said goodbye to a very big part of my life.

And as I gave my last day testimony. My daughter saw and heard. "I had been in denial since the day I became an addict, and always thought I would never become an addict, only fools become addicts, not me. And when I started lying, I thought I was so good at it, I even believed my lies. But those that have loved me, noticed I had changed, I've have never fooled my daughter" And as I looked at my daughter, when I said what I said I saw tears come down my daughter's cheeks. "She's been too smart to fool. She's always been ten miles ahead of me, maybe more."

Just before I graduated, I heard my director say, that I was graduating on a very lucky day, 777, July seventh, two thousand seven.

And where did my wife and I get married at, Las Vegas, Nevada. You can say, I'm living to my 777. And we have.

But we haven't met yet. Didn't know it then, but God will bless me, with the love of my life.

As I said, I had to stay in sober living, for another ex amount of time. And didn't know where God was taking me in life.

Two months go by, after my graduation, and lord and behold, didn't think about it much after I meet up with a very pretty lady.

I was on my way to visit my parents, like I have always done, on one of my last day of work, and spend a day or two with them, and then report back to work.

And as I sat quietly, on the train, listening to my music earphones, this attractive lady and a lady friend of hers, aboard the train, called the blue line. And we started a small conversation, but I was too blind to see what was ahead of me. She had given me a card, and she told me to call her, but as I said, I was too blind to see, and didn't call her. And that was a mistake. And I honestly can tell you, I can't imagine, where I would be, without the love of my life, my wife.

Without her love and support, I would have probably stayed working for minimum wage, oh my god. I really believe that, I would have been stuck on stupid, literally speaking. As I said, I didn't call her, and if we would have not seen each other again, two months later, I would have been lost in the wind.

Remember we're talking about two thousand seven, and I'm working for Vons, and I'm getting paid, eight dollars and fifty cents, per hour. Can you see what I'm talking about, lost in the wind.

Couldn't see what God was trying to tell me, so God gives me another chance of his love.

And the lady I had met on the blue line, as I had just arrived from another visit from mom and dad, as I was about to aboard my bus, this nice lady, sees me, and tells me, why haven't I called her. It was two months later, and we bumped into each other again. This has always been a very unique loving relationship, with my wife and I. I never believed I would ever experience the real strength of love, by God giving me this beautiful lady I'm now married to.

When she asked why I hadn't called her, I was lost of words, with nothing to say to her. And I'm on a bike, like a bum, and why was she interested in me, to this day, I don't understand. But as love will be as it is, we're not supposed to understand love, we're to love, unconditionally.

I throw my bike on the bus, jumped in the bus, flying like a bat out of hell, to my apartment, threw myself on my bed, throwing out my wallet, emptying it, looking for her card, like my life depended on it. And I didn't think I had her card, and then I found it. I really think, God put it there.

Yes, I really believe God put her card back in my wallet. Come on guys we all know our wallets, or we should. I could have sworn I threw her card away a few days before. And the next thing I'm doing is calling her, acting like nothing was wrong. And she answered very nonchalant, "Hello" I responded, "it's only me" she says, "oh hello" I say, "I can't believe I found your card, and you know, I find you very attractive" And she's probably heard that before, so it wasn't no surprise to her. But she says, "Oh thank you" And the next thing, I'm asking her out for a date. "Say listen, would you like to have a cup of coffee at Starbucks" And this would be the first date of the rest of our lives. But I didn't think so then, because I had to tell her, the dark world I just crawled out of, and I had just graduated from a rehab center, because this lady looked like a very clean respectable attractive lady, which I didn't think, she should be with. But I would have to see, what she thinks after our first date, and I tell her my whole life story.

I couldn't believe it, after I told her my story of mishaps, and where I once worked at, and how I lost it all. I also had to tell her, "I don't see what you see in me, because I don't have anything to show for, and I'm pushing sixty years, and I'm working for Vons, for eight fifty an hour and that's all I have to give" "So what do you think of that" And what did she say, "Well you don't do that anymore" I couldn't believe that, but she gave me hope, when she told me that. And hope would be in our lives together, because you see, this nice lady had, had a stroke two years before our meeting, and when she had to leave for a short while, and we're walking to the train station, I tell her that I'm not going to look for anyone, that I'll be waiting for her. And she tells me, "Why do you want to waste your time with an old and crippled woman" My immediate reply, "First of all, you're not an old woman, and we can both work things out together" And we have, because that was the beginning of a beautiful everlasting love, and we lived together for about four years, before we got married. Got married in Las Vegas, and what do they say, "What happens in Vegas stays in Vegas" And that's true, because we got married in Vegas and stayed in Vegas.

I have never regretted our marriage. Oh, we have our differences like all couples do. There's no perfection in relationships.

If they're were perfections in anything we do, we wouldn't need God. At least that's what I've heard, but I'm kind of skeptical about that. I think we'll always need God.

And when I first brought my girlfriend to meet my mom and dad, it became so quiet as we entered the house, as I introduce my beautiful girlfriend to my mother and father, you should have seen my mother's eyes, and my girlfriend's eyes, they were glued wide open, staring at each other. For me, it was a beautiful sight, because now that I thought back, about all the older women I had known, all of a sudden they all turned into tramps. And I'm not just saying that, because if they would've been true relationships, I would have stayed with them.

My girl, climbed on to my moms bed, because remember I wrote, my mother had a broken foot, and she had become bedridden for two years, when they first met.

ROBERT GARCIA

They held hands as they spoke with smiles. I really believe, God was there with us, that day, when my girl and my Mom met for the first time.

Oh my Dad, you should have seen him, I'm in the living room, Dad in the dining room, and with his index finger, he's flipping it, for me to come over to where he is, wanting me to go to the kitchen with him. The first thing Dad says, "where did you meet her, she's a pretty girl, and you better marry her before someone else does.

Oh, and when my girlfriend and I got into our first argument, and I went to the house without my girl, you should have seen the looks on both of Mom's and Dad's faces, asking me where was my girl at. Telling them we got into a fight of words, and I cussed her. Dad got outrageous, telling me, "What is wrong with you" While Mom stares at me, flipping her index finger, to come over to her. And we get inches away from each of our faces, as she says, "Go after her", No one had to say anymore, I ran out and into my car and gone with the wind, bat out of hell. If you can picture that, my girlfriend had a doctors appointment in downtown L.A. and I had to drive from Mom and Dad's house, which was about twenty miles, and I must arrived within ten minutes. And I was so happy to see my girlfriend, and she was safe and sound, still a little sore at me, but no more harsh words. Just holding hands for the rest of our lives.

All the meanwhile, I've filed for disability with social security and the V.A., and it became kind of tricky not to work. Because we're not supposed to work, when we're filing for disability. Hello!!

My only problem and question was, so how does one eat, if we're not receiving any money. And does anybody care, the answer, nobody cares. To each his own, in this world. Well something had to give, either receive general relief or something, as I continued working. And my work, my wife to be, and our financial situation was my focus. And that's all that mattered to me.

I've always heard that strong love, is possible, when there's loyalty and devotion, in a relationship. And I have never had that, until I met this wonderful lady, love was growing between us, because it's become an unconditional love, that I never thought I would ever have.

God is never in a hurry but he's always on time. But my only wish, I wish God would had been a little in a hurry for me, because I was already too old when I fell in a dark world of drugs. But what can I say, but shut up, and be grateful. Of course I should be grateful, or I would be dead for sure.

All along I've painted you all a life story of myself and the three deathly times I should have died, and now through God's grace, love and blessings, I'm now living a life I thought I shouldn't have deserved. But who am I say, if I deserved this life or not. God is powerful and his love is indescribable, because I'm lost of words to describe my life I live now. No matter how many words there might be, I'll never have enough words and time to paint you a colorful picture of our lives together, my wife and I.

How's a song go, "We've only just begun"

Then our very first date arrived, which was the same day she was catching a flight to Guam. And what she informs me next, kept my mouth open for too long. She says, "Do you have a passport", thought to myself, me a passport, got to be kidding me, naturally I said no. And the next thing she says, "When I get back, you have to apply for a passport", And that scared the shit out of me, and also thinking to myself me apply for a passport.

I'm sure all of you remember, I've been through a truck crash, was deployed to Vietnam, shot at numerous times, saw comrades get killed. Years later, I became a cocaine addict, in and out of jail for eight years, and when I met this lovely lady, had just graduated from a rehab center, and now she's asking me to apply for a passport.

I was thinking very negative about myself, which goes without saying, because of my past life. Being so sure, no way I'm going to get a passport. I have a drug record. And where were we going to fly, didn't have a clue, because I didn't really think I was flying anywhere. Well only God was the only one, that knew if I was going to fly or not, and the judge. In my mind, I have to go see the judge, she'll tell me, if I will fly or not. Thought, if I go see the judge, was afraid, she might laugh at my face. And yell out loud, "You want to apply for a passport, and you want to fly, where", but that's not what happened.

So I had to sit tight, behave myself, and wait for my wife to be. Before she left, she told me she had two children that worked for two major airlines. As I waited for my lady, working at my job at Vons, went on visiting my parents, and being as normal as I can be. Went to N/A meetings, close by the folks home.

And my lady queen arrived from Guam, and I was so happy she had arrived. If you could have seen my face, and my parents could see the love on my face, and didn't know it was so obvious. But why would I hide, a special love, which I don't believe I've ever felt. This lady would become my love of my life. I have always thought she could have been with someone much better than me. But that's how I thought then.

It just goes to show you, like God showed me, the way of love and happiness, like I thought would never be possible, for me personally. To us people, things look impossible, but to God, everything is possible. To a lot of non believers, they'll say, unbelievable. Well believe it people, because if you don't believe in God before you leave this life, you're bound to lose the second life.

Becoming a Christian and falling in love, is a many splendored thing to have, had changed me, by falling in love with God and my wife.

Receiving my wife to be at the airport, I jumped for joy, as I ran up to her, and picked her up, and swung around a couple of times. I was so happy to see her back home, I took her out to dinner. And at this restaurant, I bought her a rose, and we were serenaded. What beautiful memories of our life, my wife and I.

And the word beautiful, can only describe just a percentage of the love I feel in my life today.

Remember "DIED THREE TIMES LIVED ONCE"

As some of you can already can tell, I'm at my climax of my life, and in my happiest part of my life, after dying three times.

I will soon paint you the picture that's in my heart, where my wife and her children that work for two major airlines, have flown me with my wife and her children, around the world.

Some of you recovered addicts, may not believe me, and that's okay and it's not important if you believe me or not. What is important, is that my wife and I have flown to Italy, France, Spain, the Philippines, Japan, and Guam, at least three times. And to you brothers and sisters, I feel like I've been in heaven since I met my wife.

As I said before, I was trying to get a V.A. claim approved, and/or get a social security claim approved as well, and of course it takes a long time for a response.

But that didn't stop my wife to get me on an airline to Italy, oh my god.

I don't think I have to tell you, the only airline I have ever flown on, was to Vietnam, and back. So this first flight in years, to Italy, scared the hell out of me. The take off, the landing, and the turbulence, oh wow. But after a few more flights, around the world, the flights were in God's hands, like my life has always been in his hands. All three times when I faced death in the face, and should have gotten killed, my life has been in God's hands.

I've tried my best of my ability and capability, to describe my life as a colorful motion picture of a true tragic love story. And I've never dreamed of having a nightmare, a fantasy and reality, all in one life time, as I've lived my lives as I have.

And my journey is not over yet, until God says it's over.

I keep saying, God is never in a hurry, but he's always on time. But we're the ones that are out of time, and always in a hurry, and for so many of us, we're still late.

As long as I live my life on this side of the fence, I'll always feel incredible about how God has rewarded me his love and blessings. And the very reason why I feel incredible, and amazed about my life's results, after a lot of wrong doings I've committed. It's unbelievable, but I have no choice but to believe what has happened to me, because God gave it to me, and I have to believe what God has given me. God is an awesome God. And he's also a forgiving God. But it's always been hard to forgive myself.

Both my wife and I live happily in Las Vegas, and financially secured from the V.A. and social security, but I'm also grateful for my mother. There had been a military award letter that I received, forty years before Mom passed away, at her home, but I had never seen that military award letter, from a Lt. General, due to the fact, mother had forgotten to give it to me. But it was God's timing for me to receive the military award letter, because of lives I had saved in Vietnam. And I had never had the intention to save lives to receive an award, because that was far from my mind, when I was at war against the enemy.

In the Marine Corp, we're all trained to save our comrade's lives. I was too busy trying to save lives, than to think about any award. But

I also have to be very thankful, and grateful, for the Marine that was watching what I had done, during a few war situations. I now look at it this way, after decades past, God sent someone to witness what I was trying to accomplish. And I did it to the best to my utmost ability.

I had to frame my gratitude for God's love, and hang it on my wall, by hanging my award, from a general, and hang my wife's picture, as my reward of love from God.

I've mentioned this before, I fell deeply in love with my wife, and have overlooked her disability, because I have always felt an unconditional love for her.

Some of my wife's relatives, and a close friend of mine of over sixty years, have told me, I have a very unique love for my wife. And my answer has always been, because I love her.

Awe, she'll feel at times, sad and kind of depressed, because she can't help me out with things that I have to do, as I maintain our home. But I have to always remind her, that we both accepted this love and life of ours.

We never leave each other's sight, maybe an half an hour to take a shower, or maybe to do some cooking. But what the heck, I love this lady of mine. I can't help it.

Sometimes I've wondered, who's more disabled than who, me or her. Since I met her, she has been an inspirational lady, which I fell in love with. Although she had a stroke, before I met her, I overlooked her disability, and I fell deeply in love with her.

Check this out, she has been flying on the airlines, since the eighties. And then when she had a stroke in two thousand five, you would think, she would stop taking flights. No way, not my wife. I'm not talking about domestic flights, I'm talking about flying to the Philippines, to Japan, to Guam, to Europe, and back to the States. Here I am, I'm lucky, I took an airplane to Vietnam, and that's all the flying I did, until I met my lovely wife.

She was born in the Philippines, I was born in the States, but I have lived a more shallow life than she has. You think I'm bragging about my wife, you damn straight I am. And why shouldn't I be, because of my wife, I was able to purchase my first home. And we have purchased three homes, since we have been together. And we have purchased three new Chevy traverses.

I was never able to purchase anything, with my past two wives.

Check out this funny one, as I said, my wife, even though she had a stroke and before she had a stroke, she has flown around the world, and I have a sister, that lost her husband, and all I did was advice her to go somewhere on a bus, and she almost made me fall off my chair, I laughed so hard, when she told me, "all by myself brother" It blew my mind, I couldn't believe she said that.

Oh, now let me tell you about my wife's children and all her rest of her family. Since I met my wife, I have more love than I would have ever would imagine, from all over the world. We're talking, from Texas, Philippines, Guam, California, oh, and Australia. Can you people see what I'm talking about.

My family, dysfunctional, and that's to say the least, arrogant, and violent. And I have an ancestry to prove it.

I also have two sisters, which I feel ashamed to call them that. Thank God, I only have two. And poor Dad, he has been sadly hurt by not just his daughters, but also by his only son, me. And I also have God, that has helped me help Dad. His daughters have never helped him, but abuse him.

When I said, Dad's son helped him, that's exactly what I did. Being ashamed of myself, under my addiction, I prayed to God, to help me make amends to Dad, under my emotional stupor, as I shedded some tears, God all of a sudden, threw me an idea. Boom, God clearing my heart and mind, gave me the thought of helping Dad, open a claim at the V.A. I thought, wow, God is good and his love is strong.

Dad will never know it, but he has always been Vulnerable, with a capital V. Evil has always seen Dad come around, and take what they can take, and then laugh at him. So sad.

Even his own brother took advantage of him, by also abusing him, and actually took Dad's business away from him. I couldn't believe it, when I saw it happening. But such has been done over a half a century ago now. But it doesn't really matter when anything that bad happens, I call it how I see it. Bad is bad. A waste trash business, now that's a billion dollar business, by today's standards. You would think Dad would learn, and not be so trusting, even by his family. Because in business, you're not supposed to trust anybody. But Dad trusted everybody. And Dad's problem was trusting people, and Dad's own family whom he trusted, aren't people, they're snakes. if you don't believe me about calling people snakes. Watch a snake, the way they slide on the ground, and see what they catch and take it away. That's what I've seen this woman, that's related to me, that's what I've noticed what her husband has always acted on people, he's always come sliding up to you, and see what he can take away.

Wonder if any of you people believe that bad seeds are born everyday. I'm sure there are a few of you that do know, out there. I really believe there are bad seeds in everything. In crops that we eat, to the different animals that we eat, and then the actual snakes. But there are also people that are snakes as well. And I also believe, these kinds of people that are lying jealous, and greedy, will manipulate and steal from anyone that is vulnerable. The reason I bring this up, because unfortunately I have relatives that are evil as hell. And I was once possessed, and evil as well. This is why I can recognize those types of people.

I'm not going to elaborate about these evil people that I'm related to, it just wouldn't make sense, in my life's writings. Because we all have a price to pay, when we face judgement day.

Through my life, and my rights and wrongs, and my wrong choices, I have found out that God has always been there for me. I've become a God fearing man. Oh, yes, God has scared the living daylights out of me, because on how he has saved me from dying three times. And now I'm living a life, I would have never dreamed of. I call my life, miraculous.

And also through my life, when I had doubts, I found faith, hope and love, through God's blessings.

When I try to reminisce about my life, and think as to how many times God tried knocking on my heart's door, and I wouldn't answer, he has proven to me, what a patient loving God he is.

When I finally opened my heart to God, he blessed me with love. And how has he blessed me, many of you might ask.

I have constantly repeated, by telling you all, how my Lord saved me three times from dying. And the beautiful life, I now live. That's one of my biggest blessings.

Next God has me meet a beautiful lady, I'm now married to. She then supported me and motivated me in opening a V.A. claim. Then my wife motivated me in opening a social security claim. And then, when my dear mother passed away, this so called sister of mine, while she was cleaning the house, Mom and Dad once lived in, she found an award letter from the Marine Corp, finding out, it was an award letter, with a medal of Valor. That letter proved to be a very important decision for the V.A., to approve me compensation, for the rest of my life. Then my dear wife motivated me, and convinced me to see if I would qualify to buy a house. And let me tell ya, in my life before my current wife, I have never been able to buy any house. And since we've been married, my wife and I have purchased three homes. You think that's all, no it's not.

Another amazing part of our lives, since we've been together over seventeen years, not only homes, that we have purchased, we have purchased seven vehicles. Three of them, brand new Chevy Traverses. God put us on an airline a half of dozen times and we traveled the world, under my wife's children's benefits. Do you think I've been blessed, oh yes I have. Above and beyond.

And during my rehab program, I have never thought it to be real, and I have never thought it to be true. There were a couple of guys that told me I had a strong spirit. But since then, I've grown to realize, that can only be true because of God's strong spirit. And guess what happens next, God introduced me to a lady, with a strong spirit as well. I'll show you how strong our spirits are together, my wife and I.

We'll be having a conversation, like we have through the years, and out of nowhere, I'll go to say something, and she'll say, "I was just thinking the same thing" And that hadn't happened just once, no no, it happens all the time.

One of my big memories of my rehab days, as a in patient, at various meetings, I recall people saying, when and if anyone of us recover from our addiction. Your spouse will have already divorce you, you have lost a beautiful career, all of your possessions, but the biggest part of our loss, is ourselves. You will be lost in the wind, if you don't ask for forgiveness and help from God. That's without a doubt.

When I had fallen on my hands and knees, and had lost everything, thinking there was no hope, lost, God found me. And when that happened, I couldn't believe the change in my life. When I had gone completely the wrong direction, God turned me one hundred and eighty degrees to go the right direction. For those of you that understand what I'm saying, then you know. But for those of you, that this has never happened, then you won't understand, and probably won't believe me. Because you see, anything that happens to us, with God as our lord and savior, its not physical by no means, it's completely spiritual.

I will probably never be able to put my love feelings for my wife, in plain English words. Because I have a strong love for her, that I have never felt for anyone else.

My wife will never know the amount of love I have for her, but it's first God's love, is the very reason I found my wife in the first place.

As I said, I have a very strong feeling of love for my wife.

And here's another reason, besides loving her from the bottom of my heart, she also a lot of love for people, and has a big heart.

Although it's been quite a few years, but I will never forget what my brother in law, whose married to my wife's sister, in Guam, told me about my lovely wife.

We had flown to Guam, to celebrate my wife's sister and brother in law's fiftieth anniversary. And I have to say, we had a beautiful time at their anniversary celebration. A lot of food and a lot of friends and relatives. And within my wife's family relatives, they have shown me more love, in a short time, and all the time, my wife and I have been married, than my whole family have shown me, excluding my daughters, in all my life. Shameful but it's true. I've always been known to speak my mind.

And this is what I have to say. We arrived in Guam, was welcomed with love, from her sister, brother in law, and their family. My wife's family have continually treated me with warm love, whereas on the other hand, my family doesn't know what love is. Like I said, I speak my mind.

My sister in law and her husband and family, threw a big anniversary celebration at the Hyatt hotel. It was so beautiful, to say the least. Talking, listening, and laughing. Hardly any consumption of alcohol, and there was no smoking around a buffet.

Brother in law and I, talked and laughed, as if we've known each other for years. I'll forever cherish those moments, sacredly in my heart and soul. Such a wonderful, happy event.

And then brother in law took me to the buffet, and wanting to talk to me about a loving incident, as we got our food, because of his sister in law, my wife, wouldn't accept that the doctors in the Philippines, were going to amputate his legs. He tells me with emotion, "I'm walking today because of my sister in law, your wife" As I catch the emotion in his eyes, I asked, "How is that, do you want to tell me the story", as he responds, "Of course", as he walked into the story, I listened very carefully.

He started telling me, "well as we are now in our fiftieth anniversary today, and getting old, and when I was much younger, around thirty five years old, I had very bad knees, and I didn't know why my knees were in so much pain and becoming so weak", "So I went to my doctor, and he tells me, he had to run some tests, to see what's wrong with my knees" And I didn't dare interrupt what he was saying. It was becoming so interesting to me, by the moment. As he continued, "So as my doctor continued his testing on my knees, it was becoming hard for him to tell me what is happening to my knees and to my legs" Now he wasn't the kind of man to cry out, but I could see, as he told the story, he was trying very hard not to show too much emotion. As I tell him, "And then what happened", I was so quiet, because I wanted to know everything about this woman I'm falling in love with. So he continues, "Well the time came, when my doctor finally had to tell me the sad and bad news" And it was very bad news, because I was imagining, what if that happened to me. As his eyes looked so sad, and then he became happy, when he says to me, "Well as I said, my knees had become very

ROBERT GARCIA

bad, because of my cartilage in my knees, and that he was so sad to tell me, that he's going to have to amputate my legs" I stared at him, I couldn't take my eyes off of him. Because as he spoke, I noticed he was walking very good. So something good must had happened. As he winds up his happy end of story. So he ended up telling me, "Well as you can see, I'm walking very good today, because of your wife" but he didn't stop there, "your wife couldn't accept that my doctor was going to amputate my legs, and I'm walking today because of her, because she has a heart, and went back to the States to talk to another doctor. "And that doctor wanted to see me, to see what he could do, and I thank God and I thank my sister in law" "Because when I went to see that other doctor, I couldn't believe what that doctor told me, that he was not going to cut my legs off, brother in law, I went home and cried", as I respond to him, "well you're about to make me cry brother" and he ends by telling me, "And that's been now, forty years ago"

And I have thought so much about that story, since he told me, and it's no wonder, my wife and I have a very unique love.

Just so you remember what I told you, we have an unconditional love, because of her condition and disability, because she had a stroke, two years before we met, but that didn't stop me from falling in love and marrying her.

We've even been approached, and people have complimented me, as to how I love my wife. Believe me people, I don't love and kiss my wife in public, to impress anyone. Because when I kiss my wife in public, I'm thanking God, for giving me this beautiful lady to marry. And that my friends, as God as my witness, is my loving truth.

I've painted you an ugly beginning of my life, when I was in a truck crash, and we should have been killed.

Deployed to Vietnam, shot at numerous times, while watching my comrades get killed.

Becoming a drug addict, and wanting to commit suicide, by jumping off a freeway bridge.

Now I'm ending my beautiful painting of my life, as how my wife and I live today.

Through thick and thin, and my asking for God's help, and he in return, saved me. Thank You Lord.

"DIED THREE TIMES LIVED ONCE"

Printed in the United States
by Baker & Taylor Publisher Services